Enigma Books

Also published by Enigma Books

Klaus-Michael Mallmann
and
Martin Cüppers

Nazi Palestine

The Plans for the Extermination
of the Jews in Palestine

Enigma Books

Publications of the Ludwigsburg Research Unit
Stuttgart University, Vol. 8
Edited by Klaus-Michael Mallmann

Copyright © 2005 by WBG (Wissenschaftliche Buchgesellschaft), Darmstadt
Copyright © 2010 by Enigma Books for the English Translation

Translated from the German by Krista Smith

Original German title:
Halbmond und Hakenkreuz: das Dritte Reich, die Araber und Palästina

First English Edition

Library of Congress Cataloguing-in-Publication

Mallmann, Klaus-Michael
    [Halbmond und Hakenkreuz. English]
    Nazi Palestine : the plans to exterminate the Jews in Palestine / Klaus-Michael Mallmann and Martin
Cüppers ; [translated from the German by Krista Smith]. -- 1st English ed.

    p. ; cm.

    Original German title: Halbmond und Hakenkreuz: das Dritte Reich, die Araber und Palästina.
    "Publications of the Ludwigsburg Research Unit, Stuggart University, Vol. 8"--T.p. verso
    Includes bibliographical references and index.
    ISBN: 978-1-929631-93-3

    1. Jewish-Arab relations--History--1917-1948. 2. Palestine--History--1917-1948. 3. Jews—Palestine--
History. I. Cüppers, Martin, 1966- II. Smith, Krista. III. Title. IV. Title: Halbmond und Hakenkreuz.
English

DS119.7 .M3513 2010
956.9404

Contents

Introduction

The economic and financial restructuring known as "globalization" has radically transformed societies and national economies that for better or worse have become increasingly interconnected. But the lowering of barriers and greater interaction has created a clash of cultures and even violent resistance to the cultural, economic, and financial standardization that the West has imposed on the world through a form of non-violent coercion. An increasingly militant encounter between Western values and the most radicalized, fundamentalist elements of Islam turned violent since the 2001 attacks on New York, taken as the symbol of Western domination and oppression. The struggle between the West and Islamic radicalism has not stopped over the course of the intervening years, from Afghanistan to Chechnya to Iraq, and present among these new conflicts the 60-year Israeli-Arab and Palestinian antagonism that appears destined to remain without a tangible solution.[1]

This book offers no prognostications regarding the conflict; rather, by examining the past structure of the clash in Palestine, the authors seek to trace and analyze the historical dimensions of the origins of the broader conflict in one of its most important arenas. This volume returns to a very specific period in German history and examines the relations of the Third Reich with the Arab Islamic world. The shared hatred of the Yishuv (Hebrew for "settlement"), and of the Jewish minority in the British Mandate of Palestine, created an increasing convergence leading to a momentous shift in German foreign policy, which in the late 1930s switched its focus from seeking the acceleration of Jewish emigration to providing direct support for Arab nationalists. The ideo-

---

1. Primarily Lewis, Wut; on Iran: Küntzel, Spaltung.

logical consensus, the shared perception of common threats, the protection of one's specific cultural identity, and notions of achievement, was quickly followed even before the outbreak of World War II by shipments of weapons and financial support given to the Islamic nationalists. Direct German intervention in the Arab world began with the arrival of the Afrika Korps in Libya in February 1941. For the National Socialists, this event was directly related to far-reaching strategic plans for the conquest of the entire Middle East.

Numerous joint German-Arab plots intending to expel the British from their land route to India were also to eliminate the Jewish national homeland promised by the Balfour Declaration. The culmination of these plans came in the summer of 1942, when the extermination of the Jews that had begun in Europe was to be expanded to the Yishuv as well, with the active assistance of local Arab collaborators. Although the German units required for this undertaking were ready and waiting for their marching orders, Rommel's defeat at El Alamein prevented the implementation of these plans. Collaboration with the Arabs did not end, however, with the military defeat in Egypt. The Axis forces landing in Tunisia in the fall of 1942 was followed by plans to foment revolution in the states of the Maghreb using Arab agents and to launch infiltration attempts in the Middle East. This came at the same time as the broad effort at recruitment of Muslims into the Wehrmacht and SS (Schutzstaffel). Certain Arab expatriates knew about the killing of the European Jews and, in view of the looming defeat, personally advocated a partial expansion of the extermination efforts.

Until now there has been no comprehensive and scientific study of the period between 1933 and 1945 tracing the development of German-Arab relations, with an analysis of their philosophical affinities, and a discussion of the joint schemes shared by the Germans and the Arabs. In general, existing studies end with the outbreak of the war in 1939 or, at times, with the pro-Axis coup in Iraq in March-April 1941, thus omitting the decisive phase of 1941–1942—the period of the impending occupation of the Middle East. In addition, many authors tend to be largely uncritical, by playing down the relationship between Arab nationalists and National Socialists, and dismissing anti-Semitic propaganda and action in the Islamic world as an expression of cultural differences, and, warning in this regard, against a "Eurocentric" view. One significant exception is Matthias Küntzel's study *Djihad und Judenhaß* (Jihad and Anti-Semitism). Though Küntzel writes without examining archival sources, he convincingly conveys the ideological affinities that existed between National Socialism and political Islam.[2] Reference should also be made to Klaus

---

2. Küntzel, *Djihad*.

42. Paucker, born in 1921 in Berlin, and Bauer, born in 1926 in Prague, escaped to Palestine during the second half of the 1930s, fleeing the National Socialists. Both understood the fundamental danger that a German invasion would pose to the Yishuv, and both acted accordingly. Paucker volunteered for the British army in 1941 and was a member of the Royal Engineers in Egypt and Italy until the end of the war. Bauer, 16 in 1942, joined the Haganah and was prepared to retreat to the Carmel Mountains near Haifa ready to engage in armed resistance from there. Paucker celebrated his 85th birthday in January 2005, and Bauer turned 80 the same year. We congratulate them both wholeheartedly and wish them a long life ahead.

Gensicke's impressive biography of Haj Amin el-Husseini, the Grand Mufti of Jerusalem and a loyal supporter of Hitler.[3] The fact that the Palestinian Jews' very existence was under direct threat because of the presence of the Einsatz-kommando of the security police and the SD (Sicherheitsdienst) assigned to the Afrika Korps has been until recently completely overlooked by academic researchers.[4] Helmut Krausnick, who is still considered the leading expert on the Einsatzgruppen,[5] had joined the Nazi Party (NSDAP) in January 1932 while he was still a student.[6] In 1942, despite severe war shortages, he was rewarded with a second printing of his dissertation.[7] He understandably failed to undertake that research.

****

We must thank the many people whose assistance made this book possible: Wissenschaftliche Buchgesellschaft in Darmstadt immediately declared itself ready to accept the volume into its program, and its editor, Daniel Zimmermann, attended to the book's development in exemplary fashion. At the archives we visited, we found many professionals who were ready to listen and eager to help. We would also like to thank several colleagues who offered advice, criticism, and help: Dr. Andrej Angrick (Berlin), Dr. Jochen Böhler (Warsaw), Dr. Jürgen Matthäus (Washington, D.C.), Dr. Dan Michman (Ramat-Gan/Jerusalem), Dr. Jacek Młynarczyk (Warsaw), Dr. Wolfram Pyta (Stuttgart), and Stephen Tyas (St. Albans). Dr. Manfred Rommel (Stuttgart) willingly provided us with information about his father, the former commander of Afrika Korps. Special thanks go to Heidrun Baur (Ludwigsburg). For months she obtained mountains of literature, collected texts, proofread, compiled back matter, and generally did much more than should be expected of a secretary at our research center.

We would like to dedicate this book to two great Jewish historians, whose lives were closely connected to the events that we describe and analyze here: Dr. Arnold Paucker, director of the Leo Baeck Institute in London from 1959 to 2001, and Dr. Yehuda Bauer, professor emeritus for Holocaust studies at the Hebrew University of Jerusalem and director of the International Institute for Holocaust Research at the Yad Vashem memorial from 1996 to 2000. Both kindly shared their personal recollections and impressions of Palestine in 1941–

---

3. Gensicke.
4. Addressed for the first time by Mallmann/Cüppers.
5. Krausnick, *Hitlers*.
6. BAB, NSDAP-Zentralkartei 3200/L 0083, Helmut Krausnick membership card; cf. Berg, p. 405.
7. Krausnick, *Holsteins*.

Nazi Palestine

The Plans to Exterminate the Jews in Palestine

Chapter I

Jihad in Palestine:
The Arab Rejection of the Jews

Until the end of World War I, Palestine was a remote province of the Ottoman Empire.[1] At the turn of the century, the land was neither overpopulated nor intensively used; rather, it was sparsely settled—estimates suggest about 400,000 residents. The great majority were ethnic Arabs. Most were Sunni Muslims, but a minority of Christians of Arabic origin lived in the cities as well. In addition, a small Jewish population of Sephardic descent, which had been present for centuries, was concentrated in Jerusalem, Hebron, Tiberias, and Safed. For this old Yishuv—just 25,000 people in 1870—settlement in the Holy Land was a religious imperative; Zionism as a motive and idea was foreign to them.[2]

Jews of Ashkenazy descent did not go to Palestine until the First Aliyah ("ascent"), after 1881, when the murder of Czar Alexander II and the subsequent pogroms and restrictions led to the mass emigration of Jews from the Russian Empire. The vast majority went to the United States; by 1914, only

---

1. Porath, *Emergence*, p. 1ff.; cf. Gerber.
2. Krämer, *Geschichte*, p. 154ff.

about 70,000 had emigrated from Eastern Europe to Palestine. While the first of these were refugees seeking a new Diaspora, the immigrants of the Second Aliyah, after 1905, were significantly different.[3] They were primarily adherents of a socialist-influenced Zionism who left Russia after the failed revolution of 1905 in order to recultivate the land of their ancestors through manual agricultural labor. This new Yishuv saw itself as part of the dawn of a new nation and was inspired to create a classless society in a Jewish land free from anti-Semitism or pogroms. Although Theodor Herzl, the founder of political Zionism, gave little thought to the existing Arab population, the project had nothing in common with existing Western colonialism in Africa and Asia. Colonies were generally acquired in order to control raw materials, mineral resources and exploit the labor of the native inhabitants. Palestine, by contrast, did not offer a favorable economic situation for the Jewish immigrants. It involved the need for massive irrigation and cultivation, back-breaking work and years spent waiting for the rewards of their labor, and consciously renouncing most forms of relative prosperity and urbanity. This was the only way, the Jewish pioneers believed, they could free themselves from the ghetto and its mentality and transform their historical claim to Erez Israel into a moral claim as well.[4]

World War I turned Palestine into a battlefield between British, Ottoman, and German troops. In 1917, moving out from Egypt, the Anglo-Egyptian expeditionary force under General Sir Edmund Allenby conquered Sinai, Negev, and the Gaza Strip, with heavy losses suffered on both sides. On November 16 it took Jaffa, and on December 9, Jerusalem. Northern Palestine, however, remained in Ottoman hands until the late summer of 1918. Haifa fell on September 23 and Damascus on October 1. The Armistice of Mudros, signed by British and Ottoman representatives on October 30, ended the war in the Levant but left Palestine in a highly ambiguous situation.[5] During the war, the British had made vague promises to three different groups. In order to draw the Arabs to the British side and encourage them to revolt against the Sultan, Sir Henry MacMahon, the high commissioner in Egypt, promised Hussein bin Ali, the sharif of Mecca, that a pan-Arab empire would be created; however, no mention was made in their correspondence as to whether Palestine would be included as well.[6] In the Sykes-Picot Agreement of May 9, 1916, Great Britain and France agreed on the boundaries of their respective spheres of influence in the region for the period after the war, and outlined the division of the areas

3. Brenner, p. 55ff.
4. Laqueur, pp. 227ff., 287ff.
5. Fromkin, p. 305ff.
6. Ibid., pp. 173ff., 218ff.; Cohen, *Origins*, p. 14ff.; cf. Antonius.

that were expected to be inherited from the "sick man on the Bosporus." France was to control the area south of Anatolia between Mosul and Acre, and the British were to receive the adjacent territory to the south from Amman to Baghdad, while international control was proposed for Palestine.[7]

Even more significant was the explanation that the British foreign minister, Lord Arthur Balfour, gave to Lord James Rothschild on November 2, 1917. He promised that the government "views with favor the establishment in Palestine of a national home for the Jewish people, and will use their best endeavors to facilitate the achievement of this object, it being clearly understood that nothing shall be done which may prejudice the civil and religious rights of existing non-Jewish communities in Palestine or the rights and political status enjoyed by Jews in any other country."[8] These goodwill gestures, intended to mobilize Jewish communities throughout the world in support of London, certainly represented a diplomatic breakthrough for Zionism, but they were far from explicit. "Palestine" could mean the whole area or just a part of it. "National home" was not a term defined under international law and seemed to mean an ill-defined entity somewhere between a formal state and the right of domicile. And "views with favor" implied no binding guarantee whatsoever on the part of the British Empire.[9] Nevertheless, the San Remo Conference on April 25, 1920, decided to incorporate the Balfour Declaration into the peace treaty concluded with Turkey at Sèvres and to grant the Palestinian mandate to Great Britain. Article 2 of the San Remo resolution (which was ratified by the League of Nations on July 24, 1922) provided, for the first time, an international legal basis for the promise made by the British foreign minister to create a homeland for the Jews. Problems associated with the flexibility of his phrasing would soon emerge, however.[10]

While the area was still under military administration, the Arabs carried out numerous anti-Jewish assaults. In late 1919, Bedouins attacked Jewish settlers in Galilee. In March 1920, eight Jews were killed in an attack on Tel Hai. Among them was Joseph Trumpeldor, a dentist and former czarist officer who, together with Vladimir Jabotinsky, had led the Jewish Legion that fought on the British side in 1917–18 in Palestine. He was considered a quintessential Zionist pioneer and afterward gained the status of a national legend.[11] The Muslim violence in Jerusalem on April 4, 1920, assumed far greater propor-

7. Fromkin, p. 188ff.
8. *The Times*, Nov. 9, 1917; cf. Hyamson, p. 26ff.; Fromkin, p. 276ff.; Cohen, *Origins*, p. 41ff.
9. Brenner, p. 88.
10. Fromkin, p. 403ff.
11. Ibid., p. 446; Brenner, p. 69f.; cf. Porath, *Emergence*, p. 31ff.

tions. On that day, three religious holidays coincided: Jewish Passover, Christian Easter, and Muslim Nebi Musa. The Arabs streaming into the city for the procession were called upon to unite with Syria, where Feisal, the son of Sharif Hussein, had just proclaimed an independent kingdom.[12] The Muslims shouted, "Palestine is our land. The Jews are our dogs!" As the pilgrims crossed the Jewish quarter, aggression and pillaging ensued. The violence, which continued until April 8, resulted in 5 dead, 216 injured, and 18 seriously injured among the Jews.[13] Those who saw it simply as a "national demonstration for independence and freedom"[14]—in the words of a German Arabist— closed their eyes to the anti-Semitic violence and glorified terrorism. According to Colonel Richard Meinertzhagen, a British intelligence officer of Jewish descent, the leading functionaries of the military administration had encouraged the Arab aggression to discredit Zionism.[15] Giving credence to this theory is the fact that Jerusalem was empty of British troops during that time and the fact that the crowd chanted, "The government is on our side."[16]

The punishment imposed afterward was also mild. Musa Kazem el-Husseini, the mayor of Jerusalem and one of the Nebi Musa agitators, was removed from office and replaced by Ragheb Nashashibi. Haj Muhammad Amin el-Husseini, another agitator, who had fled to Syria afterward, was sentenced in absentia to 10 years' imprisonment. He was not to be required to serve even a single day. Part of the tragedy was that Sir Herbert Samuel, a British liberal of Jewish descent, had become head of the newly established civil administration of the mandate at that time and wished to make peace with the Arabs.[17] To achieve this, he decided to play the Husseinis and the Nashashibis—the two most powerful families in the country, both of which descended from the Prophet—against one another, under the "divide et imperat" principle, in order to neutralize them. Because a Nashashibi was now mayor of Jerusalem, so a Husseini had to hold the highest spiritual office in the Holy City for there to be a balance of power. Samuel chose, of all people, Amin el-Husseini, whom he considered to be a "moderate man."[18] In September 1920, Samuel pardoned el-Husseini and allowed him to return. In the vote to elect the Mufti of Jerusalem on April 12, 1921, el-Husseini was only fourth behind other respected scholars from equally well-regarded families, but Samuel overturned the vote and announced el-Husseini's appointment on May 8. With this appointment, el-

12. Kedourie, *England*, p. 142ff.; Porath, *Search*, p. 4ff.
13. Lesch, p. 201ff.; Wasserstein, p. 60ff.; Krämer, *Geschichte*, p. 245ff.; Segev, p. 142ff.
14. Hollstein, p. 128.
15. Meinertzhagen, pp. 56, 79ff.
16. Fromkin, p. 447.
17. Caplan, p. 2ff.; Wasserstein, p. 73ff.
18. Bentwich/Bentwich, p. 191f.

Husseini reached the crucial position of power from which he, more than any other, would for decades radicalize and reinforce the ideologically charged nature of the Arab struggle against the Jews of Palestine.[19] "Able, ambitious, ruthless, humorless, and incorruptible, he was of the authentic stuff of which dictators are made," in the judgment of one British historian.[20]

Amin el-Husseini, whose exact date of birth is not certain (1893, 1895, or 1896), studied for a short time at the Al-Azhar University in Cairo in 1912–13, and was involved in the formation of an anti-Zionist association of Palestinian students. He joined the Ottoman army as an officer but in 1916 joined an Arab undercover group advocating autonomy. In 1917 he deserted while on medical leave in Jerusalem, defected to the insurgents under Sharif Hussein, and returned to his hometown with Allenby's forces.[21] Despite his meager theological education, el-Husseini became, thanks to the British vote, the highest Islamic legal authority in Palestine. He had the final word on interpretations the Koran and especially the oral traditions compiled in the Sunna. The fatwa instrument, with his opinion also binding on the sharia tribunals, made him the last instance of judicial control for public and private law.[22] The chairmanship of the Supreme Muslim Council—reestablished in December 1921 with British support in order to supervise the religious foundations, the awqaf—also provided him with significant financial resources and instruments of power as well as an extensive patronage network.[23]

Meanwhile, there was a new uprising in Palestine, by Arabs protesting the appointment of a Jew as high commissioner.[24] The starting point was Jaffa, where the mob attacked Jewish shops and establishments on May 1, 1921; the particular target was an immigrants' home that sheltered men as well as women and was therefore viewed as immoral. The Arab police looked on while even children were killed and many a victim's skull was split. Among those murdered was the well-known Jewish writer Joseph Chaim Brenner. The unrest began to subside in Jaffa with the imposition of a state of emergency on May 3, but it flared up again four days later in the rural areas—where, however, the aggression was met with armed resistance. By May 7, 47 Jews and 48 Arabs had been killed. The most significant result of the unrest was the independence of Tel Aviv. The city on the outskirts of Jaffa was awarded autonomy, and thou-

19. Porath, "Al-Hājj," p. 130ff.; Porath, *Emergence*, p. 184ff.; Jbara, p. 41ff.
20. Marlowe, p. 5.
21. On his early life, but with many inaccurate details: Wiesenthal, p. 3ff.; cf. Schechtman, p. 15ff.; Jbara, p. 13 ff.; Elpeleg, p. 1ff.; minimizing the importance: Zimmer-Winkel; Mattar, *The Mufti of Jerusalem*, p. 6ff.; cf. Green, p. 12.
22. Krämer, *Geschichte*, p. 259ff.
23. Kupferschmidt, p. 17ff.; Porath, "Al-Hājj," p. 137ff.; Porath, *Emergence*, p. 194ff.
24. Schmitz-Kairo, p. 153.

sands of Jewish residents of Jaffa fled there.[25] On November 2, 1921, the anniversary of the Balfour Declaration, Arab thugs ransacked the Jewish quarter in Jerusalem's Old City; five Jews and three Arabs were killed, the latter by explosive devices used for self-defense.[26]

Despite the extreme Arab violence, the British government found it difficult to identify those responsible. Colonial secretary Winston Churchill, during his visit to Palestine on March 28, 1921, was told by Musa el-Husseini that the Jews were responsible for the fall of the czarist empire and the defeat of Germany and Austria.[27] And some British newspapers expressed increasing sympathy for the Arabs and concern about the cost of the Empire's new engagement in Palestine. Both of these elements became part of a pattern of British behavior that would continue throughout the end of the 1930s. In a memorandum dated July 1, 1922, Churchill made it clear that the United Kingdom did not intend to allow Palestine to become "as Jewish as England is English." Further immigration would be allowed, but only to a degree compatible with the needs of the economy. In addition, Transjordan was separated from Palestine, and Jewish immigration to Transjordan was prohibited.[28]

Thus began a spiral of Arab extortion. After every outbreak of violence, a British commission of inquiry would be established to identify the causes, and every final report would determine that the Arabs were afraid of being displaced by the Jews. To reduce the unrest, the commissions always recommended the same remedy, in varying dosages: setting limits to Jewish immigration. The victims were thus perceived as being at fault, and the Arabs realized that by attacking Jews they could force the British Empire to impose new restrictions. Every curb on immigration reinforced the Arab inclination toward violence. Thanks to this vicious circle, the Balfour Declaration—which was completely unacceptable to the Arabs—and the mandate constructed on it began to be viewed in an increasingly unfavorable light in Great Britain as well. At the same time, the Arabs developed their own strategy of rejection. Since they refused to acknowledge the mandatory power, they also boycotted the self-governing institutions it proposed and the regional elections planned for them.[29] In addition, the Arabs' perception of themselves as double victims of colonialism and Zionism led to the formation of a self-victimization perspective (still present today) that precluded any questioning of the chosen

25. Wasserstein, p. 100ff.; Lesch, p. 204ff.; Segev, p. 188f.
26. Segev, p. 204.
27. Wasserstein, p. 96f.
28. Stewart, *Relations*, p. 25f.; Caplan, p. 21ff.
29. Krämer, *Geschichte*, pp. 236, 252; cf. Porath, *Emergence*, p. 123ff.

direction. And it seemed that only violence could offer the prospect of success-ful change. Looking forward, this combination of factors clearly suggested that further escalation was more likely than a decrease in tensions.

Nevertheless, Jewish immigration continued unabated. The Third Aliyah, with its 35,000 immigrants arriving between 1919 and 1923, was triggered pri-marily by the pogroms in the Ukraine in 1919–20 and was strongly shaped by the Zionist labor movement. A 1922 census showed a total population of 752,048 in Palestine, of which 589,177 were Muslims and 83,790 were Jews. The Fourth Aliyah, which started in 1924, had a notably different social com-position, as the immigrants came primarily from Poland and significantly strengthened the urban middle class in Palestine. The climate had changed markedly in the meantime. The United States, which had previously taken in the majority of the Jewish refugees from Central and Eastern Europe, intro-duced substantial legal hurdles to immigration in 1921 and 1924 with a quota system, and the Soviet Union, previously the country of origin of most socialist-oriented immigrants, hindered emigration. In 1932, Palestine's popu-lation totaled 1,052,872, of which 771,174 were Muslims and 180,793 were Jews.[30] Given these figures, the Arab fear of being swamped by a wave of Jews was completely groundless, as the Arab population, with its much higher birth rate, was growing faster than the Jewish population. However, facts by them-selves are not always decisive but rather the perceptions and interpretations of those facts.

Indeed, Jewish-Arab relations in Palestine in the 1920s were by no means harmonious, but they were not clouded by additional major clashes until the end of the decade. Not until 1929 did the latent conflict come to a head and acquire a new ideological slant. The escalation was sparked by a dispute over the Western Wall, the remaining 28-meter-long section of the perimeter wall of the Herodian temple. The Jews, who considered these last remains of the Second Temple as sacred, had prayed there since the Middle Ages. But the Muslims also revered the wall as a holy place. For them, it was part of the "sacred site" (Haram ash-Sharif), along with the al-Aqsa Mosque and the Dome of the Rock, where the Prophet Muhammad, according to Islamic tradition, tethered his horse Buraq before his night journey to heaven. The Western Wall, which was under the control of the awqaf and therefore the Mufti, was the Jews' holiest place of prayer; for the Muslims, the Haram was the third most important location after Mecca and Medina. It would have been hard to find a source of friction that carried more symbolism.[31]

---

30. Stewart, *Relations*, p. 20; Brenner, p. 64f.
31. Wasserstein, p. 222f.; Kolinsky, *Law*, p. 31ff.

The conflict escalated on issues of status. The first clashes at the Western Wall came on September 24, 1928, the Jewish Day of Atonement (Yom Kippur), when believers erected a portable partition to separate the men from the women and set up chairs for the elderly. Because the Muslims saw this as a violation of the status quo, the British police stepped in and removed the alterations under the protest of the Jews.[32] Afterward, the Mufti systematically spread the rumor that the Zionists were planning to destroy the mosque and rebuild their temple. On August 16, 1929, the Prophet's birthday,[33] the Muslims were called upon during Friday prayers to defend the sacred site. Shouting rallying cries such as "God is great," "The wall is ours," and "Kill the Jews," 2,000 believers streamed from the Haram mosque to the Western Wall, beat up praying Jews, and burned Torah scrolls.[34] Exactly one week later, on August 23, the Arab excesses escalated further. Thousands of farmers from the surrounding area, armed with clubs and knives, set out for Jerusalem and attacked residents in the Jewish quarters of Mea Shearim and Yemin Moshe. The wave of violence quickly spread throughout the entire city and out to the suburbs.[35]

But this was just the prelude. That same afternoon, the rumor that Jews were slaughtering Arabs in Jerusalem reached Hebron, and a genuine massacre ensued there. Sixty-seven Jews were killed, including a dozen women and three children under the age of five. Meanwhile, the violence continued in Jerusalem and then spread throughout the country. Six kibbutzim were completely destroyed, and Arabs even attempted to attack Tel Aviv. On August 30, 20 Jews were killed in Safed. Viewing such anti-Jewish massacres as "unrest directed against the Zionist power politics in Palestine"[36] completely distorts the facts. When the violence finally abated after a week (due to British police actions), 133 Jews and 116 Arabs had been killed and 339 Jews and 232 Arabs injured. All the Jewish casualties were victims of Arab aggression, while most of the Arab casualties resulted from British intervention.[37] Despite all the previous eruptions of violence, the events of August 1929 were different in nature. They marked a turning point in the relations between Arabs and Jews in Palestine—a turning point that would cloud the 1930s and 1940s as well. The idea of peaceful cooperation and coexistence, which previously had been the

32. Elpeleg, p. 16ff.; Krämer, *Geschichte*, p. 268f.
33. The birthday of the Prophet falls in the month of Rabi Al Awwal in the Muslim calendar. The equivalent month in the Gregorian calendar fluctuates from one year to the next. Hence, a different date is seen below in Chapter 2.
34. Krämer, Geschichte, p. 270; Segev, p. 339; Lesch, p. 209f.
35. Segev, p. 343ff.
36. Hollstein, p. 111.
37. Segev, p. 346ff.; Porath, *Emergence*, p. 258ff.; Lesch, p. 210f.; Krämer, *Geschichte*, p. 271; minimizing the importance: Mattar, *The Mufti of Jerusalem*, p. 33ff.; Mattar, "Role," p. 104ff.; cf. Friedman, p. 462f.

hope of many Jews, now proved to be an illusion. What remained was antagonism, a hardening desire for self-assertion, and an increasing tendency to think in terms of military categories. It was significant that the Jewish Brit Shalom organization, which worked for understanding between the ethnic groups and a binational community—Martin Buber was one of the group's founders in 1925—dissolved quietly in 1933 because it had no partner on the Arab side with whom it could have a dialogue.[38]

The British, whose police had shown itself incapable of protecting the Jewish minority, began a reorganization of the security forces[39] but also sent a commission of inquiry to the Mandate under Sir Walter Shaw. The commission's March 1930 report, though it identified the Arabs as being responsible for the massacres, yet again identified Jewish immigration as the key factor in the instability of the region. On this basis, Colonial Secretary Lord Passfield issued a white paper on October 20, 1930, with a new statement of British policy in Palestine. He called for significant restrictions on immigration and redefined the criteria for determining the land's capacity to absorb population growth. The quotas were not based, as before, primarily on the state of the Jewish economy; rather, immigration would now be allowed only to the extent that Arabs would not be crowded out of the labor market. This position pushed responsibility over to the Jewish side. Zionist protests finally led to the nullification of the Passfield White Paper. Prime Minister Ramsay MacDonald retracted it in an open letter in February 1931.[40]

Although the Mufti was not convicted of being responsible for the pogroms, Sir John Chancellor, high commissioner of Palestine, noted presciently, "The worst thing that happened to this country was the grant of extraordinary powers to the President of the Supreme Moslem Council from which Haj Amin derived his strength."[41] In fact, when called before the Shaw Commission, el-Husseini invoked *The Protocols of the Elders of Zion* to prove the existence of a Jewish plot in Palestine and explained, "The House of Commons is nothing more than a council of the Elders of Zion, from which we can expect no justice!"[42] Thus, the most resilient document of modern anti-Semitism—a literary forgery promoted by the czarist secret police in 1903 that supposedly confirmed a Jewish conspiracy to achieve world domination—came under discussion in Palestine as well, where it had circulated at least since

38. Brenner, p. 87; Segev, p. 446ff.
39. Kolinsky, "Reorganization," pp. 155–179.
40. *The Times*, Feb. 14, 1931; Kolinsky, *Law*, pp. 71ff., 141ff.; Porath, *Movement*, pp. 3ff., 27ff.
41. Kisch, p. 203.
42. Jorda, *Araber-Aufstand*, p. 194; cf. Cooper, "Palestinian," p. 9; Wasserstein, p. 234; Cohen, *Year*, p. 20; Krämer, *Geschichte*, p. 273.

1921.[43] After 1917, the *Protocols* became a best seller of the anti-Semitic Communist International (Comintern), and the book was specifically and emphatically praised in Hitler's *Mein Kampf* (My Struggle): "Because once this book becomes the common property of a people, the Jewish menace can be considered as broken."[44]

In addition to the fundamental ideological slant of his anti-Semitism, which in certain respects catapulted him to the "highest" European levels, the Mufti also brought about the Islamization of the conflict by 1929. By distinguishing himself as a defender of sacred sites and a champion of the Arab nation, he projected himself into the spotlight of Islamic opinion. At the same time, he leveraged the religious motivations of the fellah population, which previously was not affected by Jewish immigration and did not directly owe allegiance to his family.[45] Arab nationalism, anti-Semitism, and Islamism thus merged in a practically inseparable symbiosis. In 1929, the Mufti also won a new ally whose support he could hardly have expected. On October 16, 1929, the secretariat of the executive committee of the Communist International passed a resolution on the "uprising in Arabistan," in which it interpreted the massacres as a validation of the new ultra-left-wing direction of the Comintern, criticized the small Jewish-dominated Palestinian Communist Party for not noticing that the religious national conflict was becoming a general national anti-imperialist peasant action, and called for the Arabization of the section "from top to bottom."[46] On October 26, 1930, in an open letter, the Executive Committee complained about the inadequate implementation of this directive and appointed an Arab-dominated central committee for the first time. The 7th Party Congress of the Palestinian Communist Party, which billed itself as the "party congress of Arabization," found new groundbreaking words: "In Palestine, as a colonial land, the Jewish national minority under the Zionist influence plays the role of an imperialist agency to suppress the Arab national liberation movement."[47] Thus el-Husseini unexpectedly found a loyal partner, and the Soviet Union established the terminology underpinnings that would last many decades.

On October 13, 1933, an Arab general strike broke out. It turned against immigration, with Jews and Jewish buildings being attacked in Haifa. Violent demonstrations, in which the Arabs used firearms and dynamite on a large scale for the first time, faced determined opposition by the police; a total of 27

43. Wild, "Rezeption," p. 519; cf. Wistrich, p. 281f.
44. Hitler, p. 337; cf. Cohn; Sammons.
45. Schechtman, p. 39ff.; Elpeleg, p. 26ff.; Jbara, pp. 90ff., 103ff.
46. Flores, p. 267f.
47. Ibid., p. 270.

Arabs who attacked the British were shot.[48] In January 1935, at the al-Aqsa Mosque, el-Husseini issued a fatwa that was subsequently printed and distributed throughout the country. In it he declared that Palestine had been entrusted to the Muslims and denounced as traitors and unbelievers all those who would sell this "holy Islamic land" to the Jews. Supported by the Koran, he threatened these traitors and unbelievers with business boycotts and the denial of Muslim burial. Shortly thereafter, an association of Islamic religious and legal scholars, the Central Society for the Promotion of the Good and the Prevention of the Reprehensible, was established to monitor land sales and address immoral behavior such as unseemly attire, unauthorized encounters between men and women, and offensive scenes in literature, film, and theater.[49] With these initiatives, the Islamization of the Arab national movement took another step forward.

Hitler's rise to power in Germany in 1933, along with increasing anti-Semitism in other European countries, launched the Fifth Aliyah. In 1933, Jewish immigrants numbered 30,327; in 1934, 42,359; and in 1935, 61,854. In 1937, the population of Palestine was 1,401,794 of which 883,446 were Muslims and 395,836 were Jews (who thus made up less than one-third of the total). Within three years—between 1933 and 1935—the Jewish population had almost doubled. This growth contributed in particular to the expansion of Tel Aviv, Jerusalem, and Haifa, but Jews still lived in unconnected enclaves scattered throughout the mandate territory. As a result of British restrictions, immigration levels decreased considerably in the following years. In 1936, 29,727 Jews arrived; in 1937, only 10,536; in 1938, 12,868; and in 1939, 16,405.[50] In the mid-1930s, just when a safe asylum for the Jews would have been particularly important, the doors in Palestine and elsewhere were closed ever tighter. As Dr. Chaim Weizmann, president of the Zionist organization, lamented, the world was divided into countries in which the Jews could not live and countries to which they could not emigrate.[51] The share of immigrants from German-speaking areas increased sharply after 1933—from only about 2.5 percent of annual immigration previously to 17 percent in 1933 and 52 percent in 1938.[52] In contrast to the Jews from Eastern Europe, the immigrants from Germany were generally not motivated by Zionist idealism but by the tangible threats of the National Socialists. Upon arrival in Palestine, the immi-

---

48. Kolinsky, *Law*, p. 172ff.; Lesch, p. 214f.; Krämer, *Geschichte*, p. 297f.
49. Krämer, *Geschichte*, p. 295; Kolinsky, *Law*, p. 185.
50. Stewart, *Relations*, p. 20f.; Krämer, *Geschichte*, p. 280f.
51. Wasserstein, p. 237.
52. Melka, *Axis*, p. 46.

grants were therefore often confronted with the wry question, "Do you come out of conviction or from Germany?"[53]

As the immigration restrictions indicate, the British also viewed Jewish immigration in an increasingly critical light. Many members of the mandate government already saw the Balfour Declaration, which in London was regarded as the basis for the British presence in Palestine, as the greatest obstacle to the formation of a normal colonial government. Some were pro-Arab, and some even anti-Semitic; certainly the majority were anti-Zionist.[54] Viennese author Franz Schattenfroh, who wrote the anti-Semitic best seller *Wille und Rasse* (Will and Race) and traveled to Palestine during the second half of the 1930s, noted that "British police officers, most of whom are Mosley supporters, like to raise a hand and salute the swastika flag, for example, whether they are passing on foot or by car. Many English officers and officials who knew next to nothing about the Jewish question in their homeland become convinced anti-Semites in Palestine."[55]

Given the prior history and the growing wave of immigration, anti-Semitism was particularly widespread among the Arabs of Palestine. Beginning in the early 1930s, a process of political party formation led to the creation of national networks that reached beyond the traditional family and patronage structures. On August 4, 1932, the pan-Arab Istiqlal (Independence) Party was founded by Auni Abd el-Hadi; it advocated a strategy of non-cooperation with the mandate government and the non-payment of taxes. In December 1934, the Nashashibis' National Defense Party was formed, which espoused cooperation with the British. The Mufti responded in March 1935 by creating the Palestine Arab Party, which repudiated all Jewish rights in Palestine. This party found a close ally in the Reform Party created by Dr. Hussein al-Khalidi in June of that same year. The establishment of the relatively moderate National Bloc Party in October 1935 concluded the party formation process. Despite differences regarding details, all the parties were in agreement in their demands for an Arab state and their animosity toward Zionism.[56]

A radicalization of the youth organizations took place at the same time. The Young Men's Muslim Association and the Arab Boy Scouts became overtly militant organizations.[57] And the motto of al-Futuwwa, the youth section of the Mufti's party, founded in February 1936, proclaimed, "Freedom is my right, independence my goal, Arabism my precept, Palestine my land

53. Brenner, p. 106.
54. Krämer, *Geschichte*, p. 187.
55. Schattenfroh, p. 55.
56. Schiller, p. 95ff.; Elpeleg, p. 34ff.; Krämer, *Geschichte*, p. 299ff.; Porath, *Movement*, p. 62ff.
57. Kolinsky, Law, p. 170f.

alone."[58] Turned around, this meant the Jews had no right to exist. The new powers also included various covert Arab organizations that preached and practiced jihad as "holy war." In Galilee, the Islamic group Green Hand emerged in October 1929; it attacked Jewish settlements until 1931, when it was disbanded by the British. In August of that same year, the Organization for Holy War was formed under the leadership of Abd el-Qadir el-Husseini, a close relative of the Mufti; by the end of 1934 it was providing underground military training to 400 youths. Other groups, such as the Young Rebels, operated in 1935 near Nablus and Tulkarm. They were generally established through the initiative of local leaders of the Istiqlal Party or the Young Men's Muslim Association. It remains unclear to what extent the Mufti already supported (at least secretly) these gangs.[59]

Another critical element in the process of ideologically charging and radicalizing Arab patterns of behavior was the impetus provided by Islamic fundamentalist Izz al-Din al-Qassam (the Hamas brigades that carry out suicide attacks against Israelis bear his name even today). As imam of Haifa, he took part in 1928 in the founding of the Young Men's Muslim Association, declared jihad to be the personal responsibility of every believer, and proclaimed the ideal of the martyr (shahid) who sacrifices himself for the cause of Islam and is rewarded in paradise. The ideal starting point for the agitation and the resulting recruitment of combatants was his mosque, as the British avoided the interior. In November 1935, al-Qassam decided that the time was ripe for an uprising and went into the mountains with part of his group. After they had murdered a Jewish police officer in northern Samaria, they were confronted by a British patrol and shot. Al-Qassam's burial procession became a triumphal march, and his grave a place of pilgrimage.[60] That such a terrorist, even after September 11, 2001, could still be labeled in Western scholarly literature as a martyr who bore witness to "his faith and the Palestinian cause"[61] can be explained only by a mixture of blindness and the author's uncritical infatuation with his subject. And the characterization of al-Qassam as "a deeply religious shaykh and a man of integrity, social concern, and eloquence" is also miles off the mark.[62] Al-Qassam reduced the concept of jihad—which previously, as "striving in the way of God," had been a relatively open concept—to the war against unbelievers and declared this militant version to be the authoritative interpretation of the Koran, thereby eliminating any potential for tolerance in one of the

58. Krämer, *Geschichte*, p. 301.
59. Ibid. p. 302f.; Elpeleg, p. 37ff.; Porath, *Movement*, p. 118ff.
60. Schleifer, p. 61ff.; Lachman, p. 59ff.; Nafi, Shaykh, p. 185ff.; Segev, p. 301ff.
61. Krämer, *Geschichte*, pp. 302, 307.
62. Mattar, "The Mufti of Jerusalem and the Politics of Palestine," p. 234.

world's great religions and providing spiritual cover for any violence. Some of al-Qassam's surviving followers would play a significant role in the impending Arab revolt.[63]

The date for the beginning of this first intifada was chosen with care. Great Britain's demonstrated weakness in the Abyssinian crisis and shortly thereafter in Spain, the ascent of Japan and Germany, and the developing Berlin-Rome axis revealed the vulnerability of the Empire and portended a power shift in the Middle East as well.[64] The fact that, for the first time, a Western country—Germany—had excluded the Jews made their defenselessness clear and unleashed additional incentives.[65] The actual provocation for the revolt was arbitrary: on April 15, 1936, Arabs shot two Jewish settlers. In retaliation, Jews killed two Arabs the following night. Incidents of this nature had occurred dozens of times without leading to extensive unrest. This time, however, the reaction was different. On April 19, Arabs killed nine Jews in Jaffa,[66] and on April 25, Sir Arthur Wauchope, Chancellor's successor as high commissioner, was surprised by the news that all six Arab parties had joined forces as the Arab Higher Committee under the chairmanship of the Mufti and declared a general strike. The new alliance demanded an end to Jewish immigration, a ban on selling land to Jews, and the formation of an Arab government.[67] The Communists, though remaining outside the Islamic consensus, immediately declared their unconditional support.[68]

That the Arab majority was ostensibly induced to take this step due to "fear of a massive Jewish arms buildup, which they could not counter with anything comparable,"[69] would be clearly refuted afterward. The report of a regular German informer at the end of 1935, according to which the Arabs would be able to carry out only "peripheral slaughters in remote areas of Jewish colonization that are not rapidly reachable by either the Haganah [the Jewish defense organization] or the military,"[70] would soon be disproved by the uprising itself. The general strike immediately developed into a national armed revolt, directed first against the Jews and then increasingly against the British. Muslim functionaries appealed to the population in the name of Islam to unite with the rebels and join the revolt. Snipers fired from strategic points at patrols, passersby, and vehicles. British police stations were stormed, telephone

63. Lachman, p. 78ff.
64. DGK Jerusalem to AA, Feb. 12, 1936, PAAA, R 78338; Wirsing, p. 152; Sheffer, "Principles," p. 111f.; Pratt, p. 12ff.
65. O'Brien, p. 129.
66. Cohen, *Palestine*, p. 10.
67. Schiller, p. 106f.; Porath, *Movement*, p. 162ff.; Kalkas, p. 241ff.
68. Flores, p. 281ff.; Jorda, *Araber-Aufstand*, p. 203.
69. Krämer, *Geschichte*, p. 308.
70. Hamburg-Bremen Information Agency to AA on Nov. 28, 1935, PAAA, R 78338.

and telegraph wires cut, and roads and railroad tracks destroyed by mines. The Arabs attacked Jewish settlements, destroyed their fields and plantations, cut down fruit trees, and slaughtered livestock.[71] The peasant gangs were soon reinforced by guerrillas from Syria and Iraq who were active in Palestine under the rebel leader Fawzi al-Qawuqji.[72] From then on, jihad and paramilitarization would become the definitive hallmark of Palestinian nationalism.[73]

By October 12, 1936, when the general strike was stopped thanks to the intervention of Arab governments,[74] the toll stood at 306 dead and 1,322 injured. The civilian population suffered 277 deaths (187 Muslims, 80 Jews, and 10 Christians), while the military and police had 29 deaths to mourn.[75] Although relative peace had returned to Palestine by mid-October, a rekindling of the insurrection seemed possible at any time. The rebels had not been disarmed, the influence of the Arab Higher Committee had not been reduced, and the position of the Mufti remained untouched.[76] "Cross-border arms smuggling is very active and could amply supply the population," reported the German consul general Dr. Walter Doehle in early 1937. "The situation in Palestine can be characterized as follows: in the time since the strike was called off, the terrorist activities (attacks on roads and settlements) have never completely stopped. Only in comparison to the peak of the turmoil in the summer months, when there was actual combat, can a reduction be noted, but throughout this period one could never speak of security in the area."[77] General John Dill, commander-in-chief of the British troops in Palestine, wryly noted to the War Office that an armed ceasefire would be the best description of the situation.[78]

It became clear that the mandatory power's "peace organization"—which included the Palestine Police Force, composed of British, Arabs, and Jews; the Transjordan Frontier Force; and two infantry battalions—was already overburdened in preventing demonstrations and riots in the cities. And everyone knew that the Arab police, which made up the backbone of the security structure in the predominantly Arab-settled areas, had proven unreliable because the officers were at the mercy of the insurrectionists' reprisals and, as "collaborators and traitors," represented preferred assassination targets.[79] At

---

71. Hurewitz, p. 67ff.; O'Brien, p. 131ff.; Porath, *Movement*, p. 166ff.; Krämer, *Geschichte*, p. 316ff.

72. DG Baghdad to AA, Dec. 17, 1936, PAAA, R 102806; Jorda, Fauzi, p. 261ff.; Arnon-Ohanna, p. 234ff.; Swedenburg, "Role," p. 190ff.

73. Schiller, p. 111ff.

74. Rose, p. 213ff.; Cohen, *Palestine*, pp. 18ff., 25ff.; Sheffer, "Involvement," p. 63ff.

75. Report by Foreign Service/AA, Jan. 19, 1937, PAAA, R 104786.

76. Schechtman, p. 51.

77. DGK Jerusalem to AA, Feb. 17, 1937, PAAA, R 104791.

78. Schiller, p. 137.

79. Ibid., p. 123.

the same time, al-Qassam's shadow fell grimly across the land. The anti-Jewish struggle was glorified as a religious duty, and the Palestinian conflict was positioned in a pan-Islamic and pan-Arab context.[80] Moreover, the open threat of annihilation now hung over the Yishuv: "As long as the Jews want to establish a national home in Palestine, peace will be impossible here," declared the Arab Higher Committee. "Whenever the English remove their hands from this land, we will throw and chase all the Jews in a stampede into the sea!"[81]

On August 8, 1936, the British ordered another commission of inquiry, under the chairmanship of Lord William Robert Peel. He was not able to travel to Palestine until three months later, however, due to the continuing unrest. The Mufti did not mince words with this commission, either: "Give us independence, and we will deal with the Jews ourselves!"[82] When he was asked whether the Jews could be integrated or assimilated, he answered simply, "No." The next question was whether the Jews should then be expelled or "somehow removed." "We must leave all that to the future," said the Mufti, and el-Hadi, leader of the Istiqlal Party, answered tellingly, "This is not a question that can be decided here." He also did not hesitate to call on the Third Reich as a key witness. When 60 million Germans could not endure the presence of 600,000 Jews, how could one expect the Arabs to accept the presence of 400,000 Jews in a much smaller country?[83]

The commission, mindful of the Balfour Declaration, did not wish to concur with this type of solution to the conflict, which hinted at the ultimate culmination in mass murder. Instead, in its report published July 7, 1937, it made a downright revolutionary proposal. It recognized Jews and Arabs as "national communities" whose differences had proven insurmountable. Because unification was highly unlikely in the foreseeable future, clinging to the idea of a Palestinian citizenship represented a ruinous illusion: the incompatible national aspirations of Arabs and Jews prevented them from uniting in the service of a single state.[84] Cantonizing on the Swiss model would thus not go far enough. Peace would be possible only if Palestine were partitioned and two independent states—one Jewish and one Arab—were formed. The commission therefore recommended dividing the country into three zones: a Jewish state comprising the coastal plain from Tel Aviv to Acre and Galilee, a British mandate remnant consisting of the sacred sites in Jerusalem and Bethlehem as well as a narrow corridor to the Mediterranean, and an Arab state incorporating the rest

---

80. Küntzel, *Djihad*, p. 40.
81. Jorda, *Araber-Aufstand*, p. 196f.
82. Ibid., p. 296; cf. Jbara, p. 154ff.; Schechtman, p. 51ff.
83. Laqueur, p. 536f.
84. Krämer, *Geschichte*, p. 327.

of Palestine and Transjordan. Thus, concluded the commission, although partition "offers neither party all it wants, it offers each what it wants most, namely freedom and security."[85]

Although the Peel Plan represented a radical shift away from the previous questionable approaches to resolving the conflict, it found few supporters. In the House of Lords, the first high commissioner in Palestine, now Viscount Herbert Samuel, argued against the plan based on a view that was shared by many other British politicians: in the planned Jewish state, 225,000 Arabs would live alongside 258,000 Jews; conversely, there were numerous Jewish enclaves within the future Arab part of the territory. Due to the hardships it would impose, he categorically ruled out a population exchange like the one 10 years earlier between Greece and Turkey. The Peel Plan, he prophesied pointedly, would in reality create a Saar Territory, a Polish Corridor, and half a dozen Danzigs and Memels in an area the size of Wales.[86] At the 20th Zionist Congress in mid-August 1937 in Zurich, Weizmann criticized the limited size of the Jewish territory. He declared, however, that the Jews had only one choice: they could become either a minority in all of Palestine or a compact Jewish majority in a part of Palestine.[87] While this signaled extremely reluctant agreement, the Arab Higher Committee and the Mufti immediately and fiercely opposed the partition plan. They criticized in particular the British government's "greatly mistaken" idea "that the Arabs and Jews are two combating parties that both have equal rights."[88] In addition, el-Husseini had a very personal reason for his abrupt dismissal of the proposals. The unification of the remainder of Palestine with Transjordan would have meant the end of his political power and the triumph of his enemy, Emir Abdullah, in Amman.

Immediately following the announcement of the Peel Plan, the Arab revolt flared up in Palestine once again. On September 26, 1937, Lewis Andrews, the district commissioner of Galilee, became the first senior British official to be murdered. The United Kingdom's response to this provocation was a significantly intensified reaction. In the early morning hours of October 1, the police arrested all the members of the Arab Higher Committee except the Mufti, deported them to the Seychelles Islands, and dissolved the committee, and all subcommittees. In addition, el-Husseini, who had been hiding on the grounds of the Haram ash-Sharif (the Noble Sanctuary) since July, was removed from his position as president of the Supreme Muslim Council and the awqaf. But the British did not dare enter the Haram. On October 12, el-Husseini fled from

85. O'Brien, p. 142; cf. Hurewitz, p. 72ff.; Porath, *Movement*, p. 220ff.; Krämer, *Geschichte*, p. 325ff.
86. Laqueur, p. 539.
87. DGK Zurich to DG Bern, Aug. 19, 1937, PAAA, R 104788.
88. Memorandum by Arab Higher Committee, July 23, 1937, PAAA, R 104789.

Jerusalem to Lebanon dressed as a Bedouin. In exile in Beirut, he built up new guerilla units[89] while the French mandatory power there declared that the Palestinian conflict "n'est pas notre affaire."[90] "It is suspected, however, that after the arrest of the previously recognized leaders, who to some extent attempted to exercise a moderating influence on the radical elements, the leadership of the Arab national movement will pass to local terrorist organizations that are determined to carry out the struggle against the Jews and English by means of individual acts of terrorism," prophesied the German deputy consul general, Herbert Dittmann, at the time. "The existence of such organizations—with few but extremely determined members—can hardly be doubted."[91]

Shortly before, from September 8 to 10, a pan-Arab conference had taken place in Bludan, Syria. The conference participants recommended the renewed use of force, organized foreign arms purchases accordingly,[92] and at the same time issued an open threat: Great Britain must choose between its friendship with the Arabs and its friendship with the Jews. It must withdraw the partition plan, "or we shall be at liberty to side with other European Powers whose politics are inimical to Great Britain."[93] This attempt at blackmail, which would be repeated a year later at another conference in Cairo,[94] was bound to elicit a reaction in London. But first, beginning on October 14, the British were confronted with a rapid surge in violence in Palestine that dwarfed the events of the previous year.[95] "Entire English patrols would often disappear without a trace," observed Franz Schattenfroh. "On almost all residential streets in Palestine, one frequently sees the charred remains of buses and cars of all kinds that were stopped by shots to the tires and then burned with everyone inside or blown up with bombs."[96] Schattenfroh, who apparently had first-hand knowledge of these events, was able to report in detail on the methods of the "Arab guerrillas" as well: "All attacks—recently against Jewish auxiliary police in particular—are organized in those headquarters and the underground, and it is noteworthy that in three years not a single assassin has been caught in the act, even though such attacks are consistently carried out in broad daylight and in the middle of the chaos of traffic. Usually the perpetrator walks away quite innocently; a veiled woman or a boy follows him and hands him the weapon at

89. Elpeleg, p. 47ff.; Jbara, p. 163ff.
90. Laurens, p. 68.
91. DGK Jerusalem to AA, Oct. 5, 1937, PAAA, R 104788.
92. DGK Jerusalem to DGK Beirut, Oct. 16, 1937, PAAA, R 104789; Kedourie, "Bludan," p. 107ff.
93. Marlowe, p. 145f.
94. Ibid., p. 151f.
95. DGK Jerusalem to AA, Oct. 22, 1937, PAAA, R 104789; cf. Krämer, *Geschichte*, p. 332ff.; Hurewitz, p. 81ff.; Nevo, "Activity," p. 178ff.; Kolinsky, "Collapse," p. 153ff.; Lesch, p. 221ff.; Porath, *Movement*, p. 233ff.
96. Schattenfroh, p. 53f.

the last minute, and then takes it back again and disappears after the gun has been fired. Therefore during the subsequent search of the entire quarter, no weapons are found on any Arab men."[97] The British were reluctant to perform body searches of Arab women, and children could slip through anywhere anyway.[98]

"The heavy-handed policy has had no success," reported Doehle at the end of 1937. Even though the British imposed martial law and demolished the houses used by the insurgents to shoot from, the disturbances again escalated into guerrilla warfare. The consul general predicted, "The harsh approach of the mandate government has bred in the Arab population a fanaticism and hatred that could have serious consequences."[99] The second year of the uprising brought a total of 97 deaths: 32 Jewish civilians, 21 representatives of the mandatory power and security institutions, and 44 Arab civilians (most of them died as a result of the guerrillas' terrorist activities).[100] At the same time, however, the United Kingdom began moving away from the Peel Plan. For the eight months ending in March 1938, the immigration quota was reduced to 8,000. "Officials returning to England make no secret of the fact that if the present policy is pursued, they have no desire for further service in a country where they are forced to risk their lives for a pro-Jewish solution," observed Berlin's ambassador in Jerusalem. He stated further: "News reports from England give the impression that because of the pro-Jewish agitation in Parliament and in the press, more voices have emerged in support of the Arabs and the implementation of a real colonial policy."[101]

Doehle was completely correct in his prediction. In December 1937, Prime Minister Neville Chamberlain brought his authority to bear in support of the Foreign Office policy. The new commission under Sir John Woodhead, instructed in 1938 to reassess the Peel partition plans on location, was given the option of discarding them altogether if necessary. The commission, which stayed in Palestine from the end of April to July, was totally boycotted by the Arabs, though they understood the significance of its mission. In its November 9 report, the Woodhead Commission conceded the impossibility of developing a realistic partition plan in view of Arab opposition. Both of the proposed state structures would be too small to survive economically. It would be impossible to create a Jewish state that would include only a few Arabs yet at the same time be large enough to allow space for additional immigrants. Population

97. Ibid., pp. 61, 64.
98. Krämer, *Geschichte*, p. 334.
99. DGK Jerusalem to AA, Dec. 29, 1937, PAAA, R 104789.
100. Schiller, p. 163.
101. DGK Jerusalem to AA, Dec. 29, 1937, PAAA, R 104789.

exchanges would only further complicate the situation. With this report, the British government was offered a devastating critique of the Peel Plan.[102] Already well prepared in this respect, the government published a white paper that same month in which it repudiated a solution to the Palestinian conflict based on the principle of partition taking a position that it would sustain until 1947. While the Chamberlain government rejected the Peel Plan as "impracticable," it declared at the same time that peace could only be achieved through an understanding between Jews and Arabs.[103]

This prediction in late 1938 was even more astonishing considering that that year represented the peak of violent terror—206 Jewish civilians, 175 representatives of the mandatory power and security agencies, and 454 Arab civilians were killed.[104] In addition to these 835 deaths, the British noted the deaths of 1,138 armed Arab guerrillas.[105] "With the exception of individual cities such as Jerusalem, Haifa, and Tel Aviv, the insurgents control the country," reported Dittmann to Berlin in mid-September 1938. "The insurgent Arabs, though initially numerically weak, succeeded in drawing virtually the entire Arab population of Palestine to their side. The means employed to achieve this goal were, in accordance with the Oriental character and fanaticism of the insurgents, often downright barbarous, as the insurgents employed not only the weapon of propaganda but widespread individual terror, and had no qualms about killing their own people. No consideration was taken of age, scholarship, or previous merit. Anyone who did not place himself wholeheartedly on the side of the Palestinian freedom fighters—whether he was an official in the service of the mandate government or a Muslim cleric or a simple peasant—and was under suspicion of collaboration with the English was sentenced to death by the insurgents and murdered." Near Jaffa, for example, two dead Arabs were found, "one with his heart torn from his body and the second with his throat slit and his tongue pulled through." Both had placards attached with the inscription "This is how we treat traitors to the national cause." In addition, underground sharia tribunals were established to rule on "criminal offenses" in their own ranks and "the fate of abducted Jewish hostages." To Dittmann, the consequences were obvious: "These means have not failed to achieve their purpose. Today the insurgents can rightly claim that they are not fanatical loners but supporters of a popular movement." And further: "The Arabs are feeling and experiencing for the first time that it is

---

102. Cohen, *Palestine*, p. 41ff.; Cohen, *Direction*, p. 244ff.
103. Laqueur, p. 544.
104. Schiller, p. 163.
105. *The Times*, Jan. 2, 1939; Stewart, *Relations*, p. 90.

possible to create a unified, fanatical people, and also to impose their will on the English, who previously seemed unassailable."[106]

"A certain disappointment is noticeable among the Arabs, over the fact that the Munich Agreement peacefully resolved the European conflict that they had been anticipating for years," commented Doehle one month later regarding the reaction to the conference that temporarily relaxed tensions over the Sudetenland crisis in October 1938.[107] He confirmed at the same time a "further exacerbation of the situation" in the Middle East: "The insurgents' activities have caused the mandate government to close most police stations, administrative offices, and courts in the insurrectionist area. It can be claimed without exaggeration that the rebels currently control the majority of Palestine and that they also wield complete power over the Arabs located in areas ruled by the British. [...] People speak of a day government and a night government, but it is clear that the so-called Arab night government rules most of Palestine by day as well. Even in Jerusalem it carries out punitive measures during the day and uses its agents to bring suspects out of the city."[108] One month later, the German consul in Haifa reported that until recently, "Arab gangs from outside the area [...] attacked local Jewish settlements in the evenings, plundering and killing even women and children." He also mentioned that "in Haifa, starting about 10 days ago, individual Jewish workers are being shot almost daily in their workplaces and on the streets, with no perpetrators being detained."[109] During this time, the Arabs continually ravaged the land cultivated by the Jews; estimates suggest 200,000 destroyed trees.[110]

Despite the high number of Jewish victims, the Jews in Palestine were not the only targets of the Arab revolt. The Arabs would also turn on other Arabs within their own ranks. While Arab terrorists took the lives of 547 Jews between 1936 and 1939, they also killed 494 Arabs—an almost equal number.[111] Motives included readiness to compromise with the Jews and the British, support for the Nashashibis (publicly repudiated as too moderate), pro-Western attitudes, vendettas, and pure greed. "In Haifa, the Arab business community in particular has suffered under the terrorism of the insurgents," related Dr. Wilhelm Melchers, the German consul there, with regard to the situation in the north. "Arab merchants whose patriotism is unimpeachable have received threats and extortionary letters from the insurgents, forcing them to pay sums that are sometimes beyond their means. Anyone who does not pay

---

106. DGK Jerusalem to AA, Sept. 14, 1938, PAAA, R 104790.
107. Ibid., Oct. 11, 1938, PAAA, R 104790.
108. Ibid., Oct. 20, 1938, PAAA, R 104789; cf. Lesch, p. 222ff.
109. DK Haifa to AA, Nov. 23, 1938, PAAA, R 104790.
110. Sykes, *Kreuzwege*, p. 199.
111. Bowden, p. 147; Kolinsky, "Collapse," p. 162.

or flee in time is a marked person. Creditors with larger debts are in particular danger. They have left Haifa in droves and have fled to Syria, Egypt, and Cyprus. Old feuds and family disputes are being rekindled under the guise of politics and paraded before the insurrectionists' tribunals in the mountains. The accused are summoned there or abducted, and are lucky if they get off with only fines or contributions to the insurgents. This situation has created the opportunity to wage vendettas under political pretexts."[112] Doehle saw much of the same in Jerusalem: "In Palestine there can hardly be a single respected Arab who has not already been questioned by agents from the Arab headquarters and, depending on the outcome of the inquiry, either issued a certificate of indemnity or sentenced or banished."[113] At the same time, the *New York Times* reported, "More than 90% of the casualties of the last few days have been inflicted by Arab terrorists on Arabs."[114]

Germans traveling to Palestine at the time also noted the intra-Arab terrorism and described it enthusiastically as a necessary straightening of the Arabs' own ranks: "In addition, there exist Arab tribunals that operate rather cavalierly and administer justice in all areas relating to the national struggle and national honor." For example, the leaders of the rebellion proclaimed that "with the exception of extremely urgent cases, the Arab population was absolutely forbidden to apply for passports from the English authorities. Anyone who disobeyed was sentenced and, not infrequently, shot in broad daylight in the middle of the street," declared Franz Schattenfroh.[115] And Mufti biographer Kurt Fischer-Weth wrote effusively, "An official sits gloomily in the darkness of a cave in the rock, which is being used as a prison. He did not relay important information about official activities to the insurgents in a timely manner, because he feared for his job. [...] Now he fears for his head, not for his job ... A shopkeeper sits in the furthest corner of the cave and calculates while beads of sweat form on his forehead. He should have calculated sooner. When the collectors for the revolutionary army came, he fobbed them off with many words."[116] The former SA (Sturmabteilung) spirit inside author Fischer-Weth had no doubt revived and was guiding his pen.

Due to the massive internally directed terror campaign, progress toward developing a civil society in the Arab part of Palestine was abruptly halted. The Arab sphere abolished the rule of law, disconnected itself from the legal system of the British mandate government, and judged according to its own discretion,

---

112. DK Haifa to AA, Nov. 23, 1938, PAAA, R 104790; examples in Schechtman, p. 73ff.
113. DGK Jerusalem to AA, Oct. 20, 1938, PAAA, R 104789.
114. *New York Times*, Oct. 15, 1938.
115. Schattenfroh, p. 63f.
116. Fischer-Weth, p. 84f.; similarly Jorda, *Araber-Aufstand*, pp. 217, 302; Wirsing, p. 155.

using unlimited, unrestrained force. The insurgents imposed their will on society, replaced laws with arbitrary decisions, and kept the areas "liberated" by them beyond any legal jurisdiction. The last remnants of freedom and open dissent vanished, making way for extortion and intimidation, censorship and mental terror. A monitoring and denunciation association was established to pursue "enemies of the revolution" and "un-Islamic" deviationists. Politics, religion, personal enmities, family feuds, and ordinary crime merged into a colorful mélange.[117] While legal certainty, human rights, and individual liberty were thus being abolished, the Mufti triumphed in exile. The uprising against the Jews and the British gave him the opportunity to eliminate all opponents within his own camp—those Palestinians who supported a two-state solution and who wanted to negotiate with the Jews rather than shoot them.[118] Arab intellectuals from Haifa asked el-Husseini at that time for a fatwa against murder, but he flatly refused.[119]

The depth of the tyranny of forced conformity was demonstrated by the new dress code for the Arab population, aggressively enforced in August 1938. "It was suddenly decreed that anyone who identified with the Palestinian national cause must wear the same headdress as the insurgents—kaffiyeh and agal (headcloth and double cord)," reported Dittmann in September of that year. "This order has been obeyed by Mohammedans as well as Christians, gentlemen as well as peasants, so that today the centuries-old headdress of the urban Arabs, the tarboosh, has completely disappeared, and the cities of Palestine have a completely different external appearance."[120]

This decree was also enforced by terror, as Fischer-Weth describes smugly: "On a tree-lined street in the Old City of Jerusalem, the police find them: two Arabs lying facedown, clearly felled by shots to the back, but with the bullet holes carefully covered by that familiar headdress known in Europe as a 'fez' but in the Orient as a 'tarboosh.' One of the two dead is a prominent lawyer, the other an affluent homeowner. The bullets from which they bled to death did not come from Jewish or British firearms ... The two are Arabs who have been shot by Arabs. They committed the crime of disregarding the latest instructions issued by the general of the guerrilla forces, which a few days earlier had been posted on every street corner in Jerusalem."[121]

The insurgents also forced Arab women—even Christians—to renounce Western dress and veil their faces.[122] Women who refused were berated as

117. Arnon-Ohanna, p. 244ff.
118. Küntzel, *Djihad*, p. 152f.
119. Elpeleg, p. 50.
120. DGK Jerusalem to AA, Sept. 14, 1938, PAAA, R 104790; similarly Jorda, *Araber-Aufstand*, p. 405.
121. Fischer-Weth, p. 82f.; similarly Schattenfroh, p. 64.
122. Swedenburg, *Memories*, p. 181ff.; Segev, p. 402f.; Schechtman, p. 47f.

whores, and their hats were torn from their heads.[123] At the same time, one of the most important rebel leaders reminded the women of the punishments that awaited them should they persist in their foolish frivolity.[124] When the German Leopold von Mildenstein traveled through Palestine, the picture he saw was not terribly pleasing: "Some Arab women are sitting across from me. The very old are no longer veiled, though one would welcome it if they were. The others are often only by a bolt of fabric."[125] The enforcement of the veil requirement was still ardently romanticized in Western scholarly literature as late as 2002. Against those "women of the Jerusalem aristocracy," who as socialites liked to stroll around "dressed in the European style and with their faces uncovered," a seemingly very Islamic argument was presented: "Islamic scholars and activists, from the Mufti and the 'Society for the Promotion of the Good and the Prevention of the Reprehensible' to Izz al-Din al-Qassam, spoke out against these signs of Westernization (the female Jewish settlers went out in public half naked, according to conservative opinion), against moral degeneracy, for morality and decency, and, in this context, also for the veil."[126] The significance of the fact that this explanation simply did not exist previously in Islam appears to be irrelevant to some Arabists.

While this repression was being aggressively enforced under an Islamic decree, the cracks in the British-Jewish relationship widened. The closer Europe slid toward war, the more London was seeking an appeasement policy toward the Arab states. The British believed that in the event of a conflict, Arab support, or at least their benign neutrality, was required, and British actions opposing the Arab revolt in Palestine clearly constituted the greatest obstacle to this. Maintaining good relations with the Jews, by contrast, was not a cause for concern. The British were confident about the Jews, because in the event of war they would have no choice but to support the British side. The option of an alliance with the Third Reich was not available to them, though it certainly was to the Arabs. Consequently, consideration toward the Jews decreased, while it increased toward the Arab world.[127] Of course, the British were aware of the Arabs' affinity for the National Socialists, but it was precisely this tendency that promoted rather than discouraged the search for cooperation. The fundamental strategic situation was all too clear: the Arabs were located precisely on the central land route to India, the heart of the Empire, and on the Mediterranean, the shortest sea route to the Asian subcontinent. It

---

123. *The Times*, Sept. 5, 1938.
124. Swedenburg, *Memories*, p. 182.
125. Mildenstein, *Land*, p. 54.
126. Krämer, *Geschichte*, p. 338.
127. Bethell, p. 37ff.; O'Brien, p. 137ff.; Segev, p. 476ff.; Kedourie, "Great Britain," pp. 93–170.

was at this weak link in particular that a clash had to be avoided at all costs. Fear regarding the defensive capability of the Empire in the event of a new world war became the dominant theme.[128]

When a final British-Arab-Jewish attempt to reach agreement on the Palestinian conflict began on February 7, 1939, at St. James Palace in London, the conference was little more than window dressing. All the parties knew that the partition plan was no longer under consideration, and they suspected that the promise made in the Balfour Declaration was up for negotiation, as was future Jewish immigration. This marked the beginning of the policy that Chamberlain would summarize as follows before the Palestine committee of the Cabinet on April 20: "If we must offend one side, let us offend the Jews rather than the Arabs."[129] Even the German ambassador in London seemed very certain about this matter at the beginning of the conference: "Essentially, all signs indicate that the Palestine problem will be resolved, with the support of the English, in the Arabs' favor."[130] The Arabs declined to negotiate directly with the Jews, and neither side expressed interest in a binational state. On March 15 the British government offered the parties a series of final proposals, but both rejected them. That same day, the Wehrmacht marched into Czechoslovakia. Two days later, the conference adjourned without reaching any conclusion.[131]

On May 17, 1939, His Majesty's Government published a white paper written by colonial secretary Malcolm MacDonald, son of the former prime minister, that would settle the Palestine conflict and remain officially valid throughout World War II. This unilateral declaration by the British government contained the most favorable proposal the Arabs had received since the beginning of the mandate. Neither partition nor an independent Jewish state was considered. The issue of a "national home for the Jewish people" was declared closed. Within 10 years, a Palestinian state with an Arab majority was to obtain its sovereignty. During the coming five years, only 75,000 Jews would be allowed to enter the country. After that, further immigration would be possible only with Arab consent. In addition, Jews were forbidden to purchase land in heavily populated Arab areas. The British government did not, according to the key sentence of the white paper, intend that "Palestine should be converted into a Jewish State against the will of the Arab population of the country."[132] During the House of Commons debate on May 23, Churchill

---

128. Cohen, "Strategy," p. 157ff.; Omissi, p. 14ff.
129. Segev, p. 478; cf. Zweig, "Palestine," p. 206ff.
130. DG London to AA, Feb. 16, 1939, PAAA, R 99387.
131. Bethell, p. 61ff.; O'Brien, p. 149ff.; Laqueur, p. 544ff.; Porath, *Movement*, p. 281ff.
132. Hurewitz, p. 98ff.; Cohen, *Palestine*, p. 66ff.; Sykes, *Kreuzwege*, p. 213ff.

declared, "I regret very much that the pledge of the Balfour Declaration, endorsed as it has been by successive Governments, and the conditions under which we obtained the Mandate, have both been violated by the Government's proposals."[133] He refused to support the white paper. Meanwhile, the Arabs celebrated in Palestine, and the Union Jack was burned for the first time in Tel Aviv. The white paper was regarded by the Jews as capitulation before Arab nationalism as well as a reward for the three-year uprising.[134] Nevertheless, Weizmann wrote to Chamberlain on August 29, on the eve of the world war: "The Jews stand by Great Britain and will fight on the side of the democracies."[135]

133. DNB, May 23, 1939, PAAA, R 99387.
134. Hurewitz, p. 108.
135. Weizmann, p. 253.

Chapter II

Nazi Sympathies:

Middle East Supporters of the Third Reich

Because the Middle East also considered itself as a victim of the Paris peace treaties following World War I, observers there marveled at the way Germany was able to throw off the chains of Versailles after 1933 and achieve a renaissance as a powerful state. Growing separation from the Western democracies and the values they had imported—parliamentarianism and rule of law, universal human rights and secular constitutions, freedom of opinion and pluralism—prepared the ground in the Orient for authoritarianism and a mystical glorification of the nation and the people. The Third Reich's openly proclaimed and enforced anti-Semitism and the fact that German and Italian policy was on the road toward confrontation with the mandatory powers increased the Axis powers' appeal as potential allies for Arab nationalism. Germany—by contrast with Great Britain, France, and Italy—had never been a colonial power in the Middle East, which represented an additional advantage. This perception promoted not only the rise of Islamic fundamentalist movements but also the formation of numerous paramilitary parties based on the Führer principle and organized along the lines of their European models.[1]

In particular, Hitler the individual was held in great esteem in the Arab world, and in the Islamic world as a whole. After his ascent to power, he received praise, as in the following: "May God preserve you. Every day I bring my prayers for you to God. The news of Your Highness's patriotism spreads the best fragrances in the whole world," wrote a sheikh from Palestine. "I am ready at any time to serve your regime with 100 soldiers on horseback. I am waiting for Your Highness's signal. [...] May you always remain my Lord."[2] And from Jerusalem he received the following telegram: "The Arab youth of Palestine respectfully ask the only Führer of Germany to prevent the sale of the German Schneller School and its land to the Jews, so that this sale does not contribute to the Jewification of the Holy Land."[3] An Iraqi newspaper, under the headline THE ONLY MAN STANDING TALL IN GERMANY, noted, "Germany must be proud of its Führer, and Iraq offers Germany its most cordial congratulations and salutes the German nation and its Führer."[4] "Is this man not called by God? To save the German people from the snare set in the name of humanity by the Jews and their various organizations. These Jewish organizations, which externally seem to bring blessings, are in reality pursuing destructive goals," claimed Dr. Zeki Kiram, and he asked himself when Arabia would wake up as well. "Now I say, Arabia will wake up on the day God sends a faithful man who believes in his actions and who summons the people of Arabia like Hitler has summoned the German people."[5] In this Führer cult laced with anti-Semitism, the potential for alliances between Islam and National Socialism and between Arab nationalism and the "new Germany" had actually emerged early on.

Hitler's popularity did not wane; rather, it intensified as the war advanced toward the Middle East. Beginning in 1938, articles appeared in various Arab newspapers in which Hitler was placed on a level with the Prophet Muhammad.[6] "For months the embassy has received notifications from various sources pointing out that throughout the country, clerics are coming forward and speaking to believers about old secret prophesies and dreams indicating that God has sent the twelfth imam to the world in the form of Adolf Hitler," reported ambassador and SS-Brigadeführer Erwin Ettel from Teheran in early 1941. "So without any action on the part of the embassy, an in-

1. Cf. Steppat, p. 271ff.; Marston, p. 19ff.
2. Rahal Scheiban to Hitler, July 18, 1933, BAB, R 43 II/1420.
3. AA memorandum, July 27, 1935, BAB, R 43 II/1420.
4. DG Baghdad to RMVP, Aug. 25, 1934, BAB, R 43 II/1420.
5. Kiram, p. 60.
6. Höpp, "Koran," p. 444.

creasingly widespread notion has emerged that the Führer (and therefore Germany) is the knight in shining armor. [...] A printer in Teheran produced images in his publishing house of the Führer as well as of Ali the first imam. For months these large pictures were hanging, right and left, on the door of his shop. Every insider understood this juxtaposition. It meant that Ali is the first and Hitler the last imam." The advantages of this perception were obvious to Ettel: "One way to encourage this development would be to clearly focus on Muhammad's struggle against the Jews in the past and the Führer's struggle in the present. If the British can be equated with the Jews at the same time, extremely effective anti-English propaganda will be circulated among the Iranian Shiite population."[7] National Socialist anti-Semitism could thus be stretched back into history, religiously legitimated, and actively used in the present.

When the German Reich conquered France in 1940, participants at mass demonstrations in Damascus, Homs, and Aleppo sang a new song that included the words: "No more monsieur, No more mister / In heaven Allah, on earth Hitler."[8] And just one year later the rhymes had become: "Pourquoi t'enfuir quand l'Allemand approche? / Français à la religion de chien. / Qui t'a dit de partir en guerre? / Dieu est au ciel, Hitler est sur la terre."[9] (Why flee when the Germans come? / Frenchman who practices the dog's religion. / Who told you to go to war? / God is in heaven and Hitler is on earth.) In Yemen at that time, only Italian radio broadcasts were heard,[10] and King Ibn Saud of Saudi Arabia informed Hitler that he had "the greatest respect and admiration for Germany's Führer."[11] Egypt's King Farouk sent him a message in the spring of 1941 saying that "he was filled with great admiration for the Führer and respect for the German people, whose victory over England he fervently wished for. He was united with his people in the wish that German troops, as deliverers from the unbearably brutal English yoke, would appear in Egypt as soon as possible."[12] At this time, pictures of Hitler were being displayed in shop windows of Baghdad,[13] and in Cairo the French physician Pierre Schrumpf-Pierron, who was working for the Abwehr, reported: "In the Islamic world, the Führer is credited with supernatural powers. They are convinced that he has a 'jinni,' a useful spirit that tells him what he must do and how he must act. In addition, he is the prophet who opposes the Jews."[14]

---

7. DG Teheran to AA, Feb. 2, 1941, PAAA, R 60690; on the individual: Döscher, p. 168; Bajohr, p. 242ff.; similarly: special report on Iran, June 11, 1941. BAB, NS 19/2414.
8. Aglion, p. 217.
9. Collet, p. 169f.
10. Stark, p. 31.
11. Annex to report by DG Djidda, Feb. 18, 1939, ADAP, ser. D, vol. 5, p. 679.
12. DG Teheran to AA, April 15, 1941, ADAP, ser. D, vol. 12/1, p. 466.
13. Kohlhaas, p. 53.
14. Schrumpf-Pierron/Cairo to von Papen, May 12, 1941, BA-MA, RH 2/1765; Buchheit, p. 234.

Although Hitler represented a great propaganda image of the Third Reich in the Arab world, translating his key work, *Mein Kampf,* was problematic because it contained a decidedly anti-Arab passage. Hitler had scornfully rejected the Muslims' "holy war," spurned alliance with a "coalition of cripples," and stated in a very imperialistic, colonialistic style, "As a völkisch man, who appraises the value of humanity on racial principles, I am prevented by the recognition of the racial inferiority of these so-called 'oppressed nations' from linking the fate of my own people with theirs."[15] Although a complete Arab edition of the original *Mein Kampf* did not appear in Beirut until 1960,[16] numerous partial translations, prudently omitting the incriminating lines, were already circulating in Egypt, Morocco, Iraq, and Lebanon before the war.[17] The Germans never produced an Arabic translation, though in 1936 Hitler had agreed that such a work should exclude "those passages that do not appear suitable for translation, considering the current political situation and the sensibilities of the Arab peoples."[18] Even the term "anti-Semitism"—which experts on the Middle East had cautioned against using, as Arabs are also Semites[19]—did not create problems; the Germans simply explained that the term applied exclusively to Jews.[20] The Mufti, however, insisted to Alfred Rosenberg, who was responsible for the philosophical and ideological training and instruction of the NSDAP, that the term should be prohibited. Rosenberg finally agreed to give the press instructions to that effect in order to avoid the impression that the Germans were "lumping the Arabs together with the Jews."[21] But in the Arab world, Hitler's symbolic value as a campaigner against the Jews, the British, and the French was always more important than those minor irritations.

In the summer of 1933, Hitler received an Egyptian journalist, who repaid the favor with a series of articles that "contributed considerably to dispelling the distrust that the Jews had tried to create between Egypt and Germany."[22] The following year, the first Hitler biography appeared in Cairo, and by 1935 it was circulating among the intellectuals of Fez, Morocco. It depicted the Jews'

---

15. Hitler, p. 747.

16. Wild, "Kampf," p. 207.

17. DG Baghdad to AA, March 29, 1934, PAAA, R 121232; DG Baghdad to Eher-Verlag/Munich, July 17, 1934, PAAA, R 121232; RMVP to AA, Dec. 10, 1937, PAAA, R 104800; Vernier, p. 74ff.; Wild, "Socialism," pp. 147–163; Simon, p. 36.

18. RMVP to AA, Nov. 12, 1936, PAAA, R 121232; Wild, "Socialism," pp. 163–170.

19. DG Baghdad to RMVP, May 17, 1934, PAAA, R 121232; Schrumpf-Pierron/Cairo to von Papen, May 12, 1941, BA-MA, RH 2/1765.

20. Groß/NSDAP Office of Racial Policy to al-Gailani, Oct. 17, 1942, in Weltkampf: Die Judenfrage in Geschichte und Gegenwart 3 (1944), p. 168; as facsimile in Höpp, Shadow, p. 231.

21. Hagemeyer/AR to AR, May 17, 1943, reprinted in Poliakov/Wulf, p. 369.

22. DG Bulkeley to AA, Oct. 5, 1933, BAB, R 43 II/1423.

domination of Germany, for which the only remedy was their extermination.[23] In 1937 a senior Egyptian police officer acted as "panegyrist of the German police" and gave lectures in which he promoted "modeling the Egyptian police organization as closely as possible after the German example."[24] It was during this time that the nucleus of modern Islamism, the Egyptian Muslim Brotherhood, grew into a mass organization. The movement, founded in 1928 by the cleric Hassan al-Banna, a friend of the Mufti, had only 800 members in 1936; two years later that number had jumped to 200,000.[25] The driving force behind this increase was mobilization for the Arab revolt in Palestine, in which the anti-Jewish passages of the Koran[26] were interwoven with the anti-Semitic combat methods of the Third Reich, and hatred of the Jews was transformed into jihad.[27] Boycott campaigns and violent demonstrations with the rallying cry "Jews out of Egypt and Palestine" were the result.[28] In October 1938, anti-Jewish treatises, including Arabic versions of *Mein Kampf* and *The Protocols of the Elders of Zion,* were distributed at an Islamic parliamentarians' conference "for the defense of Palestine" in Cairo.[29]

While the Muslim Brotherhood was an anti-Western association that called for a return to an original Islam, fought the secular state and parliamentary democracy, and saw in the Koran and Sunna the source of all legality,[30] the Young Egypt movement, founded in 1933 by Ahmad Hussein, was initially an ultranationalist youth and student party. Fascist salutes and uniforms, torchlight processions, and the cult of the Führer, as well as a growing penchant for street fighting, pointed to European sources of inspiration, despite the party's anti-Western orientation.[31] In 1936, Hussein and a delegation of his paramilitary Green Shirts took part in the Nuremberg Rally.[32] After 1936, during the Palestine campaign, Young Egypt also turned toward Islamic fundamentalism, and in March 1940 the organization changed its name to become the Islamic Nationalist Party.[33] The party's ruthless anti-Semitism did not change. Hussein declared in 1939 that the Jews were the clandestine promoters

---

23. Cao-Van-Hoa, pp. 15, 19; Baida, Bild, p. 22.
24. AA to RK, July 20, 1937, BAB, R 43 II/1424.
25. Awaisi, p. 98; cf. Lia, p. 151ff.
26. Cf. Lewis, Meer, p. 137ff.; Lewis, "Antisemitism," p. 60ff.; Lewis, Juden, pp. 13ff., 140ff.; Bouman, p. 93ff.; Kiefer, p. 27ff.; Rabinovich, "Antisemitism," p. 255ff.; Nordbruch, p. 244ff.; Gessler, p. 49ff.
27. Küntzel, Djihad, p. 22.
28. Krämer, Jews, pp. 139–154; Lia, pp. 235–247; Awaisi, pp. 34–89; Mayer, pp. 41–82; cf. Jankowski, "Government," p. 428ff.; Jankowski, "Responses," pp. 1–38.
29. Krämer, Jews, p. 146f.
30. Mitchell, pp. 14, 203, 225, 254ff.
31. Jankowski, Rebels, p. 9ff.; Erlich, p. 105ff.
32. Schröder, Deutschland, p. 58.
33. Jankowski, Rebels, pp. 41, 72ff.; Porath, Search, p. 189.

of religious and moral degeneration, and that one could rightly say, "Look for the Jews behind every perversion."[34]

By contrast, the Syrian Social Nationalist Party, founded in Damascus by Antun Saadeh in 1932, and the Lebanese Phalange, formed in 1936 and also structured according to the Führer principle, were markedly secularist and totalitarian. They claimed a völkisch superiority and also based their external symbols—a swastika-like flag and the raised-hand salute—on those of the NSDAP.[35] Because the Syrians still saw Palestine as South Syria, they vigorously supported the Arab revolt by sending money, smuggling weapons, and deploying gangs.[36] Anti-Semitism was also creating a stir in Transjordan, which, under the Hashemite Emir Abdullah, was the most moderate country in the region.[37] "I would not advise any Jew to venture as far as Kerak," reported the German consul general in Jerusalem after a trip there in late 1933, "because he would hardly make it out alive."[38] And the British ambassador in Amman acknowledged in February 1941, "There has been a certain amount of pro-Nazi talk."[39] In Saudi Arabia, in turn, Ibn Saud declared in 1939 that the Mufti was his "personal friend," offered the use of his territory as a staging ground for German weapons shipments to Palestine, and openly acknowledged his pro-Nazi affinities: "All Arabs and Mohammedans throughout the world have great respect for Germany, and this respect is increased by the battle that Germany is waging against the Jews, the archenemy of the Arabs."[40] There as well, anti-Semitism proved to be the strongest link between the Third Reich and the Middle East.

The Palestine question also served to strengthen political Arabism in Iraq. In February 1928, 40,000 Iraqis had protested in Baghdad against the visit of British politician Sir Alfred Mond, who had helped formulate the Balfour Declaration. In this first anti-Zionist mass demonstration in the Arab Islamic world, Jewish shops were looted and set on fire.[41] In 1936, numerous Jews were killed on the streets of the Iraqi capital,[42] and mass protests featuring anti-Jewish assaults were launched again one year later when the partition plan came to light. "We will sacrifice ourselves for Palestine" and "The Jews are the agents of imperialism" were the battle cries.[43] In his 1939 book *These Are Our*

---

34. Shamir, "Influence," p. 207.
35. Yamak, pp. 53ff., 76ff., 101ff., 124ff.; Mendel/Müller, pp. 2ff., 10ff.
36. DGK Beirut to AA Aug. 7, 1937, PAAA, R 104787; Khoury, p. 535ff.
37. Shlaim, pp. 39ff., 54ff.
38. DGK Jerusalem to AA, Dec. 20, 1933, PAAA, R 97229.
39. Dieterich, "Jahreszeit," p. 79.
40. Annex to report by DG Djidda, Feb. 18, 1939, ADAP, ser. D, vol. 5, p. 680.
41. Sluglett, p. 159f.
42. Haim, p. 192; Simon, p. 64.
43. DG Baghdad to AA, July 17, 1937, PAAA, R 104787.

Aims, Dr. Sami Shawkat, the Iraqi minister of education, called for the annihilation of the local Jews as a precondition for national rebirth.[44] That same year, a mob lynched the British consul in Mosul in broad daylight as soon as the death of King Ghazi became known. Under the influence of alcohol, the king had lost control of his car, and people almost automatically interpreted this as the doings of the British secret service.[45] And when Hitler proclaimed in his Reichstag speech on February 20, 1938, "I would advise the members of the English House of Commons to concern themselves with and inquire into the verdicts of the military courts in Palestine and not the verdicts issued by German courts," he received an enthusiastic response in Iraq.[46]

When Baldur von Schirach, head of the Hitler Youth organization, visited Iraq in 1937, he stressed the similarities between the pan-Arab renaissance and the German racial awakening, and invited a local Hitler Youth delegation to the next NSDAP party congress.[47] In September 1938, 30 Iraqis went to Nuremberg, where they were received by Hitler and then enjoyed a two-week vacation in Germany as guests of the Hitler Youth.[48] The visit was not without effect. The following year, Sami Shawkat created the al-Futuwa youth organization, modeled after the Hitler Youth. Membership was compulsory for all students in the upper grades of secondary school. The members wore uniforms patterned after those of the Germans and were subject to soldierly discipline and paramilitary training.[49] During this same time period, the Muthanna Club in Baghdad—of which Shawkat and his brothers Saib and Naji, both of them government ministers, were prominent members—became the intellectual center of radical pan-Arabism and pro-Nazi attitudes.[50] In northern Iraq, in Kurdistan, which was then in opposition to the central power of monarchy in Baghdad, the mood was not much different. A future lieutenant in the German military who traveled through the area in 1935–36 saw large portraits of Hitler in teahouses and reported on the attitude of the Kurds: "They spoke enthusiastically of freedom-loving Germany and her national hero, the Führer, though they knew little about him other than that he would make Germany great again and that he shared the same enemies as the Germans: the English and the Jews. These facts were enough to make the Kurds feel very close to

---

44. Wild, "Socialism," p. 137.
45. Simon, p. 38f.
46. DG Baghdad to AA, Mar. 3, 1938, PAAA, R 104785.
47. Vernier, p. 92f.; Watt, pp. 195–204.
48. Khadduri, *Iraq*, p. 173.
49. Simon, p. 80ff.
50. Khadduri, *Iraq*, p. 166f.

Germany."[51] Here as well, the Third Reich clearly won the hearts of Muslims through its anti-Semitism and cynical anti-imperialism.

In French North Africa, Hitler and Nazi Germany also found new friends. "Vive le chancelier Hitler. A bas la France" could be read on the walls of Moroccan houses in 1934,[52] and in August of that year, the local Jews in Constantine, Algeria, were the target of a pogrom in which 23 were killed.[53] "In every conversation with the Arabs, they express how pleased they are about our anti-Semitism," reported a German captain after a 1939 trip through North Africa. Even the French colonial officers there showed "great appreciation for National Socialism" and exhibited a "remarkably strong anti-Semitic attitude."[54] In October of that year flyers were circulating in Morocco commenting on the world war that had just begun: "Don't you know that there is no one left in Paris—that nest of Jews—able to destroy German aircraft? [...] What happened to the cowardly French will also happen to others of their ilk, the English Jews. The evidence is what they did in Palestine with our Muslim brothers, whom they bully and force into subjugation under the Jewish dictatorship."[55] In Spanish Morocco, the Hitler salute was given Islamic legitimation in that individuals shouted "God is great" as they extended their right arms.[56] After the defeat of France, swastikas were painted on the walls of medinas, and in Casablanca people sang, "My hope rests on the Germans."[57] The situation was similar in Tunisia: "Arabs in Tunis are extremely pro-German," reported a German major in May 1941. "Arabs and Jews are mortal enemies. Night of May 19-20 in Gabès there was a pogrom with at least 7 Jews dead."[58]

It is not surprising that Muslim Palestine fit into this context perfectly. With regard to the 1932 German presidential election, a Palestinian newspaper commented: "But in terms of the position of the Arabs in Palestine [...] toward these elections [...], though we have no voting rights, we do have a wish and a hope. And perhaps, because the Jews are our adversaries [...], then our wish and our hope remains Hitler, naturally, [...] based on the rule: The enemy of my enemy is my friend."[59] Many stood unreservedly behind the coercive measures of the Third Reich: "The Jew [... is] an international communist," wrote

51. Lt. Müller/[Abwehr]Ausl/Abw II, Dec. 5, 1942, Operation Mammoth, BA-MA, RW 5/271.
52. Baida, Bild, p. 22.
53. Abitbol, p. 18.
54. Capt. Xylander/GenStdH, Mar. 10, 1939, report on trip through Tunisia and Algeria, Jan. 19–Feb. 18, BA-MA, RW 5/413; similarly RFSS to Hitler, Jan. 21, 1943, Gen. Weygand, BAB, NS 19/2289.
55. Baida, "Wahrnehmung," p. 195.
56. Harras, p. 206.
57. Baida, "Wahrnehmung," p. 196.
58. Maj. Hofweber to DAK, May 21, 1941, BA-MA, RH 23/109.
59. Abbasi, p. 168f.

another newspaper. "In my eyes, Germany is right to drive such people out of the fatherland, because they represent a danger to all the countries in which they live."[60] This view studiously ignored the fact that it was because of these measures that the number of Jews in Palestine had increased; thus, Nazi Germany actually accelerated the "Jewification" of the country and explicitly promoted it through the Haavara Agreement, as discussed below. Stubborn silence prevailed with regard to this aspect of German anti-Semitism.[61] "Who is the greater genius, the Jews or Hitler?" asked the *Alam Arabi* newspaper, and interpreted the facts in its own way: "Now when major Jewish capitalists leave Germany, they must spend their millions on German goods to bring into Palestine. In that way the German gain and the Jewish loss is doubled."[62] Evidently, the anti-Semitism that was being repeated was sometimes greater than the anti-Zionism.

On March 31, 1933, the Mufti visited the German consul general, Heinrich Wolff, in Jerusalem and assured him that the Muslims "welcome the new German regime and anticipate the spread of fascist anti-democratic state leadership to other countries." A German boycott, to target the wealth of the Jews, would find "enthusiastic support throughout the entire Mohammedan world."[63] Just three months later, he was able to report on the "intended establishment of an Arab National Socialist party."[64] The swastika was frequently seen on leaflets and walls during the October 1933 Arab strike protesting Jewish immigration.[65] "Efforts to organize Nazi Associations have been revived," reported the British police in the summer of 1934,[66] and in the fall they saw constant Nazi propaganda in the Arab press.[67] In Palestinian literature, Jews were portrayed as money-hungry, devious, and unscrupulous, and as cowards, "new Shylocks," and "sons of clinking gold."[68] There were lyrics such as these: "Step on the Jews' heads / to free Buraq and Haram. / You young men, close ranks; / attack them by the thousands. / O God, how beautiful death is / in the freeing of Haram and Buraq."[69]

Khalil as-Sakakini, an Arab Christian teacher in Jerusalem, wrote in his journal that Hitler had opened the eyes of the world. Before he came to power, people feared the Jews and their boundless influence. But Hitler had shown the

---

60. Ibid., p. 171.
61. Ibid., p. 175.
62. AA to RK, Nov. 12, 1934, BAB, R 43 II/1420.
63. DGK Jerusalem to AA, Mar. 31, 1933, PAAA, R 78325.
64. Ibid., June 27, 1933, PAAA, R 78325.
65. Jorda, *Araber-Aufstand*, p. 3.
66. Criminal Investigation Department Jerusalem, Periodical Appreciation Summary No. 9, June 15, 1934, NAK, FO 371/17878.
67. Ibid., No. 13, Sept. 20, 1934, NAK, FO 371/17878.
68. Altoma, p. 64ff.; Osta, pp. 21ff., 221ff.
69. Wild, "Judentum," p. 278.

world that they were really harmless. The Germans were the first to confront the Jews and had no fear of them. Hitler put them in their place, according to the accomplished conspiracy theorist as-Sakakini, and Mussolini, through the occupation of Ethiopia, dealt the British a blow. When news arrived in Jerusalem that on January 13, 1935, a majority of Saar residents had voted for reunification with Germany, as-Sakakini celebrated this development together with the victory of Husseini in the local elections in Jerusalem. For him, the two successes belonged together.[70]

The "God-fearing freedom fighter" Hanaf Hassan wrote to the German consul in Haifa, the "representative of Hitler the Great": "God protect him and all Germany. [...] No Arab will forget the friendship of the Germans throughout the world for the help they granted in aid of the Arabs in Palestine. The land of Palestine does not belong to us Arabs alone, but also to the Germans, and I hope, Mr. Consul, that you will help us free the Holy Land from the Jews, and I hope that we are all brothers, God willing."[71] The Third Reich also enjoyed strong support among the students at a private secondary school in Bir Zeit, near Ramallah. When an English teacher gave her students a novel by Benjamin Disraeli to read, the class rebelled. "But he's a Jew," the students protested. The teacher then tried to steer the discussion to the question of what makes a man important. She suggested that this was someone who had influenced the spirit of his times and asked the class to compile a list of important men. Most of the students named Adolf Hitler first.[72]

According to the German consul in Jaffa, Timotheus Wurst, in late March 1936 the Muslim Palestinians were "deeply impressed by fascist, particularly National Socialist, teachings and views. National Socialism, with its anti-Jewish notions, has struck a chord among the Arabs of Palestine, who find themselves in a desperate and almost hopeless defensive battle against Zionism. Among the Arabs, fascism and National Socialism have in many cases become the standards against which all other political systems and teachings are measured, and, in the eyes of many Arabs, Adolf Hitler is without a doubt simply the most important man of the 20th century. Our Führer's popularity is so great that there can hardly be a single Arab, even the lowliest peasant, who doesn't know the name of Hitler." Like the Boy Scouts, the Istiqlal Party in particular has "embraced the National Socialist theses to the greatest extent. The Istiqlal Party organ, *The Defense*, has a markedly National Socialist orientation."[73] One year later, the *Völkischer Beobachter* printed an interview with the party's presi-

70. Segev, p. 450f.
71. Copy (undated), PAAA, R 104790.
72. Segev, p. 451f.
73. DK Jaffa to AA, Mar. 1, 1936, PAAA, R 78338.

dent, Auni Abd el-Hadi. In the interview, he admitted proudly that while he was interned by the British he had thoroughly worked through the English translation of *Mein Kampf*.[74]

It should not be surprising that the Arab revolt did not change such attitudes after 1936, but rather strengthened them. The rebels often displayed the swastika as a challenge to the Jews and the British,[75] and on Muhammad's birthday on June 4, 1937, in Palestine as well as in many other parts of the Arab world,[76] German and Italian flags and pictures of Hitler and Mussolini were on view.[77] "A critical factor in the Arabs' current sympathy toward Germany is the admiration that our Führer enjoys," reported Doehle, Wolff's successor as consul general in Jerusalem, that same year. "The periods of unrest often gave me the opportunity to discover just how widespread this sympathy is. When confronted with threatening behavior by an Arab crowd, an individual who identified himself as a German would generally be allowed to pass unhindered. But if a person identified himself using the German greeting 'Heil Hitler,' the Arabs usually became enthusiastic, cheering the individual and fervently returning the German greeting. The enthusiasm for our Führer and the new Germany is likely so widespread because the Palestinian Arabs, in their struggle for existence, long for an Arab Führer, and because they feel that they are on the same side as Germany in the battle against the Jews."[78]

Anyone who drove through Arab territory with a swastika pennant had nothing to fear and was met with rapturous cheers. Werner von Hentig, head of the Foreign Office's Political Department VII (which was responsible for the Middle East) from 1937 to 1939, was thus able to "safely visit the entire country under the protection of the German flag."[79] The approximately 2,500 German settlers in Palestine—almost all were members of the pietistic Temple Society that had established seven planned colonies since 1868[80] and showed a great affinity for the Third Reich[81]—carried swastika emblems and pennants with them. These identified them as Germans, as specifically required by the insurgents, and allowed them to drive around the country unmolested.[82] While overall only 5 percent of non-Jewish German citizens living in foreign countries belonged to the NSDAP, the share in Palestine amounted to 17 per-

74. *Völkischer Beobachter*, Jan. 23, 1937.
75. Jorda, *Araber-Aufstand*, pp. 156, 187f., 257.
76. *New York Times*, May 23, 1937.
77. DGK Jerusalem to AA, June 4, 1937, BAB, R 43 II/1421a.
78. Ibid., Mar. 22, 1937, PAAA, R 104791.
79. Hentig, p. 329; similarly Jorda, *Araber-Aufstand*, p. 148.
80. Cf. Carmel.
81. Balke, p. 79ff.; Schmidt, p. 461ff.
82. DGK Jerusalem to AA, Sept. 14, 1938, PAAA, R 104790.

cent.[83] Franz Schattenfroh also characterized the relationship between Arabs and German colonists as excellent: "When, for example, a German has to ride in a Jewish bus because on certain routes there is no other means of transportation, and the bus is stopped by Arabs, the German (if he is able to prove that he is German) can go wherever he wants, but the others will be shot."[84] If non-German Europeans ended up in a similarly dangerous situation, the Arab enthusiasm for the Third Reich could save them as well: "In extreme distress, the young Swede cried out, 'I'm a German! Heil Hitler!'" reported Iwo Jorda, a German traveling in Palestine. "It worked. The leader of the gang stepped back, raised his hand in salute, excused himself, and led the Swede to the mukhtar where he was bandaged and cared for."[85] Although the Germans in Palestine were officially required to maintain neutrality,[86] in 1937 even the Jewish affairs department of the SD in Berlin knew that "the anti-Jewish influence of members of the NSDAP's foreign section on Arab circles in Palestine [...] had often been noticeable in recent years."[87]

Hitler also frequently declared his sympathy for the Muslims in Palestine. "Arab fantasies about a German intervention, based on the fact that the Führer shows interest in the Palestine question, can be explained by the Arabs' desperate situation in their struggle against the Jews and the English," Doehle decided in 1938.[88] Indeed, as early as the summer of 1938, the insurgents turned to the consul general and requested weapons and money from Germany.[89] In December of that year, the Mufti inquired into the matter with Dr. Fritz Grobba, the German ambassador in Baghdad: "Germany would secure the eternal thanks of all Arabs if it were to assist them in their current distress and help them achieve victory."[90] In January 1937, members of the Arab Higher Committee paid a visit to Grobba, who noted the following about their position: "The only great power that is interested in an Arab victory over the Jews in Palestine, and that the Arabs have full confidence in, is Germany. The Arab Higher Committee therefore counts on German assistance."[91] In July the committee repeated its request to the Third Reich's ambassador in the Iraqi

---

83. McKale, *Swastika*, p. 120.
84. Schattenfroh, p. 65f.; similarly Kossak-Raytenau, p. 37.
85. Jorda, *Araber-Aufstand*, p. 139.
86. DGK Jerusalem to AA, July 7, 1936, PAAA, R 104785; cf. Balke, p. 216ff.
87. Memorandum on the Jewish problem (undated/Jan. 1937), BAB, R 58/956; likewise Schmidt, p. 467.
88. DGK Jerusalem to AA, Oct. 28, 1938, PAAA, R 104790.
89. Ibid., July 7, 1936, PAAA, R 104785.
90. DGK Jerusalem to DG Baghdad, Dec. 17, 1936, PAAA, R 102806; on the individual: Grobba; Nicosia, Grobba, p. 206ff.; Flacker, p. 18ff.; Schwanitz, *Geist*, p. 127ff.
91. DG Baghdad to AA, Jan. 6, 1937, PAAA, R 104785.

capital.[92] In parallel, el-Husseini established secret contacts with the Italian consul in Jerusalem.[93]

Shortly before the revolt flared up again in the summer of 1937, forcing him to flee, the Mufti visited Doehle again and informed him that he wished to send "a representative to Germany incognito."[94] In September the Arab Higher Committee tried its luck with Julius Seiler, the German consul general in Beirut, who sided fully with the committee in its efforts to defeat the partition plan: "The only means to achieve this seemed and seem to lie in the Arab attempts to intimidate the Jews through terrorism while at the same time exerting pressure on the English."[95] In November, Dr. Said Abd al-Imam, founder of the Arab Club of Damascus and a radical pan-Arabist, appeared in Berlin as the Mufti's representative[96] and delivered some delicate proposals: in exchange for material and nonmaterial support for the "Arab independence movement," he promised "the promotion of a pro-German atmosphere, which would also be evident in the event of war; the propagation of National Socialism in the Arab Islamic world; and the use of all available means in the struggle against the establishment of a Jewish state in Palestine."[97] Shortly before Christmas 1938, the leader of the revolt in the northern district of Palestine applied directly to "Adolf Hitler, the great Führer of Germany, who has brought his nation eternal honor and glory": "Great German Führer, I do not wish to introduce the Jews to you. You know them and their history, and you knew them before we were acquainted with them. [...] Receive the greetings of one who sees his example in Muhammad the leader, and his precepts in the teachings and commands of the holy Koran. The servant of the fatherland and religion, the jihadist Joseph Said Abu Durra."[98]

In November, the Mufti again informed Seiler that "the insurgents in Palestine urgently need weapons."[99] In the spring of 1939, el-Hadi, the leader of the Istiqlal Party, remained in Germany as the guest of Reichsleiter Rosenberg, and on April 1 was received in the Foreign Office. "The Palestinian Arabs are still forced to engage in costly guerrilla warfare against the English in Palestine because that is the only way they can eventually come into their own," he admitted, and mentioned twice that he "always thinks about German

---

92. Ibid., July 17, 1937, PAAA, R 104787.

93. Nafi, "Arabs," p. 4.

94. DGK Jerusalem to AA, July 15, 1937, PAAA, R 104787; cf. DGK Jerusalem to AA, Aug. 10, 1937, PAAA, R 104785.

95. DGK Jerusalem to DGK Beirut, Sept. 22, 1937, PAAA, R 104788.

96. Al-Imam to RMVP, Nov. 24, 1937, PAAA, R 104800; Geiger/NSDAP Damascus to RMVP, Dec. 1, 1937, PAAA R, 104800; cf. Rabinovich, Germany, p. 196.

97. RMVP to AA, Dec. 14, 1937, Annex 3, PAAA, R 104800.

98. DGK Jerusalem to AA, Dec. 23, 1938, PAAA, R 104785.

99. DGK Jerusalem to DGK Beirut, Nov. 29, 1938, PAAA, BA 61148.

assistance."[100] After the failure of the London conference, Consul Wilhelm
Melchers in Haifa experienced the Arabs' "jubilation and celebratory moods"
and heard the cry "Long live the Mufti" everywhere. But after numerous Jews
were killed by Arab bombs and bullets during these supposed independence
celebrations, and the Irgun, the revisionist Jewish resistance organization,
responded by setting off two explosive charges that killed 29 Arabs in the train
station and in the bazaar, demonstrators stormed the consulate and, said
Melchers, "wanted to make me ask the German government for help."[101]

As has been shown, it was the Third Reich's dictatorial orientation, aggres-
siveness, Führer cult, and, especially, its hatred for the Jews that brought it
popularity in parts of the Arab world and in the broader Islamic world. It was
precisely the most chilling characteristics that allowed the "new Germany" to
become an example and that set the pattern for the future. Or, in other words,
it was not despite but because of their virulent anti-Semitism that Hitler and
the Germans gained the sympathies of the Muslims of the Middle East. It is
therefore fundamentally incorrect to speak of an "ideological and strategic
incompatibility" between Arab nationalism and National Socialism.[102] Moreover, Muslims from every country in the larger region, not least Palestine, tena-
ciously pursued the alliance with National Socialist Germany, even though the
Germans avoided playing the Arab card for a long time. In any case, in the
Middle East a powerful indigenous sounding board had already emerged for
the National Socialists before the beginning of the war.

Therefore, the notion that in 1939 "the political, social, and not least
military resistance potential of Palestinian society [...] had been destroyed for
years to come,"[103] that "the Arabs were largely disarmed and the Zionists better
equipped than ever," and that the country had even been "pacified [...] when
war broke out,"[104] is seriously inaccurate. Aside from the fact that no systematic disarming of the rebels had taken place, unparalleled ideological agitation
attested to the fact that in the Muslim part of Palestine an eliminationist anti-
Semitism had taken root that was no less intense than the German hatred for
the Jews, and that even anticipated it in terms of practical implementation, to
the extent that the Arabs already had the necessary power to do so. Not least
because of German arms deliveries (as discussed below), the revolt flared up
again in the fall of 1939.[105] In the summer of the following year, the Deutsches
Nachrichtenbüro (the DNB—official German news agency) reported:

100. Memorandum by Woermann/AA, April 1, 1939, PAAA, R 29899.
101. DK Haifa to AA, Mar. 3, 1939, PAAA, R 104790.
102. Nicosia, "Nationalism," p. 351.
103. Baumgarten, p. 36.
104. Krämer, *Geschichte*, p. 344f.
105. Seifert, p. 80f.; Jorda, *Araber-Aufstand*, pp. 438f., 441.

"According to reliable estimates, 20 percent of Jewish orange plantations have been completely destroyed, and 40 percent of all irrigation installations. Consequent loss of new crops estimated at 33 percent. Agitation in Arab circles against Jewish immigration steadily increasing."[106] According to an estimate by the Jewish Agency's news bureau, approximately 60 percent of the country's non-Jews supported the National Socialists.[107] In addition, many former activists were returning from exile at that time.[108] And in May 1941, "along the coast of Palestine, the Arabs saw small groups of British soldiers land in fishing boats, unarmed and completely exhausted: the survivors escaping from Greece and then from Crete. Full of hope, the Arabs saw with their own eyes how hard the proud power of Great Britain had been hit."[109] From then on they waited even more expectantly for the arrival of the Germans.

---

106. DNB report, July 25, 1940, PAAA, R 99388.
107. Segev, p. 505.
108. Khalaf, p. 80.
109. Jorda, *Araber-Aufstand*, p. 433.

Chapter III

Shifting Priorities:

Jewish Emigration and Germany's Arab Policy

The foreign policy of the Third Reich after 1933 was initially shaped by guiding ideas that were not geared in any way to favor the Arabs. First, there was the desire for unrestricted rearmament. This implied avoiding any major conflict with Great Britain and, if anything, seeking an alliance with that great power. And second, there was the intention to "get rid of" as many German Jews as possible, as quickly as possible. This implied that a significant number of those expelled would choose Palestine as their new home, therefore strengthening the Yishuv. These fundamental interests of the National Socialist regime did not take Arab wishes into consideration at all and prevented any immediate show of unity. Nevertheless, this early lack of alignment was not permanent, and a creeping priority shift can be detected on the German side.

The original spurned love would be transformed into a complete harmony of interests by the year 1941.

The August 25, 1933, Haavara (Transfer) Agreement between the Anglo-Palestine Bank and the Reich Ministry of Economics represented an attempt by two extremely different partners to derive mutual advantages from their respective predicaments. The Third Reich was facing a worldwide boycott campaign with possibly ruinous effects on the German balance of trade. The Jews of Palestine were facing a situation in which the British mandate authorities allowed only a limited number of immigrants, based on the economic capacity of the land to absorb them; beyond that number, entry was granted only to Jews with assets of at least 1,000 pounds sterling. To increase the number of Jews who would qualify through this proof of assets—also called a "capital certificate"—the following system was agreed upon: The emigrants would sign over their liquid assets to a trust office in Germany, which, in turn, provided the required amount of currency for the certificate. The balance would be used to finance the export of German goods to Palestine. After their arrival in Palestine, the emigrants would receive partial repayment of their assets, after the deduction of an emigration tax and various other fees. The Third Reich benefited since Jews were thus encouraged to leave Germany, and German goods could be sold abroad. The Jews on the other hand could claim to have conserved Jewish capital without the Germans having received an equivalent value in the form of liquid currency. On the basis of this agreement, approximately 20,000 prosperous Jews—37 percent of all German Jews who emigrated to Palestine—left their country of origin with a portion of their assets.[1]

The Arab revolt created doubts about the usefulness of the agreement. "We have done little to strengthen and support the Arabs' sympathies for the new Germany, and we have disregarded the danger that the Arabs could become our opponents, thanks to our assistance in the construction of the Jewish national home and the Jewish economy," warned Consul General Doehle in March 1937.[2] Though this concern would prove to be unfounded, it showed a change in that the Arabs now played a role in German calculations. When the first news of the Peel Commission's partition plan leaked out in the summer of that year, alarm bells went off in Berlin. Foreign Minister Konstantin von Neurath put the Haavara Agreement up for negotiation and issued the following statements: "(1) The formation of a Jewish state, or a Jewish-led state entity under the British mandate's sovereignty, is not in the

---

1. In-depth: Feilchenfeld/Michaelis/Pinner, p. 18ff.; cf. Barkai, p. 245ff.; Yisraeli, "The Third Reich and the Transfer Agreement," p. 129ff.; Black, p. 120ff.; Nicosia, *Hitler*, p. 73ff.; Bauer, Freikauf, p. 15ff.; Kolinsky, *Law*, p. 195ff.; Wistrich, pp. 285ff., 292ff.; from the participants' perspective: Marcus, p. 179ff.
2. DGK Jerusalem to AA. Mar. 22, 1937, PAAA, R 104791·

German interest, because a state of Palestine would not absorb the Jews of the world but instead strengthen the power base of international Jewry through international law, as the Vatican state has done for political Catholicism or Moscow for the Comintern. (2) Thus, Germany has an interest in strengthening the Arab community to counter any such increase in the power of the Jews."[3] Although this position did not yet mean providing material support, it indicated the future direction. The Germans began to observe the Middle East to a greater degree.[4]

While the Reich Ministry of Economics and the Middle East department of the Foreign Office supported the Haavara Agreement, the foreign section of the NSDAP continued its long campaign against it, because, according to the new argument, it "facilitated the establishment of a Jewish national state with the help of German capital."[5] The German affairs department of the Foreign Office shared this position and argued for an "increase in the pressure for Jewish emigration [...] through the tightening of domestic Jewish legislation."[6] The dispute was not resolved until Hitler personally decided in early 1938 "that Jewish emigration from Germany should continue to be promoted using all available means" and that Palestine would remain a target country.[7] However, the fact that Grobba in Baghdad and Doehle in Jerusalem received the directive in June 1937 to "express the German interest in the Arab nationalist efforts more clearly than before" underlined the growing weight the Third Reich now assigned to the "Arab cause."[8]

The SD's interest was also colored by Palestine's status as the most important target country for emigrating German Jews—particularly in light of the restrictive immigration policies of most European and North American states. The complete expulsion envisioned by the SD implied tolerance of the Zionist organizations active in Germany, which, in contrast to assimilation-oriented Jewish groups, were able to continue their work largely unopposed.[9] The other side of the segregation promoted by the Nuremberg Laws was the "use of all available means to promote the Zionist emigration of Jews from Germany."[10] Even while, in view of the British partition plan, the Haavara Agreement created acrimonious conflict within the government and the NSDAP in 1937,

---

3. RAM to DG London, DG Baghdad, and DGK Jerusalem, June 1, 1937, PAAA, R 29899; cf. Nicosia, *Hitler*, p. 177ff.
4. Rabl, "Osten," pp. 293–302; Rabl, "Nah-Ost-Nachtrag," pp. 402–404; Björkman, "Erfolge," pp. 350–356.
5. Note by head of NSDAP foreign section, June 5, 1937, PAAA, R 27266.
6. Note by Bülow-Schwante/AA, June 11, 1937, PAAA, R 29899.
7. Note by Clodius/AA, Jan. 27, 1938, ADAP, ser. D, vol. 5, p. 660; cf. Nicosia, *Hitler*, p. 217ff.
8. Note by Bülow-Schwante/AA, June 22, 1937, PAAA, R 99387.
9. RMVP to AA, Oct. 4, 1938, PAAA, R 104785.
10. Comment by Wisliceny/SDHA, April 7, 1937, Jewish question, BAB, R 58/991; cf. Wildt, *Judenpolitik*, pp. 12ff., 40ff.

the SD's Jewish Affairs department made the following proposal: "Pressure will be brought to bear on the Reich Deputation of Jews in Germany, so that it will oblige the Jews emigrating from Germany to go exclusively to Palestine, and not to any other country. Such a measure is entirely in the German interest and is already being prepared for through the Gestapo measures."[11]

And in early 1939, when the concept of forced deportation, as developed by Adolf Eichmann in Vienna, was extended throughout the old empire through the establishment of the Reich Central Office for Jewish Emigration, Palestine remained on top of the list as the target country for German Jews. At the office's first meeting on February 11, 1939, Reinhard Heydrich approved even illegal emigration there: "He explained that in principle any illegal emigration must fundamentally be opposed. The situation in Palestine, however, was such that illegal transports were going there from many other European countries (which were just transit countries themselves), and under these circumstances Germany could also avail itself of the opportunity, though without official involvement."[12] This line was also further pursued by the Gestapo and SD during the first two years of the war.[13]

In Palestine itself, Dr. Franz Reicher, the representative of the Deutsches Nachrichtenbüro in Jerusalem, was active on behalf of the SD's Jewish Affairs department.[14] He furnished Berlin with reports on the general situation in the country and, after 1937 at the latest, was in official contact—in his role at the news agency—with the Mufti of Jerusalem.[15] When Herbert Hagen and Adolf Eichmann of the Jewish Affairs department set off on a trip to the Middle East to survey the situation on-site in late September of that same year, Reicher was to put them in contact with el-Husseini. "Dr. Reichert will arrange a meeting with Emir Abdulah [*sic*] and the Mufti of Jerusalem, as well as other Arab politicians," reported Eichmann beforehand.[16] The planned discussion did not take place, however, because the two SD emissaries could not obtain visas due to the unrest that had flared up again in Palestine on October 15. Eichmann and Hagen were nevertheless able to report that the "common Arab [...], upon hearing the name Hitler, perks up his ears and indulges in outbursts of joy." They also recounted sympathetically "that all Arab-ruled countries send money to Palestine via Syria, and also smuggle in weapons, in order to enable the

---

11. SDHA II 112 report, June 17, 1937, Feivel Polkes, BAB, R 58/954.

12. CdS to AA, Feb. 14, 1939, ADAP, ser. D, vol. 5, p. 788.

13. Kimche, *Roads*, p. 15ff.; Avriel, p. 28ff.; Ball-Kaduri, p. 387ff.; Ofer, p. 98ff.; Bauer, Freikauf, p. 75ff.

14. SDHA II 112, Jan. 15, 1938, activity report July 1–Dec. 31, 1937, BAB, R 58/991; cf. Balke, p. 196ff.

15. SDHA II 112 to II 1, May 3 and Aug. 9, 1938, BAB, R 58/563; statement by Dieter Wisliceny, July 26, 1946, YVA, TR 3/129.

16. SDHA II 112 to II 1, Sept. 2, 1937, BAB, R 58/623; to the East German journalist Polkehn, p. 73, this represented a Zionist fabrication: "The inventor of this story seems to be the well-known Zionist Simon Wiesenthal."

victory of the Palestinian Arabs over the Jews and the English."[17] Thus, a pro-Arab bias was gaining strength in the Jewish Affairs department of the SD as well.

Hitler's foreign policy options, which constituted a key focal point until the end of the 1930s as a result of his wish for an understanding or even an alliance with Great Britain, initially hampered German engagement in Palestine. Accordingly, a pivotal role fell to the Empire, as Hitler saw it as a natural partner, while France was considered an eternal mortal enemy and Italy was an acknowledged ally.[18] The high point of this alliance-pursuing phase, which lasted from 1933 to 1937, was the Anglo-German Naval Agreement of June 18, 1935. In return, the Third Reich expected recognition of Germany's role as dominant power on the Continent. The situation remained unchanged as Germany and Italy subsequently drew closer together.[19]

Requests for German arms deliveries for the Arab revolt in Palestine were therefore coolly dismissed initially. "I explained to him that we wished to maintain good relations with England, and therefore, despite all our sympathies for the Arabs, we could not support an anti-English uprising," noted Grobba on his December 1936 conversation with Fawzi al-Qawuqji, the Mufti's emissary. "He responded that the uprising was not ultimately aimed at the English, with whom the Arabs had always been friends, but rather against the Jews in Palestine, that included many communists." But this argument also failed to convince. "I countered that the hostilities would still be directed at the English, and that we could not participate in that," said the German ambassador in Baghdad.[20] Berlin reacted with equal reservation to the Mufti's suggestions in the summer of 1937. "The decision to support the Arabs with money and weapons," according to Legation Councilor Schumburg of the Foreign Office's German Affairs department, "was to be abandoned in consideration of the development of German-English relations."[21] And Vice Consul Dittmann in Jerusalem impassively informed el-Husseini that the visit of his representative "to Berlin appears premature."[22]

However, a radical change in position must have taken place by 1938 at the latest, because a June 18, 1939, "conversation note f. Admiral C."—that stood for Wilhelm Canaris, the head of the Abwehr—stated unambiguously: "The Grand Mufti had his representative communicate to me his sincere thanks for

17. SDHA II 112, Nov. 4, 1937, Palestine trip report, BAB, R 58/954.
18. Hildebrand, p. 79.
19. Petersen, pp. 461–492; Michaelis, p. 50ff.
20. DG Baghdad to AA, Dec. 17, 1936, PAAA, R 102806; cf. Nicosia, *Hitler*, p. 165ff.
21. Note by Schumburg/AA, Aug. 7, 1937, ADAP, ser. D, vol. 5, p. 642; similarly note by Pol VII/AA, Aug. 7, 1937, ADAP, ser. D, vol. 5, pp. 642–645.
22. DGK Jerusalem to AA, Aug. 10, 1937, ADAP, ser. D, vol. 5, p. 645.

the support provided thus far. It was only through the funds provided by us that he was able to carry out the revolt in Palestine." The author—whom the unsigned text indicates must have been Colonel Hans Pieckenbrock, head of the Abwehr's *Amts*gruppe I. which was responsible for foreign military espionage—determined that the rebellion was subsiding and that providing further assistance to the Mufti would therefore be inappropriate. He reasoned: "The ability to resume the uprising at any time, however, must be ensured. I therefore intend to maintain the connection with the Grand Mufti." And he stated that "resources would be provided for the victims of the uprising."[23] At this point, the Abwehr, which reported directly to the OKH (Army High Command) had long been involved on the Arab side in Palestine and positioned itself to engage in terrorism in a country that could be a potential enemy in the coming world war.

The point in time when this shift from non-intervention to active involvement took place cannot be identified exactly, although plausible assumptions can be made. The German sources remain unclear about it, and the Mufti also spoke in riddles concerning the matter: "I was the first to seek direct relations with Germany and to bring about the collaboration with Germany already many years before the war."[24] It is certain that German weapons were used in the Arab revolt in Palestine;[25] however, it remains unclear whether these were World War I weapons or modern equipment. The British seized relatively little military equipment from Germany,[26] which does not allow us to draw conclusions about the timing and extent of the deliveries. It is certain that in 1938 Canaris, together with Major Helmuth Groscurth, the head of Abwehr II at the time, met with the Mufti in Baghdad and remained in friendly contact afterward.[27] The admiral—negatively fixated on England since World War I, with his traditional German navyman's hostility to the British—would have seen this as a chance to compensate for past losses. His old confidant and representative Grobba, a vehement supporter of pro-Arab alignment, could have arranged the contact.[28]

Groscurth's diary provides the only precise indication of the timing. Under August 29, 1938, it says, "Conversation with Ambassador Grobba from Baghdad. Arab movement should be activated immediately."[29] If interpreted as instruction from Berlin rather than as Iraq's wish, this would mean that the

23. OKW/Ausl/Abw I conversation note, June 18, 1939, IfZ, Nbg. Dok., PS-792.
24. Note by Mufti (undated/Dec. 1943), PAAA, R 101101.
25. Jorda, *Araber-Aufstand*, p. 206.
26. *The Times*, Nov. 28, 1938, and Feb. 23, 1939; Stewart, *Relations*, p. 97; Melka, *Axis*, p. 36f.
27. Abshagen, p. 316; Reile, p. 174.
28. Kohlhaas, p. 21; DG Baghdad to AA, May 2, 1939, ADAP, ser. D, vol. 6, p. 334.
29. Groscurth, p. 106.

decision to provide financial support and perhaps also arms deliveries must have been reached during the crisis in German-British relations following the annexation of Austria (March 12, 1938). As the famous Hossbach Memorandum reporting Hitler's statements on November 5, 1937, records,[30] Hitler had at that point decided to pursue his expansion plans—"capturing new lebensraum in the east and ruthlessly Germanizing it"—without England, since an alliance with the British Empire could not be realized according to his conditions. Although Hitler did not wish to implement his agenda in conflict with Britain, he believed he could conclude from previous experience that the Downing Street government would ultimately decide not to actively resist. British behavior in response to the Abyssinian crisis of 1935–36, the Spanish Civil War after 1936, and shortly thereafter the annexation of Austria in 1938 seemed to confirm this notion. The previous aim, "friendship and partnership with England," was now replaced by the motto "preferably no antagonism."[31] When Hitler set a course aiming at the dismantling of Czechoslovakia in the spring of 1938 and again encountered British opposition to his hegemonic plans, he used the Arab revolt in Palestine to prevent possible interference with his project.

At a secret conference with the military leadership on July 14, 1938—at which Hermann Göring, Wilhelm Keitel, Josef Goebbels, and Heinrich Himmler participated, among others—Hitler explained that he wanted to choose a time to attack Prague when Great Britain was heavily engaged in Palestine and would therefore have no interest in becoming entangled in conflicts in Central Europe as well.[32] Keitel seems to have understood these thoughts as instructions, which he then passed along to Canaris, his direct subordinate. Canaris in turn delegated the issue to Groscurth, the head of the appropriate Abwehr unit. After that, weapons from the Abwehr were transported by sea to Lebanon, and from there to the coast of Palestine with the help of Arab fishing boats, in order to fuel the conflict in the Mandate.[33] In 1939, when a military clash with Great Britain grew increasingly likely, the last doubts probably disappeared, and when the world war became a reality there certainly were no more reservations. Now the extension to Palestine was just a question of time and range. In August 1939, when Captain Wilhelm Kohlhaas was called to Abwehr II in Berlin, the issue had long been on the agenda: "The

---

30. Reprinted in Wendt, pp. 191–202.
31. Cf. Henke, p. 99ff.
32. Ibid., p. 158; Neubert, p. 119f.; Nicosia, *Nationalism*, p. 363f.; they draw on a Brauchitsch briefing in Colvin, p. 220.
33. Kiernan, p. 71ff.; Schiller, p. 176; facsimile of British report in Dekel, p. 231ff.

many fantasies aimed at Israel and Jerusalem could be countered by referring to the inaccessibility of the Orient for air deployment," he recalled later.[34]

The creeping priority shift was now also evident in German radio propaganda aimed at the Middle East. The Italians had already begun broadcasting Arabic programs via Radio Bari in March 1934, in preparation for the war in Abyssinia, while the Third Reich held back out of consideration for British interests.[35] Although there were only 10,000 listeners who paid the radio fee in Palestine in 1935, the public playing of news and music in Arab coffeehouses was extremely popular.[36] Radio Bari was soon well regarded there; in 1937 the British mandate administration estimated that 60 percent of all radio owners in Palestine regularly listened to Radio Bari programs, and declared apprehensively, "There is little doubt that the Bari broadcast enjoys wide publicity."[37] The implication was certainly that the broadcaster owed its popularity to the raw anti-British tone it had taken on after the beginning of the Arab revolt.[38]

Prior to the outbreak of World War II, the Third Reich followed suit. On April 25, 1939, from Zeesen, south of Berlin, the most powerful shortwave transmitter in the world broadcast its first Arabic program.[39] The broadcast consisted of music, readings from the Koran, news, and "chats" about current events. It portrayed Germany as a powerful opponent of the Arab world's enemies and disparaged the Jews, the British, and the French.[40] There was nothing but derision for Arabs who wanted to negotiate with the Zionists. Thus, Emir Abdullah of Transjordan was regularly mocked as "Rabbi Abdullah."[41] Franz Schattenfroh, on his trip to Palestine shortly before the war began, was so impressed by the effect of the broadcasts that he expressed the hope that the Arabs there "have by now also learned something from German radio propaganda, which the Arabs take in very attentively and positively."[42]

The writings of German visitors to Palestine likewise reflected the priority shift toward vehement pro-Arab alignment. "The events of 1939 clearly attest that world Jewry is pressing for a decision in Palestine, and that it is ready to take—with bloody terror and with weapons—what it has not achieved in 20 years of negotiations," summed up Heinrich Hest that same year. He con-

---

34. Kohlhaas, p. 13.
35. MacDonald, p. 195; Michaelis, p. 50; Barbour, p. 58, and Arsenian, p. 419, give the incorrect date of September 1935; cf. Baker, p. 98ff.; Melka, Axis, p. 7ff.
36. Report from Palestine, Nov. 12, 1935, NAK, FO 371/18958.
37. Ibid., Aug. 26, 1937, NAK, FO 395/547.
38. MacDonald, p. 197ff.
39. Schwipps, p. 58; Steppat, p. 269; on the refusal by the AA in 1938: Neubert, p. 113ff.; Barbour, p. 63, Arsenian, p. 419, MacDonald, p. 204, and Melka, *Axis*, p. 226, incorrectly give 1938 for the beginning of the broadcasts.
40. Baker, p. 102ff.
41. Barbour, p. 65.
42. Schattenfroh, p. 69.

cluded, "English colonial policy in the Middle East has been reduced to acting as a stooge for world Jewry."[43] At the same time, he attested that the Arabs were claiming "the most natural human right, that of self-defense."[44] He also knew the future winner of this conflict: "The more ruthlessly the Jews [...] try to destroy the physical existence of these Arabs, the greater the Arabs' vital energy will become, and the stronger their will to resist."[45]

In the book he completed in February 1940, Hermann Erich Seifert predicted: "The more world Jewry threatens in Palestine, and the more the two democracies [Great Britain and France] unmask their brutal tyranny, the clearer it will become to what degree the Arabs are ready for a decisive struggle for freedom. Evidence of the strength to fight has long been present in the individual countries. Today the Arab world is waiting for the most advantageous moment, but then the Middle East will be the first to soar out of the British Empire."[46] Here, any consideration for the United Kingdom was no longer heard. Great Britain was categorized as a lackey of the Jews, and many predicted that the Arab world would rise up against the British and the Jews. Kurt Fischer-Weth, the Mufti's biographer, also knew that the Arab world was "waiting for its cue to—at the right moment—again take up the fight that is prescribed by history for a vital and revolutionary people."[47] He predicted that in the event of a war, "the Arabs of Palestine will be ready and waiting for battle until the opportunity comes that they are waiting for."[48] The prognoses were clear.

"The Arab recognized the threat posed by the Jew before the good-natured German did, and he determinedly countered it with strength and passion. He fights the Jew whenever and however he can, and here in Haifa, in particular, the battle never ends," wrote Karl Kossak-Raytenau, who traveled through Palestine in 1938 as a special correspondent for the National Socialist paper *Der Angriff*. He described the situation in the port city and praised the Muslims there as shining examples in matters of violent anti-Semitism: "On Mount Carmel, volleys of gunfire are constantly ringing out, and the Arabs especially like to shoot at the buses that go up Carmel from Haifa and are used almost exclusively by the Jews."[49] He also knew about the Third Reich's function as a role model: "We Arabs," he quoted a leader of the insurgents as saying, "follow Germany's rise with great interest and affection, because several

---

43. Hest, p. 5f.
44. Ibid., p. 48.
45. Ibid., p. 72.
46. Seifert, p. 90f.
47. Fischer-Weth, p. 94f.
48. Ibid., p. 85.
49. Kossak-Raytenau, p. 18.

years ago, before Adolf Hitler came to power, Germany found itself in a similar situation to the one we Arabs face in Palestine."[50] And he did not forget to draw parallels between the two images of the enemy. "The Jews want to destroy us. Here, like everywhere, they are parasites, and the English support them," the insurgent continued, his voice fading away with Islamist longing for a leader. "The Arab is awakening! He slept for a long time, and Allah took his hand away from him because many of us forgot Allah! But in his goodness and mercy he has awakened us, and he who knows the way will also send us a leader to guide us to freedom! Glory and praise to the most merciful of the merciful! There is no god but Allah, and Muhammad is his prophet!"[51]

The shift in emphasis was portrayed most clearly by Leopold Itz Edler von Mildenstein, as he visited Palestine twice and published reports and two books with clearly differing perspectives.[52] In the summer of 1934 he visited the country for the first time as a journalist for Goebbels's *Angriff* and subsequently published a 12-part series there under the title "Ein Nazi fährt nach Palästina" (A Nazi Goes to Palestine).[53] The series also formed the basis for his 1938 book *Rings um das brennende Land am Jordan* (Around the Burning Land by the Jordan). Despite all the anti-Semitic views and the wish to "free" Europe from the Jews, he regarded the Zionist project for the most part positively, interpreted the Jewish settlement activity as a "recovery" derived from reacquired roots, and saw Palestine as the target country for emigrating German Jews. But he also warned: "In recent years, Palestine has become a political volcano about which we know only one thing for certain: that the next eruption is as sure to come as the last—the only question is when."[54] Mildenstein's series of articles found a prominent reader: Reinhard Heydrich, who promptly appointed the author to lead the Jewish Affairs department at SD headquarters. Mildenstein worked there from March 1935 to July 1936 and, as a "solution to the Jewish question," promoted emigration, which was to be pushed through conscious dissimilation.[55] Thus, it is not absolutely necessary to agree with the claim that "the Untersturmführer [was] just as little anti-Semitic as was his clumsy right-hand man Adolf Eichmann." In the early summer of 1939, Mildenstein, now active in the foreign press department of the Reich Ministry for Propaganda, took a second trip to Palestine, which he documented in *Naher Osten—Vom Straßenrand erlebt* (The Middle East—Experienced from the Side of the Road), published in 1941. He positioned himself unconditionally on the

50. Ibid., p. 54.
51. Ibid., p. 56f.
52. Cf. Kaiser, pp. 407–423; Wistrich, p. 288f.; Balke, p. 208.
53. *Der Angriff*, Sept. 26–Oct. 9, 1934.
54. Mildenstein, *Land*, p. 63.
55. Drobisch, p. 240; Wildt, *Judenpolitik*, pp. 19f., 29, 49, 80f.

side of the Arabs and anticipated their victory in the struggle against the Jews
and the British. The current calm was deceptive, wrote Mildenstein: "Englishmen, Jews, and Arabs—all three know this and avoid each other. No Arab
enters the Jewish part of the city unnecessarily, and no Jew or Englishman goes
to the Arab Old City. They hate and boycott each other in silence, with
clenched fists in their pockets, waiting for the day the conflict will begin."[56]
The section of the book addressing Palestine purposefully ends with a conversation between the author and an Arab engineer in a German restaurant in
Jaffa. "We know today that we must first achieve two things before we can
attack again: we must be certain of the active help of the other Arab states this
time, and we must destroy the traitors and corruptible subjects in our own
ranks beforehand," Mildenstein quoted the engineer as saying; he concluded
with the prophecy that "the stimulus must come from the outside, but it will
find us ready to complete the work here."[57] In 1941, when the book appeared,
any reader would have understood this as a reference to the Wehrmacht, when
Rommel's Afrika Korps was already in Cyrenaica! And some would also have
immediately recognized the annihilation of the Jews as being part of the work
to be completed.

Although the Germans still encouraged illegal Jewish emigration from
areas in Europe under German control to Palestine until 1941, the priorities
shifted markedly as the world war came closer. Nazi consideration for Great
Britain waned appreciably, and support for the Arab side seemed to grow daily.
The Third Reich saw the Jews of Palestine as bitter enemies in the coming
clash, while the Arabs were increasingly viewed as assets. The Germans therefore supported them with weapons, supplied propaganda points, shared their
perspectives on international events, and appreciated the prestige that Germany and Hitler enjoyed in that part of the world. Finally, the Germans increasingly saw in the Grand Mufti of Jerusalem a key partner in the Middle
East, and glorified his life and work in writings that were absolutely hagio-
graphic.[58]

In view of this unequivocal shift in the parameters of Germany's relations
in all sectors, one simply cannot claim, "The Arab cause in Palestine—which
for a short time in 1938 and 1939, at most, seemed a convenient means to influence events in Europe—was not among the interests of National Socialist
Germany."[59] And it is even more erroneous when the same author, a few pages

56. Mildenstein, *Osten*, p. 115.
57. Ibid., p. 119f.
58. Björkman, "Mufti," p. 307ff.; Fischer-Weth, p. 47ff.; Hartmann, p. 430ff.; Klingmüller, p. 413ff.; Hüber,
Hadsch, p. 139ff.
59. Nicosia, *Hitler*, p. 286.

later, inconsistently claims to find that "the Hitler regime, in 1938 and 1939, no longer attached any value to the Arab factor."[60] The exact opposite was the case. Likewise, there is no evidence for an alleged "growing animosity toward Germany in the Arab world due to the role Germany played in illegal Jewish immigration to Palestine."[61] Rather, it was a process of a steadily growing consensus and a shared enmity that would lead to solidarity in the event of war.

---

60. Ibid., p. 296; similarly Yisraeli, "The Third Reich and Palestine," p. 343.
61. Nicosia, *Hitler*, p. 286.

Chapter IV

War in North Africa and Mesopotamia:
Cyrenaica and Iraq

The key foundations of the Berlin-Rome axis formed in October 1936 included, from the beginning, German recognition of the Mediterranean as an Italian "mare nostrum" in line with Mussolini's ancient imperial aspirations.[1] Mussolini saw Italy as trapped in the Mediterranean, with the British Empire and France denying free access to the oceans. From this interpretation, he derived a vision for his country that involved prying open the "bars of the Italian prison"—meaning Gibraltar, Corsica, Tunisia, Malta, Cyprus, and Suez—and ending the strategic naval superiority of Great Britain in this body of water.[2] The conclusion of the Pact of Steel with Germany on May 22, 1939, which obliged each country to aid the other in the event of war, was intended to create the alliance structure to achieve this. The German Reich thus recognized an Italian claim on the Middle East as future areas of influence, but this acceptance was provisional. In view of Italy's increasing military weakness, it would gradually be withdrawn.

---

1. Bessis, p. 330.
2. Deakin, p. 23; Michaelis, p. 55f.

Only following Italy's belated entry into the war on June 10, 1940, did the Mediterranean become an active military battleground. But while Mussolini was greedily focused on part of the French spoils, he failed to seize the opportunity for a surprise attack against the British Empire's Mediterranean strongholds. Although the defeat of France and, especially, the retreat of the British at Dunkirk were encouraging signs to the Arab world, there was no sign of a rapid collapse of the United Kingdom. The British still occupied the Mediterranean's entry and exit points—Gibraltar and the Suez Canal—and, via Malta and Cyprus, controlled passage to its central and eastern parts.[3] Even though Britain had been forcibly driven from the continent and was the Axis powers' only remaining wartime enemy, it was not about to opt for the defensive. While the Battle of Britain raged,[4] the Third Reich, by controlling the Channel and the Atlantic coast, was able to contain the British through naval and air strategy. But in mid-September the planned invasion had to be abandoned,[5] and British air and naval forces in the Mediterranean seized every opportunity available. Their most effective attack came during the night of November 11–12, 1940, when 20 torpedo bombers from the aircraft carrier *Illustrious* sank a large portion of the Italian fleet while at anchor in the harbor of Taranto. With this success, Great Britain reasserted and secured its naval supremacy in the Mediterranean—a supremacy that Italy would be unable to challenge again on its own.[6]

At that point, the German army was not yet present in the new theater of operations. Hitler, who by the end of July 1940 had already decided to prepare his attack on the Soviet Union in the spring of 1941, was hindered by his contradictory intentions and the situation at sea and on the ground. The desire to invade England; the need to consider the plans of his main ally Mussolini, and Spain, Vichy France, and Turkey, which he wanted to either draw to his side or neutralize; the reality of the weakness of the German navy; and especially the planned war in the east—all precluded intervention in the Mediterranean in the last half of 1940.[7] Hitler therefore favored a policy of separate spheres, in which Germany would pursue its goals of continental hegemony north of the Alps while Italy would independently attempt to reestablish its "Roman Empire in the Mediterranean" to the south.[8] This was compatible with Mussolini's conception of waging a parallel war that he intended to fight in the

---

3. Hillgruber, *Hitlers*, p. 126ff.
4. Keegan, p. 135ff.
5. Cf. Klee.
6. Schröder, *Deutschland*, p. 29; Reuth, *Entscheidung*, p. 25.
7. Dessouki, p. 33ff.
8. Note by Woermann/AA, July 21, 1940, ADAP, ser. D, vol. 10, p. 215f.; AA circular order, Aug. 20, 1940, ADAP, ser. D, vol. 10, p. 425f.

Mediterranean arena while anxiously protecting his problematic autonomy vis-à-vis his Axis partner.[9]

Libya served as the starting point for the Italian offensive against Egypt, which the Duce insisted upon despite the opposition of the Italian high command. The offensive began on September 13, 1940, by General Graziani but was suspended just three days later after the capture of Sidi Barrani and a territorial gain of 90 kilometers. On October 28, Mussolini ordered his troops to cross the Albanian border into Greece after handing the Greeks an ultimatum they rejected. The following day, British forces landed on Crete, and in early November, in the Athens area. Once the highly motivated Greeks began to counterattack and push the Italian army back into Albania, Mussolini decided in early December to appeal to Berlin for help in order to avert what was clearly imminent defeat. Thus, six months into the war, Italy in effect abandoned its policy of parallel warfare. On December 8, the British also launched a counteroffensive on the Libyan-Egyptian border, and soon threatened Bardia and Tobruk.[10]

Because of these rapid setbacks on all fronts, Italy was facing an inevitable military disaster. Moreover, the oil fields of Romania, which were vital to the Third Reich, were now within the range of the Royal Air Force installed on the island of Crete. To forestall both dangers, Hitler also abandoned his policy of separate spheres and opted for a sustained "cleansing" of the southern European flank prior to the initiation of Operation Barbarossa, which had been postponed to the late spring or early summer of 1941.[11] In Directive No. 18, dated November 12, 1940, he ordered a panzer division be held ready for deployment in North Africa, preparations be made for air attacks on Alexandria and the Suez Canal, and an invasion from bases in Bulgaria into Greece be planned for German units.[12] On December 10 he ordered the relocation of the 10th Air Corps from Norway to Sicily. The most important assignment for the corps was "fighting against the English fleet, especially in the harbor of Alexandria, as well as enemy naval traffic through the Suez Canal and through the straits between Sicily and the North African coast."[13] And on January 11, 1941, he ordered German forces to "assist in the fighting in the Mediterranean arena": "Tripolitania must be held, and the danger of a collapse on the

---

9. Gruchmann, "Chancen," p. 461f.
10. Reuth, *Entscheidung,* p. 23ff.
11. Note by Schmidt/office of RAM, Nov. 19, 1940, Hitler-Ciano conversation on Nov. 18, ADAP, ser. D, vol. 11/2, p. 509ff.; cf. Hillgruber, *Hitlers,* p. 339ff.
12. OKW/WFSt/Abt. L, Nov. 12, 1940, Directive No. 18, ADAP, ser. D, vol. 11/1, p. 444ff.
13. OKW/WFSt/Abt. L, Dec. 10, 1940, deployment of German flying units from Italy, ADAP, ser. D, vol. 11/2, p. 697; cf. Gundelach, vol. 1, p. 92ff.

Albanian front averted."[14] Thus, the states bordering the Mediterranean became potential targets for Germany's war effort.

Despite these support measures, the Italian defeat initially continued to run its course. Bardia and Tobruk fell in January 1941; Benghazi, the capital of Cyrenaica, was occupied on February 6. By mid-month the British had destroyed most of Marshal Rodolfo Graziani's army and taken 130,000 prisoners of war. Not until their offensive ended—as a result of the formation of a new focal point in the Greek-Aegean area, at El Agheila on the southeastern corner of the Gulf of Sidra—and the first successes of the 10th Air Corps (in action since January 10) became apparent, did British pressure lessen in North Africa. The danger of losing Tripolitania as well was thus averted.[15] Protected by German aircraft and shielded by the Italian navy, 15 German ship squadrons reached Tripoli between the beginning of February and the end of March, transporting 25,000 men, plus vehicles and supplies.[16] The Luftwaffe bomber and fighter squadrons also attacked Malta and British convoys, the harbor of Alexandria, and began to mine the Suez Canal flying out of the Dodecanese Islands.[17]

Now Palestine was within range of the Axis powers. As early as 1940, Italian bombers had been taking off from Rhodes to attack the coastal cities, and in 1941 the Luftwaffe began to participate as well. The primary targets were Tel Aviv, Jaffa, and especially Haifa, where the oil pipeline from Iraq ended and large refineries were located. Hundreds of Jews and Arabs died in these attacks.[18] Nevertheless, the bombardment was observed "with great satisfaction" by the Arabs, who, "flocking exultantly from Acre on the other side of the bay and from the mountains of Ras en Nakura, watched this spectacle and danced with joy," as Iwo Jorda describes it. "The leaflets dropped by the Italian airmen were not necessary to explain the meaning of this attack."[19] In view of the extension of the war to the Middle East, the German government, in agreement with Italy, broadcast a statement on December 4, 1940, declaring that Germany was in complete sympathy with "the struggle of the Arab lands to obtain their independence."[20] Although the statement was very general and made no mention of any future goals, it generated a "warm response through-

14. OKW/WFSt/Abt. L, Jan. 11, 1941, Directive No. 22, ADAP, ser. D, vol. 11/2, p. 894.

15. Reuth, *Entscheidung*, p. 41ff.

16. Rich in material on this: BA-MA, N 316/v.36.

17. Gundelach, vol. 1, p. 102ff.

18. Ibid., pp. 253, 267; OKW/Ausl/Abw I, Dec. 7, 1940, report from Palestine, BA-MA, RL 2 II/486; report by LFSt/Ic, June 11, June 12, and July 8, 1941, BA-MA, RL 2 II/486; OKW/Ausl/Abw I , Mar. 26, 1941, Middle East, British measures in Egypt and Palestine, BA-MA, RH 2/1784; Ritter to AA, June 9, 1941, PAAA, R 29885; cf. Segev, pp. 489, 492.

19. Jorda, *Araber-Aufstand*, p. 438.

20. Radio broadcast, Dec. 4, 1940, PAAA, R 27326.

out the entire Arab world," reported Dr. Wilhelm Melchers, who had succeeded Hentig as head of Political Department VII (dealing with the Middle
East) in the Foreign Office at the end of 1939.[21]

With the end of the Italian parallel war, the Axis partner's military operations became integrated into the broad framework of overall German strategy;
at the same time, however, the previously sacrosanct Italian primacy in the
Middle East was increasingly being called into question.[22] "Due to Italy's hegemony in the Mediterranean—that is, the absolute control of the sea route
[through the Suez Canal] to the central African territories that we must regain,
as well as the oil resources in the Middle East—it seems essential that the
Reich secure for itself at least one land connection to the Persian Gulf that is
independent of these maritime routes," asserted Franz von Papen, the German
ambassador in Ankara, in October 1940.[23] Lieutenant Colonel Bernhard von
Lossberg of the Wehrmacht command staff was even more explicit in January
1941: "The German decision to allow the Italians freedom in their political
work in the Mediterranean region as well has proven a failure in the Arab
countries. The Italians have no interest in independent Arab states because
they want to play the key role there themselves later. Valuable relations in
Arabia have been broken off or worsened in the last few months." From this
analysis he identified two essential consequences for the future: "(1) It is high
time that we direct the political work in the Middle East from Germany, and
that we act quickly and forcefully to do so. (2) This includes acknowledging the
independence of the Arabs as a war aim of the Axis. In this regard, we would
do well if we did not need to promise the Arabs a merely 'tolerable' resolution
to the Jewish question in Palestine, but rather could make every necessary con-
cession on this matter in good conscience."[24] In plain language: only the denial
of Italian colonial aspirations and the promise of Arab autonomy could guarantee a radical "solution to the Jewish question" in this area.

That same month, Lossberg contacted the Middle East department of the
Foreign Office with regard to this issue; he argued against the "political first
option" given to the Italians and used the current relative military strengths to
support his case: "Today, after Italy's various defeats, further consideration
would hardly be possible, because it would be evident that in reality the Italians
no longer had the upper hand in the areas in question." In view of impending
further losses, the OKH held "the view that we could not let things drift in the
Middle East, but that we must instead become more active in our warfare,

21. Note by Melchers/AA, Dec. 11, 1940, ADAP, ser. D, vol. 11/2, p. 706.
22. Hirszowicz, *Germany*, p. 57ff.; Melka, *Axis*, p. 204ff.
23. DG Ankara to AA, Oct. 3, 1940, ADAP, ser. D, vol. 11/1, p. 207.
24. OKW/WFSt/Abt. L to OKW/Ausl/Abw, Jan. 7, 1941, PAAA, BA 61179.

especially to prevent the worse—for example, the loss of North Africa."[25] Joachim von Ribbentrop decided in early February 1941 that "great consideration should be shown for Italian sensibilities" in this matter; however, at the same time he granted a loophole for independent German action. "Considering that the Italians have thus far left the Arab question hanging, we can take the initiative ourselves in appropriate situations, but we must always involve the Italians in a timely manner and defer to them externally," maintained Undersecretary of State Dr. Ernst Woermann, who was head of the political department.[26] Thus, Italy's "political first option" was effectively eliminated, as it could now be circumvented with ministerial approval whenever the situation seemed to require it. It now served only as a screen behind which the conflicts of all involved would be—more or less openly—played out.

On January 21, 1941, Hitler ordered the launch of Operation Sunflower in support of the Italians in North Africa.[27] For this purpose, the 5th Light Division was transported by ship from Naples to Tripoli.[28] This "blocking force," which was strengthened in May with the addition of the 15th Panzer Division,[29] was designated as the German Afrika Korps.[30] Tactically, it was directly subordinate to the Italian commander-in-chief in Libya and could be deployed only in its entirety.[31] On February 12, Lieutenant General Erwin Rommel took over leadership of the corps. Rommel had made a great name for himself as commander of the 7th Panzer Division in the French campaign, but he had also come under criticism for his unorthodox and risky actions.[32] However, Hitler, who knew Rommel well since he had served as commander of the Führer's headquarters in the Polish campaign, thought very highly of him. "General Rommel is the boldest panzer general we have in the German army," he wrote to Mussolini on February 5.[33] Indeed, Rommel soon developed grand plans. On March 8 he informed the Army High Command that it would be advisable to initiate an offensive before the beginning of summer, in order to first regain Cyrenaica and then push forward into Egypt.[34]

Although scarcity of transport capacity and bottlenecks in the fuel supply demonstrated early that the logistical backup for long-range operations was very thin, the German Afrika Korps and the Italian Ariete and Brescia divi-

25. Note by Melchers/AA, Jan. 16, 1941, PAAA, BA 61179.
26. Note by Woermann/AA, Feb. 4, 1941, ADAP, ser. D, vol. 12/1, p. 16.
27. OKW/WFSt/Abt. L directive, Jan. 21, 1941, ADAP, ser. D, vol. 11/2, p. 963f.
28. OKH/GenStdH/Op.Abt., Feb. 10, 1941, Operation Sunflower, BA-MA, RH 2/457.
29. Ibid. to DAK commander, Mar. 21, 1941, BA-MA, RH 2/457.
30. OKW/WFSt/Abt. L, Feb. 19, 1941, Operation Sunflower, BA-MA, RH 2/457.
31. Ibid., Feb. 5, 1941, behavior of German troops in Italian theaters of war, BA-MA, RH 2/459.
32. Cf. Reuth, *Rommel*, p. 55ff.; Fraser, *Rommel*, p. 119ff.; Rutherford, p. 38ff.
33. Hitler to Mussolini, Feb. 5, 1941, ADAP, ser. D, vol. 12/1, p. 25.
34. Rintelen to OKH, Mar. 8, 1941, BA-MA, RH 2/459.

sions, also under Rommel's command, began the offensive on March 31. On April 4 they took Benghazi and on April 8 Derna, and then circled Tobruk and surrounded the fortress with its important harbor on April 11. That same day, Rommel's rapid units conquered Bardia; on April 13, Sollum; and two days later, Halfaya Pass, taking them across the Egyptian border. Within two weeks, they had regained Cyrenaica and compensated for Graziani's territorial loss. Except for Tobruk, the British quickly lost everything they had taken from the Italians the previous winter.[35]

At the same time, German divisions overran the Balkans. On April 6, the Third Reich attacked Yugoslavia and Greece. Belgrade surrendered on the 17th of the month, and Athens followed on the 21st. This German assistance strategy restabilized the situation in the eastern Mediterranean for the Axis powers. Within the German-Italian sphere of control, only Crete—which Hitler viewed essentially as a British aircraft carrier enabling strikes against the Romanian oil fields of Ploesti—was still in British hands. The failed attempt of the British Middle East high command in April 1941 to check the advance of Rommel in Cyrenaica while at the same time holding the British positions in Greece had greatly overextended the British forces. The 58,000-strong British expeditionary corps was compelled to hurriedly evacuate its positions in Greece, leaving behind its heavy equipment. These events resulted in an immense loss of power and prestige for the British Empire, especially in the Middle East.

The loss became even greater when Operation Mercury—the conquest of Crete, ordered on April 25[36]—led to the complete occupation of the island on June 1. This victory came at the cost of substantial German casualties, but it proved that air supremacy over an area could trump naval supremacy.[37] From that point on, the air forces of the Axis powers enjoyed undisputed control of the Ionian and Aegean Seas and threatened the Levant and the bases of the Mediterranean fleet. In addition, a second supply route had now been opened from Greece to Benghazi and Derna.[38] During that period, Churchill, as he stated shortly thereafter in a secret session of the House of Commons,[39] was envisioning the loss of Egypt, Palestine, Malta, and Cyprus—the end, in effect, of British dominance in the Mediterranean. He could not anticipate at that point that the Third Reich would not seize this opportunity. Because of the upcoming campaign against the Soviet Union, truly decisive operations were no

35. Reuth, *Entscheidung*, p. 54ff.; Kühn, p. 13ff.; Lucas, p. 45ff.; Heckmann, p. 58ff.
36. OKW/WFSt/Abt. L, April 25, 1941, Directive No. 28, reprinted in Hubatsch, p. 115ff.
37. Hillgruber, *Hitlers*, p. 465ff.
38. Activity of the 10th German Air Corps in Italy, Jan.–May 22, 1941, BA-MA, RL 7/689; cf. Gundelach, vol. 1, p. 254ff.
39. Eade, p. 58f.

longer feasible for the German land and air forces, as would happen during the anti-British uprising that broke out in Iraq in April 1941.[40]

When the war began, Amin el-Husseini, the former Grand Mufti of Jerusalem, immediately selected Mesopotamia as the next location for his exile. Fearing arrest by the French mandatory power, he went into hiding in Beirut on October 14, 1939; then two days later, he suddenly appeared in Baghdad, where he was received as an honored guest.[41] Although the British insisted that he should remain completely isolated and prevented him from carrying out any political activities, el-Husseini was revered as an Arab national hero in Iraq and quickly became the center of an influential circle of opposition officers and politicians. Rashid Ali al-Gailani became the local head of the emerging junta that was to take power. Al-Gailani, a jurist, born in 1894 to an influential family, had already served several times as an Iraqi minister and even as prime minister in 1940. He had spent a number of weeks in Berlin in 1936 and since then had raved about the Third Reich.[42] Unity prevailed in Iraqi support for the Axis, the refusal of Iraq to declare war on Germany as the British requested, hatred for the British Empire, and radical pan-Arabism.[43]

While even the pro-British prime minister Nuri as-Said occasionally flirted with the Axis after the German victory in the west in 1940,[44] the Mufti and al-Gailani aggressively approached the Germans.[45] Their contact was Hitler's former vice chancellor, Franz von Papen, who since April 1939 had represented the Third Reich in Ankara and was considered the first point of contact for Arab nationalists throughout the Middle East.[46] Naji Shawkat, the Iraqi minister of justice, visited him on July 5, 1940, and delivered a letter from the Mufti that contained congratulations on the victory over France and a solicitation of German support for the Arab cause. "The Arab national government will take up the fight in Palestine again as well," Shawkat also promised.[47] Osman Kemal Haddad, the Mufti's private secretary, visited von Papen on August 6 and declared that on behalf of the Iraqi junta he would proceed to Berlin and Rome for preliminary negotiations. Once in power, the junta would support the "struggle of the Axis powers against England in all areas [...], particularly through a new revolt in Palestine."[48] The German ambassador in

---

40. Cf. Gruchmann, "Chancen," p. 472ff.
41. Nevo, "Amin," p. 7; Mattar, "Amin," p. 270ff.
42. Hüber, El-Gailani, p. 153ff.; Hamdi, p. 45ff.
43. Khadduri, *Iraq*, p. 162ff.
44. Khadduri, "General," p. 329ff.
45. Cf. Melka, *Axis*, p. 114ff.
46. Roth, p. 107ff.; cf. von Papen, p. 499ff.
47. DG Ankara to AA, July 6, 1940, ADAP, ser. D, vol. 10, p. 118; Mufti to von Papen, June 21, 1940, ADAP, ser. D, vol. 10, p. 119; cf. Nafi, *Arabism*, p. 366ff.
48. Ibid., Aug. 6, 1940, ADAP, ser. D, vol. 10, p. 341.

Ankara subsequently served as a diplomatically protected mail drop for Haddad's correspondence with the Mufti and the Committee for Cooperation between Arab Countries that he had founded in Baghdad—to which leading notables from Iraq, Syria, Saudi Arabia, and Palestine belonged.[49]

On August 26, in Berlin, Haddad conferred on the Mufti's behalf with Grobba, who had been serving as Middle East expert in the Foreign Office since his return from Baghdad. Haddad called for a joint German-Italian declaration of independence for the Arab states as well as the recognition of their right "to solve the Jewish question in the interests of their nation and people, following the German-Italian model." He hinted at a secret agreement by the future Iraqi government and promised "the organization of large-scale uprisings in Palestine-Transjordan against England, centered in Syria, with weapons seized from the French and with financial support from the Axis powers."[50] On October 18, on the basis of this understanding, Secretary of State Ernst von Weizsäcker and Haddad reached an agreement on the already discussed German-Italian declaration.[51] At the same time, Shawkat sought out von Papen again and declared the Arabs' readiness to "immediately unleash new unrest [in] Palestine. [...] Everything is ready."[52] In Rome Ambassador Hans von Mackensen also appeared determined to support the Mufti financially, in order to enable him "to resume assassinations, disruption of the oil pipeline connections, and so forth, to harm the English, as he proposed."[53]

In mid-February 1941, Haddad returned to Berlin and delivered a personal letter from the Mufti to Hitler.[54] The letter portrayed his struggle against "perfidious Albion" and the Jews, "that dangerous enemy whose secret weapons are finance, corruption, and intrigue." He declared, "The particularly warm sympathy of the Arab peoples for Germany and for the Axis is virtually an accomplished fact," and promised that "freed from certain material limitations, the Arab people are ready everywhere to act against the common enemy to the best of their abilities and to rise enthusiastically with the Axis to perform their part in the well-deserved defeat of the English-Jewish coalition."[55] With this statement, an official offer of alliance was on the table. On February 26, Woermann assured Haddad of "ready" financial support.[56] On March 23, Hitler

---

49. Roth, p. 111f.
50. Note by Grobba/AA, Aug. 27, 1940, ADAP, ser. D, vol. 10, p. 459ff.; AA to DG Rome, Sept. 9, 1940, ADAP, ser. D, vol. 11/1, p 38f.
51. Note by Grobba/AA, Oct. 18, 1940, ADAP, ser. D, vol. 11/1, p. 272ff.
52. AA to DG Rome, Sept. 12, 1940, ADAP, ser. D, vol. 11/1, p. 57.
53. DG Rome to AA, Sept. 14, 1940, ADAP, ser. D, vol. 11/1, p. 67; cf. Khadduri, *Iraq*, p. 179ff.; Gensicke, p. 59ff.; Höpp, Alī, p. 572ff.
54. Note by Grobba/AA, Feb. 18, 1941, PAAA, BA 61123.
55. Mufti to Hitler, Jan. 20, 1941, PAAA, R 27326.
56. Note by Woermann/AA, Feb. 26, 1941, PAAA, BA 61123.

approved the draft response developed by Weizsäcker,[57] which stated, "Germany recognizes the complete independence of the Arab states, or, where independence has not yet been achieved, the right to achieve it."[58] One day later, Woermann conferred with Canaris and the leaders of the Abwehr: "There was agreement that the primary political route to the Arab world should be via the Grand Mufti and his secretary."[59] The pact with the devil was concluded.

Much more documentary evidence of German weapons smuggling in the Orient can be found after this legalization of the coalition. In mid-April 1941 the Abwehr sent 15,000 carbines, 200 light machine guns, and 300 submachine guns to Palestine.[60] On May 11, the following message was received from Baghdad: "Mufti's need very urgent, as major undertaking planned for Palestine in near future."[61] Three days later, a motor glider carrying weapons took off from Salonika in the direction of Syria. On May 15, 400 light machine guns were transported by air from Athens to Iraq; four days later, bazookas and ammunition followed.[62] On May 21 Italian aircraft delivered 60 light machine guns to Mosul for the Mufti's "Palestinian undertaking."[63] In addition, by May 24 the Mufti had received cash totaling $35,000, paid out by the German Foreign Office.[64] On May 27 and 28 the Abwehr sent 20 railway cars toward Palestine; they contained, among other things, 15,000 carbines, 300 submachine guns, and ammunition.[65] On June 1, the Foreign Office promised the Mufti "further financial support."[66] Shortly thereafter, another German "weapons ship" set out from Salonika to Palestine.[67] These reports alone, in a span of barely two months in the spring of 1941, indicate how significant the Middle East had become in the calculations of the Third Reich.

"If the political and military requirements are met through a pan-Arabic movement in the interior and money, weapons, and German support, a spark is all that is needed for an Arab uprising to break out in Palestine," concluded the Middle East arms dealer Hans Steffen in early April 1941. He predicted, "Based on my information, the mood in Iraq is ripe for attack. They are just waiting for the signal from the Germans." But he also warned that the revolt "should take place only in concert with German operations—no earlier and no

57. Memorandum by office of RAM, Mar. 23, 1941, PAAA, BA 61123.
58. StS./AA to Mufti, Mar. 11, 1941, PAAA, R 27326; cf. Hirszowicz, *Reich*, p. 126ff.
59. Note by Woermann/AA, Mar. 26, 1941, PAAA, BA 61123.
60. Note by Davidsen/AA, April 19, 1941, PAAA, BA 61148.
61. Gehrcke [=Grobba] to AA, May 11, 1941, PAAA, R 29884.
62. OKW/Ausl/Abw II war diary, May 14, 15, and 19, 1941, BA-MA, RW 5/498.
63. Gehrcke [=Grobba] to AA, May 21, 1941, PAAA, R 29884.
64. Note by Melchers/AA, May 24, 1941, PAAA, R 29884.
65. OKW/Ausl/Abw II war diary, May 29, 1941, BA-MA, RW 5/498.
66. AA to DG Teheran, June 1, 1941, PAAA, R 29885.
67. Gehrcke [=Grobba] to AA, June 3, 1941, PAAA, R 29885.

later. Isolated, it runs the risk of being put down early."[68] But this is exactly
what happened in Iraq. When German troops reconquered Cyrenaica, drove
the British from Greece, and consequently marched forward victoriously on all
fronts in the Mediterranean, the junta around the Mufti saw the right moment
for a coup, setting the stage for an armed conflict with Great Britain. El-
Husseini, in any case, often said afterward that he was "one of the major
factors—even the initiator—of this war."[69]

During the night of April 1–2, 1941, Iraqi officers overthrew the govern-
ment in Baghdad. They installed a successor to the regent Abdul Illah (guardian
of the underage heir to the throne, Feisal II), who had fled, and appointed al-
Gailani as the new prime minister.[70] Since the Wehrmacht's offensive in the
Balkans had created a southeastern European base for operations in the
Orient, the geostrategic situation of the British Empire in the Mediterranean
had now become precarious. The oil supply seemed endangered by the new
Iraqi government, which threatened to open the door to the Third Reich in the
Middle East. In Iraq, the British had only the right to march through the
country; they also maintained an aviation school at the Habbaniya air base west
of Baghdad, which had been fortified because of the war. In addition, troops
from India were sailing toward Iraq to reach Baghdad. When the soldiers
landed in Basra on April 18 the conflict escalated. On April 30 Iraqi troops
occupied the mountain ranges around Habbaniya and surrounded the base.[71]

In Berlin and Rome, where a request for help from al-Gailani was received
on April 18, officials were totally surprised by this early move. "Immediate
intervention by German air force units in Iraq is out of the question, as Iraq is
beyond the range of the Luftwaffe," noted Ribbentrop on April 21 for Hitler.
"Arms transports to Iraq appear possible, using individual Ju aircraft, but only
via Syria."[72] The Reich foreign minister knew, however, that this would require
the consent of Vichy France, which, though conquered, was still the mandatory
power. In addition, the landing under way on Crete severely limited German
actions in the southeast. Churchill defied the commander of British forces in
the Middle East, Sir Archibald Wavell, who had recommended negotiations
with Iraq,[73] and on the evening of May 1 issued the order to attack.[74] The
prime minister personally gave the commander of the base at Habbaniya the

---

68. Hans Steffen, early April 1941, the situation in Arabia, BA-MA, RH 2/1764.
69. Note by Mufti (undated/Dec. 1943), PAAA, R 101101.
70. Khadduri, *Iraq*, p. 212ff.; Schröder, *Deutschland*, p. 74ff.
71. Schröder, *Deutschland*, p. 78ff.; Schröder, *Irak*, p. 41ff.; Stewart, *Relations*, p. 241ff.
72. Note by RAM, April 21, 1941, ADAP, ser. D, vol. 12/2, p. 494; cf. Melka, *Axis*, p. 220ff.
73. Connell, p. 436f.
74. Melka, *Axis*, p. 253f.

encouraging counsel, "If you have to strike, strike hard."[75] The next day, British aircraft attacked Iraqi positions while troops from Basra began marching toward Baghdad; at the same time, a Transjordanian formation was proceeding there as well.[76] With just a few sorties, the Royal Air Force eliminated the small Iraqi air force and broke through the encirclement; on May 6 al-Gailani's troops retreated from the Habbaniya area.

While German soldiers had just taken the Greek mainland, though the British still held Crete, this sudden shift was not at all convenient to Berlin. On May 3 Ribbentrop sent Grobba, who had "worked undercover there regularly, even after the outbreak of the war," as German liaison to Baghdad, hoping that "from our central office Iraq will then bring the entire Arab world into revolt against England."[77] That same day, Hitler ordered that "everything possible be done with regard to military support."[78] The means to do so were provided on May 5 by Deputy Prime Minister Admiral François Darlan, who agreed on behalf of the French government to make available the stocks of weapons in Syria and allow German aircraft to use Syrian airfields for stopovers.[79] On May 11 Rudolf Rahn arrived in Beirut as the representative of the German Reich and, together with General Henri Fernand Dentz, commander of the French army in Syria, set in motion the arms and ammunition transports for Iraq.[80] Two days earlier, on the radio, the Mufti had called for jihad against Great Britain and appealed to all Muslims to help in the "holy war."[81]

On May 11 Grobba arrived in Iraq and was enthusiastically cheered as "emancipator and deliverer" by the people of Mosul.[82] Abwehr captain Kohlhaas, who accompanied him, was also able to report happily "that the name of the Führer is known even to the humblest Arab."[83] For this reason, Grobba called for the swastika to be carried "in any appropriate form" as an identifying mark.[84] That same day the Luftwaffe's Sonderkommando Junck reached Mosul with 12 heavy fighters and 12 bombers. On May 12, the Iraqis cheered the low-altitude flight over Baghdad from the streets and rooftops. However, Major Axel von Blomberg, the squadron leader and son of the former minister of

---

75. Grobba, p. 228.
76. DG Ankara to AA, May 2, 1941, ADAP, ser. D., vol. 12/2, p. 570f.
77. Note by RAM, May 3, 1941, ADAP, ser. D., vol. 12/2, p. 573.
78. Note by Hewel/RAM staff, May 3, 1941, ADAP, ser. D., vol. 12/2, p. 574; cf. Hirszowicz, *Reich*, pp. 114ff., 144ff.
79. DG Paris to AA, May 5, 1941, PAAA, p. 618ff.; KTB Halder, vol. 2, p. 399; minutes of the German-French military negotiations on May 21, 1941, BA-MA, RW 34/10; cf. Jäckel, p. 161ff.
80. Rahn to AA, May 11, 1941, PAAA, R 29884; Rahn, p. 152ff.
81. Khadduri, *Iraq*, p. 224; Schechtman, p. 110; Elpeleg, p. 61.
82. Address by Grobba/AA, May 11, 1942, the controversy over the English policy in the Middle East, BAB, NS 19/3847; Grobba, p. 236.
83. Report by Capt. Kohlhaas, June 16, 1941, battles in Iraq, BA-MA, RH 24-68/2.
84. Gehrcke [=Grobba] to AA, May 17, 1941, PAAA, R 29884.

war, received a fatal shot to the head during the celebratory gunfire that was the local custom.[85] Although the aircraft immediately began attacking British targets in Iraq, they soon suffered significant losses. A lack of desert equipment such as auxiliary cooling systems, special tires, and sand filters; missing supplies; inadequate coordination with the Iraqi army; and the complete absence of any air defense led to the failure of the German Luftwaffe mission. By May 27 just two aircraft were still able to fly, and they took off for Syria two days later.[86] Grobba and his entourage fled there as well on May 31.

On May 29, as British troops came closer to Baghdad, al-Gailani and the Mufti decamped and crossed the Iranian border.[87] Two days later a ceasefire was negotiated, but the soldiers of the United Kingdom remained outside the capital to await the return of the regent. The failure of the coup had brought tempers in Baghdad to the boiling point. Before he fled, Al-Gailani made sure weapons were distributed to the al-Futuwwa youth,[88] and the English journalist Freya Stark was told, "Become a Muslim and we will take care of you while we kill the others."[89] The anger of the mob was directed in particular against the local Jews. During the British advance, they were suspected of espionage, and some had been beaten and arrested.[90] "There is no shortage of fearful pessimists, friends of Nuri as-Said and the Jews, who covertly or overtly work to sabotage the efforts of the Mufti and Gailani, who is fighting like a lion," el-Husseini informed the Italian ambassador shortly before fleeing.[91] When the Jews of Baghdad wished to welcome the returning regent on June 1, this was the signal for a pogrom in which primarily Iraqi soldiers, police officers, and youth participated. According to official figures, 110 Jews—including 28 women—were killed and 204 injured on June 1 and 2. In addition, 586 Jewish businesses and 911 homes were looted and destroyed.[92] On June 9, the Italian embassy in the Iraqi capital reported, "In Baghdad, Jews are still being attacked and robbed."[93] The pogrom was a foretaste of what would have happened in many locations had German soldiers reached the Arabian Peninsula.

Despite the debacle in Iraq, the entire region remained in the German field of vision, particularly since the conquest of Crete was reaching its victorious conclusion and Rommel's troops had set foot in Egypt. To avoid a recurrence

85. Sonderkommando Junck war diary, May 12, 1941, BA-MA, N 475; Grobba, p. 241.
86. Gehrcke [=Grobba] to AA, May 27, 1941, PAAA, R 29884; cf. note by Kramarz/AA, May 16, 1941, the state of military support for Iraq, ADAP, ser. D, vol. 12/2, p. 694ff.; Gundelach, vol. 1, p. 241ff.; Schröder, *Deutschland*, p. 107ff.; Schröder, *Irak*, p. 73ff.
87. Gehrcke [=Grobba] to AA, May 30, 1941, PAAA, R 29884.
88. Schröder, *Irak*, p. 57.
89. Stark, p. 169.
90. Kedourie, Sack, p. 307; Cohen, *Farhûd*, p. 8.
91. DG Rome to AA, May 27, 1941, ADAP, ser. D, vol. 12/2, p. 741.
92. Cohen, "Farhûd," p. 10ff.; Rejwan, p. 126ff.
93. Translation of report by DG Baghdad, June 9, 1941, PAAA, R 29885.

of the confusion over authority that had arisen at the beginning of the effort to assist the Iraqi rebels, Hitler issued Directive No. 30, "Middle East," on May 23. "The Arab independence movement is our natural ally against England in the Middle East," it declared, and stated that a military mission under the code name "Sonderstab F" would be deployed to support Iraq.[94] Sonderstab F would be placed under the command of Luftwaffe General Hellmuth Felmy, who in World War I was the commander of Air Unit 300 on the Sinai front and who was also Grobba's brother-in-law.[95] Planned as a higher-level head-quarters for the entire Middle East, by the end of May it included around 40 officers, noncommissioned officers, and men.[96] Contact with al-Gailani and the Mufti, who reached Teheran on June 2,[97] was also maintained. Just days earlier, Weizsäcker had told Ambasssador Ettel that "we are very anxious that the Grand Mufti be convinced that we will further support him and the Arab struggle for independence." Both the Mufti and al-Gailani were also granted future financial support.[98] Officials in Berlin were delighted to hear from Ettel on June 5 that the "Grand Mufti and Gailani are filled with unshakable faith in the Führer and Germany's final victory, in which they also see the victory of the Arab struggle for freedom."[99]

But the British were also very active. Because they viewed the arms deliveries from French supplies in Iraq and the stopovers of German aircraft in Syria as proof that Vichy France was actively siding with the Third Reich, a campaign against the French mandate began immediately after the occupation of Iraq.[100] British troops attacked Syria on June 8 and conquered Damascus on the 21st of the month. That same day, the hesitant Wavell was replaced by Sir Claude Auchinleck, the former commander-in-chief in India.[101] While Rahn and Major Meyer-Ricks, the Ia officer of Sonderstab F, saw as their primary task the organization of the Arab guerrillas, the French army suffered 9,000 dead and wounded during its fierce resistance.[102] On July 9, Beirut was captured; three days later German personnel took refuge in Turkey, and on July 14

94. OKW/WFSt/Abt. L, May 23, 1941, Directive No. 30, reprinted in Hubatsch, p. 120ff.
95. Grobba, p. 234.
96. OKW/Ausl/Abw, May 24, 1941, Iraq military mission, BA-MA, RH 24-68/2; cf. OKW/Ausl/Abw II war diary, May 24, 1941, BA-MA, RW 5/498.
97. DG Teheran to AA, June 3, 1941, PAAA, R 29885.
98. StS./AA to DG Teheran, June 1, 1941, PAAA, R 29885.
99. DG Teheran to AA, June 5, 1941, PAAA, R 29885.
100. Melka, *Axis*, p. 325ff.
101. Connell, p. 458ff.
102. Sonderstab F, July 4, 1941, report covering June 26–July 4, BA-MA, RH 24-68/2; note by Rahn/AA, July 30, 1941, report on the German mission in Syria, May 9–July 11, ADAP, ser. D, vol. 13/1, p. 198ff.; cf. Hirszowicz, *Reich*, p. 184ff.

an armistice was concluded.[103] Germany thus dropped its "certain restraint" toward France. "In the propagandistic handling of the Arab question," stated Ribbentrop, "the Arab wish to attain complete freedom should be emphatically supported."[104]

While the British were pacifying Iraq and occupying Syria, and the situation in the eastern Mediterranean was consequently turning in their favor, Rommel had attempted several times to take Tobruk. The attacks, however, were costly and not successful. And when the German military leadership began to concentrate fully on the eastern campaign, the supply situation quickly became catastrophic. Aside from the German Afrika Korps, the only forces remaining in the Mediterranean were the 10th Air Corps, which had been transferred from Sicily to Greece, and the Southeastern navy's weak units. At the same time, Malta acquired greater importance for the British after the German Balkan campaign. As a heavily fortified base for the Royal Air Force, as well as a submarine and light naval vessel refueling base, it continually disrupted the Axis powers' critical supply lines to Tripoli. The strengthening of Malta's air defenses and the addition of new aircraft and ships meant that the Italian air force had become ineffective against the island, just as the Italian navy had been for quite some time.[105]

Rommel, who did not learn about Hitler's plans for war in the east until May 1941, found himself at a great disadvantage, and the situation was getting worse. Because of Operation Barbarossa, additional troops would not be provided;[106] convoys were being intercepted and sunk by the British on an increasingly regular basis; and for the limited amount of supplies that did get through, the supply lines to the rear were completely overextended.[107] Although the harbors of Benghazi, Derna, and Bardia became available after the conquest of Crete, and were beyond the range of the British aircraft based on Malta, their capacity was limited.[108] By the end of October, 15 German U-boats had been transferred to the Mediterranean. They achieved some spectacular successes against the Royal Navy but remained ineffective against British submarines and the Royal Air Force, the two greatest threats to the German-

103. Welck to AA, July 14, 1941, PAAA, R 29925; cf. Warner, p. 122ff.; Schröder, *Deutschland*, p. 150ff.; Roshwald, p. 62ff.

104. RAM to AA, July 20, 1941, ADAP, ser. D, vol. 13/1, p. 158.

105. Reuth, *Entscheidung*, p. 60ff.; Gundelach, vol. 1, p. 279ff.

106. Warlimont, p. 142ff.

107. DAK/Ia to OKH, July 25, 1941, BA-MA, RH 2/599.

108. Consideration of the strategic situation in the eastern Mediterranean after the occupation of Greece and Crete (undated/June 1941), BA-MA, RM 7/234; notes on Göring-Pricolo conversation, Oct. 2, 1941, BA-MA, RL 7/691; cf. Reuth, *Entscheidung*, pp. 70ff., 108ff.

Italian supply lines. In September, Axis losses—nine ships—exceeded anything previously documented in the Mediterranean.[109]

Although the rapid advance to Tobruk and Sollum was proving to be a Pyrrhic victory, Rommel, who had been promoted to general of the panzer forces, planned a new offensive into Egypt in the summer of 1941. It was to be carried out by Panzer Group Afrika, which was formed on August 15 and placed under both the German Afrika Korps and the Italian 21st Infantry Corps.[110] In the hypertrophic atmosphere of the early eastern campaign, the Army High Command called on Rommel in all seriousness to "submit a plan for resuming the offensive after the seizure of Tobruk."[111] In August Rommel was still convinced that it would be possible to successfully advance as far as the Suez Canal.[112] And the operational department of the high command still believed this possible in early September, given an improvement in the naval transport situation, a strengthening of the German air forces, and timely provision of supplies.[113] Rommel also assessed the situation in the Middle East as "extraordinarily favorable," as "the majority of English forces" were "currently tied up in the Middle East" in view of the German threat from the Caucasus.[114] Not until late fall would the appraisals become more sober, but even then they were intermingled with overly optimistic projections. The Foreign Armies West department determined that the British armed forces now had "freedom of action" in the Orient but believed that "no evidence exists yet of a large-scale attack in Cyrenaica."[115]

Rommel's troops received extremely positive signals from the opposing side during this time. As early as April, captured Indian soldiers in the British armed services volunteered "for immediate deployment in the German Afrika Korps" and were consequently separated from the other prisoners of war.[116] At the same time, it was reported "that the German advance at Tobruk and events in Iraq are beginning to have an effect on Egyptian opinion. Pro-English posi-

109. Head of naval warfare to Hitler, Sept. 23, 1941, BA-MA, RM 7/234; cf. Reuth, *Entscheidung*, p. 101ff.
110. DAK/Ia war diary, Aug. 15, 1941, BA-MA, RH 19 VIII/6.
111. OKH/GenStdH/Op.Abt. to DAK, June 28, 1941, BA-MA, RH 2/460; cf. Reuth, *Entscheidung*, p. 88ff.
112. OKH/GenStdH/Op.Abt., Aug. 13, 1941, memorandum on the DAK proposal for the continuation of the offensive against Egypt, BA-MA, RH 2/599; cf. Heckmann, p. 124ff.
113. Ibid., Sept. 2, 1941, comments on the DAK proposal regarding the continuation of the offensive, BA-MA, RH 2/599.
114. Kdo. PzGr Afrika/Ia to commander-in-chief of Italian armed forces in North Africa, Sept. 6, 1941, BA-MA, RH 19 VIII/7.
115. OKH/GenStdH/Abt. FHW, Nov. 7, 1941, assessment of the enemy situation in the Middle East, BA-MA, RH 2/1521.
116. Telex from LFSt/Ic, April 14, 1941, BA-MA, RW 4/v.657; OKH/GenStdH/Abt. FHW to OKW, April 18, 1941, BA-MA, RW 4/v.657.

tion is becoming weaker."[117] Future president Anwar el-Sadat, an officer at the time, described the situation as follows: "The Egyptians openly expressed their schadenfreude. They demonstrated on the streets, chanting. [...] They saw the defeat of the English as the only way to get the enemy out of the country."[118] Konstantin von Neurath, who had been serving as the Foreign Office's liaison officer in the Afrika Korps since May, and who was in charge of the propaganda unit,[119] exacerbated the situation with flyers on the "racial issue." He praised the anti-Semitism of the Third Reich: "Germany grew tired of its countless Jews, who sat like maggots in its flesh, as professors, lawyers, artists, doctors, and, not least, industrialists and merchants. After 1933, Hitler cleaned house." The underlying "racial idea" he explained as, "He accepts every people as God's will except the corrupt, exploitative Jews." Neurath promised the Arabs on behalf of Germany, "Rather, it will take part in your struggle against the English and the Jews with warm sympathy and, God willing, soon with more."[120]

But none of this happened in 1941. On November 18 the British lined up in North Africa for Operation Crusader—the offensive against Rommel, who was forced on December 8 to abandon the siege of Tobruk and evacuate his defensive line on the Sollum front. On January 12, 1942, after four weeks of retreat, the majority of the German-Italian units were back to their original positions on the Gulf of Sidra, where they had started from in March 1941, when they had originally moved to the east. The pendulum had swung back, and for the time being Rommel's attempt to seize Egypt had failed.[121]

---

117. DG Budapest to AA, April 10, 1941, PAAA, R 29533.
118. Sadat, *Gerechtigkeit*, p. 43.
119. AA express letter, April 18, 1941, PAAA, R 60747; AA to Neurath, May 30, 1941, PAAA, R 60747.
120. VAA PzGr Afrika to AA, Nov. 17, 1941, PAAA, R 60747.
121. Reuth, *Entscheidung*, p. 118ff.; Gundelach, vol. 1, p. 318ff.

Chapter V

After Barbarossa:

Germany's Mediterranean Strategy in 1941–1942

Operation Barbarossa, the German attack on the Soviet Union that began on June 22, 1941, created a temporary obstacle to increased intervention in the Middle East, but in the minds of the German strategists it was to be only a short delay. They believed that the eastern campaign could be concluded successfully by the fall of 1941, and then all forces would be free to move into the next target arena, the Mediterranean. Conquering England itself had proven unfeasible, but the German navy still viewed the British Empire's main sea routes as vulnerable. Therefore, after crushing the Soviet Union, Germany would seize every opportunity to bring Great Britain down and thereby cement Nazi hegemony in Europe.[1] The Middle East would be an easy prize that would be practically handed to the German Reich on a plate; the Germans would not have to fight the weakened Italians very long to grab it. Palestine would therefore become part of the German sphere of interest and there is no basis for the assumption that the Jews would have been treated differently

---

1. Hillgruber, *Hitlers*, p. 377ff.

there than in the Soviet Union. Here Hitler did not mince words. "It is good if the fear that we will exterminate the Jews precedes us. The attempt to found a Jewish state will be a failure," he announced on October 25, 1941, in the presence of Himmler and Heydrich.[2]

The plans for the controversial southeastern combat theater were completed before the beginning of the eastern campaign. On June 11, 1941, the OKW submitted Directive No. 32, which outlined the "preparations for the period following Barbarossa." It assumed that the bulk of the German army and air force would be available again for new assignments in late fall, "after the defeat of the Soviet Russian armed forces." In addition to securing and exploiting the "newly won territory in the east," which was expected to be achieved with 60 divisions and a single Luftwaffe fleet, "continuing the battle against the British positions in the Mediterranean and Middle East" would be the focus of all military efforts. In November, "the primary attack against the Suez Canal would be carried out from Cyrenaica by German and Italian troops." And "German pressure from the east in the direction of the Suez Canal would be considered" as well. For this purpose, "motorized expeditionary corps" were to be assembled in Bulgaria and the Caucasus "to later pave the way through Turkey and Syria to Palestine, and through Iran to Basra." The "utilization of the Arab independence movement" was also explicitly mentioned. The Arabs were clearly viewed as a fifth column of the Third Reich: "The more forces that are tied up by timely disturbances, the more difficult the English situation will become in the Middle East during major German operations." All Arab questions were to be directed to Sonderstab F, to which all "the best experts and agents" would be assigned.[3]

In July and August of 1941, the various departments in the OKH Army High Command were working feverishly on the details of the operations. They performed comprehensive scheduling and logistics calculations, inquired about the focal points of the three planned attack groups, debated the best solution for crossing Anatolia, weighed the various alternatives' requirements for troop deployments and timing, studied the terrain and transport options, discussed climatic conditions, assessed the enemy situation, speculated on the enemy's likely tactics, and even considered the time required to prepare German divisions for desert warfare.[4] While Operation Barbarossa pressed forward successfully, the staff was already busy with the next project. Closer examination

---

2. Jochmann, p. 106; *Dienstkalender Himmlers*, p. 246.
3. OKW/WFSt/Abt. L, June 11, 1941, Directive No. 32, BA-MA, RH 2/1520; cf. lightly corrected version of June 30, 1941, BA-MA, RW 4/v.538; cf. Hirszowicz, *Reich*, p. 197ff.
4. BA-MA, RH 2/630–633.

shows that the great pincer movement in the Middle East was hardly "a pipe dream that Hitler wasted no thought on."[5]

In July 1941, Sonderstab F, which was directly subordinated to the chief of the OKH, established its headquarters at Cape Sounion, near Athens; at the same time, its head, General Felmy, was named military commander of southern Greece. "Sonderstab F maintains and seeks, to the extent possible, connections with anti-English forces in the Middle East and supports them with the objective of preparing for later operations through timely attacks," as the staff instructions stated. In addition, the unit was authorized to organize weapons deliveries in the area, as well as training leaders and—together with Abwehr II—saboteurs "for anti-English movements." The Army High Command also received the order to deploy a special formation of battalion strength, "fully equipped with auxiliary weapons and motorized."[6] Further, Oskar Ritter von Niedermayer, a Middle East veteran of World War I and a professor at the University of Berlin, was reactivated and sent to Cape Sounion as an adviser. Niedermayer, Felmy, and Grobba had been officers together in Army Group F in Palestine in 1917–18.[7] Finally, former guerrilla leader Fawzi al-Qawuqji, who had fought against Britain in Iraq and Syria and had been flown out seriously wounded, was transferred to Sonderstab F after his recovery.[8]

The unit, composed of "specially selected German troops and men from the Eastern countries, who are all Mohammedans" and accustomed to desert service conditions, would be increased from 125 men in mid-July 1941 to 2,300 by mid-September.[9] This took place primarily through the addition of the new Sonderverband 288, which was trained and equipped in Potsdam as "the core unit for deployment in the Arab region," according to the plan. It would operate "broken up into individual smaller units together with Arab tribesmen and volunteers."[10] Because most of this special formation was transferred to Rommel's panzer army in Libya at the end of November,[11] however, Sonderstab F was again reduced to the quite modest size of 257 men and limited

5. Schröder, *Irak*, p. 11.
6. OKW/WFSt/Abt. L, June 21, 1941, staff instructions for Sonderstab F, BA-MA, RW 4/v.538.
7. Seidt, pp. 43ff., 307, 316ff.
8. Moellhausen to AA, June 26, 1941, PAAA, R 29925; cf. OKW/Ausl/Abw conversation note, July 25, 1941, Fawzi al-Qawuqji memorandum on the war against the British in the Iraqi-Syrian area, BA-MA, RW 4/v.252; Höpp, *Zwischenspiel*, p. 26.
9. Sonderstab F to AOK 12, July 8, 1941, BA-MA, RH 24-68/2; OKW/WFSt/Abt. L, June 20, 1941, Sonderstab F, BA-MA, RW 34/10.
10. Sonderstab F, July 21, 1941, assignment and organization orders, BA-MA, RH 24-68/2; OKW/WFSt/Abt. L, Sept. 21, 1941, staff instructions for Sonderstab F, PAAA, BA 61179; Grobba to AA, Sept. 23, 1941, PAAA, BA 61179.
11. Sonderstab F order, Nov. 25, 1941, BA-MA, RH 24-68/4.

itself to the training of future leaders of insurgent tribes.[12] But their number initially remained minimal as well, because Turkey would not issue transit visas to Arab nationalists who had taken part in al-Gailani's coup in Iraq, and it blocked their departure for Germany.[13] In mid-September 1941 only 27 Arabs were receiving military training at Cape Sounion as part of the so-called German-Arab Battalion of Sonderstab F.[14]

In this context, the Palestinian Germans who were in the German army took on a special significance; 232 of those liable for military service had fled immediately before the war broke out.[15] These must have been almost exclusively members of the Hitler Youth, as the Palestinian National Committee had registered virtually 100 percent of male youth.[16] Because this was a small but highly ideological and also mostly Arabic-speaking segment, it was by no coincidence that many of the young Palestinian Germans, after their basic training in 1940, were assigned to the Special Action Regiment Brandenburg 800.[17] This innocent-sounding name actually hid a unit, still being formed, that was subordinated to the Abwehr's *Amts*gruppe II and designed for commando missions behind enemy lines.[18] Palestinian German "Brandenburgers," according to one planning scenario, were to blow up the Suez Canal as early as 1940.[19] They took part in the coup in Iraq,[20] made up three companies of the above-mentioned Sonderverband 288,[21] and were appointed as instructors in the German-Arab Special Battalion.[22] At the same time, the Abwehr also tapped the available pool of Muslims in German-controlled Europe. Thus, 24 Iraqi students were recruited by Abwehr II in May 1941.[23] And the Germans were subsequently able "to enlist numerous informers and agents of Arab nationality, who, after their training in Germany, especially at the Brandenburgers' Quenzsee military school, achieved outstanding results in their homeland."[24]

In addition to these military plans and preparations, Turkey was under the spotlight. The question was whether the country could be persuaded to come

---

12. Sonderstab F to OKW/WFSt/Abt. L, Dec. 3, 1941, BA-MA, RH 24-68/4; Von der Orientarmee zur Balkanfeuerwehr (undated/1976), BA-MA, RH 24-68/51.
13. DG Ankara to AA, July 12, 1941, PAAA, R 29925; Tillmann, p. 314.
14. Grobba to AA, Sept. 23, 1941, PAAA, BA 61179.
15. Note by Hentig/AA, Sept. 30, 1939, PAAA, R 29533; AA to NSDAP national leadership, July 30, 1942, PAAA, R 98813; Schwarz/NSDAP Palestine to Wolff, Mar. 18, 1941, BAB, NS 19/186; Balke, p. 126ff.
16. Cf. Balke, pp. 84f., 93ff.
17. Brockdorff, p. 59; Kohlhaas, p. 15; Spaeter, p. 250.
18. Abshagen, p. 235ff.; Leverkuehn, p. 25ff.; Buchheit, p. 307ff.
19. Buchheit, p. 317f.
20. Grobba, p. 234; Kohlhaas, p. 26.
21. Grobba to AA, Sept. 23, 1941, PAAA, BA 61179.
22. Hellmuth Felmy/Walter Warlimont, *German Exploitation of Arab Nationalist Movements in World War II* (undated), NARA, Foreign Military Studies, P-207.
23. OKW/Ausl/Abw II war diary, May 16, 1941, BA-MA, RW 5/498.
24. Brockdorff, p. 400.

over to the side of the Axis or whether it would need to be overpowered and forced to grant passage. A bilateral treaty of friendship was signed on June 18, 1941,[25] and Berlin was gratified to hear that Turkey was elated at the German attack on the Soviet Union.[26] But the fact that Great Britain—which had also concluded a treaty of friendship with Turkey on October 19, 1939, as a reaction to the Hitler-Stalin Pact[27]—was a bordering state to the south limited Turkish mobility and weakened the impact the Germans had hoped to achieve with the newly negotiated agreement. For this reason, Berlin strengthened its efforts to entice Turkey with spoils of war from the assets of the Soviet Union. The idea was a pan-Turanian solution, as Hitler outlined it on March 17, 1941: "The Caucasus should later be handed over to Turkey but utilized by us."[28] This idea of a Greater Turkish expansion to the east was subsequently extended to the Muslim Turkic peoples of the Soviet Union as well,[29] but it did not work as bait to lure Turkey into the war as the Nazis had hoped. Playing the pan-Turanian card would presuppose a German victory over the Soviet Union, and Ankara wished to wait for that to happen first.

At the time of Directive No. 32, the preparations by the Nazi intelligence apparatus (both Abwehr and *Amt* VI of the RSHA) for operations in the Middle East were proceeding at full throttle. On February 6, 1941, Canaris told Grobba that he wished that the Foreign Office would give the Abwehr an assignment for its intended activities in the Arab region.[30] "For reasons of secrecy," said Canaris, it would not be advisable "for the Abwehr to inform the Italians about all its measures."[31] On March 7, Woermann put down on paper some comprehensive "notes on the Arab question," according to which the Arabs were to be of use "by carrying out acts of sabotage and creating uprisings." He concluded: "The Grand Mufti and his people are already active in this regard and have achieved certain limited successes in Palestine. Further organization in this regard should be primarily the concern of the Abwehr, which thus far—in keeping with the wish of the Reich foreign minister—has imposed great restraint, particularly out of consideration for Italy. Further relaxation of these restrictions, also as regards the enhancement of the intelligence service, is necessary in the context of the conflict with England." He specified: "Acts of sabotage could be carried out in Egypt, Transjordan, and

---

25. German-Turkish treaty of friendship, June 18, 1941, ADAP, ser. D., vol. 12/2, p. 876; cf. Krecker, p. 153ff.

26. DG Ankara to AA, June 22, 1941, ADAP, ser. D, vol. 12/2, p. 901.

27. Krecker, p. 51ff.; cf. Weber.

28. KTB Halder, vol. 2, p. 320.

29. Note by StS./AA, Sept. 10, 1941, ADAP, ser. D, vol. 13/1, p. 386f.; note by RAM, Nov. 13, 1941, ADAP, ser. D, vol. 13/2, p. 636f.; cf. Krecker, p. 205ff.; Glasneck/Kircheisen, p. 99ff.; Kunz, p. 19ff.

30. Rintelen to AA, Mar. 21, 1941, ADAP, ser. D, vol. 12/1, p. 267.

31. Tillmann, p. 199.

Palestine, and against English installations in Iraq. At the moment, an uprising would make sense only in Palestine and Transjordan."[32]

On March 24, he conferred with Canaris; Captain Leopold Bürkner, the head of the Abwehr's foreign branch; and Colonels Hans Piekenbrock and Erwin Lahousen, the heads of the Abwehr's *Amts*gruppe I and *Amts*gruppe II, respectively, regarding this matter. Woermann was to immediately carry out the "development of a secret network of informers throughout the Middle East." In Palestine, "power plants, oil pump stations, factories, and water and electrical supplies" were to be sabotaged. "Uprisings in Palestine and Transjordan will automatically be sparked by weapons deliveries, for which better opportunities will emerge as soon as Thrace [Salonika] is in German hands."[33] Ribbentrop approved this arrangement on April 9 and called for "immediate and rapid initiation of all our activities in that area."[34] Consideration for Italy, which had thus far caused the Third Reich to refrain from significant engagement in the Arab world, was eventually to be permanently consigned to history.[35] When Grobba spoke with Ribbentrop about it, he was told, "This is just temporary."[36]

An Oriental department had existed in the Abwehr since the summer of 1940, under Major Franz Seubert in Foreign Armies West,[37] and there were certainly communication links and informers. However, a so-called Kriegsorganization, that is, an intelligence infrastructure in the countries themselves, was missing. This was quickly corrected in the summer of 1941. In July, an Abwehr control center for the Middle East was established under Lieutenant Colonel Meyer-Zermatt in Ankara. At the same time, Captain Paul Leverkuehn took over the branch in Istanbul, which would soon become a German intelligence hub. Meyer-Zermatt was attached to the German embassy in Ankara, and Leverkuehn to the consul general in Istanbul. Canaris and Piekenbrock made an inspection visit at the beginning of August.[38] Bases were also established in Tetuan and Tangier in Spanish Morocco so agents of Abwehr II could influence the local Arab and Berber tribes.[39] Captain Rudolf Roser was operating Beirut; he had been there since September 1940 as a representative of the German-French armistice commission. His many connections, which

32. Woermann/AA, Mar. 7, 1941, notes on the Arab question, ADAP, ser. D, vol. 12/1, p. 195.
33. OKW/Ausl/Abw file note, Mar. 25, 1941, planned Abwehr measures in the Middle East, IfZ, Nbg. Dok., NG-089.
34. Note by Woermann/AA, April 9, 1941, ADAP, ser. D, vol. 12/2, p. 413f.
35. Cf. Gensicke, p. 67ff.
36. Grobba, p. 214.
37. Seubert, p. 2; Buchheit, p. 233f.
38. Rich in material on this: PAAA, R 101832, 101881, 101883; Paul Leverkuehn, *Orient 1940–1944*, BAK, N 1146/13; NAK, WO 208/4558; Leverkuehn, p. 161; Reile, p. 344; Buchheit, p. 279f.
39. Leverkuehn, p. 104; Storch de Garcia, p. 7.

pertained not least to Palestine, were significant.[40] Before long, the Abwehr was able to deploy radio informers in Beirut, Damascus, and Alexandria[41] and slip Arab saboteurs from Sonderstab F into the Middle East.[42]

In late July 1941, Abwehr I, which was responsible for the secret network of informers, listed 34 existing contacts in the Middle East; 22 additional contacts were being prepared, and 24 more were planned. Nine of them had special relations with Palestine. A "German scholar" was among them, as were an "international artist and hotel thief" with a Norwegian passport and an "Indian maharajah" characterized as "totally anti-English." Germans were clearly in the minority. There were Bulgarians, Swiss, and Greeks, and also an English prisoner of war who had "voluntarily declared himself willing to collaborate" because he was a "fanatical opponent of the Churchill regime." This prisoner had previously worked in the cipher department of the British headquarters in Cairo, so he told a "plausible story of a long flight from Crete" after which he was dropped by parachute over Egypt so he could take up his old position again. Communications channels included dead drops and safe houses, radio equipment and mail using the diplomatic courier. The agents were being directed from various Abwehr stations in Germany, in occupied Europe, and in friendly foreign countries.[43] These efforts were assisted by the intelligence network of the Mufti, which initially worked exclusively with the Abwehr and extended "from Morocco to north India."[44] Seubert later recalled that "very powerful Abwehr radio receivers, first in Athens and then at the Bulgarian station and later at the Abwehr station in Vienna, were able until the last day of the war to maintain contact with any agent transmitters that remained undetected" and received from them reports about ship and troop movements as well as the mood in the country.[45]

At the same time, the SD foreign intelligence service of *Amt* VI of the RSHA was also giving greater attention to the Middle East. The service had been relatively insignificant under the leadership of Brigadeführer Heinz Jost, but his successor, Standartenführer Walter Schellenberg, who took over the position on July 2, 1941, immediately identified the expansion and improvement of the effectiveness of *Amt* VI as one of his key tasks.[46] In view of Operation Barbarossa, the most important area of operation for *Amt* VI C—

40. Leverkuehn, p. 162ff.; Schröder, *Deutschland*, p. 52.
41. Buchheit, p. 238.
42. Sonderstab F to OKW/Ausl/Abw, Dec. 5, 1941, BA-MA, RH 24-68/4.
43. OKW/Ausl/Abw I, July 28, 1941, characteristics of contacts in the Middle East, BA-MA, RH 24-68/2.
44. Seubert, p. 3; cf. Buchheit, p. 234.
45. Seubert, p. 7.
46. RSHA organizational plan as of Jan. 1, 1941, BAB, R 58/840; BAB, SSO Walter Schellenberg; Schellenberg, p. 182ff.; cf. Kahn, p. 255ff.; Browder, p. 418ff.; Querg, pp. 165ff., 206, 223ff.; Wildt, Generation, p. 391.

which was responsible for the Soviet Union and the Middle East, and was led by Sturmbannführer Dr. Heinz Gräfe—was the new theater of war in Eastern Europe, but the Middle East also came increasingly under consideration.[47] Hauptsturmführer Dr. Erich Hengelhaupt, took over the three Russian departments, VI C 1–3.[48] Hauptsturmführer Peter Weirauch received departments VI C 4–11, covering the Far East and India. He had joined the völkisch youth movement in 1924, and became a member of the NSDAP and the SS in 1933.[49] The leadership of department VI C 12, which was responsible for Turkey, Iran, and Afghanistan, was under Hauptsturmführer Kurt Schuback, who had interrupted his studies in 1934 in order to work full-time with the Hitler Youth as a specialist in the area of cross-border and foreign intelligence. In 1938, he transferred to the SD Oberabschnitt in Königsberg, where he "was significantly and deeply involved in preparations for the action in Poland." He belonged to an SD unit and was employed by *Amt* VI as "intelligence chief for the political intelligence unit in Riga, Latvia" beginning in early 1940.[50] Obersturmführer Heinz Tunnat served as Schuback's deputy; he joined the SS in 1934, became a commissioner at the Hannover headquarters of the criminal investigation department, and in 1941, as a candidate for superintendent, belonged to Einsatzkommando 9 in Belarus—he was therefore an expert in mass murder and in the killing of Jews.[51]

In 1940, Hauptsturmführer Herbert Hagen took over the Arab department, VI C 13—then still called VI D 5—which was responsible for Syria, Transjordan, Iraq, Palestine, and Egypt. He had been head of the SD's Jewish affairs department since the end of 1937 and was probably valued as a Middle East expert because of his background. He joined the SS in 1933 and in 1938–39 belonged to the Einsatzkommandos for Vienna and Prague.[52] In January 1941, he was replaced by Obersturmführer Hans-Joachim Weise, who had joined the NSDAP in 1928 after secondary school and training as a textile technician. Weise wore the Gold Party Badge and transferred from the SA to the SS in December 1930. He was a key contributor to the development of the so-called Rauhe Alb in Württemberg. In Nazi Germany, after temporarily working

---

47. BAB, SSO Dr. Heinz Gräfe; cf. Wildt, *Generation*, p. 152ff.
48. BAB, SSO Dr. Erich Hengelhaupt; cf. Mallmann, "Krieg," p. 332.
49. SS membership card, curriculum vitae, BAB, SSO Peter Weirauch; curriculum vitae, BAB, RuSHA Peter Weirauch.
50. SS membership card, curriculum vitae, personnel review, BAB, SSO Kurt Schuback; marriage license application, BAB, RuSHA Kurt Schuback.
51. SS membership card, curriculum vitae, recommendation for promotion, BAB, SSO Heinz Tunnat; curriculum vitae, BAB, RuSHA Heinz Tunnat; BAL, B 162/2402; verdict of Berlin district court, June 22, 1962, BAL, B 162/14138.
52. Service record, curriculum vitae, CdS to RFSS, Oct. 15, 1941, BAB, SSO Herbert Hagen; curriculum vitae, BAB, RuSHA Herbert Hagen; interrogation of Herbert Hagen, Nov. 19, 1962, BAL, B 162/1327, p. 1263ff.; interrogation of Herbert Hagen, Nov. 13, 1964, BAL, B 162/16704.

as an auxiliary police officer, he found a position as a telephone operator at the Thüringen NSDAP district office. In early 1938, he transferred to SD headquarters in Berlin. After practical training in the Jewish Affairs department there, he joined Einsatzkommando Prague in March 1939, and in the fall of 1940 completed a colonial service course for the security police and SD at the officers' school in Berlin-Charlottenburg.[53] In the summer of 1941, Weise was replaced as department head by Sturmbannführer Wilhelm Beisner, but remained as Beisner's deputy and at the end of the year took on the role of an RSHA liaison officer for the exiled Mufti, who had just arrived in Germany.

Beisner had joined the SA in August 1930 as a student, and became a party member as well one month later. In November 1932, he switched to the SS. After studying economics, he worked for three years as a desk officer for the southeastern countries in the foreign policy department of the NSDAP directorate. After a brief military training course by the armed SS, he was deployed as part of the German Selbstschutz organization in Poland in October 1939. In August 1940, Beisner joined *Amt* VI full-time and was charged with the development of an intelligence network in the Balkans. In April 1941, he led Commando Zagreb of Einsatzgruppe Yugoslavia.[54] The third man in the Arabian department was Eugen Faber, a Palestinian-German who had established a National Socialist-oriented youth group in Palestine in the spring of 1933. He brought the group into the Hitler Youth organization in 1934 and served as one of its national leaders after that. In 1939, Faber escaped to Germany and was transferred to *Amt* VI after his training as a Brandenburger.[55] Essentially, it was a group of young men in their 30s who occupied leadership positions in *Amt* VI C at that time. Despite their youth, they nevertheless had considerable political experience—approximately 10 years each, or more—in the NSDAP, Hitler Youth, and SS. These men no longer needed explicit orders; they had long been guided by ideology.

Like the Abwehr, *Amt* VI C also used Turkey as an intelligence hub. The Austrian Ludwig Moyzisch, posing as an aide to the commercial attaché in Ankara, took over operations there at the end of 1940.[56] Although he was identified by the British secret service as "actually head of the Gestapo in Turkey"

---

53. SS membership card, BAB, SSO Hans-Joachim Weise; curriculum vitae, BAB, RuSHA Hans-Joachim Weise; SDHA II 112 to I 1, May 16, 1939, BAB, R 58/954; curriculum vitae, BA-ZA, ZR 358; interrogation of Hans-Joachim Weise, Jan. 12, 1965, BAL, B 162/16704; general information on training for the colonial service: PAAA, R 99229.
54. SS membership card, curriculum vitae, BAB, SSO Wilhelm Beisner; curriculum vitae, BAB, RuSHA Wilhelm Beisner; RSHA IV Gst, May 16, 1941, deployment of the security police and the SD in the former Yugoslavia, BAB, R 58/241; RSHA telephone directory, May 1942, BAB, R 58/927; interrogation of Wilhelm Beisner, Nov. 4, 1960, BAL, B 162/Vorl. AR 1650/67, p. 6ff.
55. Balke, pp. 93f., 130, 132, 213, 222, 238.
56. Police attaché list, Oct. 16, 1943, YVA, TR 3/542; Moyzisch, pp. 17, 100f., 105, purports to have been only an "attaché to the German embassy."

the following fall,[57] he nevertheless created a Turkish-Arab-operated intelligence network for the Middle East.[58] In December 1941, Waldemar Fast, a Palestinian-German, became his right-hand man. Fast joined the NSDAP in Jerusalem in 1934. He was a travel agent, spoke fluent Arabic, and was involved on the Arab side in the uprising in Palestine. Suspected of espionage, he succeeded in leaving the Mandate shortly before the war broke out. In December 1939 he found employment at the RSHA and by 1941 had advanced to the rank of Untersturmführer.[59] Three other German staff members were active in Istanbul as well. Like the Abwehr, VI C also maintained a four-person branch for North Africa, attached to the German consulate general in Tangier.[60]

The Abwehr and VI C also sent feelers into Iran. In October 1940, the SD sent two Untersturmführers, disguised as businessmen, to Teheran to establish an intelligence apparatus there.[61] The two were Franz Mayr of Munich[62] and Roman Gamotha of Vienna. The latter had joined the Hitler Youth at age 15. In 1936, while in his second university semester, he was "permanently" expelled due to his activities in the Nazi Party, after having already completed a 10-month sentence in jail for, among other things, participating in attacks with explosives.[63] In the spring of 1941, Major Dr. Julius Berthold Schulze-Holthus was also sent to Iran, ostensibly as consular secretary in the north Persian city of Tabriz, to carry out aerial reconnaissance for Abwehr I in the nearby Soviet Union. Two additional Abwehr agents were sent to southern Iran.[64] In July, Major Strojil—posing as an aide to the German military attaché—was also sent to Teheran, to work in the Kriegsorganisation Orient and serve as a sabotage expert.[65] When British and Soviet troops entered Iran from the north and south on August 25, 1941, and the Iranian forces ceased their resistance just two days later,[66] Schulze-Holthus, Mayr, and Gamotha successfully avoided internment. While Gamotha evaded capture in northern Iran,[67] the other two went into hiding in Teheran and were picked up there by the networks of pro-Axis army and police officers.[68]

57. M.I.3, Sept. 30, 1941, Axis Fifth Column Activity in Turkey, NAK, WO 208/4558.
58. CdS VI C 12 to RFSS, Jan. 20, 1943, BAB, NS 19/2236; Schellenberg, p. 310f.
59. SS membership card, curriculum vitae, BAB, SSO Waldemar Fast; curriculum vitae, BAB, RuSHA Waldemar Fast; personnel review, BAB, SSO Kurt Schuback; Balke, pp. 213, 236, 261.
60. Police attaché list, Oct. 16, 1943, YVA, TR 3/542; Storch de Garcia, p. 7.
61. RFSS, deployment of SS leaders in Iran (undated/May 1943), BAB, NS 19/2235.
62. SS membership card, BAB, SSO Franz Mayr.
63. SS membership card, memorandum by Munich reentry control station, BAB, SSO Roman Gamotha.
64. Madani, p. 261ff.; Hirschfeld, p. 256f.
65. OKW/Ausl/Abw II war diary, July 3, 1941, BA-MA, RW 5/498.
66. Stewart, *Sunrise*, p. 109ff.; Jaschinski, p. 168ff.
67. RFSS, SS-Hstuf. Gamotha's Iron Cross 1st Class award (undated/May 1943), BAB, NS 19/2235.
68. Schulze-Holthus, *Iran*, p. 121ff.; Schröder, *Deutschland*, p. 256f.

German radio propaganda in the Middle East also became significantly more aggressive during this time, as it intensified its anti-Semitic agitation. "The Arabs must realize that large parts of Syria, Transjordan, and Iraq, not to mention Palestine, will be relinquished to the Jews; that England will repay the Jews in this way, at the expense of the Arabs, for their help in a potential English victory; that our land will become an object to be bartered for Jewish espionage, Jewish betrayal, and Jewish acts of sabotage," postulated Fawzi al-Qawuqji in July 1941 in an official Abwehr position paper on propaganda,[69] and Grobba immediately assented on behalf of the Foreign Office.[70] In the broadcasts, the Allies were ridiculed as Jewish-controlled or as the "united Jewish nations." Cleverly intermingled with quotations from the Koran and Arabic music were attacks on the Jews as being the complete opposite of Islam: the Jew is the enemy, and killing him pleases Allah.[71] After 1945, German generals Felmy and Warlimont admitted on record to the Historical Division of the U.S. Army that the primary content of the German radio broadcasts had consisted of anti-Semitism because "the only real political rallying point among the Arabs was their common hatred of the Jews."[72]

The content was coordinated in consultation between the Foreign Office; the OKH Wehrmacht Propaganda IV, the department responsible for foreign propaganda; and the Reich Ministry for Propaganda.[73] The key roles were played by Grobba and by Mildenstein, who now worked in Goebbels's ministry as an expert on the Middle East. The translation took place in the Iranian, Arab, Indian, and Turkish sections of Reichsrundfunk; in addition to German editors, each section had a staff of 10 to 15 native speakers and translators.[74] After October 24, 1941, Radio Athens aired two Arabic broadcasts per day, which were produced directly by Sonderstab F.[75] The Germans also made use of the Arabs in the training battalion at nearby Cape Sounion, whose songs were recorded on records and then played back.[76]

"Our policy in the Middle East must [...] first of all meet the needs of the war effort and be dedicated to defeating England," noted Woermann on November 6, 1941. "The primary goals will be the permanent disengagement of England from the Middle Eastern region and the permanent safeguarding of

69. OKW/Ausl/Abw, July 25, 1941, propaganda, PAAA, R 29885.
70. Note by Grobba/AA, Aug. 7, 1941, propaganda against England in the Middle East, PAAA, R 29885.
71. Arsenian, p. 420f.; further examples in Schnabel, p. 258ff.
72. Hellmuth Felmy/Walter Warlimont, *German Exploitation of Arab Nationalist Movements in World War II* (undated), NARA, Foreign Military Studies, P-207.
73. Ritter to AA, May 26, 1941, PAAA, BA 61179; Trentow/Kranhold, p. 34f.
74. Interrogation of Irmtraud Kaiser, Aug. 30, 1945, NAK, FO 371/46781.
75. Activity report of Wehrmacht propaganda officers of Sonderstab F for Oct. 26–Dec. 15, 1941, BA-MA, RW 4/v.184.
76. Activity report of Wehrmacht propaganda officers of Sonderstab F for March 1942, BA-MA, RW 4/v.184.

German influence on the oil sources there." There was no mention of Italy. The undersecretary of state also recorded Ribbentrop's decision "that consideration for France can now cease." From then on, the Third Reich would engage in its own great power politics in the Middle East. Woermann recommended that Hitler receive the Mufti soon, because in him "one of the leading personalities of the Arab world is available to us." He also advised that an agreement be concluded with al-Gailani, who would be arriving shortly as well, and called for the "establishment of an Arab leadership council in Berlin." Finally, he emphasized that warfare in the Arab world would be different than warfare in the Soviet Union: "Before the operations begin, the Foreign Office must exercise its influence on the Wehrmacht, as the war will be fought on the territory of friendly peoples, so completely different presuppositions apply than, for example, in the Russian war theater."[77]

Here, Woermann adapted a German concept from World War I: jihad made in Germany. On November 14, 1914, the sheikh ul-Islam, by order of the sultan and at the wish of the Germans, had read out a fatwa in the great mosque of Mehmed the Conqueror, announcing the "holy war" of the Muslims behind enemy lines. He assured his listeners of martyr status if they were killed, and even promised special benefits in paradise.[78] Middle East expert Max von Oppenheim, head of the Berlin-based Intelligence Bureau for the Orient, was the instigator of this maneuver, which targeted the British, French, and Russians. Although the sultanate and caliphate had since been abolished in Turkey, the vestiges of Muslim traditions of this kind could still be exploited. For this reason, on July 25, 1940, the now 80-year-old Oppenheim forwarded to the Foreign Office his "Memorandum on Revolutionizing the Middle East," in which he claimed: "In Palestine, the struggle against the English and the Jews should be taken up again and vigorously pursued. [...] A government under the Mufti should be installed in Palestine." And Oppenheim—although of Jewish descent himself—also concluded, "Of the Jews, only those who were there before the world war should be left."[79] His conservative German outlook lacked the imagination required to envision the impending Holocaust.[80]

"The presence of the Grand Mufti in Germany is one factor whose significance cannot be overestimated. This is a piece of good fortune that must be exploited completely," advised Eberhard von Stohrer, the former German ambassador in Cairo, and pointed to important parallels. "National Socialist con-

---

77. Note by Woermann/AA, Nov. 6, 1941, Middle East questions, PAAA, BA 61179.
78. Cf. McKale, *War*.
79. Quoted in Schwanitz, "Oppenheim," p. 57.
80. Cf. Schwanitz, "Djihad," p. 18ff.; Schwanitz, "Paschas," p. 28ff.

cepts are found in many Islamic principles. Thanks to his battle with the Jews, the Führer has already gained an outstanding position among Muslims."[81] The former Cairo agent Schrumpf-Pierron, now senior war consultant with the Abwehr in Berlin, viewed the situation in much the same way: "The structure of Islam also has much in common with National Socialism: authority above, 'democracy' below." And he knew who the Germans' real allies were. The solution to the "Jewish question" in Palestine, he said, is "a power problem that only National Socialism can solve in a ruthless manner, but that must above all conform to the wishes of the Arabs and Syrians. Italy cannot interfere in this."[82]

"While this report on my trip was being printed, the war that the English and the Jews were always speaking about, and that they were busily preparing for, became a reality," Franz Schattenfroh wrote at the end of his Palestine report. He reasoned on behalf of the country: "Then it will be time to finally eliminate the poisonous seeds that for countless centuries have weakened, endangered, and created continual unrest in our land; then the time will come to solve the Jewish question on our terms. And only then, when this has happened, will there be peace in this world again!"[83] And a Dr. Karl Wuck, also from Vienna, wrote to the Foreign Office in the summer of 1941: "There will be no peace in the Middle East or in all of Europe, and the people will not be free from the troublemakers, until the Jews are smoked out of their Palestinian Zionist state. [...] It is not enough to eliminate the Jews in Europe, Egypt, and other areas once every two hundred years, because they keep coming. [...] Just as the Czechs are isolated, and the Poles, Slovenes, and Serbs, the Jews could also be enclosed and isolated in their Zionist state, and destroyed there root and branch."[84] In September 1941, Fawzi al-Qawuqji in turn told an old comrade in Syria, "I will come with Arab and German troops to help you."[85] Thus, the ideological course for an independent German Middle East policy had been set.[86]

Numerous maps and a booklet prepared in mid-October 1941 by the Army General Staff underscored the intensity of the Nazi war plans. These materials were intended to instruct the military on the conditions in the area to be conquered. The introductory booklet, which contained a large number of photos and detailed text, provided information on the climatic, geographic,

81. Stohrer to StS./AA, Nov. 18, 1941, PAAA, R 29533.
82. Schrumpf-Pierron to von Papen, July 8, 1941, BA-MA, RH 2/1765.
83. Schattenfroh, p. 96f.
84. Dr. Karl Wuck/Vienna to AA, June 28, 1941, PAAA, R 99388.
85. Letter, Sept. 4, 1941, BA-MA, RH 24-68/3.
86. A "lack of systematic and coherent conception of the Middle East," as Shamir, *East*, p. 174, suggests, can hardly be assumed in light of these extensive plans and preparations.

demographic, and economic conditions in Palestine and Transjordan. The officers to whom this booklet was furnished learned, for example, that the coast appeared "hostile to landings," the roads were well developed, and the "north-south longitudinal connections" would favor an invasion. The strategists had also already included the Jewish minority in their war plans; the Germans planned to appropriate the Jews' housing space on a grand scale: "Lodging of troops possible only in newer European settlements; not advisable in Arab homes, which are cramped and present health hazards." However, the military did not fear potential conflict with the Muslim majority at all, as one unifying element could always be explicitly identified: "Anyone who fights against the Jews can always count on the sympathies of the Arab population."[87]

At the end of October 1941, Hitler deemed "that the campaign in the east had not only been won but for the most part was definitively concluded" and ordered the 10th Air Corps to resume providing escorts from Sicily for all sea transports to North Africa as well as suppressing Malta.[88] In addition, Field Marshal Albert Kesselring, the new Commander-in-Chief South, was charged with coordinating these assignments and received as reinforcements the 2nd Air Corps, which had previously been deployed in the east.[89] Two days earlier, Hitler had informed the Italian foreign minister, Count Galeazzo Ciano, of the new war aims: "In and of itself, of course, the conquest of the Caucasus is not decisive to the outcome of the war, but one could ascribe such importance to a seizure of Iran, Iraq, Syria, and Palestine."[90] The "time after Barbarossa," anticipated in Directive No. 32, appeared to have begun.

But then suddenly, events began to spin out of control. Two almost simultaneous occurrences fundamentally changed the situation. The Soviet counteroffensive outside Moscow on December 5–6, 1941, forced the Wehrmacht into retreat for the first time.[91] This caused the permanent collapse of Hitler's "world blitzkrieg plan,"[92] and the "period after Barbarossa" now slipped into a nebulous future. As in World War I, the German Reich was facing a two-front war of attrition. At the same time, however, the Japanese attack on Pearl Harbor on December 7 opened another theater of war.[93] And when the Japanese sank the brand-new British battleship *Prince of Wales* and the cruiser *Repulse* off Malaya on December 10, and took Singapore on February 15, 1942, it became

87 .GenStdH, Department for War Maps and Surveying, booklet, Oct. 15, 1941.

88. Hitler to Mussolini, Oct. 29, 1941, ADAP, ser. D, vol. 13/2, pp. 580, 584.

89. OKW/WFSt/Abt. L, Dec. 2, 1941, Directive No. 38, ADAP, ser. D, vol. 13/2, p. 763f.; cf. Gundelach, vol. 1, p. 329ff.

90. Note by Schmidt/office of RAM, Nov. 30, 1941, Hitler-Ciano conversation on Nov. 29, ADAP, ser. D, vol. 13/3, p. 735.

91. Primarily Reinhardt.

92. Reuth, *Entscheidung*, p. 128.

93. Keegan, p. 364ff.

clear that the cards had been completely reshuffled and the previous assumptions now applied only to a very limited degree.[94] In view of this dramatic transformation of the conflict into a world war, which Hitler immediately followed on December 11, 1941, with the German declaration of war against the United States, the fact that British troops finally liberated Tobruk on December 8 and thus ended the eight-month siege now seemed of little consequence. It was clear to those involved that the war in the Far East would soon draw a large share of the British troops designated for Africa. Hitler could wager that Japan's entry into the war would split the Anglo-American forces over two oceans and, at least initially, avert the danger of a second front in Europe. The December 8 order to the German Army in Russia to cease offensive activity and shift to the defensive "in order to create the conditions for the resumption of major offensive operations in 1942" was therefore not an admission of defeat.[95] Even though Barbarossa had failed, 1942 was to bring the greatest expansion of the Third Reich.

---

94. Ibid., pp. 374, 378.
95. OKW/WFSt/Abt. L, Dec. 8, 1941, Directive No. 39, ADAP, ser. D, vol. 13/2, p. 801.

Chapter VI

The Grand Mufti:
Axis Ally

After their flight from Iraq, el-Husseini and al-Gailani arrived in Teheran on June 1, 1941.[1] The Persian capital, however, would turn out to be only a temporary residence for the two Arab leaders. Their situation became extremely precarious after British and Soviet troops occupied Iran on August 25 and pressured the Shah to abdicate. While al-Gailani was able to obtain a Turkish entry visa and leave for Istanbul, the Mufti was initially stranded in Teheran. Sensing the danger of being captured by the British, he fled to the Japanese embassy.[2] Colonel Lahousen of the Abwehr was relieved to confirm on September 3 that the Mufti was "safe" at that location.[3] Because this asylum, in the eyes of el-Husseini, was not to be permanent, he now faced—after his flights from Jerusalem, Beirut, and Baghdad—a fourth escape from the British sphere of control. Dressed in women's clothing and with the help of Italian legation counselor Mellini, he succeeded in escaping to Istanbul.

---

1. Gehrcke [=Grobba] to AA, May 30, 1941, PAAA, R 29884; Gensicke, p. 71.
2. Grobba, p. 249; Schechtman, p. 116f.
3. OKW/Ausl/Abw II war diary, Sept. 3, 1941, BA-MA, RW 5/498.

From there he was flown to Rome on October 10.[4] On the 27th, he met with the Duce for the first time. The two seem to have taken to each other— probably not least because Mussolini, during the discussion, expressed marked hostility toward the Jews and the idea of a Jewish state in Palestine. The Mufti, for his part, made an "intelligent impression" on the Duce.[5]

One week later, el-Husseini traveled on to Germany. On November 6 he arrived in Berlin where, in the presence of press representatives, he was received by Grobba, among others.[6] Al-Gailani also arrived in the capital of the Reich shortly thereafter, on the 21st. He had been temporarily stranded in Istanbul after his flight from Teheran because the Turkish government refused him an exit visa. Reich press chief Paul Schmidt came openly to his assistance in this situation, and al-Gailani was immediately flown to Berlin in a German airplane.[7] There, however, the Iraqi did not receive quite the same attention. Although he met with Ribbentrop in early December, he had to wait until July 1942 for a meeting with Hitler.[8] El-Husseini, in contrast, was able to call on Weizsäcker immediately after his arrival; three weeks later he had an appointment with the Reich foreign minister.[9]

On November 28, 1941, the Mufti was received by Hitler as well. This first meeting between the two radical anti-Semites was also attended by Ribbentrop, Grobba, a note taker, and two German interpreters.[10] According to one of the interpreters, the beginning of the meeting was affected by Hitler's behavioral peculiarities. During the greetings, Hitler avoided taking the outstretched hand of the Mufti, and the Führer also declined to drink coffee with his guest in accordance with Arab tradition.[11] In response to an interpreter's cautious remark about the Arab practice, Hitler snapped that he did not permit "anyone at all to drink coffee in the headquarters"; he angrily disappeared for a few minutes, unceremoniously leaving his visibly bewildered guest standing there in the meeting room. Attempting to be polite after his return, he finally had a member of the SS bring el-Husseini a glass of lemonade.[12]

---

4. DG Rome to AA, Oct. 13, 1941, ADAP, ser. D, vol. 13/2, p. 524; Grobba, p. 249; Gensicke, p. 74f.

5. *Frankfurter Zeitung*, Oct. 28, 1942; Gensicke, p. 75; Lewis, "Meer," p. 180; cf. Carpi, *Mufti*, p. 104ff.; at a meeting with Secretary of State Weizsäcker, the Turkish ambassador attempted to find out whether the Mufti had traveled to Italy via Turkey, and the diplomat said he "felt reluctant to meet the Grand Mufti other than privately and in ordinary dress," but he would willingly monitor him more closely, memorandum by StS./AA, Nov. 15, 1941, PAAA, R 29835.

6. *Deutsche Allgemeine Zeitung*, Dec. 6, 1942; note by Grobba/AA, Nov. 6, 1941, ADAP, ser. D, vol. 13/2, p. 611f.

7. Grobba, p. 249; Gensicke, p. 91f.; Dieterich, *Kailānī*, p. 48.

8. Note by Grobba/AA, Dec. 2, 1941, PAAA, BA 61123; Gensicke, p. 92.

9. Gensicke, pp. 77–84; note by Loesch/AA, Nov. 28, 1941, ADAP, ser. D, vol. 13/2., pp. 714–718.

10. On the meeting: Carpi, *Mufti*, p. 109;

11. Schechtman, p. 123; Gensicke, p. 86.

12. Quoted in Gensicke, p. 86, note 34; cf. Schechtman, p. 123.

After that bizarre prelude, Hitler refrained from further irritating his guest during the conversation that followed. The Mufti expressed his thanks for the honor of the reception, and assured Hitler of the admiration of the entire Arab world. The people there, el-Husseini said, have "complete confidence in the Führer, who is fighting against the same three enemies that are the enemies of the Arabs, namely, the English, the Jews, and the Bolsheviks. The Arabs are ready to join in this battle on the German side, and not only negatively—for example, through acts of sabotage or creating unrest—but also positively, by forming an Arab legion to fight alongside German troops."[13] In connection with this offer, el-Husseini brought up his own request. He spoke of the desire of the Arabs of Palestine, Syria, and Iraq for independence and unity, and argued that a public declaration by Germany on the issue at this time would have an extremely positive effect. It would encourage and arouse the Arabs and facilitate his secret preparations for an uprising in the Arab world to coincide with the arrival of the Axis powers. He attempted from the outset to dispel the German chancellor's misgivings about the possibility that Turkey and France might react negatively to such a declaration.[14]

Hitler assured the Mufti of his basic agreement and then promptly turned to the theme that was particularly close to his own heart, as well as that of his guest. He emphasized that Germany supported "an uncompromising struggle against the Jews"; this "would include, of course, opposition to a Jewish homeland in Palestine, which is nothing more than a national hub for the destructive influence of Jewish interests." Then he spoke about the current situation. "Germany is determined, step by step, to call upon one European nation after another to solve the Jewish problem, and to turn to non-European peoples with a similar appeal at a certain point," Hitler declared. With these words he allowed the Mufti a first glimpse of the extermination of the Jews that had just begun on the Continent. He added that Germany would soon find itself "in a life-or-death struggle against two strongholds of Jewish power," Great Britain and the Soviet Union.[15] The Reich would "of course" provide "positive and practical help" to the Arabs, who were engaged in the same ideological struggle against the Jews, "because platonic assurances are pointless in a struggle for one's very existence, where the Jews can use the British instruments of power for their own purposes."

13. Note by Grobba/AA, Dec. 1, 1941, PAAA, BA 61123; additional notes on the meeting exist that differ in certain details from Grobba's account, cf. note by Schmidt/office of RAM, Nov. 30, 1941, ADAP, ser. D., vol. 13/2, pp. 718–721.
14. Note by Schmidt/office of RAM, Nov. 30, 1941, ADAP, ser. D., vol. 13/2, p. 719; cf. note by Grobba/AA, Jan. 2, 1942, PAAA, BA 61123.
15. Note by Schmidt/office of RAM, Nov. 30, 1941, ADAP, ser. D., vol. 13/2, p. 720.

The declaration the Mufti wished for, however, would be counterproductive in the current military situation. But soon the German armies would reach the southern edge of the Caucasus; then liberation would come for the Arab world as well. Germany's only goal in the region would then be "the destruction of the Jews living in the Arab territory under the protection of the British."[16] By that, Hitler could only have meant the Yishuv and the Jewish communities in the neighboring countries. The Mufti was "absolutely at ease and satisfied" with these assurances. Nevertheless, he asked again whether it would be possible to at least make a secret statement in the desired form. When Hitler replied that he had just provided one, el-Husseini thanked him again, affirmed his trust one more time, and took his leave.[17]

The Mufti subsequently settled in Berlin and assembled an extensive staff. The Germans provided him with a monthly sum of 75,000 reichsmarks, and he received additional generous contributions beyond that.[18] In the following years, nothing would change in the fundamental position of Germany and Italy toward the desire for an official guarantee of independence for the Arab countries.[19] Nevertheless, after the face-to-face meeting between Hitler and the Mufti, Arab nationalist leaders made continuous and varied efforts to wring from the Axis powers the desired declaration of support for the independence of the countries of the Middle East. In January 1942, el-Husseini communicated to the Foreign Office his wish that the Reich government provide a commitment with regard to the future of the Arab countries—if possible before his trip to Italy, planned for early February. Aware of the difficulty of issuing a public declaration, he wished only for a precautionary "confidential letter," whose contents would not be made known to France or Turkey.[20] Al-Gailani had obtained from Ribbentrop a similar secret declaration with regard to Iraq in mid-December 1941; the Mufti was therefore jealously intent on obtaining at least something adequate for the sphere of influence he laid claim to. With regard to his own position, he also wanted Germany to recognize him as spokesperson or even leader of the Arab countries. In this context, el-Husseini argued that he had, after all, been the instigator of the uprisings in Palestine and Syria, besides being "Germany's first friend."[21]

These wishes remained unfulfilled. Because Germany was still seeking permission to march through Turkey in preparation for an offensive in the Arab

---

16. Ibid., p. 720f.; Grobba differed on this issue: "Germany has no interests there other than the destruction of the power that is protecting the Jews," note by Grobba/AA, Dec. 1, 1941, PAAA, BA 61123.
17. Note by Schmidt/office of RAM, Nov. 30, 1941, ADAP, ser. D., vol. 13/2, p. 720f.
18. Cooper, "Palestinian," p. 18.
19. Gensicke, pp. 95–98; Höpp, "Alī," pp. 569–581.
20. Note by Grobba/AA, Jan. 27, 1942, ADAP, ser. E, vol. 1, p. 310f.; Tillmann, p. 334.
21. Woermann/AA to DG Rome, Dec. 20, 1941, ADAP, ser. E, vol. 1, p. 66f.; Grobba, p. 260f.

region in early 1942, diplomatic advances in this direction were clearly given priority. The Germans would put off both the Mufti and al-Gailani for the time being, without making substantial concessions, in order to "keep them active and to ensure that the population would be ready to cooperate when a military invasion took place."[22] After both had again solicited, in a joint letter to Weizsäcker on April 28, regarding "the sovereignty and independence of the Arab countries currently suffering under English repression," along with the "elimination of the Jewish national homeland in Palestine," they finally accepted the wording suggested by the Axis.[23] This version—whose contents, with the necessary agreement of the Arab side, was to be kept secret—was in the style of an official written reply and was signed on May 3 by the Italian foreign minister and two weeks later by the German foreign minister, and then delivered to the Mufti and al-Gailani. Despite the disappointing outcome, both conveyed their "vigorous thanks for the sympathetic furtherance of their political aims."[24] Al-Qawuqji, however, frustrated with the meager yield, commented that the documents were "just symbolic and not an agreement."[25]

The German government did not make a formal declaration on the "recognition of the independence of the Arab countries and the promotion of their unity" until November 2, 1944, long after the last German troops had left Africa and the Caucasus and the war was militarily lost for Nazi Germany. The declaration, by then without any practical value, contained what the Mufti had urged for so long.[26] In his numerous attempts to obtain a declaration of independence from the Axis, el-Husseini no doubt had various complementary motives. First, in the event that the declaration became public, it would have more forcefully pulled onto the Axis side the parts of the Arab world that were willing to collaborate. Second, one can also read in his efforts the wariness that he must have felt regarding Axis plans when contemplating the prospect of a German-Italian conquest of the Arab region. Although the Mufti knew that Hitler had no territorial claims on the area, the Italians very much regarded it as their own sphere of influence. For this reason, the Mufti wanted to forestall the feared Italian formation of colonies—for example, in Palestine or Lebanon— as soon as possible through a clearly worded declaration. Third, the power-conscious el-Husseini attempted at the outset to thwart potential rivals for the leadership of a Greater Arab empire by personally obtaining a guarantee of

22. Note by Woermann/AA, Mar. 12, 1942, ADAP, ser. E, vol. 2, p. 61; Gensicke, p. 97.
23. Mufti and al-Gailani to RAM, April 28, 1942, PAAA, R 27828.
24. RAM to Mufti, April 28, 1942, PAAA, BA 61124; RAM to al-Gailani, April 28, 1942, PAAA, BA 61124; Italian foreign minister to Mufti, April 28, 1942, PAAA, R 27828; Italian foreign minister to al-Gailani, April 28, 1942, PAAA, R 27828; note by StS./AA, May 15, 1942, PAAA, BA 61124.
25. Quoted in Höpp, "Ali," p. 582.
26. Schröder, *Deutschland*, p. 204.

independence for the Arab countries. A public Axis declaration would no doubt have emphatically underscored his own claim to power in the Greater Syrian Empire that he was aiming for—with relation to Germany and Italy as well as the Arab world.[27]

Despite their many joint initiatives to obtain a guarantee of independence from the Axis, the el-Husseini-al-Gailani duo did not represent an amicably cooperative team pursuing common interests in the service of the Arab cause. Instead, their relations were characterized by increasing rivalry soon after their arrival in Germany. The conflict came to a head in the spring of 1942, while Afrika Korps was successfully advancing toward Egypt. The causes of the dispute lay in the mundane desire of each individual to prevail as the sovereign leader of a hoped-for Greater Arab Empire. Both jealously sought to neutralize the other as an unpleasant rival.

After the first intrigues, el-Husseini created a new state of affairs in June 1942. In an interview with Ettel, he claimed to be the president of a secret organization called the "Arab Nation." The secret society was founded by Sharif Hussein of Mecca, the leader of the uprising against the Turks in World War I. This organization would take on the real leadership role in the Arabs' struggle for independence, and it would claim members and representatives in all the Arab countries. Al-Gailani, the Mufti continued, had also joined the organization, and it was thanks to the de facto acknowledgment of his position that he had become the Iraqi prime minister. Finally, el-Husseini told Ettel that he intended to have the Germans recognize his leadership role in the secret organization; this would have represented the virtual realization of his plan to establish himself as the undisputed leader of the Arab world.[28]

Al-Gailani categorically denied the existence of such an organization and called the account a complete fabrication by the Mufti. He stressed that he was responsible only to himself and to the King of Iraq.[29] In any case, el-Husseini managed to get rid of Grobba, his unloved contact at the Foreign Office, with those wild claims. Ettel was given the assignment in his place on June 29, 1942; from then on, Grobba served as the contact person only for al-Gailani.[30] But the conflict between the exiled Arabs was in no way defused. Meanwhile, the Germans appeared anxious to reconcile the two parties. Given the extensive petty jealousies, there was increasing perplexity among the Germans. Legation counselor Hans-Ulrich Granow from Rome only provided the recommendation that both politicians be treated identically in order to avoid further irrita-

---

27. Too one-dimensional: Höpp, "Alī," p. 582f.; Tillmann, p. 352.
28. Note by Ettel/AA, June 26, 1942, PAAA, R 27324; Gensicke, p. 100f.
29. Note by Woermann/AA, Sept. 12, 1942, PAAA, R 27324.
30. Ettel/AA to RAM, Sept. 22, 1942, PAAA, R 27324; Bajohr, p. 246.

tion. They were to take their trips and make their visits separately whenever possible. In the event that an encounter was nevertheless unavoidable, the two were to take turns granting precedence to each other.[31] The OKH, observing the escalating conflict, also requested that at least the development and training of the Muslim volunteers in the German-Arab Battalion be kept out of those disputes. At the end of August, the military even considered disbanding the Arab unit due to the increasingly untenable situation.[32]

The friction quickly grew into an open clash with Ettel and Grobba as well. Thus, the Mufti's aversion to Grobba escalated even further and culminated in November 1942 in the following statement: "Dr. Grobba fights me with the same methods the Freemasons used to fight me. It is truly painful and unfair that while the English and the Jews are engaged in a fierce campaign against me, I am being fought with the same ferocity by a German official such as Ambassador Grobba."[33] El-Husseini also initiated new attacks against his Iraqi adversary in the fall. Via a nephew, he had the text of the German-Iraqi military accord, negotiated by al-Gailani, disseminated in Arab exile circles in Berlin and Paris and spread the rumor that the former prime minister had thoughtlessly surrendered Arab interests to the Axis powers.[34] Through all these intrigues, the Grand Mufti finally gained the upper hand. The climax of the dispute came in November 1942 during preparations for the opening of the Central Islamic Institute. On the question of priority of rank at the grand opening festivities, al-Gailani had to take a backseat; shortly thereafter, Grobba was recalled from his duties and demoted to archive service in Paris.[35] Thus, the side that (not coincidentally) was also favored by the Nazis over the Foreign Office also finally prevailed. It was not just within the RSHA that the view "that the Grand Mufti outshines Gailani in every dimension" became the norm. The Mufti's policies also offered the Germans significantly greater ideological links. Al-Gailani, in contrast, pursued his own nationalistic interests far

---

31. DG Rome to AA, May 8, 1942, ADAP, ser. E, vol. 2, p. 328ff.

32. OKW/WFSt telegram, Aug. 23, 1942, PAAA, BA 61125; Ritter/AA to Grobba/AA, Aug. 25, 1942, PAAA, BA 61125; OKW/WFSt to AA, Aug. 23, 1942, PAAA, R 27828.

33. DG Rome to AA, Nov. 5, 1942, PAAA, R 27325; cf. note by Ettel/AA, Sept. 3, 1942, PAAA, R 27324.

34. Gen.kdo. zbV. telex, Oct. 22, 1942, PAAA, BA 61124; Gen.kdo. zbV. telex, Oct. 28, 1942, PAAA, BA 61124; note by Grobba/AA, Nov. 21, 1942, PAAA, BA 61124; memorandum from head of OKW/Ausl/ Abw II, Dec. 1, 1942, PAAA, BA 61124; note by Ettel/AA, Dec. 12, 1942, PAAA, R 27325; in November, to Woermann, al-Gailani threatened to leave Germany because the dispute had taken on an "intolerable form" to which he was no longer willing to subject his "personal dignity," note by Woermann/AA, Nov. 12, 1942, PAAA, BA 61124.

35. Translation of note by al-Gailani, Dec. 21, 1942, PAAA, R 27324; note by Tismer/AA, Dec. 29, 1942, PAAA, R 27324; note by Woermann/AA, Dec. 30, 1942, PAAA, R 27324; Höpp, "Muslime," p. 22ff.; Bajohr, p. 245f.; Grobba, p. 310f.; Schwanitz, "Geist," p. 139.

too narrowly, and his reserve toward Germany's Italian ally likely had a negative impact as well.[36]

The Mufti, however, did not simply lose himself in rivalry and intrigues after his arrival in Berlin. His personal history in Palestine and his decades-long struggle against the Yishuv and English authority prepared him to play a prominent role in exile as an Axis collaborator. After his escape in 1937, he was never isolated from the current developments taking place in the Middle East; he had contacts who updated him regularly on events in Palestine. The influence of his clan, which remained dominant there and whose members served effectively as local representatives, guaranteed the Mufti an enduring, powerful base after his escape and kept open the crucial option for him to reassume power himself one day in an independent Palestine. He worked consistently toward this goal while in exile in Berlin and Rome.

The relentless dissemination of anti-Semitic propaganda was a key ingredient of el-Husseini's work in Europe. Countless meeting minutes, speeches, memorandums, letters, and other statements attest that his hatred for the Jews was the fundamental impetus driving him. His call for "the abolition of the Jewish national homeland in Palestine" was always one of the key points in his attempts to obtain a guarantee of independence from the Axis after his meeting with Hitler.[37] He expressed himself in greater detail in March 1942 in an interview with the Arab journalist Sanki. Asked about Jewish intentions in the Middle East, he answered: "The efforts of the Jews know no limits. The Jews use Palestine as a base for their devilish aims against the rest of the Arab countries: Egypt, Syria, Transjordan, and Iraq. Essentially, the Jews want to extend their domination over the entire Middle East. Their tactic to achieve this goal is to first conquer these countries economically, in that they first push them into an acute crisis, which strangles them, in order to bring them under Jewish control more easily."[38]

During a conversation with Ettel at the end of June, the Mufti emphasized that "Arab interests are in complete harmony with German interests." In addition to unity in opposing England and communism, consensus prevailed in particular in both sides' hostility toward the Jews. "Germany," said the Mufti, "is the only country in the world that does not hesitate to fight the Jews on its own soil; rather, it has uncompromisingly declared war on world Jewry. In this conflict with the Jews, the Arabs feel the closest connection with Germany."[39]

---

36. Note by Ettel/AA, Sept. 3, 1942, PAAA, R 27324; DG Rome to AA, Aug. 7, 1942, PAAA, R 27324; Hirszowicz, "Germany," p. 74.
37. Mufti to RAM (undated/Mar. 1942), PAAA, BA 61123.
38. Interview with Mufti (undated/Mar. 1942), quoted in Höpp, *Mufti-Papiere*, p. 36.
39. Note by Ettel/AA, June 26, 1942, PAAA, R 27324.

Similarly, he stressed in a memorandum in the fall of 1942: "A number of strong ties connect the German and Arab peoples. Germany is the only power that is trying to definitively solve the Jewish problem and that is present to destroy the power of Great Britain and communism. These are issues of critical importance to the Arabs; any of these ties would be enough to strongly join the two nations together."[40]

On the occasion of the opening of the Central Islamic Institute in Berlin on December 18, 1942, el-Husseini gave a speech that provides an example of his constantly recurring pattern of argumentation. On the one hand, he argued in an Islamic fundamentalist manner, in that he emphasized: "Among the bitterest enemies of the Muslims are the Jews and their accomplices, who since time immemorial have expressed hostility toward the Muslims and confronted them everywhere with guile and cunning." On the other hand, however, the Mufti did not act merely as a religious zealot. To spread hatred against the Jews, he relied equally on the central anti-Semitic stereotype of National Socialist ideology, as another passage from the same speech shows: "In England as well as in America, only the Jewish influence rules. It is the same Jewish influence that is behind godless communism, which is averse to all religions and principles. It is also what has set the peoples against each other in this grueling war, whose tragic outcome benefits only the Jews. The confirmed enemies of the Muslims are the Jews and their allies—the English, the Americans, and the Bolsheviks."[41]

On April 21, 1943, in Frankfurt, during a visit to World Service, the self-proclaimed International Institute for the Elucidation of the Jewish Question, el-Husseini presented both the Islamist and racial-ideological sides of his anti-Semitism. Following the welcoming address by the director, el-Husseini gave a speech in which he spoke about his faith in great detail. He claimed that the Jews were the first people to oppose the Muslims "1,350 years ago." He then offered his listeners some deeper insights into his beliefs and, in this context, highlighted the significance of the Koran, the book "that depicts the Jewish character so well." El-Husseini said that the Koran lists all the attributes of the Jews; in addition "it burdens them with the eternal curse and condemns them to never make good because they carry the divine curse. This divine curse expresses itself in the ignoble character of the Jews and their propensity for evil."

He then abruptly switched to the racial-ideological argumentation pattern. He offered the following statement, among others, in striking Stürmer style: "The Jews can be compared to disease-carrying insects. If they are far away,

---

40. Translation of memorandum by Mufti (undated/Oct. 1942), PAAA, BA 61124.
41. Speech by Mufti at opening of Central Islamic Institute, Dec. 18, 1942, PAAA, R 27327.

one can believe them to be peaceful creatures, but if a person is stung by them and afflicted with the illness, then only radical remedies can help." He also invoked an argument that had recently come back in vogue in the Middle East. "It would be wise," he said, "to send the Jews as a gift to the people who defend the Jews. With the Jews in their country, they would then quickly join our ranks." In conclusion, el-Husseini did not forget to explicitly emphasize the similarities between the Germans and the Arabs: "Germany is also the only country that has finally decided to resolve the Jewish question once and for all. This, of course, is of interest to the Arab world first and foremost. [...] Until now, each has fought this danger separately—now we will fight it together. In this fashion we will also reach our goal together."[42]

Even after the defeat of the Axis in North Africa in May 1943, when the prospect of "liberation" for the Arab countries was clearly nil, el-Husseini did not end his anti-Jewish diatribes. To mark the anniversary of the Balfour Declaration, he organized a protest rally in Berlin on November 2, 1943.[43] His speech on this occasion was again full of anti-Semitic stereotypes and agitation against the Yishuv. Obviously informed about the annihilation of the European Jews, he said: "Germany is also fighting the common enemy, who oppressed the Arabs and Mohammedans in their various countries. It identified the Jews accurately and decided to find a final solution to the Jewish danger that would remove their harm from the world." The conclusion of the speech consisted of an appeal to fight without compromise. "Do not fear your enemies and their propaganda," he cried out, "and remember that you have never in history clashed with the Jews and not seen them lose. God has ordained that there will be no stable regime for the Jews and that no state will come into being for them. Perhaps you have been tasked with this. I have not the slightest doubt that we will be victorious over them despite the active assistance of the barbarous Allies."[44]

During the final phase of the war, el-Husseini gave a radio address on the occasion of the Islamic New Year's celebration on December 17, 1944. In that speech, which was broadcast to the entire Arab world, he declared: "We will not be satisfied with less than what the free nations have fought for—genuine independence that does not allow entry to foreigners and that leaves no room for Jews, in which the entire Arab fatherland is available to the Arab people alone."[45] Wilhelm Melchers, the former German consul in Haifa who tempo-

---

42. Translation of speech by Mufti during visit to World Service, April 21, 1943, USHMM, RG 71.005.D7, Box 248.
43. RFSS to Mufti, Oct. 31, 1943, BAB, NS 19/2637.
44. Speech by Mufti, Nov. 2, 1943, PAAA, R 27327.
45. Radio address by Mufti, Dec. 17, 1944, quoted in Höpp, *Mufti-Papiere*, p. 233.

rarily looked after the most important Arab exiles for the Foreign Office after the fall of 1943, expressed himself very clearly on the topic of el-Husseini's radical anti-Semitism. Melchers pointed out to American officers interrogating him in 1947 that the Mufti was "a confirmed enemy of the Jews and made no secret of the fact that he would like to see them all killed."[46]

As some of the diatribes cited indicate, el-Husseini's anti-Semitism was also no longer targeted only at the Palestinian Jews. Since he had been specifically informed about the current status of the Final Solution, he seized the initiative and called for its completion in European countries where implementation appeared to be less than energetic. In particular, he kept an eye on the regimes in Hungary, Romania, and Bulgaria, which were allied with the Third Reich and in his opinion were not acting forcefully enough against the flight of their Jews to Palestine. Whenever he detected evidence of this negligence, he became active and used his access to the highest governmental authorities to voice his opinions. Here as well, he identified the "Arab cause" with the annihilation of the Jews.[47]

At the end of 1942, Dieter Wisliceny, the German "Jewish affairs adviser" to the Slovakian government, negotiated with the representatives of the Joint Distribution Committee in Bratislava regarding the possibility of allowing Jewish children from Slovakia, Poland, and Hungary to emigrate to Palestine. An exchange for German civilian internees, under the mediation of the Red Cross, was planned. "I was called to Berlin by Eichmann, who disclosed to me that the Grand Mufti had found out about the planned action through his intelligence service in Palestine," explained Wisliceny in 1946. "He protested vigorously to Himmler on the grounds that these Jewish children would be adults in a few years and would represent a strengthening of the Jewish element in Palestine. Himmler then vetoed the entire action and issued a prohibition for future cases as well, stating that no Jew would be allowed to leave the German-controlled territories for Palestine."[48] Endre Steiner, who had negotiated with Wisliceny on the Jewish side, confirmed this state of affairs that same year: "He [Wisliceny] declared that the Mufti was in very close communication and collaboration with Eichmann, and therefore—in order not to be denounced by the Mufti—German officials could not accept Palestine as a final destination." The Mufti was, according to Wisliceny, "an implacable archenemy of the Jews and had also always been a proponent of the idea of exterminating the Jews."[49]

---

46. Wilhelm Melchers affidavit, Aug. 6, 1947, USHMM, RG 71.000.D7, Box 248.
47. Summarizing: Schechtman, p. 154ff.; Gensicke, pp. 149ff., 159ff.; Ofer, p. 189ff.
48. Statement by Dieter Wisliceny, July 26, 1946, YVA, TR 3/129.
49. Endre Steiner affidavit, Feb. 6, 1946, YVA, TR 3/281.

This type of solution then became the rule whenever a similar "problem" arose. In December 1942, the German ambassador to Bucharest reported that the Romanian head of state, Marshal Antonescu, had allowed 75,000–80,000 Jews to emigrate to Palestine upon payment of a premium.[50] The objections of the Foreign Office were as follows: This step "represents an unacceptable partial solution in the context of the European solution to the Jewish problem enacted by the German government." In addition, it would "greatly strain the trust of our political friends in the Middle East," because "sending in 80,000 Jews who are on the side of our wartime enemy would play directly into the enemy's hands."[51] The Mufti may have intervened in this instance as well. At a minimum, he argued for the primacy of extermination. In February 1943, when it became known that Great Britain had offered to take 5,000 Jewish children from Bulgaria to Palestine, Undersecretary of State Luther reacted in similar fashion: because "these 5,000 Jews would be brought up under the English influence to become propagandists against our anti-Semitic measures," he advised "very strongly" against it. "Also, such a measure would not be consistent with our policy toward the Arab peoples."[52]

In this case, there is again evidence of the direct involvement of the Mufti.[53] "The Jewish threat to the entire world, and especially to the countries where Jews live, has become a reality for most nations, causing them to take self-protective measures. The Axis powers and their allies were among the first to recognize that stopping these hostile elements—and the disruption they cause through espionage, moral decline, the propagation of communist ideas, and the crippling of the economy—has become a national emergency," he declared to the Bulgarian foreign minister. The Mufti explained that this had led to an "outburst of rage by world Jewry": "England, America, and Russia are acting on behalf of the Jews." He recommended sending them "where they will be under tighter control, for example, to Poland. That way you will avert the danger and perform a good, rewarding deed for the Arab people."[54] Not Palestine but Poland, the scene of extermination, was thus what he anticipated for the European Jews. A few days later, el-Husseini also approached Ribbentrop: "Thanks to our common interests, the friendly Arab people have without any hesitation taken the side of the Axis powers in this defensive battle against communism and against the Anglo-Saxons. The Arabs are waiting for their friends, the Axis powers and their allies, to provide the solution to the world's

---

50. DG Bucharest to AA, Dec. 12, 1942, ADAP, ser. E, vol. 4, p. 492.
51. Luther/AA to DG Bucharest, Jan. 9, 1943, ADAP, ser. E, vol. 5, p. 52f.; similarly Luther/AA to DG Bucharest, Jan. 23, 1943, ADAP, ser. E, vol. 5, p. 134f.
52. Luther/AA to DG Sofia, Feb. 15, 1943, PAAA, R 100878.
53. Memorandum by Hencke/AA, May 12, 1943, PAAA, R 104791.
54. Mufti to Bulgarian foreign minister, May 6, 1943, YVA, TR 3/1309.

Jewish problem."[55] The Jews are agents of the English and of communism, he said, and enemies of the Arabs.[56] Just as the Holocaust was reaching its high point, el-Husseini threw the weight of the Arabs into the balance to ensure that efforts to exterminate the Jews did not lose their intensity.

As evidenced by the Mufti's initiatives to promote the strict implementation of the Final Solution in southeastern Europe, he maintained excellent relations with the SS in addition to his many contacts in the Foreign Office and the Wehrmacht. He had a warm relationship with Himmler; the two met face-to-face many times. In October 1943, el-Husseini sent Himmler a gift for his 43rd birthday and concluded the accompanying message with the words, "May the coming year bring even closer collaboration and draw us nearer to our common goals."[57] Himmler thanked his well-wisher shortly thereafter, "in genuine solidarity and in the fellowship of our common struggle."[58] On the anniversary of the "disastrous Balfour Declaration" he sent a telegram to the Arab exile expressing his "warmest greetings and wishes for the successful implementation of your campaign, until the certain final victory."[59]

In 1944, he arranged for the Mufti to be invited to Cracow for a planned international anti-Semitic conference, where, as an appointed expert, he was to make a presentation from the Arab point of view. Due to the rapid advance of the Red Army, however, the event did not take place.[60] The SS's interest in el-Husseini was also evidenced by the fact that a liaison officer was immediately assigned to him upon his arrival in Europe. This position was held after November 1941 by SS-Obersturmführer Weise from the foreign intelligence service of the RSHA. As Weise himself stated, he was "responsible for the security of his eminence during these activities and accompanied him on all his visits and travels in Germany and Italy." He worked with the Mufti intermittently until early 1944.[61]

Himmler's affinity for Islamic anti-Semitism and anti-imperialism was not limited to el-Husseini alone. After hearing examples of the fanatical admiration of Hitler in the Arab countries, he gave the RSHA the grotesque assignment on May 14, 1943, of systematically searching the Koran for passages that could be interpreted as evidence that Hitler had "already been foretold and called to complete the work of the Prophet."[62] Months later, the similarly engaged

55. Mufti to RAM, May 13, 1943, PAAA, R 100878.
56. Mufti to RAM, June 10, 1943, YVA, TR 3/1311; similar letter to Italian foreign minister reprinted in Carpi, "Negotiations," p. 122ff.
57. Mufti to RFSS, Oct. 6, 1943, BAB, NS 19/2637.
58. RFSS to Mufti, Oct. 18, 1943, BAB, NS 19/2637.
59. RFSS to Mufti, Nov. 2, 1943, BAB, NS 19/2637.
60. Cooper, "Policy," p. 71; Cooper, "Palestinian," p. 27.
61. Interrogation of Hans-Joachim Weise, Jan. 12, 1965, BAL, B 162/16704.
62. RFSS to RSHA, May 14, 1943, BAB, NS 19/3544; Höpp, "Koran," p. 443.

Berger, from the SS headquarters, regretfully reported that the research by his "scribes" had yielded no promising results.[63] Ernst Kaltenbrunner, by contrast, appeared to be more knowledgeable. He lectured in September about suitable Koran passages discussing the "return of the 'prophetic light'" that allowed "correlation with the Führer."[64] In addition, belief in the Mahdi was extremely widespread among the Muslims; he would "appear at the end of time to strengthen the faith and bring about the triumph of justice."[65] In early December, however, the head of the RSHA clarified that the Führer could "not be passed off as either the Prophet or the Mahdi." But Hitler was suitable "as the returned Isa (Jesus), foretold in the Koran, who like St. George will vanquish the giant and Jewish king Dadjdjâl at the end of the world."[66]

---

63. Chief of SSHA to chief of RFSS personal staff, Oct. 10, 1943, BAB, NS 19/3544.
64. CdS to RFSS, Sept. 3, 1943, BAB, NS 19/3544.
65. Ibid., Sept. 13, 1943, BAB, NS 19/3544.
66. Ibid., Dec. 6, 1943, BAB, NS 19/3544.

Chapter VII

Rommel and the Road to Cairo

After the military operations of the previous year, in January 1942, as a result of the British counteroffensive, Rommel ordered a retreat to the Marsa el-Brega position, where the Axis troops were to prepare themselves for a long defense.[1] The conditions for holding the front seemed favorable. For one thing, the terrain there appeared promising for a defensive battle; for another, the British 8th Army's lines of communication were now so overextended that its offensive had lost a great deal of momentum. In addition, on January 5 a convoy with a substantial quantity of supplies had reached Tripoli undamaged. On the British side, newly arrived, and largely inexperienced, tank forces had replaced the veteran 7th Armored Division. And for a short time Rommel seemed to have a significant number of armored vehicles available.[2] The detailed assessment of the situation was furnished unknowingly by a first-hand source. Major Bonner F. Fellers, the U.S. military attaché in Cairo, supplied the Pentagon with regular reports and precise appraisals of the British troops in North Africa. In late summer 1941 the Italians were able to break his

---

1. DRZW, vol. 6, p. 569f.; Gundelach, vol. 1, p. 347; Reuth, *Entscheidung*, p. 135.
2. Fraser, *Rommel*, p. 266f.; DRZW, vol. 6, p. 573ff.

radio code, and thereafter the Axis commanders had access to valuable intelligence regarding the conditions and the plans being made by the enemy.[3]

On this basis, the leadership of the German Afrika Korps decided on January 13, 1942, to seize the initiative again with an offensive relying on the element of absolute surprise. On January 21, in complete secrecy, the Germans and Italians lined up for an attack. As of the following day, the Axis units previously known as Panzer Group Africa would officially carry the title Afrika Korps. What had initially been planned more as an attack to relieve pressure developed into a broad German-Italian offensive. In the course of this advance first the town of Msus, on January 25, and four days later the town of Benghazi, a key supply port, were reconquered. By February 6, all of Cyrenaica was reconquered and the British were forced to pull back to the Gazala position.[4]

Rommel then ordered his troops to revert back to defensive positions. The British 8th Army, for the time being, no longer showed any dangerous offensive potential; but Afrika Korps also urgently needed to be refitted. Then Rommel himself left the theater of operations on February 16, flying first to Rome and then on to Hitler's headquarters. There Hitler personally presented the general with swords for the Knight's Cross and they discussed the situation in Africa at length. In this context, Rommel no doubt broached the issue of his old dream, seizing the Suez Canal with the Afrika Korps, and was largely in agreement with Hitler about that strategy. The dictator was at the same time planning the pincer movement of the Eastern Army over the Caucasus into the Middle East. Following those discussions, Rommel, who was so wildly celebrated by the Nazi propaganda effort, went on vacation.[5]

Meanwhile, on the other side, General Auchinleck, the commander-in-chief of the British forces in the Middle East, was busy improving the morale of his men. The British had just been forced to evacuate Cyrenaica again, despite their own offensive plans. On March 30, 1942, Auchinleck authored a circular to all commanders in which he called upon them to encourage their soldiers and emphatically counter Rommel's aura of invincibility. Because, as the commander-in-chief said, there was the "critical danger" that he (Rommel) "could become a bogeyman for our troops, simply because they talk about him so much." As the British commander pointed out, Rommel was in no way a superman. To fight the myth, he recommended a change in terminology: when speaking of the enemy, instead of referring to Rommel, the terms "the Germans" or "the enemy" should be used. At the end of the text, though, the

---

3. Piekalkiewicz, p. 78f.; Fraser, *Rommel*, p. 266f.
4. DRZW, vol. 6, pp. 576–586; Reuth, *Entscheidung*, p. 135f.; Gundelach, vol. 1, p. 348; Schröder, *Deutschland*, p. 186.
5. Fraser, *Rommel*, p. 271.

addition "P.S. I am not jealous of Rommel" provided evidence that even the nerves of the British commander-in-chief were not entirely untouched by the successes of his opponent.[6]

After Rommel returned to Africa on March 19, he planned a new offensive against the British, to begin in approximately two months that would again pre-empt the enemy's plans. The target of the attack would be the Tobruk fortress, which was not far from the Egyptian border. On the way there, the Germans would need to break through another British defensive line. The well-developed positions—armed with approximately 500,000 mines, according to German estimations—extended at least 60 kilometers southward from Gazala on the coast to Bir Hakeim, a desert fort held by a Free French garrison.[7] Rommel had only his marginally strengthened forces available for the offensive. At the end of November 1941, however, the 2nd Air Corps had been re-deployed from the Eastern Front to Sicily. In the following months, its missions against the strongly fortified British air and sea base on Malta allowed the Afrika Korps to benefit from significantly improved supply lines and an almost evenly balanced situation in the air.[8] Malta was not scheduled to be definitively put out of action until June, with the airborne Operation Hercules, also known as C-3.[9] The Army High Command would not approve a signifi-cant strengthening of Afrika Korps until the Eastern Army achieved additional strategic advances, thus opening up the Caucasus option. Until then, Rommel had to resign himself to the fact that he was essentially operating in a secondary theater of war.[10]

During this early phase of the Axis troops' advance, reports about wide-spread anti-English sentiment in Egypt reached the Afrika Korps. According to these reports, protests against the British in Egyptian cities featured frequent cheers for Rommel. The Germans were inspired to add fuel to the fire by in-tensifying their propaganda efforts.[11] More propaganda was evidently also directed toward other target groups during the spring of 1942. On April 10 Hans Winkler, serving as Foreign Office liaison officer for Africa on behalf of Neurath, wrote a report in which he employed a classic anti-Semitic stereotype. He pointed out that Jews might be working for the British in the cities of Libya, as they were continually transmitting situation reports by radio. In this

---

6. Circular by British Commander-in-Chief Middle East, Mar. 30, 1942, PAAA, R 60748.

7. Gundelach, vol. 1, p. 367; DRZW, vol. 6, pp. 595–598.

8. DRZW, vol. 6, pp. 588–593; Reuth, *Entscheidung*, pp. 139f., 152–155; Gundelach, vol. 1, pp. 352–358.

9. Note by Schmidt/AA, May 2, 1942, ADAP, ser. E, vol. 2, p. 315f.; Reuth, *Entscheidung*, pp. 141ff., 160–163; DRZW, vol. 6, p. 592ff.

10. Fraser, *Rommel*, p. 272ff.

11. PzAA to OKH, April 8, 1942, PAAA, R 60747; Schröder, *Deutschland*, p. 187f.

context, the liaison officer also spoke about the disdain the Arabs showed—according to his observations—toward the Jews in the country.[12]

Once adequate supplies had reached Africa, Rommel and his panzer army lined up on May 26 to begin their offensive against the Gazala position. In a feint, primarily Italian infantry attacked the center of the fortified British lines in the north. At the same time, the bulk of the motorized units under Rommel's leadership bypassed the front south of Bir Hakeim in order to force the British to fight facing the rear of their own lines.[13] The plan was largely successful. Despite the threat of encirclement faced by the panzer units, along with intermittent ammunition shortages, the army, after bypassing the front in the south, was able to push the British back out of their positions over the course of a battle lasting several days. On June 1, Sidi Muftah fell, and nine days later Axis troops took Bir Hakeim after heavy fighting. However, a large part of the French garrison, under the command of Pierre Koenig, was able to escape from the fort.[14] With the Germans pursuing the British forces in the direction of El Adem after June 10 and driving them out of the area around Acroma five days later, the entire Gazala position collapsed, and the majority of the British 8th Army was forced to pull back across the Egyptian border. In between there stood only the heavily fortified port of Tobruk, which Rommel had tried unsuccessfully to storm the year before.[15]

By June 17, the motorized Axis forces had already pushed well past Tobruk as they pursued the British to the east, driving the 7th Armored Division back east of Gambut and seizing the Royal Air Force airfields there. The British high command therefore believed that Rommel would encircle and besiege Tobruk as he had done the previous year, while at the same time attempting to push forward into Egypt.[16] In accordance with its attack orders, however, Afrika Korps performed an about-face on June 19 and lined up for a frontal assault on Tobruk from the southeast. The actual assault took place the following day, after massive air attacks. By evening, large parts of the fortifications had already been overwhelmed; the next morning, the last holdouts in the western section of Tobruk, a garrison of South Africans, surrendered as well. The panzer army took 33,000 prisoners of war and acquired 30 undamaged tanks and large quantities of fuel, ammunition, and provisions.[17] Churchill

---

12. Note by VAA/PzAA, April 10, 1942, PAAA, R 60770.

13. Gundelach, vol. 1, p. 368; DRZW, vol. 6, pp. 600–604.

14. DRZW, vol. 6, pp. 604–620; Fraser, *Rommel*, pp. 288–301; Reuth, *Entscheidung*, p. 188f.; approximately 1,000 Jews from Palestine were also part of the garrison, Sachar, p. 233.

15. DRZW, vol. 6, p. 621f.

16. Ibid., p. 626.

17. OKH/GenStdH/Op.Abt. telex, June 20, 1942, BA-MA, RH 2/615; PzAA/Ia to OKH/GenStdH/Op.Abt., June 21, 1942, BA-MA, RH 2/623; Reuth, *Entscheidung*, p. 191; DRZW, vol. 6, p. 628f.; Kirk, p. 216; Gundelach, vol. 1, p. 371f.

wrote that this defeat, for him, was one of the bitterest losses of the entire war.[18] When the bad news reached him, the British prime minister was speaking with Roosevelt in Washington: "I did not attempt to hide from the President the shock I had received. It was a bitter moment. Defeat is one thing; disgrace is another."[19] The American anxiously asked if and how he could help. When Churchill requested tanks, Roosevelt promptly sent 300 Sherman tanks to North Africa. After a German U-boat sank this shipment in the Atlantic, the same quantity was sent out again by high-speed steamer. In late summer, those tanks critically strengthened the British lines on the Egyptian front.[20]

Ultimately, the offensive again demonstrated that the British, with their comparatively antiquated combat training, were not able to deploy their armored units effectively and interact with the other military units as required by modern mobile warfare. This was a key factor in Afrika Korps's ability to repeatedly carry out its attacks successfully.[21] With the capture of Tobruk, the Axis powers now had access to an additional deepwater port. Although its unloading capacity was significantly smaller than that of Tripoli or Benghazi, a port considerably much closer to the front offered the undeniable advantage of shortening the fuel-intensive and wearing overland supply routes. However, the Axis powers were never able to ensure a secure ship route to Tobruk after its capture, and thus the precarious supply issue remained one of Afrika Korps's most pressing problems.[22]

The day after the capture of Tobruk, Rommel, who had immediately been promoted to field marshal, reported to the Army High Command that with the seizure of the fortification, the first objective of the campaign had been achieved. He then explained that the disposition of his troops, the favorable supply situation, and the current weakness of the British would allow a "pursuit deep into Egyptian territory." For this reason, he requested that Mussolini be persuaded to remove the previously imposed restrictions on movement and release all the troops under his command for immediate pursuit of the offensive.[23] Hitler approved the plans of his new field marshal, and the Italians also endorsed the advance toward Egypt. The elimination of the British base on Malta (meanwhile significantly strengthened again) by means of a German landing operation—an original precondition for the resumption of the offensive—was quietly shelved.[24]

---

18. Churchill, p. 546f.
19. Ibid.
20. Kirk, p. 224; Gundelach, vol. 1, p. 372.
21. Reuth, *Rommel*, p. 62.
22. Fraser, *Rommel*, p. 320f.
23. OB PzAA radio message, June 22, 1942, BA-MA, RH 2/462; Reuth, *Entscheidung*, p. 192f.
24. Reuth, *Entscheidung*, pp. 197–200; Fraser, *Rommel*, p. 314f.; Gundelach, vol. 1, p. 382ff.

In the course of the advance that appeared impossible a short time before, issues suddenly arose that had clearly appeared unrealistic during the preceding months. Neurath sent a telegram to the Foreign Office in Berlin on June 25, stating that Rommel was requesting the "immediate implementation of active propaganda in Egypt."[25] The following day the liaison officer made inquiries with Weizsäcker about the status of German-Egyptian relations. The secretary of state emphasized that the two countries were not at war; King Farouk was pro-German "through and through" and hostile toward England. In other circles of society, but also in the army, which had been largely disarmed by the British, there was also great sympathy for Germany. Weizsäcker said that if they went ahead using wording that emphasized that the Axis troops were coming as friends to liberate Egypt, there would be hardly any resistance from the Egyptians. Some of the population might even welcome the invasion.[26]

Meanwhile, the German-Italian offensive continued. On June 26, the panzer army reached a new British defensive position at the coastal fortress of Marsa Matruh, 350 kilometers east of Tobruk—the last harbor before Alexandria. The day before, Auchinleck had personally relieved General Ritchie as commander-in-chief of the 8th Army—clear evidence of the dramatic situation in which the British found themselves. But the new commander-in-chief could not prevent Rommel's units from breaking into the fortified lines either. Marsa Matruh fell on June 29, and at least 8,000 prisoners were captured by the Axis. However, a large number of the British forces occupying the fortress were able to withdraw to the east in time. Those units—some immediately in front of, some alongside, and some even behind the panzer army as it charged further forward—tried to reach their fallback position further to the east.[27]

After the report of the storming of Marsa Matruh reached the Foreign Office, Ribbentrop ordered intensified propaganda in Egypt and issued the relevant guidelines that same evening. According to those instructions, England had "robbed Egypt of its freedom and despite many promises had refused to leave the country. It has turned Egypt into a theater of war and attempted to drag the Egyptian people into the war in order to sacrifice them for its imperialistic plans." By contrast, "Rommel's victorious soldiers" were fighting "to liberate Egypt from the English yoke. They have no hostile intentions toward the Egyptian people; rather, they come as friends. They have only

25. Telegram from VAA/PzAA to AA, June 25, 1942, PAAA, R 29537.
26. Telegram from VAA/PzAA to AA, June 24, 1942, PAAA, R 29533; telegram from StS./AA to VAA/PzAA, June 26, 1942, PAAA, R 29533.
27. PzAA/Ia to OKH/GenStdH/Op.Abt., June 29, 1942, BA-MA, RH 2/623; DRZW, vol. 6, p. 639ff.; Fraser, *Rommel*, p. 314f.; Gundelach, vol. 1, pp. 386–389; Kirk, p. 217.

one common enemy: the English and those peoples who help them." The Nazi
foreign minister wished to send an appeal to the Egyptians stressing the theme
that the Germans and Egyptians would together pursue the goal of driving out
the British: "Be ready for this day, make General Rommel's victory easy, and
make Britain's war difficult." Finally, it was to be emphasized that "the Axis
powers are the friends of the entire Arab world. They will be awaited as
liberators also in Iraq, Syria, and Palestine, and welcomed as in Egypt."[28]

The day after the fall of Marsa Matruh, the Afrika Korps reached what was
supposedly the last British defensive position west of the Nile. The defensive
line was named after a small railway station there, which would become world
famous: El Alamein.[29] German and Italian troops were thus little more than
100 kilometers west of Alexandria. The new attack by the panzer army was set
for the morning of July 1.[30] Although the soldiers were completely exhausted
after an advance of 500 kilometers in just 10 days, the Afrika Korps had only
52 combat-ready tanks remaining, and the Royal Air Force was at last
beginning to cause serious problems. But the Germans were optimistic that
they would successfully break through and reach the Suez Canal.[31] Rommel informed the OKW on July 1 regarding the progress into Egypt. He suggested
pushing forward immediately to Alexandria, encircling the British forces there,
and then moving on to Cairo and the Suez Canal.[32] That same day, British
cryptographers deciphered a radio message from the Afrika Korps requesting
10,000 maps of the Nile delta—as soon as possible—from the Army High
Command.[33]

In the early morning of July 1, the attack on the British positions at El
Alamein began. Despite reports to the contrary during the day, the Germans
and Italians were unable to break through by evening. Rommel's otherwise
successful feints and mock assaults failed due to the British forces' superior
reconnaissance. Further offensive efforts on the following two days had the
same result.[34] On the morning of July 4, Rommel reported that he had temporarily halted further attacks and needed to revert to the defensive until his
units were regrouped and adequate reinforcements and additional supplies
arrived. The commander of the panzer army expected an interruption of ap-

---

28. Telegram from Schmieden/AA, May 29, 1942, PAAA, R 29533.
29. Schröder, *Deutschland*, p. 193; Gundelach, vol. 1, p. 388f.; Waldschmidt, p. 111; on the geographical
situation and the British forces at the El Alamein position: DRZW, vol. 6, pp. 648–651; Auchinleck had a
second defensive line prepared between El Alamein and the Nile delta, DRZW, vol. 6, p. 652.
30. Telex from PzAA/Ia to GenStdH/Op.Abt., July 1, 1942, BA-MA, RH 2/623.
31. DRZW, vol. 6, pp. 639, 655.
32. Telex from Dt.Gen.b.HQu.It.Wehrm. to GenStdH/Op.Abt., July 1, 1942, BA-MA, RH 2/462.
33. Piekalkiewicz, p. 148.
34. PzAA/Ia to OKH/GenStdH/Op.Abt., July 1, 1942, BA-MA, RH 19 VIII/23; DRZW, vol. 6, pp. 655–
659.

proximately two weeks; after that the offensive would resume.[35] The penetration of the Germans and Italians into Egypt was thus halted, but they remained convinced that the offensive would continue successfully. New attacks by the Afrika Korps on the British positions on July 10 and 13 came to nothing, however. In the following days, the Axis troops had to fight off advances by British units. Exhausted, both sides discontinued their hostilities at the end of July. The First Battle of El Alamein thus ended in a standoff, but the British had at least managed to hold their positions for the first time after a six-month retreat of over more than 1,000 kilometers from deep inside Libya to Egypt.[36]

On the Axis side, the unexpectedly successful advance of the Afrika Korps was accompanied by a massive propaganda offensive. In addition to German and Italian bombs, countless tons of leaflets, propaganda postcards, and proclamations were dropped not only over Egypt but also over Palestine, Lebanon, and Syria. By June 25, the day the Libyan-Egyptian border was crossed, 1,100,000 propaganda leaflets had been prepared, which were immediately transported to Africa in order to be dropped over cities in Egypt.[37] Several days later, Neurath reported to the Foreign Office that on July 3 "vast quantities" of leaflets had been placed into circulation and would hopefully make an impact.[38] On July 12, another 760,000 propaganda leaflets left Germany; among other things, these included 200,000 appeals by the Mufti and al-Gailani.[39] Exactly one month later, Consul General Wüster of the intelligence department of the Foreign Office delivered to his superiors a presentation on the content of various leaflets that were intended for distribution in the countries of the Middle East. These propaganda pieces alone totaled a further 1.3 million copies.[40] Among these was a leaflet designed for Egypt and Syria, "Appeal to the Arab Youth," which was intended to dissuade young Arabs from serving in the British army. England needs armies, it said, "in order to defend its policies of occupation, colonization, and tyranny, under a common flag with the Bolsheviks and the Jews. It wants to throw you into the carnage so that you will bleed to death and sacrifice the flower of your youth."[41]

A print run of 300,000 leaflets entitled "Egypt for the Egyptians" was produced, for distribution only after the fall of El Alamein. The content consisted

35. Telex from Dt.Gen.b.HQu.It.Wehrm. to GenStdH/Op.Abt., July 4, 1942, BA-MA, RH 2/462; telex from PzAA/Ia to GenStdH/Op.Abt., July 4, 1942, BA-MA, RH 2/624; Gundelach, vol. 1, p. 391.
36. Situation analysis by OB PzAA, July 21, 1942, BA-MA, RH 19 VIII/23; Fraser, *Rommel*, p. 316ff.; Gundelach, vol. 1, pp. 391–396.
37. Wüster/AA to VAA/PzAA, June 25, 1942, PAAA, R 60748.
38. VAA/PzAA to AA, July 4, 1942, PAAA, R 60748.
39. Wüster/AA to VAA/PzAA, July 13, 1942, PAAA, R 60748.
40. Ibid. to AA, Aug. 12, 1942, PAAA, R 60650.
41. Translation of leaflet (undated/Aug. 1942), PAAA, R 60650.

of an unambiguous appeal to rise up against the English. Among other things, it said: "Now it is time! Leave the ranks of the English. Refuse to serve them. Chase them out of your cities. Destroy their weapons." And further: "Welcome the Axis soldiers as friends. Protect them from danger as they will protect you. Do your utmost to help them; you will be helping yourselves. In this way you will gain political freedom and independence for Egypt. The governments of the Axis powers have solemnly declared that they will respect and protect the independence and sovereignty of Egypt."[42]

Postcards—in a print run of 100,000—with the title "Borders of the New Zionist Kingdom" were also dropped. They showed a caricature of Chaim Weizmann together with Churchill and Roosevelt standing in front of a map upon which the borders of a future Zionist state had been drawn in. In addition to Palestine, the area included all of Transjordan and Syria, as well as large portions of Iraq and Saudi Arabia.[43] The message of the drawing was clear: only if the Arabs joined the German side would they be able to oppose the handing over of their lands to the Jews by the English and Americans. Consistent with the caricature, 296,000 leaflets entitled "The New Jewish Kingdom" were prepared especially for Syria. The text of this piece also preached the "Jewish peril." It said that "American-English-Jewish statisticians" had calculated that "this new kingdom could still accommodate 17 million Jews from all over the world. No one cares that millions of Arabs, who have inherited this land from their fathers and forefathers, already live in these areas. Later, the Jews will use their well-known methods to drive the inhabitants out of the country!" Referring to current developments on the African front, it continued: "And this time, with God's help, England will not win! Because Marshal Rommel, at the head of the brave Axis troops, is already rattling the last gates of England's power! Arabs! Help your friends achieve their goal: abolishing the English-Jewish-American tyranny."[44]

With the occupation of Egypt and the advance across the Suez Canal in sight, the Germans and Italians began dividing the spoils of war, even though the fighting at El Alamein was still under way and despite the lofty propagandistic assurances of "liberation" from English oppression. In this process, conflicting ideas about the future of the land emerged. During the Afrika Korps' advance, Hitler instructed the Foreign Office to provide for the protection of the Egyptian king; the plan was kept secret from the Italians. The existence of German contacts with Egyptian officers was also kept from the Axis partner.[45]

---

42. Ibid.
43. Propaganda postcard (undated/Aug. 1942), PAAA, R 60650.
44. Translation of leaflet (undated/Aug. 1942), PAAA, R 60650.
45. Hirszowicz, *Germany*, p. 81

With regard to the future administration of the occupied territory, Mussolini suggested Rommel as commander-in-chief of the occupying army; for the civilian sector he envisaged the appointment of a so-called "delegato politico," with a German liaison staff under him to maintain contact with Rommel. The former ambassador in Cairo, Serafino Mazzolini, was designated for this post; he flew to North Africa on July 3.[46] Hitler approved of the recommendation.[47]

On July 4 the Duce added to his proposals relating to the Axis powers' future behavior toward Egypt. He pointed out that the conquered land could not be plundered because it was, after all, a neutral country rather than an enemy country. Therefore, the government would have to remain in place as well; only the local British administrative bodies were to be replaced. Clearly referring to the Germans' plundering of previous war theaters, Mussolini also stipulated that there were to be "absolutely no bulk purchases or stockpiling of goods that could lead to an impoverishment of the country's economy." To this end, he suggested the implementation of a temporary payment system for Egypt that would be placed under Italian supervision; confiscation and purchases beyond actual military requirements would be prohibited.[48] Ten days later he again underscored—with an obviously suspicious side glance at Germany—that Egypt must not be turned into "a second Greece."[49]

The German reaction indicated that the Duce's distrust was entirely justified. Although Ribbentrop assured Germany's ally of his "fundamental view that Italy has political primacy in Egypt," this stock phrase was in reality intended simply as a general reassurance.[50] The German negotiator in Rome responsible for economic issues informed the Reich foreign minister that the German-Italian economic commission proposed by the Italians was "out of the question." Other problems, Ribbentrop determined, would be better solved directly by Rommel in Egypt, as he could access the necessary expertise there as commander-in-chief.[51] A similar picture emerged in further negotiations. Italy suggested that the spoils of war obtained in the occupied Soviet Union should generally go to Germany, while those gained in Egypt should go to Italy. When Hitler was informed of this proposal, he decreed, mindful of Germany's leading role in North Africa, that "the spoils should generally go to those who capture them." In a similar vein, the Foreign Office suggested that

46. DG Rome to AA, July 2, 1942, PAAA, R 27772; Tillmann, p. 384; Hirszowicz, *Germany*, p. 82.
47. Alfred Jodl pointed out that "in the technical sense" there would probably not be an occupation army in Egypt; rather, an army would still be required for active operations, as the British would continue for quite some time to attempt to recapture the land from the west and south—note by Ritter/AA, July 3, 1942, PAAA, R 27772.
48. Note by Woermann/AA, July 4, 1942, PAAA, R 27772.
49. DG Rome to AA, July 15, 1942, PAAA, R 29533.
50. RAM to DG Rome, July 6, 1942, ADAP, ser. E, vol. 3, p. 105.
51. Report by Dt.Gen.b.HQu.It.Wehrm., July 8, 1942, PAAA, R 29537.

"independently of the issue of the future division of spoils, the first troops to arrive should secure the valuables."[52] Despite formal recognition of the Italians' "political primacy," this stance allowed the Germans to preserve the option of comprehensively exploiting Egypt's economy if required, especially in consideration of the continuation of the military offensive. In any case, the Italian side was clearly disgruntled by the general attitude of the Germans.[53]

Beyond the negotiations over the division of the expected spoils, the enemy's reaction to the advance of the Afrika Korps strengthened German and Italian confidence in their own victory. Auchinleck was already planning to retreat across the Nile after the fall of El Alamein, which even the British then accepted as likely. Destruction of the dams on the Nile was expected to provide rear cover for the defeated army, allowing it to pull back across the Suez Canal to Palestine.[54] Numerous reports and rumors about the precarious situation of the British and the mood of the Egyptian population reached the German side as well. On June 30, one day after the storming of Marsa Matruh, word arrived that the Royal Navy had begun pulling its warships out of Alexandria the previous day and were moving them toward Suez. From Cairo, numerous reports indicated that the evacuation of the city was in full swing.[55] The locals there openly taunted the anxious British in the certain expectation of the Germans' arrival. Meanwhile, on what became known as "Ash Wednesday," British military authorities, obviously preparing for an impending retreat, burned large quantities of documents.[56]

In a July 24 report on the situation in Egypt, Ettel reproduced the statements of an informer who had just been on location and who was considered reliable, indicating that Rommel's advance had caused the "nervousness of the English and the Jews to increase markedly." As evidence, the diplomat mentioned the destruction of documents in Cairo and the fact that British women and children were being "hurriedly" moved out. "Throughout Egypt," Ettel continued, "there is a noticeable exodus of Jews. They are selling their property and receiving payment in gold or U.S. dollars. The result has been a significant increase in the price of gold. Because exporting gold out of Egypt is prohibited, the Jews try to smuggle the gold out of the country in ingenious ways." The "best and most effective form of propaganda," wrote Ettel, would be to

52. Woermann/AA to AA, July 9, 1942, PAAA, R 29533.
53. Hirszowicz, *Germany*, p. 85.
54. Schröder, *Deutschland*, p. 194.
55. DG Ankara to AA, June 30, 1942, PAAA, R 27772; press department of AA, SPN, July 2, 1942, PAAA, R 27772.
56. Eppler, *Rommel*, p. 196.

use "all available means to foment the Egyptians' hatred of the English, Americans, and Jews."[57]

A late-July report by Walter Schellenberg to Undersecretary of State Martin Luther in the Foreign Office also contained numerous indications of the general agitation in Egypt in view of the current situation at the front. The head of the SD's foreign intelligence service, based on his sources, assessed that the army remained "absolutely loyal to the king." The armed forces were also "in sharp opposition" to the ruling party. The English had recently pulled out the Egyptian military forces that had been guarding the Nile dams and were preparing explosives to demolish the dams on the delta. According to the available reports, wrote Schellenberg, it seemed clear that in English military circles the loss of Egypt was being "seriously" contemplated. In the meantime, a "spirit of deep hopelessness and darkest pessimism" had taken hold among the British. Evidence of this situation was provided not least by the fact that the "Jews and anti-Axis literati" were already leaving the country. Thus, "as never before, the psychological preconditions for an uprising of the Egyptian population against the English occupying troops" were present.[58]

In a similar report from the beginning of August, an Abwehr informer provided a more complete picture of the situation. According to this individual, the Egyptian population was 95 percent "pro-Axis and harshly anti-English." Since the Axis powers' declaration regarding independence, he said, "even the animosity toward the Italians has decreased." The Axis advance started a mass exodus: "When Rommel marched into Egypt, the leading Gaullists as well as the wealthy Jews and Greeks fled Cairo (there have been no Jews in Alexandria for a long time, and no wealthy Greeks), with some going to Lebanon and some to Cape Town. Unbelievable prices were paid for a flight to Cape Town; the leading Jew, Salvator Cicurell, offered 25,000 pounds for a special aircraft. The Gaullist leader Baron de Vaux traveled as far as Kantara in the lavatory." With regard to further developments, in Cairo it was generally accepted "that the English army would be forced to abandon Egypt with Rommel's next advance." The Nile delta and the Suez Canal, as well as Palestine and Syria, would then be taken by Rommel's army.[59] During this time, Egypt's Jewish community prepared lists of prominent Zionists and antifascists, whose immediate evacuation the British had already authorized. Some of the people were actually taken to Palestine by the army as a precaution. After the first anti-Semitic abuses, the Egyptian prime minister personally attempted to calm the

---

57. Report by Ettel/AA, July 24, 1942, PAAA, R 27323.
58. CdS/VI C 13 to AA, July 31, 1942, PAAA, R 27332.
59. Summary of report by "Cuno I," Aug. 6, 1942, BA-MA, RH 2/1764.

situation by stressing that the Jews had nothing to fear; there would be no acts of discrimination against them.[60]

In view of such reports, the Axis side began preparations for a triumphant victory celebration. Mussolini planned to enter Cairo on a white horse at the head of the Afrika Korps. He flew to Libya with the horse on July 29 and set up his quarters near Derna. He wished to wait there for the certain (according to his military) occupation of the capital and the conquest of the rest of Egypt, and then be able to parade into Cairo right away.[61] As a memento of his imagined triumphal procession, he had commemorative medallions created in Italy in advance, which were to be awarded to deserving officers later on.[62]

As the propaganda products, discussions about the occupation administration, and plans for victory celebrations show very effectively, the occupation of all of Egypt seemed to be a mere formality. The conquest of Cairo, the crossing of the Nile, and arrival at the Suez Canal were all within reach at this time. After all, the route to Palestine was the same distance the Germans and Italians had covered to reach El Alamein during the ten days following the seizure of Tobruk. The German military viewed any further advance as being largely unproblematic. In Palestine and in Syria, the OKH assumed that there were only weak British occupying troops that "could hardly be fit for a serious engagement."[63] In view of the strategic circumstances in Berlin, Neurath ordered various books on Palestine and Islam, which he evidently wished to use to prepare himself for the situation during further advances in the Middle East.[64]

In the general German perception, the pincer operation that had been planned for the Arab region since 1941 appeared to be finally becoming a reality. While the Afrika Korps was preparing to cross the Suez Canal, Hitler issued the momentous orders for the summer offensive against southern Russia on the Eastern Front. Under the supreme command of General Hoth, the 4th Panzer Army set out for Voronezh, aiming to encircle and destroy the Red Army west of the Don. Scarcely two months later, German troops took the first mountain passes in the Caucasus, and on August 21 they reached the summit of Mount Elbrus.[65] Ribbentrop underscored the expectations for the

---

60. Krämer, *Jews*, p. 157.
61. Carpi, "Mufti," p. 115.; DRZW, vol. 6, p. 665f.
62. Piekalkiewicz, p. 138.
63. GenStdH/Abt. FHW situation report, May 10, 1942, BA-MA, RH 2/1521; GenStdH/Abt. FHW situation report, July 13, 1942, BA-MA, RH 2/1588.
64. AA/Ref. Inf./IVc, Aug. 18, 1942, PAAA, R 60748.
65. Fraser, *Rommel*, p. 314; Stewart, *Sunrise*, p. 221; DRZW, vol. 6, p. 677; also Roosevelt, p. 7, suggests that the Middle East was almost lost for the British thanks to Rommel's advance.

strategic situation on July 9 in a discussion with Japanese ambassador Oshima: "But if we were to succeed," said the foreign minister, "in eliminating Russia as the primary ally of England and the United States and pushing forward over the Caucasus toward the south, while Rommel, on the other side, advanced across Egypt in the Middle East, the war would be won. In any case, in the last four weeks we have come much closer to this goal than the German leadership could ever have hoped at its most optimistic."[66]

66. Note by Gottfriedsen/AA, July 10, 1942, ADAP, ser. E, vol. 3, p. 129f.

Chapter VIII

The Einsatzkommando and the Afrika Korps

In the summer of 1942, while the world seemed to be waiting for Egypt to be conquered and for Rommel's divisions to cross the Suez Canal, the Germans had already completed secret preparations to deploy a security police and SD Einsatzkommando in the area. The decision to assign such an SS unit to Afrika Korps for the upcoming operations was made in June, based on the victories at Tobruk and Marsa Matruh, as well as the further advance, which exceeded all expectations. The RSHA had previously refrained from sending its own commandos along during Rommel's journey through the Libyan desert. Now, however, such a step seemed essential given the "opposition potential" that could be expected when the troops reached the Egyptian capital and during the further movement into the Middle East—much like during the period prior to the assault on Poland in 1939 or the attack on the Soviet Union in 1941.

The relevant steps in the decision-making process surrounding the formation of the Einsatzkommando can be accurately reconstructed. In the late morning of July 1, 1942, Schellenberg spoke to Himmler about the coming "deployment in Egypt."[1] That same afternoon, the Reichsführer-SS made an hour-long presentation to Hitler at the Wolfsschanze.[2] The decision concerning the Einsatzkommando must have been made at that meeting, because Obergruppenführer Karl Wolff, chief of the personal staff of the Reichsführer-SS, immediately contacted the OKH. On July 4, Himmler was already able to report with regard to the Einsatzkommando Egypt: "Wehrmacht order to be issued tomorrow."[3] Ultimately, the order was not issued until July 13. The key passage of the deployment guidelines is recorded in the communication between the SS and Wehrmacht leadership: "With the approval of the Reichsführer-SS and the chief of the German police, the deployment of the SS unit with Afrika Korps will be regulated as follows: (1) The SS Einsatzkommando receives its technical instructions from the chief of the security police and SD and carries out its assignments under its own responsibility. It is entitled, within the scope of its mission, to take executive measures against the civilian population on its own authority."[4] The entire arrangement corresponded with the content of the text that, since the previous year, had formed the basis for the mass murders committed by the Einsatzgruppen in the Soviet Union. Central passages that had apparently "proved their worth" in practice were simply carried over verbatim.[5]

Just one week later, on July 20, SS-Obersturmbannführer Walther Rauff flew to Tobruk to receive "from Field Marshal Rommel the necessary instructions for the deployment" of his commando unit.[6] The deployment was thus imminent. The SS leader most likely did not speak personally with the prominent commander of the Afrika Korps on that day, however. Rommel was in the process of leading his troops, almost 500 kilometers to the east of Tobruk, in the decisive final phase of the First Battle of El Alamein; any transport facilities would have been much more urgently needed for supplies than for the conveyance of the Obersturmbannführer. Instead, Rauff was probably officially assigned to one of the Afrika Korps staff officers during the visit to Tobruk.[7] Thus, the statement "Disgusted with the idea, the 'Desert Fox'

1. Dienstkalender Himmlers, p. 473; on the individual Browder, pp. 418–430; on Amt VI: Kahn, p. 251ff.; Querg; Wildt, *Generation*, pp. 391–410; Mallmann, "Krieg," pp. 324–346.
2. RFSS appointment calendar, July 1, 1942, BAB, NS 19/1447.
3. Dienstkalender Himmlers, p. 477.
4. OKW/WFSt/Qu.I to Dt.Gen.b.HQu.It.Wehrm., July 13, 1942, BA-MA, RW 5/690.
5. OKH/GenStdH/Gen.Qu., April 28, 1941, regulations for the deployment of the security police and SD in army units, BA-MA, RH 22/155.
6. Recommendation for decoration by HöSSPF Italy, Feb. 25, 1945, BAB, R 70 Italien/19; British intelligence service summary, Oct. 23, 1942, NARA, RG 226, entry 11.9A, box 25, folder 637.
7. There is no record of this conversation in the Ia, Ic, or O.Qu. records of the PzAA in BA-MA; one explanation could lie in the indisputable priority of reporting on the battle at El Alamein, which took precedence over a notice about Rauff's appearance; aside from that, however, important Ic and O.Qu. files

apparently refused to discuss the matter and sent Rauff on his way" is hardly plausible; furthermore, it was based upon a highly dubious postwar declaration.[8] The RSHA unit was transported from Berlin to Athens on July 29, where it was standing by for transfer to Africa. The unit consisted of seven SS officers and seventeen noncommissioned officers and men. They were to be deployed first in Egypt and then, after the conquest of Egypt, in neighboring Palestine, where they would doubtless have been engaged first and foremost in the mass murder of the Jewish population.[9]

Using various sources, the membership of the entire leadership of this unit can be accurately identified. The commander, Walther Rauff, the son of a bank officer, was born on June 19, 1906, in Cöthen (Anhalt). In Magdeburg, where the family moved a year later, he attended school and completed his university entrance qualification in 1924. By his own admission, his parents raised him "with a national and soldierly consciousness." This preconditioning may have inspired the future SS officer to join the navy in 1924. Rauff became a lieutenant and commander of a minesweeper before he left the navy at his own request in late 1937 because of having committed "adultery." He had joined the NSDAP a few months before; in January 1938 he joined the SS as well. In April of that year Rauff was transferred to SD headquarters, where he initially specialized in mobilization affairs, and assessing which of the headquarters staff would be exempt from military service in the event of war.[10]

In this capacity, after the German attack on Poland in September 1939, Rauff participated in the security police and SD meetings under Heydrich's leadership and subsequently produced the minutes of those proceedings. Thus, the SS officer was fully informed about the mass murders that had been taking place in Poland since the beginning of the war.[11] After a voluntary interlude in the navy from 1940 to 1941, as commander of a flotilla of minesweepers on the Channel coast, Rauff returned to the RSHA at Heydrich's request and became head of *Amts* II D and VI F, which were both responsible for technical matters. The Obersturmbannführer also followed his chief to Prague when the latter was named Acting Reich protector of Bohemia and Moravia. There, Rauff led the technical communications organization of the new agency. The great respect he had for his director is shown by the fact that, according to his

of the PzAA for that day, which could indeed have contained references to the relevant conversation, have been lost.

8. Breitman/Goda/Brown, p. 154.

9. Dt.Gen.b.HQu.It.Wehrm. to OKW/WFSt/Qu.I, Sept. 14, 1942, BAB, NS 19/3695.

10. SS membership card, curriculum vitae, personnel report, BAB, SSO Walther Rauff; interrogation of Walther Rauff, June 28, 1972, BAL, B 162/3637, pp. 76f., 83f.; concise evaluation in EdH, vol. 3, p. 1195.

11. Cf. the meeting minutes signed by Rauff, BAB, R 58/825; on the mass crimes in Poland: Mallmann/Musial.

own statement, he and some "comrades" in Prague agreed that Heydrich must always be allowed to win when they played double card games together, because he "could not lose."[12]

Rauff, particularly through his activity as chief of *Amt* II D, became one of the key officers responsible for the mass destruction of the Jews. He was in charge of the technical equipment for the Einsatzgruppen in the Soviet Union—including, for example, the supply of vehicles and munitions.[13] In September 1941, he gave Friedrich Pradel, who was responsible for transport in his department, the assignment to modify vans so that people could be killed inside the sealed compartments through the introduction of carbon monoxide from the vehicles' exhaust. Soon thereafter, the first van was built accordingly. Trial gassings of Soviet prisoners of war from the Sachsenhausen concentration camp had produced promising results, and the decision was made to build additional models. By the summer of 1942, approximately 20 gas vans had been built and were being used to kill Jews in the Soviet Union and in Serbia.[14] In exile in Chile 30 years later, Rauff, when asked about his responsibility in the development of the instruments of murder, attempted to justify his part and to rationalize the mass murders at the time: "I cannot say whether I had misgivings about the use of the gas vans at the time. For me, the most important consideration was that the shootings created a great deal of stress for the men performing them, and this stress was eliminated by the use of the gas vans."[15] Clearly, it was precisely his decision-making authority and his familiarity with the process of rationalizing the extermination of the Jews that also made the resourceful Obersturmbannführer particularly well suited for the new position as head of a mobile death squad for the Middle East.

The other members of the commando's leadership cadre came from a wide variety of areas in the RSHA. Sturmbannführer Beisner, the head of the Arabian affairs *Amt* VI C 13, was appointed as a Middle East expert.[16] Obersturmführer Hans-Joachim Weise was another SS officer with close connections to Arab issues who joined Rauff's unit. Most recently as el-Husseini's RSHA liaison officer, Weise had initially received the assignment to establish an Einsatzkommando for Rommel's panzer army. By his own account, the directive came from Sturmbannführer Dr. Heinz Gräfe, who was leader of *Amt* VI C in the RSHA and thus responsible for the Soviet Union and the Far East.

12. SS membership card, curriculum vitae, personnel report, BAB, SSO Walther Rauff; interrogation of Walther Rauff, June 28, 1972, BAL, B 162/3637, p. 77f.
13. Interrogation of Walther Rauff, June 28, 1972, BAL, B 162/3637, pp. 80–85.
14. Kogon/Langbein/Rückerl, pp. 82–86; Beer, pp. 403–417.
15. Interrogation of Walther Rauff, June 28, 1972, BAL, B 162/3637, p. 87.
16. Interrogation of Wilhelm Beisner, Nov. 4, 1960, BAL, B 162/Vorl. AR 1650/67, p. 6ff.; memorandum on the interrogation of Wilhelm Beisner, Sept. 5, 1961, BAL, B 162/Vorl. AR 1650/67, p. 17f.

A short time later, however, the designated commando leader learned that the command had been transferred to the higher-ranking Rauff instead. Weise's primary task would now involve establishing communications with Arab collaborators, whom he was to recruit in large numbers to work for the Germans.[17]

Sturmbannführer Franz Hoth was responsible for the intelligence component within the commando. He was born in Stettin in October 1909 and completed an apprenticeship there before taking a position at a ship brokering agency in Brunsbüttelkoog. Hoth also became an active supporter of the Nazi cause and was the cofounder of the local NSDAP chapter. The young activist officially joined the party in December 1931. He joined the SA that same year, and in April 1933 transferred to the SS. It was supposedly his dedication to the "movement" that created problems for him with his employer. By his own account, Hoth was dismissed for this reason in August 1933, under various pretexts. After temporarily working in a fish cannery in Kiel, he gained a new perspective on life when he obtained employment at the SD headquarters in May 1934.[18] First as a desk officer in Berlin, then after April 1938 as departmental head in Oberabschnitt Donau, and after March 1940 as leader of the SD's Bremen section, he was repeatedly commended in his personnel reviews for his "exceptionally pronounced soldierly charisma," his National Socialist mind-set, and his organizational abilities.[19] In 1941, Hoth, like most of his colleagues in Rauff's commando, also completed a colonial training course at the SD officers' school in Berlin-Charlottenburg, followed that same year by a training course at the Italian colonial police academy in Tivoli, outside Rome. In July 1942, after completing this training, he joined Rauff's unit—no doubt at least in part because of his friendship with Rauff.[20]

Obersturmführer Herbert Werth was selected as head of the executive organization. Born in 1909 in Wolawapowska in the province of Posen, he studied law and political science in Berlin and Königsberg after qualifying for university admission. Werth joined the National Socialist movement during this time. He was active in the National Socialist German Students' League beginning in 1931. In August 1932 he joined the NSDAP, and in October of the following year, the SS. After completing his studies, he became a legal adviser to the German Labor Front in Königsberg and transferred one year

---

17. Interrogation of Hans-Joachim Weise, Jan. 12, 1965, BAL, B 162/16704.
18. SS membership card, service record, curriculum vitae, personnel report, BAB, SSO Franz Hoth; curriculum vitae, BAB, RuSHA Franz Hoth; report on interrogation of Franz Hoth, Mar. 15, 1946, BAL, B 162/Vorl. AR 1201/62.
19. Personnel report, BAB, SSO Franz Hoth.
20. Report on interrogation of Franz Hoth, Mar. 15, 1946, BAL, B 162/Vorl. AR 1201/62.

later, as a candidate for commissioner, to the Allenstein state police office. After passing the exam, Werth was transferred to *Amt* IV of the RSHA, the Gestapo headquarters, where he worked as an inspector until being sent to Athens.[21]

Obersturmführer Kurt Loba was given the responsibility for administrative affairs. Born in Stahnsdorf near Berlin in 1913, he began working for the police administration in Grossbeeren in 1930. Seven years later, he moved to the Gestapo office in Berlin. He had joined the SS and the NSDAP in 1933, a few weeks after Hitler came to power. He was transferred to *Amt* II at SD headquarters in the spring of 1938, and later served in the RSHA as an administrator. After he had applied for colonial service and completed a training course at the officers' academy in Berlin-Charlottenburg in the fall of 1940, the academy director called upon him to organize additional courses and supervise the participants. From there, the administrative specialist was assigned to Rauff's commando.[22]

The seventh and final SS officer in the unit, Untersturmführer Waldemar Menge, was responsible for communications. Born in August 1916 in Kirchheilingen in Thuringia, he was hired as a radio operator at SD headquarters in October 1936, following an apprenticeship and two-and-a-half years of service in the Reichswehr. He joined the SS in 1936 as well. After working as a radio operator at the Führer's headquarters during the war against Poland, Menge served as director of radio operations for the commander of the security police in Warsaw between November 1939 and April 1940. He was subsequently transferred to Tromsö, Norway, in the same capacity, before being assigned to Rauff in 1942.[23] Menge also appeared fully committed to the Nazi annihilation campaign against the Jews. Transferred to Minsk in Bielorussia after his assignment to Einsatzkommando Rauff as head of communications, Menge showed disgust at the behavior of SS-Helferin (auxiliary female staff) Lore K., who had dared to meet with a Jewish physician in the Minsk administrative office area. Shortly thereafter, in a mass execution at which Menge was also present, the doctor was killed, along with several thousand other Jews from Minsk. With reference to that specific murder, the Untersturmführer afterward told the SS-Helferin triumphantly that she could now no longer greet the man. On the same occasion, he reported on another SS officer in the administrative office

21. Curriculum vitae, BAB, RuSHA Herbert Werth; SS membership card, recommendation for promotion, BAB, SSO Herbert Werth.

22. SS membership card, BAB, SSO Kurt Loba; curriculum vitae, BAB, RuSHA Kurt Loba; interrogation of Kurt Loba, Oct. 27, 1964, BAL, B 162/16690; application by Kurt Loba for employment in the security police and in the SD for the colonies, BA-ZA, ZR 649/8.

23. Ibid Waldemar Menge; curriculum vitae, BAB, RuSHA Waldemar Menge; interrogation of Waldemar Menge, Dec. 14, 1961, BAL, B 162/1325, p. 429.

who had apparently felt faint during the shootings: "The coward collapsed, the spineless weakling."[24]

All the SS officers assigned to the Einsatzkommando were about the same age. Except for Rauff, Hoth, and Werth, all the officers were born between 1911 and 1916 and were therefore in their late twenties when they were ordered to Athens. Even the commander had just turned 36, and Hoth and Werth 32. Thus, the average age of these officers was clearly lower than that of the officers of the Einsatzgruppen in the Soviet Union, and differed even more from that of the officers of the Einsatzgruppen in Poland.[25] Aside from their relative youth, what stands out about these officers is their early adherence to National Socialism. Beisner, Weise, Hoth, and Werth—four of the seven SS officers—joined the NSDAP, SS, or SA before Hitler came to power and were therefore considered "alte Kämpfer" (old fighters). The record in this regard was held by Weise, who had joined the party at age 17. The three remaining SS officers, Rauff, Loba, and Menge, who did not join the NSDAP or one of its suborganizations until after January 1933, did not disagree with Nazi ideology. Rather, it was these officers' service in the Reichswehr or the police that represented the main reason for their later official membership in the party. And Loba and Menge, the two youngest SS officers in the Einsatzkommando, still both joined at the young age of 20.

Three members of the officer corps had already gained experience in mobile security police actions prior to their transfer to Athens. In April 1941 Beisner had led Commando Zagreb of Einsatzgruppe Yugoslavia.[26] In March 1939 Weise had belonged to one of the four Einsatzkommandos of Einsatzgruppe I, which marched into Prague when Czechoslovakia was completely occupied by the German army.[27] Hoth appeared to have been at least as active. He led an SD unit during the invasion of the Sudetenland in September 1938 and again a few months later during the occupation of the rest of Czechoslovakia. After September 1939, Hoth served in Poland as chief of the SD commandos of Einsatzgruppe I under Bruno Streckenbach; subsequently, he briefly led Group II, which was responsible for SD affairs, for the commander of the security police and the SD in the Generalgouvernement.[28] Finally, it is striking that at least four SS officers of the commando—Hoth, Weise, Loba,

---

24. Interrogation of Lore Laura K., Aug. 17, 1961, BAL, B 162/1683, p. 2025f.
25. Cf. Mallmann, *Türöffner*, pp. 437–463; Mallmann, *Menschenjagd*, pp. 291–316.
26. Interrogation of Wilhelm Beisner, Nov. 4, 1960, BAL, B 162/Vorl. AR 1650/67, p. 7; RSHA IV Gst circular, May 16, 1941, deployment of the security police and the SD in the former Yugoslavia, BAB, R 58/241.
27. Curriculum vitae of Hans-Joachim Weise, July 24, 1940, BA-ZA, ZR 358; interrogation of Hans-Joachim Weise, Jan. 12, 1965, BAL, B 162/16704; on the Einsatzkommando: cf. Mallmann, "Menschenjagd," p. 294.
28. Curriculum vitae of Franz Hoth, BA-ZA, ZR 559/13; interrogation of Georg Schraepel, April 17, 1964, BAL, B 162/3622, p. 227.

and Werth—had applied for foreign deployment in the colonies as early as 1940. Hoth and Weise even completed the six-week supplemental training course at the Berlin officers' academy together in January and February 1941, as well as subsequent officers' training at the Italian colonial police academy in Tivoli.[29]

In addition to the descriptions of the officer corps, a few statements about the men in the commandos can be made on the basis of chance archival discoveries. Friedrich Pohl, born in 1906 in Upper Silesia, applied to the police service in 1927 after secondary school, an incomplete apprenticeship as a draftsman, and five years working as a miner. From 1928 to 1936, he served in the riot police, first in Beuthen and then in Berlin. In June 1932, Pohl was among the cofounders of the then still illegal National Socialist Government Workers' Police Association. In 1936 he was transferred to the Gestapo and then to the RSHA, where he worked on internal affairs until November 1941. He then took a position in counterintelligence at the office of the commander of the security police in Warsaw, and in January 1942 he was assigned to the commander of the security police in Kraków. Pohl's next transfer, in July, was to take him to the Middle East via Athens.[30] Hauptscharführer Christoph Schölling, of the state police in Münster, almost joined Rauff's commando as well. He had already received his transfer orders and was given the assignment, as transport dispatcher, to move a number of vehicles for the commando from Italy to Africa. Due to the difficult transport situation, however, the convoy could not be shipped, and Schölling was ordered to accompany the vehicles back to Berlin.[31] Four other members of the unit came from the German capital as well. "Officers from the Berlin headquarters of the state police— Detective Sergeant Hausding, Detective Sergeant Grunert, Detective Pillasch, and Detective Däumer—were dispatched on July 29, 1942," announced a bulletin from that office.[32]

Aside from Beisner and Weise, the officers, men, and noncommissioned officers were not chosen because of their proven expertise in issues relating to the Middle East. Rather, the men were selected from the staff of the RSHA and regional offices based on the overall needs of the mobile commando.

---

29. Application by Franz Hoth for employment in the security police and in the SD for the colonies, BA-ZA, ZR 559/13; application by Hans-Joachim Weise for employment in the security police and in the SD for the colonies, BA-ZA, ZR 358; application by Kurt Loba for employment in the security police and in the SD for the colonies, BA-ZA, ZR 649/8; application by Herbert Werth for employment in the security police and in the SD for the colonies, BA-ZA, ZR 735/10; on the training course held in Tivoli beginning Mar. 1, 1941: cf. CdS/I B 1 to AA, Jan. 28, 1941, PAAA, R 99229[not in the reference list?].

30. Curriculum vitae, BAB, RuSHA Friedrich Pohl; interrogation of Friedrich Pohl, Aug. 9, 1967, BAL, B 162/8432, p. 124 ff.; interrogation of Friedrich Pohl, July 14, 1976, BAL, B 162/4409, p. 3074ff.

31. Interrogation of Christoph Schölling, July 18, 1984, BAL, B 162/Vorl. AR 209/80, p. 69.

32. Bulletin for the Berlin headquarters of the state police, No. 33, Aug. 14, 1942, BAL, B 162/Vorl. Dok.Slg. Versch. Ct. (file 179).

Officially, the deployment of the unit waiting in Athens was considered "confidential commando affairs" and was therefore subject to comprehensive efforts to maintain secrecy. However, the status of the unit was nevertheless public enough that the army postmaster had already assigned it the military postal service number 02039.[33] At first glance, the unit's total strength of just 24 men seems astonishing in light of the commando's primary task of destroying the Yishuv in Palestine. But the further history of the unit shows that during its deployment months later in the Tunisian theater of war, the commando was soon enlarged to more than four times its original strength.[34] The same would likely have taken place for the deployment in the Middle East. The original composition of the Rauff commando would thus have corresponded more closely to the character of an advance detachment, with considerable strengthening anticipated before the beginning of the actual mission.

In addition, the example of the Einsatzgruppen in Eastern Europe shows that the mass murders initiated by the Germans were often quickly supported by local collaborators and then smoothly implemented with only minimal German guidance after that.[35] Thus, a large number of the 137,346 Lithuanian Jews murdered after the beginning of December 1941 by Einsatzkommando 3 of Einsatzgruppe A were credited to the "raiding squad" under SS-Obersturmführer Joachim Hamann. Such a total would have been impossible for this 8- to 10-man German unit to reach alone, but Hamann had available numerous personnel from the Lithuanian police who performed much of the legwork and often participated in the executions as well.[36] In Riga, Latvia, the local auxiliary police unit of Victor Arajs, a Latvian nationalist and anti-Semite, soon took over the killing of a large share of Latvian Jews for Einsatzkommando 2.[37] Things were no different for the commandos of Einsatzgruppe D, which, up to the edge of the Caucasus, recruited thousands of local collaborators who then frequently assisted in murdering Jews as well.[38] Finally, Einsatzgruppen B and C, in their vast deployment territories, also routinely made use of local personnel, who proved indispensable in carrying out the mass murders.[39]

Collaboration in the annihilation of the Jews would have proceeded smoothly outside German-occupied Europe as well. As numerous reports had

---

33. Kannapin, p. 43.

34. Pz.AOK 5/Ic war diary, Jan. 11, 1943, BA-MA, RH 21-5/27; CdS/II C 1 to head of RK, April 22, 1943, BAB, R 58/860.

35. On local collaboration in the unleashing of pogroms in Kaunas, Riga, and Lemberg: Mallmann/Rieß/Pyta, pp. 61–69, 79–84, 89–96.

36. Stang, pp. 469–479; Scheffler, pp. 35–38.

37. Scheffler, p. 39.

38. Angrick, pp. 468–484.

39. Cüppers, *Wegbereiter*, pp. 172f., 198ff.; Pohl, "Einsatzgruppe," pp. 72–80; Pohl, "Hilfskräfte," pp. 206–224.

long attested, a vast number of Arabs, in some cases already well organized, were ready to serve as willing accomplices of the Germans in the Middle East. Immediately after the panzer army's arrival in Africa, the central task of Rauff's Einsatzkommando—the implementation of the Holocaust in Palestine—would have been quickly put into action with the help of those collaborators.

Chapter IX

Arab Opinion

Living in exile in Germany together with el-Husseini, al-Gailani, al-Qawuqji, and their respective supporters were numerous influential insiders who continued to command great respect and authority in the Arab world. In the summer of 1942 their common goal of driving out the British, establishing a Greater Arab Empire, and destroying Jewish life in Palestine seemed attainable. Consequently, many Arab exiles made even more forceful advances to the Axis during this decisive phase in order to improve their own position and be able to participate from the beginning in the expected "liberation" of the Arab World.

Fawzi al-Qawuqji had lived in exile in Berlin since early July 1941. After the failed anti-British revolts in Iraq and Syria, he treated himself to a luxurious lifestyle in the German capital while recovering from long years of privation in the underground resistance. In late July 1941 he wrote a memorandum addressed to General Felmy on the need for future German-Arab intervention in Iraq. In addition to discussing geography and desert warfare at length, he gave his anti-Semitism free rein in this memorandum, which was designed to ensure that the Germans would continue to consider him an ally. In terms of the propaganda content deemed most expedient, the guerrilla leader considered the "demonstration of the role of the Jews and their intrigues" to be particularly important.[1]

Thus, in view of the promising military situation, the call for freedom and independence for the Arab countries came from many sides in the summer of 1942. Former Egyptian minister Mourad Sidi Ahmed Pascha, who had been refused reentry into his homeland due to his pro-Axis stance, visited the German embassy in Geneva. Firmly convinced that the Germans and Italians would "liberate" Egypt, he offered his assistance and indicated his readiness to travel to Berlin for further discussions.[2] In Istanbul, at the same time, notable Arab nationalists who had congregated there in exile presented Legation Counselor Granow with the request for complete independence, particularly for Iraq, Syria, Lebanon, Transjordan, Palestine, and the Arab Emirates. The Axis powers were asked to provide such a guarantee within the scope of a public declaration. El-Husseini and al-Gailani were also asked by the nationalist leaders to advocate for the immediate deployment of the Arab Freedom Corps with Afrika Korps in Egypt and the adjacent Arab region "so that Arabs themselves will have the opportunity to fight for the liberation of their land from the English yoke."[3] This emphasis on the willingness to fight beyond Egypt for "liberation" and for the expulsion of the British also implied, of course, the commitment to eradicate the Jewish presence in Palestine.

The appeal to the Mufti and al-Gailani regarding the deployment of the Arab volunteers was directed to the right recipients. One of the key areas of activity for the two was to be the recruitment of Arabs for the German-Arab Battalion. The formation deployed with Sonderstab F was intended to serve first as an Axis propaganda instrument to promote Arab collaboration, and later as the core of future Arab armies that would be established through the generosity of the Germans. In the summer of 1942 the Arab collaborators' formation, like the Rauff commando, was waiting on the Greek mainland at Cape Sounion for deployment.[4] There were high expectations on both the German and Arab sides in terms of the propaganda impact that would be attained upon the formation's arrival in Arab territory. In January 1942 the Mufti and al-Gailani, in a discussion with General Felmy, had already calculated to what extent armed Arab collaboration could be expected after the arrival of the Axis troops. According to Grobba's notes from the meeting, the two explained

---

1. Memorandum by al-Qawuqji (undated/July 1941), BA-MA, RW 4/v.252.
2. DG Geneva to AA, July 1, 1942, PAAA, BA 61124.
3. Granow/AA to AA, July 1, 1942, PAAA, R 27332; Granow/AA to AA, July 4, 1942, PAAA, R 27332; translation of declaration by Arab nationalist leaders (undated/July 2, 1942), PAAA, R 27332; on the reaction of the Mufti: note by Woermann/AA, July 18, 1942, PAAA, R 27332.
4. OKW/WFSt/Abt. L staff instructions, June 21, 1941, BA-MA, RW 4/v.538; report by Kdr. Sonderstab F, Aug. 15, 1942, PAAA, R 27325; Tillmann, p. 354ff.

in detail "that virtually the entire Iraqi army, a strength of approximately three divisions, will join up with the German troops when they enter the Arab territory; that from the Greater Syrian area, volunteers in numbers equivalent to one or two additional divisions will come forward; and that perhaps tens of thousands of tribesmen will declare themselves ready to work with the German troops."[5]

The reality, however, turned out to be much more modest. Even the creation of Arab collaborator units in the Sonderstab F formation fell far short of the fanciful calculations. In early March 1942, the military officers were forced to report to the Foreign Office that the training of Arabs would achieve nowhere near the expected impact. In fact, volunteers had increasingly begun to request discharge in order to study in Germany. For this reason, the Wehrmacht urgently recommended that study opportunities with German financial support be immediately curtailed. In addition, al-Gailani and the Mufti were to be urged more forcefully to "keep the Arabs in line" better in the future.[6]

In August 1942, after more than half a year in existence, the German-Arab Battalion included only 243 Arabs; 24 men came from Iraq, 112 were Syrians or Palestinians, and 107 were from countries in northwestern Africa.[7] Given this outcome, Felmy complained that al-Gailani was not actively recruiting Arabs; instead, the former Iraqi prime minister was insisting on a military agreement with the Axis as a prerequisite for his own initiatives. In addition, both al-Gailani and the Mufti had called for a unit that would be exclusively Arab from the outset, with an all-Arab officer corps—a request that the OKH firmly rejected. In contrast to his rival, the Mufti at least made his assistance evident in the formation of the unit. Ultimately, however, he was able to make only a very modest contribution to its enlargement. Even so, thanks to his initiative and collaboration with the OKH, a formation of former Arab prisoners of war was created, which for a long time was the only Muslim formation in Sonderstab F.[8] Considering this limited success, Felmy cautioned that Germany could suffer a loss of prestige in the Arab world as a result. The general also warned that the conflict between the Mufti and al-Gailani could precipitate a general collapse of the Arab volunteer unit.[9]

The criticism expressed by the Wehrmacht regarding al-Gailani's halfhearted involvement with the German-Arab Battalion underlined yet again that the Mufti was still the most important personage among the Arab exiles. He

---

5. Note by Grobba/AA, Jan. 5, 1942, BA-MA, RW 4/v.691.
6. OKW/Abw/Abt. Ausl to AA, Mar. 6, 1942, PAAA, BA 61123.
7. Comments by Kdr. Sonderstab F (undated/mid-August 1942), PAAA, BA 61124.
8. Report by Kdr. Sonderstab F, Aug. 15, 1942, PAAA, BA 61124.
9. Ibid.; comments by Kdr. Sonderstab F (undated/mid-August 1942), PAAA, BA 61124.

worked tirelessly toward a consolidation of the German-Arab alliance, which had as its critical focus the "elimination" of the Yishuv. But even in exile in Germany he did not limit himself to anti-Semitic agitation; rather, he continued to actively pursue his vision of the annihilation of the Jews and the simultaneous creation of a pan-Arab Empire under his leadership, culminating in the establishment of a new caliphate. Zealously pushing the Axis powers to recognize the position he was striving for in the Arab world, and to safeguard it against possible rivals, the Mufti achieved considerable success, at least in Germany. Grobba proposed in February 1942 that the Palestinian be the head of state of a future Greater Syria, while al-Gailani was slated to head the government in Iraq. It appears that Ribbentrop also largely accepted, by May at the latest, el-Husseini's claim to a leadership role in Palestine and Syria.[10]

Shortly before Rommel's successful offensive resumed its course toward Egypt, the Mufti spoke on Radio Bari, and in a May 10 broadcast he again called the Arab world to pursue jihad against the West.[11] In addition to his activities in support of a military victory for the Axis, el-Husseini also initiated very specific steps to destroy the Jews in Palestine. With regard to this issue, direct communication between the Mufti and the Jewish Affairs department of the RSHA can be verified. Shortly after his first meeting with Himmler, el-Husseini paid a visit to the departmental head of *Amt* IV B 4, Obersturmbannführer Adolf Eichmann. On this occasion—the visit must have taken place in late 1941 or early 1942—Eichmann, by means of numerous statistics and charts, provided his extremely impressed guest a comprehensive view of the status of the Third Reich's "solution to the European Jewish question." The Mufti, in turn, informed Eichmann that he had already received Himmler's agreement that after the victory of the Axis powers, one of the advisers in Eichmann's Jewish Affairs department would go with him to Jerusalem to directly confront the most pressing issues. Eichmann was clearly charmed by the Mufti and met him several more times.[12] The concerns relating to the "Jewish question" in Palestine appear to have been resolved during the first meeting, however, as el-Husseini subsequently turned directly to Eichmann's relevant colleagues with regard to specific practical details. At least one discussion between the Mufti and Sturmbannführer Friedrich Suhr, the head of

---

10. Note by Grobba/AA, Feb. 7, 1942, PAAA, R 27332; note by Grobba/AA, May 30, 1942, PAAA, BA 61124.
11. Schechtman, p. 126.
12. Interrogation of Dieter Wisliceny, July 26, 1946, YVA, TR 3/129; on Wisliceny: Michman, "Täteraussagen"; Arendt, p. 37, in contrast, repeats Eichmann's defensive claim that he had been introduced to the Mufti only once, at an official function.

Amt IV B 4 b ("Jewish matters"), during the first half of 1942 was confirmed by Suhr's secretary.[13]

That same year, el-Husseini and al-Gailani also encouraged their associates to participate in SD training courses. In this connection, according to Weise, three of the former Iraqi prime minister's attendants and a confidant of the Mufti visited the Sachsenhausen concentration camp near Berlin in July.[14] Originally, al-Gailani had even wished to take part himself, because he wanted to "assess whether he could use the facilities of such a concentration camp as a pattern for equivalent institutions in Iraq."[15] Although neither al-Gailani nor the Mufti ultimately took part in the visit, their representatives paid close attention during the two-hour tour by the camp commandant. Weise, who was to depart for Athens with Einsatzkommando Rauff shortly thereafter, observed that the Arabs were extremely interested in the Jews in Sachsenhausen.[16]

It was not only the Arab exiles close to el-Husseini and al-Gailani who were striving to establish contact with the broad SS Empire. Even Indian nationalist circles were showing increasing interest. One of their leaders, Subhas Chandra Bose, had been living in exile in Berlin as well, since the spring of 1941. He clearly had great admiration for Himmler's SS apparatus and asked Himmler at a meeting in July 1942 for "special SS training" for a number of Indians in the Indian Legion that had been established in Germany.[17] That wish was soon fulfilled. Beginning in February of the following year, Indian soldiers were being trained in an RSHA course. Concerned about efficiency, Himmler specifically instructed that "the training have more of a police than an SS focus."[18]

At the end of June 1942, the capture of Tobruk must have served as the signal—both for the RSHA and for el-Husseini—to begin the practical implementation of the plans to exterminate the Jews in the Middle East. While the Einsatzkommando for the Afrika Korps was being formed in Berlin and sent to Athens to await further deployment, the Mufti intensified his work to "liberate" Palestine. He offered to travel to Egypt and engage in propaganda activities there in order to promote Arab collaboration.[19] He also called for the

---

13. Interrogation of Margaretha Reichert, Oct. 17, 1967, BAL, B 162/4172, p. 296; cf. recommendation for appointment by RMI, April 8, 1944, BA-ZA, ZR 37; recommendation for decoration by HSSPF France, Oct. 21, 1944, BAB, SSO Friedrich Suhr; Lozowick, p. 121f.

14. Note by Grobba/AA, July 17, 1942, PAAA, R 100702.

15. Ibid., June 26, 1942, PAAA, R 100702.

16. Ibid., July 17, 1942, PAAA, R 100702.

17. Von Trott zu Stolz/AA to RFSS personal staff, Aug. 21, 1942, BAB, NS 19/103; Keppler/AA to RFSS, Feb. 16, 1943, BAB, NS 19/3769; Kuhlmann, p. 262.

18. RFSS to Keppler/AA, Feb. 24, 1943, BAB, NS 19/3769.

19. Mufti to Duce (draft), Sept. 13, 1942, PAAA, R 27324.

German-Arab Battalion to be sent to Egypt.[20] On June 27, el-Husseini suggested to Ettel that he draft a public declaration promising Egypt its independence. In the Mufti's view, such a signal would "resonate greatly with the Egyptian people and lead to public resistance against the English."[21] This suggestion was promptly acted upon. The Germans and Italians circulated such a document on July 3. It stated: "In the moment in which their armed forces victoriously advance into Egyptian territory, the Axis powers solemnly affirm their unyielding intention to respect and safeguard the independence and sovereignty of Egypt. The armed forces of the Axis do not view Egypt as an enemy country, but rather enter with the goal of driving the English from Egyptian territory and pursuing military operations against England that will free the Middle East from British control."[22]

Accompanying this declaration, the Mufti announced, in a statement released to the German press on July 6, that the German-Italian victory in Egypt was creating great enthusiasm among the Arabs "because they would win the fight against their common enemies, England and the Jews, as well as the threat of Bolshevism." Rommel's successes, according to the Mufti, would have a great impact on the outcome of the war "because the loss of the Nile valley and the Suez Canal, together with the end of naval superiority in the Mediterranean and the Red Sea, would bring England's defeat in this war closer and mean the beginning of the end of the British Empire." In addition, el-Husseini attempted to articulate the close connection between the Axis and the Arab world in the common battle against the "united power of England and the Jews": "The Arab nation, which like the Axis powers suffered under the forced peace of Versailles, and which won the admiration of the Axis powers during its struggle for freedom, views the Axis forces advancing into Egypt as allies that will help it throw off its chains and free itself from its enemies. I am certain that Egypt and the other Arab countries in the Middle East will achieve their national goal of total freedom and sovereignty."[23]

El-Husseini had previously already offered to help with a concrete intervention in Egypt. On June 27, Ettel noted with regard to his suggestions: "In the course of the discussion with the Grand Mufti on June 27, he wondered whether it wasn't now time to smuggle Egyptian nationalists across the front into Egypt, through the English lines to the interior of the country, with the task of carrying out anti-English propaganda and acts of sabotage. The Grand

---

20. Note by Ettel/AA, Aug. 22, 1942, PAAA, R 27324; memorandum by Mufti to chief of OKW, Aug. 30, 1942, PAAA, R 27828.
21. Ibid., June 27, 1942, PAAA, R 27326.
22. Declaration by Reich government and Italian government, July 3, 1942, PAAA, BA 61124.
23. Press statement by Mufti, July 6, 1942, PAAA, R 27332.

Mufti believed he had suitable people available for this."[24] El-Husseini outlined his tactic of destabilizing the British position in the Middle East and preparing the region for the German invasion as follows: "Organizing and equipping guerrilla-style forces to be sent into Egypt and the other Arab countries to disrupt the enemy through the destruction of roads, bridges, and means of communication, and to create uprisings in the interior of the country. [...] Organizing regular Arab military units that will fight shoulder to shoulder with Axis troops, such units will have a positive effect on morale in the Arab countries and will appeal to the volunteers in the British army. [...] Sending weapons and ammunition to Egypt, behind enemy lines, and then to Palestine, Syria, and Iraq to prepare for uprisings and disruption of the enemy."[25]

The practical implementation of such plans to facilitate armed uprisings in the Arab world as the Axis troops approached seemed entirely realistic at that time. Numerous reports from travelers, informers, and agents regarding the atmosphere there created a telling picture of broad support for Nazi Germany and its Führer. Therefore, a Foreign Office scholar and authority on the Arab world submitted an expert report in the fall of 1942 in which he highlighted the following with regard to Arab relations with the Third Reich: "Parallels are often drawn between German and Arab history, and German unification is held up as a model for the anticipated Arab unification. German promises are accepted with absolute confidence, and the concern repeatedly expressed by leading Germans, including the Führer himself, for the current situation of the Arab people has greatly strengthened the positive feelings toward the German people." With regard to specific similarities, he wrote: "The struggle against Zionism and thus against the Jews is an undertaking that is approved by every Arab and supported to the extent it is possible. The Jews are seen as the mortal enemy."[26]

"Alexander," an informer classified as reliable, reported in June 1942 that in Syria the propaganda leaflets dropped from aircraft were much more effective than the bombings by the Axis. The leaflets were "eagerly collected" and saved like "relics." The people especially wanted leaflets containing the text written by el-Husseini himself, "because the words of the Mufti resonate strongly with the population."[27] The following month, the German vice consul in Iskenderun, Turkey, reported on the situation in Syria: "The Arabs' receptiveness to Axis propaganda continues to increase."[28] Accordingly, a German

---

24. Note by Ettel/AA, June 27, 1942, PAAA, R 27326.
25. Minutes by Ettel, Aug. 29, 1942, PAAA, R 27325; cf. [OKW] Ausl/Abw II war diary, July 13, 1942, BA-MA, RW 5/498.
26. Note by Steffen/AA, Nov. 6, 1942, PAAA, BA 61124.
27. Account of report by informer "Alexander," June 19, 1942, BA-MA, RH 2/1789.
28. Report by DVK Syria, July 24, 1942, BA-MA, RH 2/1790.

military handbook addressing political life in Syria listed almost exclusively pro-German parties and factions that would not oppose the arrival of the Wehrmacht but would instead collaborate.[29] That same year, the British secret service produced a situation analysis concluding that 95 percent of the population of Iraq was also quite positively disposed toward Germany.[30]

The Arabs, having seen Rommel's successful offensive get underway after the spring of 1942, clearly expected the Germans to march into the region in the near future. Additional hopes came with this expectation. In many countries in the Arab world, there were demonstrations of sympathy for National Socialism, and many adopted its symbolism. One informer who had traveled through Egypt in April reported that a complete change of mood had taken place there—in favor of the Germans. The majority of the population was now for the first time decidedly pro-Axis; people would pointedly greet each other on the street with the words "Heil Rommel." The same source reported from the main cities of Syria and Lebanon that during the night graffiti appeared on the walls with the words "Hitler, Ali's successor."[31]

Regarding the atmosphere in public life, an informer reported in greater detail in mid-August: "The pro-German attitude of the Muslim Arabs persists. The widely expressed wish is that the Germans will come and free the country from the occupying powers and save it from its distress. In order to be able to speak about Hitler in public, the Arabs use a series of pseudonyms; the most recent code name for Hitler is Haddsch Numur—'the Tiger.' Wishes for Hitler's victory often serve as greetings."[32] An example from a Beirut courtroom shows just how certain people sometimes were of "liberation" by the Axis. While an Arab lawyer was presenting his arguments for the defense in French, a motion was made requesting that the speech be repeated in Arabic. The presiding judge proposed simply letting the matter rest, on the remarkable grounds that "in three months the lawyer will address the court only in Arabic anyway."[33]

In Palestine, the enthusiasm for National Socialism and excitement about Rommel's advance also appeared unwavering. It was common for people to greet each other on the street with a "Heil Hitler,"[34] and one of Schellenberg's reports on the local situation said: "The extraordinarily pro-German attitude of the Arabs is due primarily to the fact that they 'hope Hitler will come' to drive

29. Kimche, *Pillars*, p. 36.
30. Simon, p. 34.
31. Vichy branch office report, April 27, 1942, PAAA, R 29533.
32. Report by informer "Antonius," Aug. 13, 1942, BA-MA, RH 2/1790.
33. DG Istanbul news and intelligence service, July 28, 1942, BA-MA, RH 2/1790.
34. Arnoni, p. 3.

out the Jews. Field Marshal Rommel has become a legendary figure. Thus, all
the Arabs today long for the arrival of the Germans; they continually ask when
the Germans will come and are downright distressed that they have no
weapons." Further, the head of the SD foreign intelligence service was able to
report on the impact of German radio propaganda: "The Arabs have great
confidence in a German victory. The German shortwave transmitter is heard
by few, but what is heard is soon spread among the Arabs—exaggerated in the
Oriental fashion and so embellished that the text is hardly recognizable."[35]

As such examples indicate, the crucial link between National Socialism and
the Arab cause—aside from the widespread fascination with Hitler himself—
was anti-Semitism. In the summer of 1942, an informer reported: "In the
Middle East, England is standing on the threshold of a defeat that will extend
from Khartoum to Iraq. The English have managed to make themselves hated
throughout the entire Middle East, especially because of their alliance with the
Jews."[36] And Ettel, who became a Middle East expert in the Foreign Office
after his expulsion from Iran, noted that same year: "The Arab question is
indissolubly connected to the Jewish question. The Jews are the mortal enemy
of the Arabs, as they are of the Germans. Anyone in Germany who is involved
with Arab politics must be a staunch and uncompromising enemy of the
Jews."[37] With regard to the situation in Iran, he noted in particular that there as
well anti-Semitic propaganda would have the best prospects for success.
Goebbels also noted in his diary on May 10, 1943, that Hitler had expressed
satisfaction with the anti-Semitic propaganda, which sometimes comprised 70
to 80 percent of German radio broadcasts abroad.[38]

In various Arab countries, evidence of steadily increasing resentment
against the Jews mounted during the German advance in the spring and summer of 1942. By this time, the Germans were not simply hoping that their anti-
Semitic propaganda would resonate with anti-Jewish attitudes in the Arab
territory and thus create common ground that could then be directed against
the Jews and against Britain's military position. Rather, during those weeks and
months there were already signs of a much more advanced, increasingly
tangible, autonomous insurgency that would involve the entire Middle East.

Regarding the situation in Egypt, an informer notified the Foreign Office
in July that forces considered pro-Axis were being disarmed by the English, as
a precautionary measure. However, that certainly did not avert the danger, as
"the disarmed Egyptians also posed a very uncomfortable threat to the

---

35. CdS/VI C 13 to AA, Dec. 21, 1942, BAB, NS 19/186.
36. Account of report by informer "Cuno I," Aug. 6, 1942, BA-MA, RH 2/1764.
37. Memorandum by Ettel/AA (undated/end of 1942), PAAA, R 27325.
38. Fröhlich, p. 261.

English. The English knew that the Egyptian soldiers would fight against them when the right moment came, especially once they were given the weapons."[39] This assessment had an entirely realistic basis, as is shown by the case of two Egyptian air force pilots who attempted to reach the German lines in early July. With orders from high in the military hierarchy and with the knowledge of King Farouk, Ahmad Sayudi Hussein took off in the direction of Rommel's headquarters on July 6 with numerous documents, secret maps, and a draft of a German-Egyptian treaty. After the unsuspecting Germans shot down the air-craft over the front—and the pilot was killed and all the secret material destroyed—a second aircraft took off the following day, piloted by the non-commissioned officer Muhammad Raduan. This time the pilot reached the German lines unharmed; however, he remained silent about his true assign-ment when he found out that his predecessor had been shot down and burned along with all the intelligence material. Raduan, who subsequently collaborated with the Germans, confirmed only that he had belonged to a secret Egyptian organization—as had his colleague who had been shot down.[40]

To intensify contacts with Egypt and prepare for the arrival of the Axis troops, the Abwehr had initiated a number of intelligence operations in the spring, without Italy's knowledge. After a failed attempt in July 1941 to smug-gle two German agents into Egypt by air, under the code name "Condor," the Abwehr planned to send its spies to Cairo by land.[41] Preparations were made for the scheme under the code name "Salam," and implementation began in early 1942. Two radio operators from the Brandenburg regiment, Hans Eppler and Hans-Gerd Sandstede, were selected; both had an excellent command of Arabic and English. They were tasked with establishing contact with pro-German circles in Cairo, including, in particular, the former Egyptian chief of general staff Aziz Ali el-Misri and the nationalist Free Officers.[42] Eppler and Sandstede were apparently even supplied with a letter of introduction from the Mufti.[43] They reached Cairo at the end of May after an adventurous trip of more than 2,000 kilometers. Contact with the Egyptians was successful, but radio communication was never established with the Abwehr, and on July 23 both agents were arrested by the British.[44]

---

39. Ettel/AA to AA, July 2, 1942, PAAA, R 27323.
40. Sonnleithner/AA to VAA/PzAA, July 28, 1942, PAAA, R 29537; Sonnleithner/AA to VAA/PzAA, July 29, 1942, PAAA, R 29537; note by Richter/AA, July 22, 1942, PAAA, R 60748; Schröder, *Deutschland*, p. 197f.
41. On Operation Condor: Faligot/Kauffer, p. 93ff.; Schröder, *Deutschland*, p. 182f.
42. Buchheit, p. 236ff.; Schröder, *Deutschland*, p. 190f.; Brockdorff, pp. 172–179; Eppler, *Geheimagent*.
43. Eppler, *Geheimagent*, p. 172f.
44. Buchheit, p. 236ff.; Schröder, *Deutschland*, p. 190f.; Brockdorff, pp. 172–179.

The above-mentioned el-Misri played a key role among Egypt's Islamists, nationalists, and anti-English forces. As a young officer, he had been involved in the resistance against the Ottoman Empire; after its collapse, he succeeded in establishing a career in the Egyptian army, which he led as chief of the general staff after 1939. Even the following year, when the British pressured him into retirement, el-Misri maintained excellent relations with the Germans, as well as with the nationalist Young Egypt movement and the Muslim Brotherhood, with whose leader, al-Banna, he was friends.[45] He also exerted a great deal of influence on the Free Officers, a nationalist secret society of Egyptian military officers. During the German-Italian advance in North Africa and the coup in Iraq, these officers had developed their own putsch plans against the British. Implementation was delayed yet again in 1941, however, on el-Misri's instructions.[46] The younger officers, Gamal Abdel Nasser and Anwar el-Sadat, who also belonged to the same circle, would later shape the postwar history of the country as presidents. Of Nasser it is known that, among other things, he was an enthusiastic reader and advocate of *The Protocols of the Elders of Zion*.[47] Sadat summed up the relationship between the Egyptian military and National Socialism when he stated concisely after the war, "We acted in complete harmony with them."[48]

The situation in Egypt—with tangible assistance, putsch plans, and widespread readiness to support the arrival of the Germans and the expulsion of the British—also existed on a similar scale in other regions of the Middle East. Because these countries, unlike parts of Egypt, were not planned to be occupied by the Axis powers, no focused assessment had yet been made of how the Arab societies there might respond to the approach of Rommel's Afrika Korps. However, available sources provide evidence indicating that in Palestine, Syria, Lebanon, Iraq, and Iran potential forces existed that had developed revolt plans and already begun terrorist activities long before the arrival of the Axis troops.

In a report from late June 1942, an Abwehr informer stressed the increasing possibility that the Arabs in Iraq, Syria, and Palestine could rise up together against the British.[49] Two weeks later, the same source reported that in Syria, Palestine, and Transjordan natives had formed a so-called anti-English committee. The members of this resistance movement were well informed about the military situation as well as the British infrastructure, including key bridges,

---

45. Schröder, *Deutschland*, p. 60ff.; Tibi, p. 172; Dessouki, p. 86; Faligot/Kauffer, p. 91f.
46. Tibi, p. 173; Arnoni, p. 5.
47. Schröder, *Deutschland*, p. 61f.; Arnoni, p. 11.
48. Sadat, *Revolt*, p. 38; Schröder, *Deutschland*, p. 61f.
49. Summary of report by "Pollux," June 30, 1942, BA-MA, RH 2/1790.

connecting roads, airfields, and military bases. Now the Arab population was just waiting for the best moment to rise up against the occupying power. All the preparations had already been completed.[50] After Allied troops were pulled out of Lebanon and Syria and transferred to the front in Egypt, anti-British protests took place in both countries in June, resulting in clashes with the remaining army units. According to various reports, some of these protests seem to have been carried out by women who were paid a daily amount of money to do so. The unrest was fueled by a secret Syrian organization that was supposedly supplied with intelligence and leaflets by the Axis powers. In any case, this organization's work contributed to the tension in the country, and discontent was increasing daily.[51]

In July, news of the existence of resistance groups surfaced in Aleppo, Syria. Likewise encouraged by the withdrawal of British and French troops, the organization was waiting for a favorable opportunity to proceed with terrorist acts against British military installations.[52] At the same time, reports poured in from the rest of the country regarding the activities of Arab terror groups that were blowing up bridges and trains as well as attacking vehicles. By the beginning of August the violence had become so intense that the British felt forced to send out a motorized battalion and an armored battalion to fight it.[53] Weeks later, however, in the north as well as the south, armed gangs were causing trouble. They carried out further attacks on rail lines and sabotaged British military installations. In addition, in the last half of September, signs of an uprising in the area of Palmyra, Syria, intensified; in the course of the revolt, the Mosul-Haifa pipeline was ruptured and the British army became embroiled in heavy fighting. A few days later, it emerged that the oil pipeline had in the meantime been blown up in several locations, and that the uprising was gaining further strength.[54]

In Iraq, evidence of anti-British activities and a strong potential insurrection also mounted in the summer of 1942. As early as mid-May, a German informer had reported that gangs were being formed there under the leadership of Iraqi intellectuals. They were active on the borders with Syria and Transjordan, with transport convoys as their primary targets.[55] On July 6, the Iraqi-Syrian railway was attacked, followed a few days later by attacks on the Mosul-

50. Summary of report by "Pollux," July 14, 1942, BA-MA, RH 2/1790.
51. Ibid., July 1, 1942, BA-MA, RH 2/1790; summary of report by "Pollux," July 2, 1942, BA-MA, RH 2/1789; report by "Pollux," July 10, 1942, BA-MA, RH 2/1790.
52. Report by "Kastor," July 23, 1942, BA-MA, RH 2/1790.
53. Summary of report by OKW/Ausl/Abw Abt. I, Aug. 6, 1942, BA-MA, RH 2/1790.
54. Report by "Pollux," Sept. 8, 1942, BA-MA, RH 2/1790; summary of report by OKW/Ausl/Abw, Sept. 21, 1942, BA-MA, RH 2/1790; report by Abwehr station Romania, Sept. 25, 1942, BA-MA, RH 2/1790.
55. Summary of report by "Pollux," May 18, 1942, BA-MA, RH 2/1789.

Haifa pipeline, which was damaged in multiple locations.[56] In August, nationalist Arabs attacked the road between Damascus and Baghdad, which had just been completed, with many casualties. Just three days after the inauguration of the roadway, terrorist attacks killed two Englishmen.[57]

Rommel's advance and the possible defeat of the British were closely followed in Palestine as well, where disturbances took place as in the other Arab countries. In July, seeing the German military successes, the fellahin suddenly began to refuse to deliver the amount of grain specified by the mandatory power to their Jewish buyers. The police were summoned, and armed conflict broke out in many villages, resulting in numerous deaths.[58] In Gaza as well, in the summer of 1942, the members of the local radical Arab organization were discussing the appropriate time to attack the British. The group belonged to the followers of el-Husseini. The local leader, Abdul al-Qudwa, who had married into this prominent family and was thus a distant relative of the Mufti, argued for waiting and appealed to his comrades' patience. Majid Halaby, a young radical who had years of terrorist experience, particularly against the Jews in Palestine, and who had been based in Gaza only since the spring of 1940, held the contrary view. In opposition to al-Qudwa, he called for an immediate attack against the British and the Yishuv. The group split as a result. Al-Qudwa drove Halaby from his house and banished him from the local extremist group. Halaby then convened meetings with his own followers. From the beginning, the young Rahman al-Qudwa, the son of Abdul, belonged to this radical faction in Gaza; at age 14, he broke with his father over the issue. Rahman then went to live with the radical Halaby and enthusiastically absorbed his crude fantasies of violence against the Jews and the British. Significantly influenced by this obscure Arab terrorist and the war years in Palestine, Rahman achieved greater popularity in later years under his nom de guerre, which was conferred on him by Halaby: Yasser Arafat.[59]

An informer's report from July 1942 indicates how heated the atmosphere in Palestine had become in anticipation of the Germans' arrival. According to this report, some units of the British 9th Army remained in Palestine to protect the Jewish population from Arab assaults, despite the critical military situation on the Egyptian front.[60] Such protective measures on the part of the manda-

---

56. Summary of report by OKW/Ausl/Abw, July 21, 1942, BA-MA, RH 2/1790.
57. Report by "Pollux," Aug. 6, 1942, BA-MA, RH 2/1790.
58. Donauzeitung, Aug. 25, 1942.
59. Kiernan, p. 101ff.; the young Arafat lived underground with Halaby until 1944, when Halaby was killed by supporters of the Mufti in Jerusalem, cf. ibid., pp. 108–112.
60. Summary of report by informer "Cuno," July 31, 1942, BA-MA, RH 2/1785; even by the fall of the following year, the situation seemed largely unchanged; according to a report by the military attaché at the German embassy in Ankara, the British in Palestine were forced to delegate military units to police service, as

tory power were urgently required during those months, as thousands of Arab soldiers deserted the British army in the course of the German advance. By 1943, 8,000 Arabs—7,000 from Palestine—had deserted with their weapons and gone into hiding, in order to be able to join Rommel's troops after the eagerly awaited invasion.[61] "The animosity between Arabs and Jews in Palestine is as great as ever," stated Schellenberg in August 1942, with regard to the tangible impact of the Arab potential for violence. "For example, before dusk all the Jews disappear from public venues and the streets, so by dark only Arabs are left on the streets."[62]

Thus, in the Middle East, an overall picture emerges that contains many conspicuous indications of an Arab movement to revolt against the British. With the appearance of Axis troops in those countries, the potential—in keeping with the thinking behind deploying Einsatzkommando Rauff—would doubtless no longer have been directed solely against British authority but increasingly at the Jewish minority as well. The situation in the Middle East during the summer of 1942 was therefore very reminiscent of that of the previous year in Eastern Europe, and there is no reason to believe that the anti-Semitic potential of Lithuanian, Latvian, or Ukrainian nationalists was any different than that of the Arabs awaiting the German Wehrmacht.[63] Knowledge of the pogroms and massacres in the western Soviet Union in the summer of 1941 allows one to imagine the will to destroy that would have been unleashed by the Arabs, especially in Palestine, once Axis troops crossed the Suez Canal, if not sooner.

"the Arabs now want to resolve the Jewish question," DG Ankara to AA, Nov. 30, 1943, BA-MA, RH 2/1791.
61. Hurewitz, p. 119; Bethell, p. 148.
62. CdS/VI C 13 to AA, Aug. 26, 1942, PAAA, R 101022.
63. Mallmann/Rieß/Pyta, pp. 61–69, 79–84, 89–96.

Chapter X

The Jews of Palestine React

The deadly threat that emerged in the summer of 1942—from Rommel's rapid advance on one side and from the open animosity of the Arabs on the other—was carefully recorded within the Yishuv. Tension gripped the Jewish communities. However, individual reactions varied considerably. Some attempted to hide in Christian monasteries to escape the approaching Germans; others procured cyanide as a precaution, preferring suicide to life under Nazi occupation.[1] Arnold Paucker, a 21-year-old volunteer in the British army at the time, recalled how the relatively unconcerned mood within the Yishuv changed during those summer months, and Rommel's advance was taken very seriously.[2] An informer working for the Germans reported that between the seizure of Tobruk and September 1942, 15,000 emigrants had arrived in Jerusalem from Egypt alone. According to his account, the mood was subdued and apprehensive.[3] In August, another informer working for the Germans spoke of numerous Jewish refugees from Egypt who, as a result of the panzer army's offensive, had sought refuge in Palestine.[4] In this highly dangerous situation, with Rommel's troops only a few days' march away and with the Arab population largely hostile and ready to collaborate with the

---

1. Segev, p. 492; Hyamson, p. 153.
2. Letter from Arnold Paucker to the authors, May 30, 2005.
3. Report by informer "Milton," Sept. 22, 1942, BA-MA, RH 2/1784; Krämer, *Jews*, p. 156f.
4. Report by "Pollux," Aug. 7, 1942, BA-MA, RL 2 II/486.

Germans when they arrived, secret chalk marks appeared on Jewish houses overnight. No one was able to explain them initially, but eventually it was revealed that the Arabs, confident of Rommel's arrival and the resulting change of government, had already staked their claims to the Jews' property.[5]

Assaults, everyday violence, and threats to their very existence were nothing new to the Jews of Palestine in the summer of 1942. Rather, the need for self-defense had long been part of the collective identity of the Yishuv. The pogrom of 1920 in Jerusalem had emphatically underscored this requirement. As a consequence of those events, the Haganah, the "Hebrew defense organization in Palestine," was founded on June 12 of that year, at the initiative of the writer Vladimir Jabotinsky. It would serve as the central armed organization of the Yishuv until the founding of the state twenty-eight years later. Not officially recognized by the mandatory power, the organization in the early years was not conceived as the expression of a Jewish executive authority or an asset to be used against the mandatory power. Rather, the arming of various members of the Yishuv was intended to serve as a purely defensive measure for all the unarmed citizens, to help bridge the gap until the arrival of British law enforcement personnel in the event of an Arab attack.[6] But when the Arab revolt broke out in April 1936, the Haganah was also largely unprepared for the scale and the organization of the Arab violence. The self-criticism that followed promoted the view that the Jewish community needed to efficiently arm itself and be better prepared for future clashes and armed conflicts.[7] Moreover, David Ben-Gurion, chairman of the Jewish Agency and the Zionist Executive after 1935, and therefore one of the most important spokespersons for the Yishuv, recognized the ideological overlaps between the National Socialists and elements of the Arab world early on. In November 1936 he had warned the Palestinian Jews about a potential invasion by Hitler and the significantly increased danger this would represent. He said it would be "the greatest catastrophe the world has ever experienced."[8]

Following the experience in the Arab revolt, the Haganah completely restructured itself. In the fall of 1939, a general staff was created to replace the regional commands, allowing for centralized leadership of the organization based on the prevailing conditions.[9] By April 1937, the Haganah had already reached a strength of 17,000 men and 4,000 women; at the same time, approximately 10,000 pistols, 4,500 rifles, and 230 submachine guns were stored

5. Koestler, p. 80.
6. Bauer, *Cooperation*, p. 182f.
7. Aronson, *Hitler*, p. 19; Pail, p. 204.
8. Quoted in Segev, p. 433.
9. Pail, p. 194.

away.[10] The revolt also led to a fundamental strategic reorientation in addition to the reorganization. After much pressure from the Haganah, the Zionist leadership abandoned its previous policy of Havlagah, restraint and measured self-control, and opened the door to possible offensive action against Arab terrorists.[11] Exclusive self-defense, the traditional image of the kibbutznik in the lookout tower, was thus superseded for the first time. Now the Haganah was ready to "cross the fence" and strike back outside its own terrain.

The most important opposition to the dominant Haganah had already formed a more militant resistance organization. In 1931, a group of officers had split off from Haganah, disagreeing with its defensive posture, and in April 1937 they finally took the name Irgun Zwai Leumi ("National Military Organization"). The organization—known as Irgun for short, or Etzel (an acronym for the Hebrew initials)—was now led by Jabotinsky.[12] Politically, it was close to the Revisionist Party, founded in 1925 by Jabotinsky after opposing the policy of the World Zionist Organization under Chaim Weizmann. This right-leaning group within Zionism called itself revisionist because, among other things, it advocated for the inclusion of Transjordan, which had been split off by the British in 1922, into the future Jewish homeland.[13] In August 1937 the Irgun abandoned its previous restraint and began responding to Arab terror with reprisals. When the British then executed its members, the organization reacted by broadening the attacks against the Arabs. The attacks widened the gulf between the revisionists and the Jewish Agency, which resolutely condemned the Irgun's course of action.[14]

The British personnel shortage, which became obvious during the revolt, ultimately proved positive for the Yishuv. The mandatory power decided in May 1936 to establish a Jewish supernumerary police force in order to maintain control over the territory without a massive troop buildup. This newly formed auxiliary police force grew quickly in numbers and importance. From 1,300 members in June 1936 and 3,000 in October, it had grown to 22,000 by July 1939. Although the men were trained and led by British officers, the entire force was in effect under the control of the Haganah and provided the legal basis for organizing Jewish self-defense in Palestine.[15]

In addition to this auxiliary police force, a special unit created by the British officer Orde Wingate soon began targeted actions against Arab terror-

---

10. Bauer, *Cooperation*, p. 183.
11. Schiller, p. 166; Katz, pp. 13f., 47f.
12. Bauer, *Cooperation*, p. 184; Katz, pp. 13–17; Morris, p. 120.
13. Morris, p. 108; Katz, p. 4f.
14. Bethell, p. 39f.; Morris, p. 147; on the radical Lehi (Lochamei Cherut Israel, "Freedom Fighters for Israel") or Stern Group (named after its leader, Abraham Stern): cf. Brenner, pp. 114–141.
15. Pail, p. 197; Bauer, *Diplomacy*, p. 11; Cohen, *Strategy*, p. 174ff.

ists. Wingate, like many other Britons, was initially sympathetic to the idealized Arab struggle for independence. But because of the perspective he gained in Palestine he became a staunch Zionist. In May 1938, he created the Special Night Squads, a mobile task force of no more than 200 men that was comprised primarily of Palestinian Jews, with only a limited number of British members.[16] Wingate's special unit broke both with the previous British defensive stance toward Arab terrorism and with the Zionist concept of Havlagah and actively prepared for the expected revolt. The unit operated at night and was thus able to directly track hostile commandos; after terrorist acts, reprisals were often carried out in the Arab villages from which the terrorists had come. The Special Night Squads were extremely successful with this new strategy. However, the unit was disbanded because of the new white-paper policy—that is, for political reasons—in the summer of 1939. Wingate was transferred to Burma, where he died during the war.[17]

The publication of the white paper in the spring of 1939 abruptly ended the hope of putting down the Arab revolt militarily. For the Yishuv, this was a bitter disappointment.[18] Weizmann, the president of the World Zionist Organization, attempted to put the Jewish community's bleak outlook—given the disappointing British policy and the German threat—into words. At the conclusion of the 21st Zionist Congress in Geneva on August 24, he said, "I take leave with a heavy heart [...], darkness prevails all around us, and we cannot see through the clouds."[19] One week later, World War II began with the German assault on Poland. In September 1939, because of the outbreak of war in Europe, the Jews in Palestine feared air attacks with poison gas. Other reactions included increased food purchases and a run on the banks.[20] The Yishuv's attitude toward the British for the next few years was characterized by Ben-Gurion in 1939 in an oft-quoted phrase: "We must fight the war as if there were no white paper and fight the white paper as if there were no war."[21] In reality, wartime events caused opposition to the white paper, and thus the Jews' direct opposition to the British was put on hold in the following years; Irgun also shared this fundamental position at least until 1944.

The British Empire's position, by contrast, was conditioned by the fear of possibly antagonizing the Arabs through a pro-Jewish policy. The mandatory power even attempted to disarm the Haganah, which in recent years had pro-

---

16. Bowden, p. 166f.; Bethell, p. 35; Pail, pp. 192, 201f.; Beckman, p. 9f; in detail: Sykes, *Wingate*.

17. Sykes, *Kreuzwege*, p. 199ff.; Schiller, p. 159ff.

18. Pail, p. 196; Zweig, *Palestine*, p. 212ff.; Zweig, *Britain*, p. 44ff.

19. Quoted in Bethell, p. 72.

20. Hyamson, p. 147.

21. Quoted in Sykes, *Kreuzwege*, p. 222; cf. Cohen, *Origins*, p. 96; Cohen, *White Paper*, p. 728; Ball-Kaduri, pp. 404–415.

vided an invaluable service in stabilizing Palestine. Thus, in early October 1939, the British police detained forty-three of the organization's members in an illegal training camp. Among them was the future Israeli defense minister Moshe Dayan. The men were sentenced to long prison terms on October 30. This was a clear signal to the Yishuv that the previous policy of arming their members would no longer be accepted.[22] Additional arrests took place in the following months.[23] The British also attempted to seal off the country from further Jewish immigration. Even when news of the mass murders by the Germans in Europe became known, the mandate administration did not change the restrictive immigration regulations. This cruelty was justified by supposedly providing protection from German spies, who could slip into Palestine disguised as Jewish refugees. The British attitude also had a negative impact on Palestine's community of Jews of German origin. Since the beginning of the war, the "Jekkes" had been under general suspicion of being infiltrated by the Gestapo or the Abwehr. For this reason, they were excluded from certain positions by the British army and had to endure discrimination in terms of advancement.[24]

With the Aliyah Beth, the "illegal" immigration, as the British designated it, the revisionists in particular attempted to respond to the changed immigration regulations of the mandatory power and help save the endangered Jews in Europe after 1939. Refugees set off for Palestine in often barely seaworthy boats and met fierce resistance from the British there. Warships patrolled the coast, attempting to prevent the refugees' safe landing. Immigrants who were apprehended were initially interned in Palestine; after 1940, as a deterrent, they were taken to an internment camp in Mauritius.[25] The adverse conditions in Palestine as well as in Europe resulted in Aliyah Beth's steady decline during the first year of the war; immigration did not increase again significantly until 1944. Nevertheless, additional ships did attempt to reach the coast of Palestine during the war years.

The names of two ships symbolize these desperate attempts. In December 1940, the *Patria* was to take on passengers from three refugee ships that the British had captured the previous month in Haifa and transport them to Mauritius. By smuggling a bomb on board, the Haganah attempted to damage the ship and prevent its departure. The explosive's power had been fatally miscalculated, however. After the explosion, the *Patria* sank, killing 252 people.[26] In December 1941, the *Struma*, a former cattle carrier, set out for Palestine

22. Cohen, *Strategy*, p. 180f.; Zweig, *Britain*, p. 158f.; Dayan, pp. 39–44.
23. Zweig, *Britain*, p. 159.
24. Gelber, p. 326.
25. Pail, p. 195; Hyamson, p. 149f.; Zweig, *Britain*, pp. 51–88; EdH, vol. 1, pp. 24–30.
26. Sykes, *Kreuzzuege*, p. 244f.; Hyamson, p. 150; Zweig, *Britain*, p. 73ff.

from the Romanian harbor of Constanţa. On board were 769 Jews who had managed to elude the Germans and their fellow Romanians. The now barely seaworthy ship stopped in Istanbul to allow the passengers to obtain immigration visas. But because the visas could not be procured there, the *Struma*, after weeks of waiting, was forcibly towed out of the harbor at the end of February and abandoned to its fate on the high seas without fuel or provisions. The ship sank shortly thereafter—possibly due to a torpedo mistakenly launched by a Soviet submarine. Only one passenger survived.[27] Despite the dangerous voyage and the inflexible attitude of the British, approximately 20,000 "illegal" immigrants succeeded in reaching Palestine during the war.[28]

The country itself experienced a rapid economic upswing after the initial crisis in the fall of 1939; full employment soon prevailed again in the Yishuv. War production on behalf of the Allies reached a total of 14 million dollars in 1941. The following year, production rose to 32.4 million dollars, which corresponded to a 40 percent share of the country's total manufacturing. In the meantime, 75 percent of the workers had been organized in the Histadrut, the Jewish labor organization. The union had a total of 126,000 members and was the country's largest industrial organization.[29] The Palestinian Jews' contribution to the victory over Nazi Germany and fascist Italy was not limited to war production alone, however. Just four months after the German attack on Poland, the Jewish Agency was able to present a list with the names of 134,000 Palestinian Jews who had declared their readiness to serve in the British army. Within a very short time, every second Jewish man and 20,000 women of the Yishuv had reported for military service.[30]

Finally, the Jews of Palestine became aware of the danger of a German attack in the Middle East after Germany had defeated France and was preparing to invade England. With the arrival of the Afrika Korps and the offensive that brought the Axis powers to the Egyptian border in April 1941, the threat level had increased significantly.[31] In the Yishuv, this led to discussions about combining forces. As a result of these deliberations, the national command declared on May 15 that the Haganah would be the Yishuv's sole defensive organization. Four days later, the Plugot ha'Mahatz (the "Striking Force"), or Palmach, for short, was established. These professionalized units, stationed in various locations throughout the country, would perform special commando

27. Zweig, *Britain*, pp. 118–134; Sykes, *Kreuzwege*, p. 246ff.; Hyamson, p. 153f.
28. Segev, p. 500.
29. Hyamson, p. 152; Hurewitz, p. 132f.; Schiller, p. 170f.; Epstein, pp. 21–26.
30. Segev, p. 490.
31. Dayan, p. 49; Bauer, *Diplomacy*, p. 124ff.

missions.[32] Itzak Sadeh, one of the key Haganah officers who had led Special Night Squad missions during the Arab revolt, was named commander of the Palmach. Many of the first members of the new organization had also previously belonged to Wingate's special units.[33] The Palmach was founded to build up the core of a future Jewish army from the many tasks of the Haganah. The first members were no longer "weekend warriors" as they had been in the Haganah; from the beginning, they were to be lodged in barracks and were to carry out "civilian" activities only as cover. The beginning, however, was difficult. Six months after its founding, the Palmach had a membership of only 460 women and men, who, moreover, could not be trained because of an inadequate budget.[34]

Nevertheless, the first deployments on behalf of the United Kingdom followed immediately after the restructuring of the Jewish self-defense organization. Because the British feared the arrival of German aircraft in Syria and their use of the fuel supplies there and in Lebanon, a sabotage commando unit was organized to destroy the refineries in Tripoli. It consisted of 23 Haganah members, led by Tsvi Spector. The assignment was to be carried out by sea, using the *Sea Lion*, a ship belonging to the British Palestinian administration that was originally intended for pursuing illegal Jewish immigrants. After a few preparations, the members of the unit boarded the ship on May 18 and set out for Lebanon. After that, no information was ever found with regard to the ship or the commandos. Evidence suggests that some men may have survived an explosion on board or fighting on land and were executed only later in captivity.[35]

When German aircraft landed in Syria a short time later, in conjunction with the intervention in Iraq, Great Britain decided to invade. Before the beginning of the military operation by Commonwealth troops and two Free French regiments, 33 Jews from Palestine (all members of the Palmach, with one exception) were also assigned to the units as scouts and local guides. Even before the attack was launched on June 8, 1941, individual Jewish reconnaissance squads had located secure road connections on the other side of the border. Moshe Dayan was heavily wounded and lost an eye in the engagements with Vichy troops during the first days of the invasion.[36] Meanwhile, in Greece, approximately 100 Jews from Palestine were killed, and up to 1,700 fell into the hands of the Germans as British prisoners of war.[37] One of them was

32. Bauer, *Diplomacy*, p. 145f.; Sachar, p. 234; Hurewitz, p. 128.
33. Ibid., pp. 139–148; Sachar, p. 234.
34. Sachar, pp. 149f., 163–167.
35. Roshwald, p. 66; Sykes, *Kreuzwege*, p. 237f.; Bauer, *Diplomacy*, p. 155f.
36. Bauer, *Diplomacy*, pp. 157–162; Sykes, *Kreuzwege*, p. 238; Dayan, pp. 51–58.
37. Hyamson, p. 153; Hurewitz, p. 127.

Yitzhak Persky, the father of future Israeli prime minister Shimon Peres. He made many escape attempts, lived in hiding in Greece for a year, fell into German captivity again, and then finally succeeded in reaching the Allied lines on his third attempt.[38]

During this time, however, Palestine had also become a real theater of war. From 1940 to 1942, German and Italian bombers carried out numerous air attacks on cities such as Haifa and Tel Aviv.[39] In a June 1941 bombing of Haifa, the casualties included the residents of a Jewish nursing home.[40] Additional air attacks in July of the following year heavily damaged the harbor, the airport, the train station, and the refineries there.[41] A German informer who was in the mandate territory in July and August 1942 counted 25 attacks during that period alone.[42] Following many such experiences, numerous air-raid shelters were built in Palestinian cities. In addition, the Yishuv established an antiaircraft corps, comprised primarily of young women.[43]

As the war increased greatly within the public consciousness, discussions took place about the appropriate response to the Nazi threat. The debate focused on priorities. One side maintained that all available forces should volunteer to join the British army, in order to effectively fight against Germany on the Allied side. The other side argued that the Yishuv should concentrate on and strengthen its own self-defense forces. The Palestinian Jews should not fight in the British army in faraway theaters of war, but instead should be marshaled locally in the ranks of the Haganah to defend their homeland.[44]

In connection with the effort to contribute to the Allied war effort, the many initiatives to create special Jewish units within the British army had a significant impact. Since the beginning of the war, Weizmann had sought the consent of the mandatory power to create such formations with their own insignia. It was his initial goal to form a division of approximately 10,000 men. Although Chamberlain refused the request, the British chief of general staff had essentially already approved the formation of a Jewish division in December 1939, which had led to euphoria among the Zionists at the time. That consent by the British military had no immediate consequences, however. Churchill, prime minister since May 1940, also gave his agreement in principle

38. Peres, pp. 63–66.
39. OKW/Ausl/Abw I to LFSt/Ic, Dec. 7, 1940, BA-MA, RL 2 II/486; report by LFSt/Ic on attack on Haifa, June 12, 1941, BA-MA, RL 2 II/486; report by LFSt/Ic on attack on Haifa, July 8, 1941, BA-MA, RL 2 II/486.
40. Segev, p. 492; report by LFSt/Ic, June 11, 1941, BA-MA, RL 2 II/486.
41. Report by "Pollux," Aug. 7, 1942, BA-MA, RL 2 II/486.
42. Report by "Milton" (undated/Sept. 1942), BA-MA, RH 2/1784.
43. Report by "Theobald," July 4, 1942, BA-MA, RL 2 II/486.
44. Bauer, *Diplomacy*, p. 174ff.; Segev, p. 494.

to an entirely Jewish unit in October of that year, but concrete measures to implement it were repeatedly postponed.[45]

The British position came from the desire—seemingly quite absurd given the reality of the situation—to avoid further antagonizing the Arabs. Thus, the military officers asserted that despite the overwhelming number of Jewish volunteers in the first year of the war, only an equal number of Jewish and Arab recruits could serve in noncombatant units. The strength of the units was consequently determined by the number of Arab volunteers, which was considerably less than the number of Jews. According to the British war secretary, only 9,041 Palestinian Arabs reported for service in the British army during the entire war. By comparison, the number of Jewish volunteers amounted to 15 times that in the first weeks of the war alone.[46] In light of the German victories in Western Europe, the British began to gradually pull back from this policy in 1940. A mixed Jewish-Arab unit, the Palestine Buffs, was formed in September. Its membership, however, was still equally balanced between Jews and Arabs.[47] In May 1941, after the Axis powers' alarming military successes in Yugoslavia, Greece, and North Africa, the British agreed to the Jewish request that this quota be abolished. From then on, the Jewish combat units were organized into companies; however, they were still not allowed to be joined into battalions or regiments with corresponding headquarters, staffs, and greater operational prominence. Not until the summer of 1942, when Palestine was under immediate threat, did the British military officers decide to create special Jewish infantry battalions from the Buffs and establish separate Arab units alongside them.[48]

After the extreme hesitation with which the Yishuv's efforts to create Jewish combat units had been considered by England, Palestinian Jews began to look around for other allies. On the other side of the Atlantic, a highly successful campaign developed in support of the Jewish army. In the United States in 1942, according to reports by the Deutsches Nachrichtenbüro, full-page advertisements repeatedly promoted the cause. Although the project initially met with widespread criticism, support grew significantly after events took an unfavorable turn for the Allies in Libya. For example, an appeal signed by 200 prominent American citizens was published advocating the creation of four to five Jewish divisions. Shortly thereafter, full-page advertisements again

45. Laqueur, p. 561; Hurewitz, p. 129.
46. Peters, p. 352; Melka, *Axis*, p. 135.
47. Hurewitz, p. 128.
48. Sykes, *Kreuzzuege*, p. 251f.; Bauer, *Diplomacy*, p. 142; Hurewitz, p. 128.

appeared in the United States, raising the telling question of how much longer the democracies could afford to continue suffering defeat after defeat.[49]

On July 2, 1942, at the beginning of the First Battle of El Alamein, when Rommel's further advance still seemed likely, Louis Levinthal, president of the Zionist Organization of America, wrote an urgent letter to Churchill. In it, he warned the British prime minister that the Palestinian Jews could be annihilated in the course of the German invasion. He referred to the Jews' long-expressed desire to defend themselves and emphasized Britain's responsibility before history to not refuse them this right.[50] At about the same time, Chaim Weizmann, in a letter to Lord Halifax, the British ambassador in Washington, confirmed the Yishuv's wish to play a more prominent role in the battle against the advancing Axis powers and in the defense of Palestine. He argued that the best way to achieve this would be to create a Jewish fighting force. The previously existing units would be merged into this military formation, which would be expanded through extensive recruiting.[51]

Following the capture of Tobruk, according to German sources, the Jewish National Council issued an appeal in which all men between 17 and 45 years of age in Palestine were called upon to report for service in the British army. The text said, "This is an imperative necessity, in order to drive back the enemy at our gate."[52] Gershon Agronsky, editor of the *Palestine Post*, commented that this was Palestine's answer to the threat posed by Rommel.[53] A few days later, the Zionist Council in Jerusalem announced that "as large a number of Jews as possible should be armed and trained to defend Palestine."[54] Considering the alarming news from the Egyptian front, such appeals could not have failed to have an effect on the British. The German military attaché in Ankara reported in July that the English had "supplied the Jewish defense force with considerable quantities of arms in the last few days."[55]

The arming of the Palestinian Jews did not meet with unreserved approval within the Yishuv, however. A German informer reported in June that the appeals to the Jews to volunteer for service with the British police had not been as successful as originally assumed. At least 80,000 volunteers had been expected, but only 16,000 individuals actually reported for service in the militia

49. DNB, Feb. 11, 1942, PAAA, R 99342; DNB, Feb. 21, 1942, PAAA, R 99342.
50. Levinthal to Churchill, July 2, 1942, quoted in Nicosia, Archives, p. 378f.
51. Weizmann to Halifax, June 20, 1942, quoted in Nicosia, Archives, p. 378.
52. Sonderdienst Seehaus report, June 23, 1942, PAAA, R 99342; similarly, the informer "Pollux" reported a few days later that an urgent radio appeal had called upon as many Palestinian Jews as possible to report to the British volunteer units, report by "Pollux," July 8, 1942, BA-MA, RH 2/1788.
53. Report by press department of AA, SPN, June 25, 1942, PAAA, R 99342.
54. Report by press department of I-Dienst, July 9, 1942, PAAA, R 99342.
55. Summary of report by DG Ankara (undated/July 1942), BA-MA, RH 2/1785.

and a total of 6,000 for the police.[56] With regard to the mood among the Jews, a German informer reported: "Immediately after my arrival in Tel Aviv at the beginning of July 1942 I observed the following peculiar circumstance: volunteer guards stood on the streets near cafés and cinema exits. These guards usually consisted of three to four young girls in English uniform and six youths of the Jewish Brigade. They stopped all passersby and the people coming out of the cinema, asked them—as well as the young people in the cafés—to show their documents, and made it clear to them that it was their duty to defend their fatherland rather than be loafing about. If the responses were evasive or negative, the girls forcefully demanded that the individuals join the armed forces. If they resisted they were publicly beaten and then loaded into waiting vehicles and taken to the enlistment office. As a result of this operation, young people were no longer seen on the streets or in cafés and cinemas; they stayed home instead."[57]

From the German point of view, the recruitment efforts seemed to achieve considerable success a few weeks after Rommel was halted at El Alamein. An informer reported in early September that all Palestinian Jews between the ages of 18 and 40 would be mobilized for service in the British army. A total of 100,000 were to be called up for army service, and an additional 36,000 Jews were to be deployed with the Palestinian police force. With regard to the Muslim soldiers, the informer reported, "The entire Arab Legion in Palestine has been sent to the Egyptian front to keep it far away from the Jewish troops."[58] Toward the end of the year, 18,800 Palestinian Jews were serving in the British armed forces, 1,600 of whom were in the Royal Air Force and 400 in the Royal Navy. In addition, the Jewish police, led by British officers, still operated as well. In view of the threat of invasion, the police—under military command since May 1942—received military training that was increasingly oriented toward defense functions. These paramilitary troops numbered about 24,000 in August of that year. Thus, a total of approximately 43,000 Jews were trained in the army or in the Palestinian police units.[59]

In September 1944, the initiatives aimed at creating Jewish military units finally led to a decision by the British war cabinet to establish the Jewish Brigade Group. This military formation was raised in Egypt in the weeks that followed; the official flag and uniform insignia bore the Star of David.[60] In

---

56. Report by "Pollux," June 18, 1942, BA-MA, RH 2/1785.
57. Report by "Milton," Sept. 22, 1942, BA-MA, RH 2/1784.
58. Report by "Pollux," Sept. 4, 1942, BA-MA, RH 2/1784; in May 1942, future Israeli prime minister Menachem Begin also went to Palestine, with the Polish army units mentioned in the report, Eckman/Hirschler, p. 68.
59. Hurewitz, p. 127; Epstein, pp. 9–13.
60. Blum, p. 18; Beckman, p. 48ff.; EdH, vol. 2, p. 671.

October the brigade was transferred to Italy, where it took part in fighting against the Germans, including the 4th Paratroop Division. The unit was then deployed as an occupation force in the northern Italian city of Tarvisio, near the border with Austria and Yugoslavia.[61] From there (and, after July, from new deployment locations in Belgium and The Netherlands), the soldiers managed to illegally gather together and attend to tens of thousands of Jewish refugees, a large number of whom were survivors of the German concentration camps. The members of the brigade then organized ships to take the refugees to Palestine. Large quantities of weapons were also stolen from the Allies' numerous arms depots and smuggled into Palestine to be used in future conflicts.[62]

But implementation of all the plans to guarantee adequate arms and military training for the Yishuv became impossible during the extremely critical period in the summer of 1942 when Axis troops were fast approaching their objectives in Egypt. Nevertheless, there were concrete preparations intended to enable the Jews to deal with that horror scenario.[63] The previous year, British military strategists had already contemplated the possibility of an Axis invasion of Palestine; however, the danger of an offensive from the north was considered disproportionately greater. For that situation, the army drew up defensive plans that envisioned blocking the German advance at the Lebanon Mountains—and thus outside Palestine—if possible. Defensive positions were also constructed in Syria and in Palestine itself in the summer of 1941. All these installations faced north, in accordance with the defensive plans. Even after months of warfare in North Africa, during which they suffered some bitter defeats due to the mobility of Rommel's panzer units, the British considered an advance through the Sinai desert as quite simply impossible. Although defensive lines did exist in southern Palestine, they had been erected only as positions to retreat to in the event of a successful German advance from the north.[64]

Thus, a grotesque situation arose in the summer of 1942 that the British positions in Palestine could have been taken from behind in the event of a successful invasion by the Afrika Korps. As late as May and June, the British were transferring supply storehouses from Palestine to Egypt, near El Alamein, to protect them from the German Army in Russia, which was expected to push forward over the Caucasus. For the same reason, General Wilson, the commander-in-chief of the 9th Army, which was stationed in Palestine, and his

61. Beckman, pp. 72–98; Blum, p. 21.
62. Blum, pp. 222–226, 235–257, 264–270; Beckman, pp. 110–116, 133–148.
63. Kimche, *Pillars*, p. 36f.
64. Bauer, *Diplomacy*, p. 184.

men worked on developing the fortifications in the north of the country, even after the fall of Marsa Matruh at the end of June. Not until July 4 did he receive instructions to prepare for the possibility of a hostile advance from the south, via the Suez Canal.[65]

Since the spring of 1941, the Yishuv had taken the conflict with the Nazis in Palestine into consideration in its defense plan. This so-called Plan A was based on the experience of the Arab revolts in the 1930s and aimed at defending all of Palestine using regional commando units.[66] In addition, the so-called Palestine Post-Occupation Scheme was developed in collaboration with the mandatory power and the Jewish Agency as a plan for Palestine after occupation. According to this plan, after the British retreat and the occupation of the country an underground resistance movement would form to carry out tasks such as gathering intelligence and organizing acts of sabotage. Approximately 100 Palmach members were trained for such assignments by the SOE—the British Special Operations Executive.[67] Finally, a nationwide radio network was established under Dayan's command, designed for intelligence gathering and communications between resistance cells.[68]

Rommel's victories in the spring of 1942 resulted in the United Kingdom taking a positive attitude toward the Palmach. Beginning in April, more than 600 Palmach members in the Mishmar HaEmek kibbutz received thoroughly professional military training by the British army, complemented by special military defense courses.[69] During this time, the Palmach even based its semi-official headquarters staff in Haifa, which was well known to the mandatory power. Thanks to recruitment and training efforts during the spring, the total strength of the Palmach nearly doubled. By mid-June, the units had more than 840 members at their command, including 90 women. When it came to arming the troops, however, alarming shortages emerged. On July 4 and 5, when the military leadership of the Yishuv transferred a Palmach company to the south of Tel Aviv and another further inland to assist in the defense against Rommel, these units were "armed" with little more than sticks; weapons from the Haganah depots did not arrive until days later.[70]

The Haganah itself was also working on a plan to evacuate the Yishuv in the event of occupation. In an emergency, as many civilians as possible would board ships in Haifa. At the same time, after the retreat of the British, those who were armed would resist the occupiers and their collaborators as long as

---

65. Ibid., p. 184.
66. Ibid., p. 144.
67. Black/Morris, p. 70.
68. Ibid.; Dayan, p. 60f.
69. Bauer, *Cooperation*, p. 198; Bethell, p. 104f.
70. Bauer, *Diplomacy*, p. 188ff.

possible from the Carmel mountains and the mountains in the north of the country.[71] Sixteen-year-old Yehuda Bauer and his father, both Haganah members, were prepared "to go to Carmel with their backpacks and rifles, in case the Germans arrived." The father told young Yehuda that he would "not fall into the Germans' hands alive."[72] For such desperate plans, the Haganah could draw on a not insignificant illegal arsenal of weapons. According to a British report, in June 1942 the organization possessed 162 machine guns, 4,545 submachine guns and other automatic weapons, 18,000 rifles, and 16,000 pistols. The same source indicated a total strength of 30,000 members, of which approximately 50 to 70 percent were armed. To that number could be added approximately 4,000 members and supporters of the Irgun.[73]

The defensive strategy for the region around Haifa, including Carmel, was known as the Plan for the North, assuming a Jewish force the size of 36 regiments. The units were to be concentrated in fortified positions in that area and defended against the Axis attacks with the support of the British navy and air force. The British, who were presented with the plan, were very skeptical. While the socialist Hashomer Hatzair supported the Plan for the North, leading representatives of the Yishuv shared the British attitude. Against the defense strategy, a counterproposal was made: in the event of a British withdrawal, the Yishuv's armed forces should be temporarily pulled out of Palestine as well, enabling them to fight alongside the British to liberate the country again in due time.[74] Thus, several plans were developed and then discarded once more, and many differing and mutually exclusive opinions were put forth. During a session of the Jewish Agency Executive, someone expressed the hope that in the event of an occupation, the Germans would allow the Palestinian Jews to live in various ghettos.[75] In short, all the defense plans and the speculation about them indicate that the Yishuv would hardly have been in a position to organize a mass evacuation in time and provide sufficient opposition to Afrika Korps and its Arab allies. On a larger scale but otherwise analogous to the armed Jewish resistance in Europe, there would have been a desperate battle against the Axis and its Arab allies in Palestine. In the end, the Yishuv would undoubtedly have been completely annihilated. The Jews of Palestine were saved only by the military developments on the North African front.[76]

---

71. Bethell, p. 140 ff.; Bauer, *Diplomacy*, p. 191f.; Sachar, p. 235.
72. Letter from Yehuda Bauer to the authors, Oct. 11, 2005.
73. Zweig, "Use," p. 290, note 45.
74. Bauer, *Diplomacy*, pp. 191–194.
75. Ibid., p. 213.
76. Letter from Yehuda Bauer to the authors, Oct. 11, 2005; letters from Arnold Paucker to the authors, May 30 and July 7, 2005.

Chapter XI

The Turning Point:
El Alamein and the End of the Caucasus Option

After Afrika Korps entered into a lull in operations at the end of July 1942, Rommel planned to begin a new offensive four weeks later. By the end of August, the Germans expected two new British divisions to reinforce the enemy front. In addition, extensive supplies of arms would arrive in early September; these arms, which were being shipped around the Cape of Good Hope, had been promised to the 8th Army by the Americans after the fall of Tobruk.[1] According to Rommel's plans, the panzer army offensive would be well underway before the arrival of these reinforcements. Until then, he calculated that the Germans would have a slight advantage in terms of the number of tanks available; this advantage would then quickly shift in favor of the British.[2] The Germans were thoroughly confident that the occupation of Egypt and the advance to the Suez Canal would succeed. Mussolini, in contrast, who had been waiting in Derna for his triumphant entry into Cairo, had already returned to Italy on July 20, deeply disappointed and physically ill. Four days later, he told his foreign minister, Galeazzo Ciano, that the Italians would now have to choose between the Germans and the English.[3]

The Afrika Korps's situation had changed drastically since the successes of June 1942. For reasons incomprehensible to the Axis, an important source of

---

1. Situation analysis by PzAA/Ia, Aug. 15, 1942, BA-MA, RH 2/1588.
2. Ibid.; telex from Dt.Gen.b.HQu.It.Wehrm., Aug. 16, 1942, BA-MA, RH 2/463; DRZW, vol. 6, p. 672f.
3. DRZW, vol. 6, p. 666.

enemy intelligence was no longer available after June 29, the day Marsa Matruh was stormed. After that day, the American military attaché in Cairo had stopped transmitting the radio messages that had been decrypted and had provided invaluable information about British strategy and tactics since 1941.[4] In addition, during an attack by the Australian 26th Infantry Brigade on the early morning of July 10, the 3rd Company of Intelligence Detachment 56 under Captain Seebohm, located in the advance positions on the El Alamein front, was involved in heavy fighting. The Australians took many prisoners and captured all the company's records. An examination of the materials, which included British radio codes, revealed how efficiently the Germans had intercepted enemy communications. This again proved to the British the urgent need to significantly strengthen their efforts at maintaining secrecy. From that point on, Rommel knew far less about the enemy's intentions.[5]

Comparisons of military strength looked increasingly unfavorable for the Axis side as well. In addition to the Allies' actual superiority in terms of tanks, which Rommel seemed to know nothing about, the Germans and Italians also had to contend with an increasingly dominant Royal Air Force.[6] As another factor, supplies took on critical importance. Within a few weeks, the already tense supply situation had worsened alarmingly. While the quantity of goods unloaded in Libyan ports for Rommel's troops amounted to 91,491 tons in July, the total for August fell to almost half that amount, at 51,655 tons. During this same time, the amount of shipping tonnage sunk by British attacks increased from 6,339 gross register tons in July to 50,562 the following month. The Royal Navy and Royal Air Force achieved 42 percent of these figures thanks to "Ultra" intelligence obtained through the British cryptologists' interception and breaking of the Germans' radio code.[7] Immediately prior to the German offensive, British air force and navy units were ordered to use the "Ultra" intelligence to target Italian convoys and supply ships. As a result, the delivery of supplies for the Afrika Korps almost came to a complete standstill.[8] Such an unfavorable supply situation, combined with the numerous additional difficulties of long supply channels with truck convoys over land, in view of the planned offensive, had immeasurably negative effects. Furthermore, the British did not have such concerns; they could rely on short, and secure supply lines.

---

4. Piekalkiewicz, p. 143.
5. Ibid., p. 158.
6. Fraser, *Rommel*, p. 326ff.; DRZW, vol. 6, p. 673; Gundelach, vol. 1, pp. 399–408.
7. Gundelach, vol. 1, pp. 409-412; DRZW, vol. 6, p. 753ff.
8. DRZW, vol. 6, p. 684.

On the British side, the military leadership at the command level was changed in August. On his way to meet Stalin in Moscow, Churchill landed in Cairo on August 3. There, in the days that followed, he came to a number of decisions regarding the leadership of the troops. General Claude Auchinleck, the luckless commander-in-chief in the Middle East (who, according to Churchill, lacked the "killer instinct," despite many military virtues), was recalled. General Sir Harold Alexander received the new command over Egypt, Palestine, and Syria, and the prime minister appointed General Gott as the new commander-in-chief of the British 8th Army. However, Gott was killed the following day when his airplane was shot down, and Lieutenant General Bernard Montgomery was named as his successor on August 7. Montgomery arrived at his new headquarters in Egypt six days later and, having just been presented with his new responsibilities, declared very confidently to his top officers that he would defeat Rommel.[9]

Despite numerous misgivings, the commander-in-chief of the German army, in consultation with General Kesselring, decided to attack at the end of August—again creating the opportunity, through the conquest of Egypt, to converge in the Arab region with the Eastern Army, which was simultaneously advancing through the Caucasus. The offensive plan called for the implementation of deceptive thrusts in the north, primarily by Italian units, in order to then use the bulk of the panzer units in the south to cross the British minefields and break through the defensive line from behind. But because the British were now in a position to decipher German communications, thanks to "Ultra," the element of surprise that had so often contributed to Rommel's victories was entirely missing.[10]

On the night of August 30, a German-Italian attack opened the Second Battle of El Alamein. The panzer offensive, which during the day had moved toward the Alam el Halfa ridge, was sidelined by evening due to a shortage of fuel and the nonstop British air attacks.[11] Because of the lack of fuel for his motorized units, Rommel was forced to shift to a defensive tactic the next day. In the hours that followed, he found out that several promised tanker ships had been attacked by the British and would not reach their destination. The decision had to be made. Supply problems, British air superiority, and a greater number of enemy tanks than initially believed forced the field marshal to order

---

9. Keegan, p. 486; Piekalkiewicz, p. 166; Waldschmidt, p. 113f.; Kirk, p. 221.

10. DRZW, vol. 6, p. 678ff.; Gundelach, vol. 1, p. 417f.

11. Kampfstaffel OB PzAA war diary, Aug. 30 and 31, 1942, BA-MA, RH 19 VIII/3; Fraser, *Rommel,* p. 327ff.; Waldschmidt, p. 114; DRZW, vol. 6, p. 682ff.; cf. VAA/PzAA telegram, Sept. 1, 1942, PAAA, R 29537.

a halt to the offensive on September 3.[12] That same day, Neurath telegraphed the news of the failure to his superiors in the Foreign Office.[13] The last chance to conquer Egypt and move further into Arab territory was lost. Given increasing British superiority, Rommel already knew that there would not be another offensive opportunity.

The officials in the RSHA also recognized the changed strategic situation. The SS commando created for deployment in the Middle East was still on standby near Athens. In the days after the Second Battle of El Alamein, however, when it became clear that a resumption of the offensive was out of the question, the plans for deploying security police and SD personnel in Egypt and Palestine had to be abandoned. By mid-September, the Wehrmacht asked the SS to repatriate the Einsatzkommando, and Himmler's consent was obtained on the 18th of the month; a few days later, Rauff's unit received the order to depart from Athens. The special returned to Berlin, where the entire unit seems to have remained together.[14]

The Mufti did not remain idle during the stalemate on the North African front. Disgruntled over the transfer of the German-Arab Battalion to the Caucasus, which took place without his knowledge, as discussed below, he intensified his contacts with the Italians. With them, he at least achieved recognition as sole Arab leader. As a tangible project, in agreement with the Comando Supremo, the establishment of an Arab center for collaboration with the Axis powers was planned for North Africa. Extensive propaganda activities were to be carried out from the center, via radio broadcasts, leaflets, and informers operating locally. However, the Mufti also planned to use the center for intelligence activities and for the organization of all types of sabotage operations in the Arab countries. In addition, el-Husseini obtained Italian consent to expand the previously formed Arab Legion and any future Arab volunteer units under his responsibility into a regular military formation with Arab insignia.[15]

Meanwhile, British special forces were busy planning a commando operation. Rommel's headquarters were to be attacked and destroyed, and the field marshal himself captured, if possible, in a plan that involved the infiltration of Tobruk by a unit of the Long Range Desert Group and the arrival of numerous

---

12. Telex from Dt.Gen.b.HQu.It.Wehrm., Sept. 5 and 7, 1942, BA-MA, RH 2/463; Kampfstaffel OB PzAA war diary, Sept. 2 and 3, 1942, BA-MA, RH 19 VIII/3; DRZW, vol. 6, p. 684ff.; Gundelach, vol. 1, p. 419ff.; Fraser, *Rommel,* p. 330f.

13. VAA/PzAA telegram, Sept. 3, 1942, PAAA, R 29537.

14. Dt.Gen.b.HQu.It.Wehrm. to OKW/WFSt/Qu.I, Sept. 14, 1942, BAB, NS 19/3695; OKW/WFSt/ Qu.I/III to HStb.Übs., Sept. 19, 1942, BAB, NS 19/2500; interrogation of Friedrich Pohl, July 14, 1976, BAL, B 162/4409, p. 3075.

15. Translation of note by Comando Supremo, Sept. 10, 1942, PAAA, BA 61125.

ships in the harbor there. In mid-September, the unit set out overland. Many Jews also took part in the operation, some of whom were emigrants from Germany who seemed particularly suited for the assignment because of their knowledge of the language and of German customs. Due to an unfortunate coincidence—one of the Jews in German uniform was recognized by a Wehrmacht soldier in Tobruk—that operation was exposed. Shortly thereafter, the British ships' landing attempt failed because the harbor was on alert. The Jewish commando members were either killed in the fighting or taken by the Germans as prisoners of war.[16]

Montgomery's extensive preparations for an offensive by the 8th Army were completed in the second half of October. The 318 Sherman tanks and numerous mobile heavy artillery from the American allies had arrived in Africa, and the British were immediately instructed in their use. The commander-in-chief planned, with his carefully prepared attack, to engage and destroy the majority of the enemy's units within the defensive lines. The trump card in the development of his strategy was the knowledge that the British could rely on clear superiority with regard to both men and material. In terms of soldiers alone, the British army had three times the manpower of the Germans and Italians.[17]

On the evening of October 23, the Third Battle of El Alamein—long expected by the Germans—began with a large-scale British artillery attack lasting five and a half hours. The main thrust by Montgomery's units was carried out that same evening, completely unanticipated by the Axis, northwest of El Alamein in the northern sector of the front. Rommel, who had been in Germany recovering because of health problems since September 22, received a call from Hitler on October 24, informing him of the British offensive. Once he was told of the seriousness of the situation, the field marshal flew from Germany the following day and reached the Afrika Korps that evening.[18] The situation proved to be extremely critical. British and Australian units had already succeeded in crossing the minefield and were therefore placed directly in front of the defensive positions of the Axis forces.

Then, on the night of November 1–2, under the code name "Supercharge," a major 8th Army attack began, aimed at forcing a breakthrough in the northern sector of the front.[19] The British succeeded in creating a break in the enemy lines, which the panzer army was able to temporarily close by the

---

16. Brockdorff, pp. 193–199.
17. DRZW, vol. 6, pp. 695–698.
18. Kampfstaffel OB PzAA war diary, Oct. 24, 1942, BA-MA, RH 19 VIII/3; Fraser, *Rommel*, pp. 339–343; Keegan, p. 488; Gundelach, vol. 1, p. 440.
19. Gundelach, vol. 1, p. 443; DRZW, vol. 6, p. 702ff.; Fraser, *Rommel*, p. 352.

evening of November 2.[20] Rommel therefore expected the worst for the next day and suggested to Hitler that a withdrawal might possibly be necessary. The response from the Führer's headquarters was prompt. In his order to stand fast, Hitler forbade retreat of any kind, grandiloquently promised reinforcements (which both sides knew did not exist), and concluded by telling Rommel, "You must not show your troops any other way than to victory or death."[21]

Following this directive, the Afrika Korps continued its increasingly hopeless defense. On November 4, however, the British again succeeded in breaking through, this time in a section of the front held by Italian troops; the Ariete Division was completely annihilated in the course of the fighting. After further breaks appeared in the front, the entire panzer army was threatened with encirclement. That afternoon, Rommel gave the order to all units to disengage from the enemy at nightfall and pull back toward the west. The commander-in-chief did not wait for Hitler's response to the announcement of this directive.[22]

Initially, Rommel believed he could stabilize his troops in the Fuka position between El Alamein and Marsa Matruh. On November 5, however, when the 8th Army again prepared to surround the panzer army with a southward flanking movement, Rommel gave the order to retreat to Marsa Matruh. In the process, virtually the entire Italian 10th Army Corps, with its Brescia, Folgore, and Pavia divisions, became prisoners of war. In further fighting, the Italian 21st Army Corps, with the Trento and Bologna divisions, was largely destroyed as well. A new encircling movement soon threatened the units that had reached the positions at Marsa Matruh, so the army leadership ordered a retreat to Sidi Barrani, then to Sollum. While circling to the west, the British recaptured Tobruk on November 12. On November 20, the defeated Axis troops retreated to Benghazi. After a stopover in the defensive positions of Buerat from December 26 to January 16, the Afrika Korps reached Tripoli on January 22, thus returning to the starting point of the operation that had begun just two years earlier with the landing of the German desert units.[23]

The Axis troops were subsequently driven further west by Montgomery's army. Tripoli was evacuated on January 23, and the last Axis forces crossed the Libyan-Tunisian border on February 2. By February 15, the rest of the Afrika

---

20. Kampfstaffel OB PzAA war diary, Nov. 2, 1942, BA-MA, RH 19 VIII/3.
21. Quoted in DRZW, vol. 6, p. 706; cf. Kampfstaffel OB PzAA war diary, Nov. 4, 1942, BA-MA, RH 19 VIII/3; Gundelach, vol. 1, p. 444; Waldschmidt, p. 119.
22. Kampfstaffel OB PzAA war diary, Nov. 4, 1942, BA-MA, RH 19 VIII/3; Keegan, p. 489f.; Kirk, p. 225ff.; Theil, p. 71; Gundelach, vol. 1, p. 445; cf. VAA/PzAA to StS./AA, Oct. 5, 1942, PAAA, R 29857.
23. Kampfstaffel OB PzAA war diary, Nov. 5–Dec. 31, 1942, BA-MA, RH 19 VIII/3; DRZW, vol. 6, pp. 725–736; Fraser, *Rommel*, pp. 358–371.

Korps had reached the newly established Mareth position in Tunisia.[24] Altogether, Rommel lost approximately 40,000 of his 100,000 men to British attacks during the 3,000-plus-kilometer retreat to the west after the defeat at El Alamein. Most of the soldiers taken into captivity or killed were Italians who were unable to keep up with the withdrawal because of a lack of vehicles. In addition, the Afrika Korps had no more than 80 combat-ready panzers left at the end.[25]

The Allies enjoyed a stroke of luck in that Hitler, with his concentration on the war in the east, never made the African front a priority and therefore did not supply it with sufficient troops and military equipment. Supply lines thus became the decisive factor. As early as 1941, and especially during the battles of El Alamein, the Axis powers were unable to adequately secure the supply lines to Africa and deliver the required quantities of war matériel and fuel. By 1943, the Germans and Italians had lost a shipping capacity totaling 1,345,000 gross tons on those supply routes alone. A further 1,195,000 gross tons were damaged. That quantity was equal to the total tonnage of Italy's entire merchant shipping fleet when it entered the war.[26]

The defeat of the Axis powers at El Alamein also affected German-Arab relations. Many Muslims in the Middle East were disappointed in their hope that Rommel's army would free their lands. The widespread pro-German attitudes did not change, however. After the failed offensive by Afrika Korps at El Alamein, when the British led German prisoners of war through Opera Square in Cairo as a sign of their victory, cheers still sounded for Rommel. The prisoners were then quickly led away through side streets.[27] In Palestine there were no fundamental changes in the positions of the political parties, but there was general bewilderment and disorientation. In the remaining years of the war, from 1942 to 1945, no one seemed capable of devising a new, alternative political program. All attempts to create parties or alliances in opposition to the Husseini power bloc, still controlled by the Mufti from his exile, were unsuccessful; any such initiatives were resolutely thwarted by his party and family members.[28]

On the Eastern Front, the Don offensive had begun under the code name "Blue I" on June 28, 1942.[29] The troops of Army Group South, in the southern sector, moved forward rapidly in the following weeks. The attacking units were then organized into a northern Army Group B under General Weichs and a

---

24. Fraser, *Rommel*, pp. 371–374; DRZW, vol. 6, p. 736f.
25. Keegan, p. 491.
26. Theil, p. 66.
27. Note by Prüfer/AA, June 17, 1943, PAAA, BA 61179.
28. Kiernan, p. 106; Khalaf, p. 90f.
29. DRZW, vol. 6, p. 868f.

southern Army Group A under Field Marshal List. The two army groups did not succeed, as originally planned, in surrounding large parts of the Red Army through a pincer movement in the direction of Stalingrad; however, on July 23, in Directive No. 45, Hitler ordered the offensive be divided. Now Weichs and Army Group B were to push forward to Stalingrad on their own. They were to capture the important industrial center on the Volga and then follow the river to Astrakhan and the Caspian Sea. At the same time, List's Army Group A was to push forward toward the Caucasus, capture the eastern shore of the Black Sea and the oil fields of Grozny, and then, moving southeast along the Caspian Sea, seize the oil wells at Baku.[30]

Both offensive movements began with marked success. The 6th Army, which belonged to Army Group B, reached the Volga near Stalingrad in the second half of August and advanced into the city at the beginning of September.[31] Meanwhile, the 1st and 4th Panzer Armies of Army Group A reached the Caucasus. On August 18, the Wehrmacht occupied three of the most important passes, and three days later reached Mount Elbrus, the highest mountain in the Caucasus; mountain troops hoisted the Nazi Swastika at the summit. The Soviets then declared a state of emergency in Transcaucasia on August 24. The occupation of Mozdok on August 25 represented the high point of the German advance.[32]

The crossing of the Caucasus and penetration into Arab territory now seemed imminent. The situation had been anticipated in a meeting between Ribbentrop, Felmy, and Grobba on May 14. In view of the expected advance to Arabia, the key points for German propaganda were defined at this meeting, in consultation with the Foreign Office and the Wehrmacht. In this connection, the two Arab exiles in Germany were to play a significant role, as Grobba noted: "The highlight of the propaganda activities of the Grand Mufti and Gailani should be an appeal by both to the Arab people to revolt against the English. The timing should be determined by us, presumably after the capture of Tbilisi. Both want to go there then. The Iraqi government should be proclaimed there. This appeal will move the Arab people to revolt [...]. When a victorious German army appears near the borders of the Arab countries, there is no doubt that the Arab people will rise up against England."

In these plans, the Arabs of the German-Arab Battalion were designated as the "framework for a new Iraqi Arab army." In the northern area of the anticipated pincer movement as well, the Germans counted on a large number of

---

30. Ibid., pp. 881–892; Gruchmann, *Weltkrieg*, p. 198.
31. Gruchmann, *Weltkrieg*, p. 199; DRZW, vol. 6, pp. 962–971.
32. Stewart, *Sunrise*, p. 221.

collaborators joining the fight when they appeared in Arab territory on the other side of the Caucasus: "We can expect that the majority of the Iraqi army—four divisions before the war between the Iraqis and the English—will join Gailani and the Grand Mufti and that numerous volunteers will also pour in from Syria and Palestine."[33] In August, during the Wehrmacht's rapid advance, the German-Arab Battalion was transferred from Greece to Stalino, together with Sonderstab F. After the crossing of the Caucasus and the seizure of Tbilisi, the unit was to march across western Iran into Iraq, in order to spearhead the propaganda efforts to promote Arab collaboration with the Axis against England.[34]

A serious conflict regarding the unit's deployment arose between the OKH and el-Husseini, who had not been informed in advance about the transfer to the edge of the Caucasus and angrily called for immediate deployment in Egypt.[35] The military agreement concluded with al-Gailani in mid-September is further evidence of how certain the enlistment of collaborators must have seemed to the Wehrmacht leadership. This agreement, in which both sides committed to the "liberation" of Iraq and Greater Syria from the British, specifically stated that the Arabs of the original battalion would serve as the core of a future Arab army. While the Germans committed to training and equipping the Arabs, al-Gailani acknowledged the alliance partner's ultimate authority. Felmy specifically agreed that the Germans would leave the Iraqi and Greater Syrian territory "no later than six months after the end of the war" and that afterward only a military mission would be maintained there.[36]

Ultimately, the military agreement never came into force. El-Husseini, disgruntled over the transfer of his Arab volunteers to the Eastern Front and jealously focused on not losing ground to al-Gailani, refused to accept the agreement during a mid-September meeting with Canaris and Felmy in Rome.[37] The military deployment of the Arabs on the other side of the Caucasus never came about either. The four Muslim companies, now 800 strong, were stationed at a camp several hundred kilometers behind the front, waiting for the mountain range to be crossed; the remaining 5,200 German soldiers in the

---

33. Note by Grobba/AA, May 30, 1942, PAAA, R 27332; with similar content: Ettel/AA to RAM, May 31, 1942, PAAA, R 27332.

34. Note by Grobba, Sept. 3, 1942, PAAA, BA 61124.

35. Note by Grobba, Sept. 8, 1942, PAAA, R 27828; the Mufti had argued to Keitel that deploying the volunteers in Egypt would have the advantage that there the Palestinian and Syrian Arabs would be "in their own country almost immediately," memorandum by Mufti, Aug. 29, 1942, PAAA, R 27828.

36. Draft of German-Iraqi military agreement (undated/Sept. 1942), PAAA, BA 61125; note by Grobba, Dec. 19, 1942, PAAA, BA 61125; in September, Hitler had also emphasized that German troops would not continue to occupy Arab territory over the long term, cf. memorandum by Hewel/AA, Sept. 12, 1942, PAAA, R 27324.

37. Note by Ritter/AA, Mar. 27, 1943, PAAA, BA 61125; memorandum by head of OKW/Ausl/Abw, Sept. 15, 1942, PAAA, BA 61125; note by Grobba, Dec. 19, 1942, PAAA, BA 61125.

battalion were deployed on the front, resulting in considerable losses for the unit.[38]

In the event of an advance over the Caucasus, the commandos of Einsatzgruppe D, moving forward with the German army, would no doubt have begun to arrest and murder the Jews living in that area as well. The first allusions to the impending mass murder can be found in the reports of the Reich Institute for the History of the New Germany. One report addressed the ancestry of Caucasians and Georgians "of the Mosaic confession," whose numbers were identified as approximately 60,000 to 70,000. Concerning this ethnic group, the institute staff pointed out that these people did not follow the Talmud.[39] Another report from October 1942 discussed Persian and Afghan Jews, whose numbers were also estimated at 60,000 to 70,000. In contrast to the Caucasians and Georgians, the Jews in Afghanistan and Persia knew the Talmud very well and followed it faithfully.[40] In response to these findings, a specialist from the Institute for the Investigation of the Jewish Question pointed out that it is "always to be suspected that the identification of members of the Mosaic confession as Iranians, Georgians, Afghans, and so on, is a matter of clever Jewish disguise, as was also common in Europe."[41] Often, it was precisely these types of classifications and pseudoscientific discourses by "Jewish specialists" that served as the prelude to annihilation, by providing the criteria by which the local killing squads or deportation experts could then select their victims.[42]

While the Wehrmacht was beginning its move over the Caucasus, attitudes in neighboring Iran were still strongly pro-Axis. The Japanese military attaché in Teheran declared that the Iranian army was "fully prepared to collaborate with the German liberators,"[43] and in February and May 1942 the Abwehr sent Persian informers there to investigate this support.[44] An Iranian diplomat reported that "at least 90 percent are pro-German. In Teheran there are swastikas on every wall. [...] Small children run behind the British officers, calling, 'Mister, Mister,' then stretch out a hand, palm up, blow on it, and say, 'Singapore.'" German radio was also "listened to eagerly."[45] The broadcasts banked on veneration for the Führer, "who was widely revered in Shiite teachings as the returning twelfth imam" and whose pictures were "found again and again

---

38. Note by Schnurre/AA, Nov. 20, 1942, PAAA, BA 61125.
39. Report by the Reich Institute for the History of the New Germany, Oct. 23, 1942, PAAA, R 27330.
40. Ibid.
41. Institute for the Investigation of the Jewish Question to AA, Oct. 27, 1942, PAAA, R 27330.
42. Angrick, pp. 326–330; Kunz, pp. 187–204.
43. DG Tokyo to AA, May 21, 1942, PAAA, R 27329.
44. Note by Ettel/AA, Aug. 11, 1942, PAAA, R 27329.
45. DK Geneva to AA, Aug. 13, 1942, PAAA, R 27329.

in even the poorest homes."[46] At the same time, the German transmissions also instigated anti-Semitic agitation. "In addition to propaganda against the British and the Soviets, anti-Jewish propaganda has good prospects for success among the Iranian people," asserted Ettel, the former ambassador in Teheran. "The majority of Iranians despise the Jews, whom they see as parasites on the body of the nation. Germany's struggle against world Jewry is thus also directed against the Jews in Iran, whom the Aryan Iranian people want to keep under their heel."[47] It is not difficult to recognize the propaganda groundwork for pogroms to come after the German invasion.

The remaining Abwehr and SD agents also prepared for the invasion in their own way. Gamotha remained in northern Iran until the fall of 1942 and built up a sabotage network there, which he used to carry out attacks on the Soviet supply lines. Then he fled to Turkey on foot and, after months of internment, returned to Germany in March 1943.[48] In October of that year, as Hauptsturmführer, he took over the leadership of the Iranian Affairs department in *Amt* VI and thus preparations for the deployment of additional agents.[49] Mayr remained in Teheran, cultivated his contacts with Iranian officers, and maintained radio communication with Berlin.[50] On March 29, 1943, six additional German agents—four SD members and two from the Abwehr— were dropped by parachute south of the capital and established contact with Mayr.[51] On August 15, however, all six fell into the hands of the British secret service during a wave of arrests targeting the Persian opposition.[52]

Nasr Khan, head of the Ghashghai tribe, offered Schulze-Holthus the opportunity to assist, as a military adviser, in preparations for an uprising by the southern Persian tribes; he accepted the offer and went to their territory. That same year, the khan had temporary airfields created for the expected German arrival[53] and began guerrilla warfare against the central administration and the British.[54] In return, he was allocated financial support of 250,000 reichsmarks, of which 100,000 were paid out in 1943.[55] Schulze-Holthus also received reinforcements from Germany. In July 1943 a four-man commando

---

46. AA/Pol VII, guidelines for propaganda in Iran, Aug. 11, 1942, PAAA, R 27329.
47. Ettel/AA, guidelines for propaganda in Iran, Aug. 24, 1942, PAAA, R 27329.
48. RFSS, deployment of SS officers in Iran (undated/May 1943), BAB, NS 19/2235; interrogation of Irmtraud Kaiser, Aug. 30, 1945, NAK, FO 371/46781.
49. Curriculum vitae, BAB, RuSHA Roman Gamotha; RSHA VI to RFSS adjutancy, Oct. 29, 1943, BAB, SSO Roman Gamotha.
50. CdS VI C 12 to AA, July 24, 1943, facsimile in Schnabel, p. 411f.; Schulze-Holthus, *Iran*, pp. 194, 206, 225, 236f., 239, 294f.; Madani, p. 463.
51. OKW/Ausl/Abw II to OKW/WFSt, May 7, 1943, BA-MA, RW 4/v. 691.
52. Schröder, *Deutschland*, p. 258f.
53. Schulze-Holthus, *Iran*, pp. 195, 198, 202.
54. Cf. Madani, p. 456ff.
55. Note by Ettel/AA, Oct. 21, 1943, PAAA, R 101101.

unit parachuted into the Ghashghai territory—three SD members and an Iranian interpreter. They brought radio equipment and explosives with them and were specifically assigned to sabotage the southern Persian oil wells.[56] The leader of the commando was Hauptsturmführer Martin Kurmis, who had been a Lithuanian expert in the SD's Memel section before Operation Barbarossa. In 1941 he belonged to Einsatzkommando 3 and then served as head of *Amt* IV in the office of the commander of the security police and the SD in Kaunas, where he was thus deeply involved in the extermination of the Lithuanian Jews. In 1942, as part of Operation Zeppelin, he led the deployment of agents in the northern Caucasus and outside Leningrad.[57] His motto was "The Reichsführer-SS is our conscience."[58]

However, the situation had clearly deteriorated in the meantime. "According to reports from our Teheran office, it would have been possible last year to provoke a major revolt in connection with the German offensive movement in the east," Kaltenbrunner reported. "Now the situation is clearly less favorable. The tribes deliberately held back and only wanted to become active in conjunction with new German operations."[59] When two of the khan's brothers—both in the service of the German Abwehr—were, while returning from Berlin, abducted by British agents in Iran and taken to Cairo, where they were imprisoned, the Ghashghai ruler came to an agreement with the Teheran government and exchanged the Germans for his brothers. In March 1944, Schulze-Holthus, Kurmis, and their companions were handed over to the British.[60] While still in a Teheran military hospital, Kurmis seized the sentry who was standing guard by his bed and dragged him headfirst out the window; both fell to their deaths in the courtyard below.[61]

The Third Reich thus found itself at an impasse in the Middle East. And, as at El Alamein, the Germans' broad strategic visions did not bear fruit in Eastern Europe either. In Stalingrad, the fighting had steadily intensified during the month of September 1942. The defenders, pressed against the Volga, resisted fiercely. A Soviet counteroffensive launched on November 19 then broke through the front to the north and south of Stalingrad and surrounded the 6th Army three days later, trapping its 250,000 soldiers in the city.[62] Faced with a similarly hopeless situation as at El Alamein two weeks earlier, Hitler

---

56. Schulze-Holthus, *Iran*, p. 274ff.
57. Curriculum vitae, BAB, RuSHA Martin Kurmis; "Zeppelin"-Hauptkdo. Süd to RSHA VI C/Z, Oct. 30, 1942, NAK, HW 19/235; RSHA VI C/Z telex, Dec. 3, 1942, BA-ZA, ZR 920/44; interrogation of Heinrich S., Oct. 18, 1959, BAL, B 162/2509, p. 4235ff.
58. Schulze-Holthus, *Iran*, p. 291.
59. CdS to RAM, June 2, 1943, ADAP, ser. E, vol. 6, p. 127f.
60. Note by Ettel/AA, Oct. 16, 1943, PAAA, R 101101; Madani, p. 470ff.; Schröder, *Deutschland*, p. 259.
61. Schulze-Holthus, *Iran*, p. 355.
62. DRZW, vol. 6, pp. 1018–1023; Gruchmann, *Weltkrieg*, p. 200f.

also forbade Field Marshal Paulus from attempting to break out. Instead, he promised to supply the soldiers by air and to send in a relief force. General Hoth's attempt to force open the pocket, which began on December 12, failed.[63] Four days later the Red Army crossed the Don northwest of Stalingrad, broke through the Italian-held front, and pushed toward Rostov. This action threatened to completely cut off Army Group A, in the Caucasus, from the front. The Wehrmacht units were therefore forced to withdraw from the Caucasus. Together with the 17th Army, part of the army group gathered on the eastern shore of the Sea of Asov and the Black Sea to form a bridgehead to the Kerch peninsula, from which a new offensive could be initiated the following year.[64]

This attack never took place, however. In the fall of 1942, within an interval of just a few weeks, the Wehrmacht units on both the African and Eastern Fronts were forced to give up their promising strategic positions and retreat, because of counteroffensives launched by superior Allied forces. The pincer movement Hitler had planned in 1941 against the British positions in the Arab world thus had to be definitively abandoned. How completely the circumstances had changed by the end of 1942 is shown not least by Iraq's declaration of war on the Axis powers the following year. In response, the Mufti suggested that the declaration regarding Arabia's freedom and independence that had secretly been promised to him and al-Gailani by the German government should now be made public for propaganda purposes. The request was rejected by the Germans. Instead, both Arab collaborators were urged to intensify their pro-German propaganda.[65]

The almost simultaneous defeats on the North African and Eastern Fronts represented the decisive turning points of World War II. After those events, the Wehrmacht would never again be able to seize the strategic initiative on a large scale. Although it could not yet be foreseen at the end of 1942, the momentum was shifting steadily toward the Allies, who forced the Axis powers to give up, one by one, all the positions they had gained through the summer. In addition, Nazi Germany and fascist Italy were less and less able to make up for the losses they had incurred. In comparison to the increasingly superior armaments industries of the Soviet Union and the United States, the Axis powers' ability to mobilize their economies for war was falling further and further behind.[66] A new theater of war in Tunisia would only confirm the general situation.

---

63. Gruchmann, *Weltkrieg*, p. 201f.; DRZW, vol. 6, pp. 1035–1053.
64. Ibid., p. 246ff.; DRZW, vol. 6, pp. 1064–1068.
65. Mufti to RAM, Jan. 28, 1943, PAAA, BA 61125; note by Prüfer/AA, Feb. 10, 1943, PAAA, BA 61125.
66. Overy, pp. 31, 241–161.

زعيم النهب الإسلامي الدولت مثل رسالة القي الأكبر السيد "أمين الحسيني" أثناء اجتماعه في برلين.

The meeting between the Grand Mufti of Jerusalem and Adolf Hitler in Berlin in 1941. The postcard was widely distributed in the Arab countries.

Jewish ambulance carrying wounded Jews following
an Arab riot in Tel Aviv, 1936.

Philosopher Martin Buber boards an armored bus in Tel Aviv, 1937.

Nazi anti-Semitic actions in Germany, 1933.

Nazi boycott of Jewish business in Bösingfeld, Germany, April 1933.

Nazi anti-Semitic boycott in Germany, 1933.

Nazi postcard inspired by the *Protocols of the Elders of Zion,* 1930s.

The famous World War I "stab in the back" in a Nazi cartoon.

Anti-Jewish pogrom in
Constantine, Algeria, 1919.

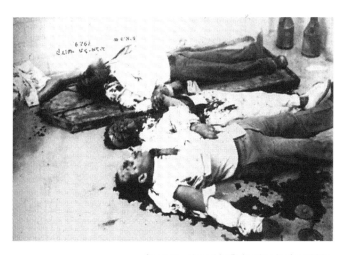

Jews murdered in Palestine in the 1920s.

Nazi propaganda postcard: King George VI offers the severed head of the Grand Mufti on a silver platter to Chaim Weizmann.

The cargo ship *Parita* with 850 European Jews is beached on a sandbar
off Tel Aviv on August 21, 1939.

The Jewish Legion from Palestine
created by the British Mandate.

The Grand Mufti inspects the Bosnian Muslim SS unit during training in Germany.

The Grand Mufti looks at equipment during his tour.

Bosnian Muslim SS volunteers, 1942.

Reichsführer SS Heinrich Himmler.

Reinhard Heydrich head of the Reich Security Office
RSHA, a key deputy of Heinrich Himmler until his
assassination in Prague in 1942.

Himmler bows low as he meets the Grand Mufti.

Walter Schellenberg, Head of the RSHA *Amt* VI, foreign espionage.

Ernst Kaltenbrunner, who replaced Heydrich as head of the RSHA, 1942-1945.

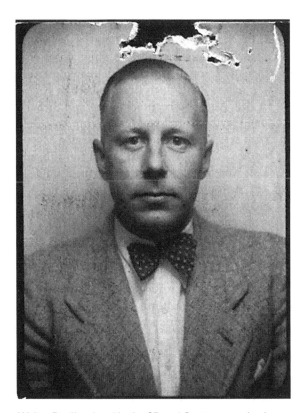

Walter Rauff, colonel in the SD and Gestapo was in charge
of the extermination team that was to operate in Palestine.
He operated in Tunis in 1942-1943.

General Erwin Rommel in the Libyan desert in 1942.

Chapter XII

Einsatzkommando Tunis:
The Second Front

In the early morning of November 8, 1942, a total of approximately 63,000 American and British soldiers landed in three separate coastal areas near Casablanca in Morocco and in the Algerian cities of Oran and Algiers. It was the beginning of the Allies' Operation Torch.[1] With the alarming German victories in the Middle East and the Soviet Union in mind, in July 1942 the British and Americans agreed to a landing in western North Africa. The preferred invasion, on the Channel coast of France, which was vehemently requested by Stalin, had to be postponed in view of the relative strengths of the Allied and Axis forces; it could not take place until the following year at the earliest. On August 14, Dwight D. Eisenhower was named Allied commander-in-chief. He was selected, among other reasons, in the hope that an American commander would be able to minimize French resistance.[2] On the day of the landing, along some parts of the coast, there was nevertheless serious resistance by French troops, who had quite varied reactions to the arrival of the Allies. By pure coincidence, apparently, Admiral Darlan, commander-in-chief of the French army, had been in Algeria since April 1942 because of his son's illness. Direct nego-

---

1. Keegan, p. 492f.; Carpi, *Mussolini*, p. 229.
2. Overy, p. 136ff.

tiations with the admiral enabled the Americans to persuade the French to ccasc all hostilities by November 10.[3]

With their landing operation, the American and British forces had gained a promising position from which to make a future advance into continental Europe from the south. From then on, the Italian mainland, in particular, had to be regarded as directly threatened. On November 9, in response to the Allied landing, Hitler ordered a bridgehead to be immediately established in Tunisia.[4] He also ordered the occupation of the rest of France, for which preparations had long been completed. The Germans paid no heed to assurances by Marshal Pétain and Prime Minister Laval that Commander-in-Chief Darlan had acted entirely of his own accord and that France had by no means changed sides. The Wehrmacht moved into southern France on the morning of November 11; the occupation, carried out in cooperation with Italy, was completed three days later without any opposition.[5]

The first German aircraft reached Tunisia on November 9. Following orders from Vichy, the French colonial army surrendered the cities of Tunis and Bizerte without opposition and withdrew toward Algeria.[6] The Wehrmacht strengthened its newly established bridgehead with the arrival of three German divisions after November 16. By the beginning of December, the troops operated under the much inflated name "5th Panzer Army"; the commander-in-chief was initially General Nehring, the former commander of the German Afrika Korps, and then, after December 8, General Hans-Jürgen von Arnim.[7] His qualities were recognized in an evaluation by General Walter Model, the commander-in-chief of the 9th Army; the succinctly worded assessment included the following statement: "He lives and leads in accordance with the National Socialist worldview."[8] The diplomat Rudolf Rahn served as the highest civilian representative of Nazi Germany and the contact person for the executive authority of the French resident-general Admiral Estéva and Sidi Moncef, the bey of Tunis, who remained in place. Italian troops also arrived at the bridgehead a few days after the Wehrmacht.[9] The Germans, in particular, were enthusiastically welcomed by the Arabs. Rahn reported from Tunis in early December that transports of British prisoners of war were being escorted

---

3. DRZW, vol. 6, p. 715ff; Keegan, p. 493f.; cf. press department of AA, SPN, Nov. 18, 1942, PAAA, R 29866; GenStdH/Abt. FHW telex, Nov. 17, 1942, BA-MA, RH 2/464.

4. Hirszowicz, *Reich*, p. 270; Carpi, *Mussolini*, p. 229f.

5. Hitler to Pétain, Nov. 11, 1942, PAAA, R 29866; DRZW, vol. 6, pp. 741–745; Keegan, p. 494.

6. Rahn/AA to AA, Nov. 21, 1942, PAAA, R 27766; Hirszowicz, *Reich*, p. 270; Gundelach, vol. 1, p. 456.

7. Carpi, *Mussolini*, p. 230; Hirszowicz, *Reich*, p. 281.

8. Quoted in Neitzel, p. 429; in addition, the British considered Arnim to be extremely anti-Semitic and anti-Bolshevik, cf. ibid.

9. Rahn/AA to AA, Nov. 15, 1942, PAAA, R 27766 Greiselis, p. 160; Carpi, *Mussolini*, p. 230; Hirszowicz, *Reich*, p. 281.

through the streets by cheers for Germany.[10] And in late January 1943, there were still frequent Arab complaints about French police arresting those who shouted "Heil Hitler" when they saw German troops.[11]

Nevertheless, the Axis troops' position in the Tunisian bridgehead was not at all secure during the first weeks. The first engagements with British forces took place on November 17, and Allied units advanced toward Tunis after November 25. In heavy fighting, American tanks moved as far as Jedeida, 25 kilometers northwest of the capital. The Germans and Italians initially considered their entire position to be directly under threat. The Mufti's emissary, who had just arrived for meetings in Tunis, was forced to quickly leave the bridgehead again.[12] Considering the situation, Nehring ordered that the front be pulled back, a decision that was sharply criticized by Kesselring; and the reason the commander-in-chief would quickly be relieved and replaced by Arnim. Then, in the days that followed, the bridgehead was again expanded to reach a main battle line that would stand for the next few weeks. The front now stretched from the Mediterranean coast, 30 kilometers west of Bizerte, via Pont du Fahs to Gabès in the south.[13]

The Allied offensive against Tunis, originally planned for December, was given up by Eisenhower on the 24th of the month in favor of supporting Montgomery's attack on the rest of Rommel's panzer army at Buerat. The field marshal, however, succeeded in withdrawing again, reaching Mareth in Tunisia by mid-February. His remaining troops thus in effect joined with Arnim's units.[14] On February 9, Kesselring ordered the two German army commanders-in-chief to carry out a coordinated attack on Eisenhower's Allied troops in the west. During this operation, on February 23, Army Group Africa was formed out of the panzer armies and the supreme command was temporarily given to Rommel.[15] The advance itself began successfully. German and Italian tanks crossed the Kasserine Pass on February 20 and reached Thala the following day, putting the entire Allied front in West Africa in danger. Due to supply problems and increasing enemy resistance, however, Rommel was forced to acknowledge that he would not be able to achieve his objective. On February 22, he ordered a halt to the offensive and withdrew his troops to the

---

10. Rahn/AA to AA, Dec. 2, 1942, PAAA, BA 61134.
11. Activity report by Feldgend. Kp. 613 Tunis, Jan. 31, 1943, BA-MA, RH 21-5/18.
12. Rahn/AA to AA, Nov. 25, 1942, PAAA, R 27766; Rahn/AA to AA, Nov. 26, 1942, PAAA, R 27766; Greiselis, p. 135; DRZW, vol. 6, p. 723f.; Gundelach, vol. 1, p. 463.
13. Gundelach, vol. 2, p. 519; DRZW, vol. 6, p. 724f.
14. DRZW, vol. 6, pp. 725, 734–737.
15. Gundelach, vol. 2, p. 536f.; Fraser, *Rommel*, p. 376f.

Mareth line in order to prepare for the now imminent attack by Montgomery from the south.[16]

As in the entire European sphere of control, the Germans had long since begun to organize the occupation regime in Tunisia, including a security police and SD commando unit. The commando was the same unit under SS-Obersturmbannführer Rauff that had been pulled out of Athens in September when the hope of conquering Egypt was thwarted. It was now being deployed in Tunisia in exactly the same strength of seven officers and seventeen noncommissioned officers and men. The instructions for Rauff's unit, as the Wehrmacht command staff explicitly emphasized, also remained the same as in July.[17] At least three additional SS officers were assigned to the commando onsite: Obersturmführer Theo Saevecke, Sturmbannführer Georg Best, and Untersturmführer Heinrich Harder.

At the time of his transfer, Saevecke had already been in Africa for six months. Born in Hamburg, he left secondary school in 1930. Regarding his reasons for leaving, he told the Race and Settlement Department nine years later that the institution was "under Jewish and Marxist leadership." After working four years as a sailor, Saevecke began a training course with the Lübeck criminal police, then attended the security police officers' academy in 1937 and passed the examination to become an inspector. By this time, the young man had already been closely connected with the National Socialist movement for a number of years. As a 15-year-old, he had been active in the Schilljugend organization of Rossbach's Freikorps; at 17 he transferred into the Lübeck SA formation, and shortly thereafter was added to the NSDAP membership book as well.[18] Following the German invasion of Poland, Saevecke was assigned to Einsatzgruppe VI in September 1939 and subsequently served as head of the murder commissariat in Posen. From there, in June 1940, he volunteered for colonial service with the security police—which just two years later would take him to Libya as the SD and security police liaison officer to the Italian police. In this role, Saevecke witnessed the advance and subsequent retreat of Rommel's panzer army, until he was transferred to Tunis at the end of 1942 to join Rauff's Einsatzkommando.[19]

---

16. Fraser, *Rommel*, p. 382f.; Gundelach, vol. 2, p. 536ff.; Keegan, p. 496f.
17. OKW/WFSt/HStb.Übs. to Dt.Gen.b.HQu.It.Wehrm., Nov. 26, 1942, BA-MA, RW 5/690; cf. Dienstkalender Himmlers, p. 617.
18. Curriculum vitae, Aug. 25, 1939, BAB, RuSHA Theo Saevecke; curriculum vitae, June 25, 1940, BA-ZA, ZR 213.
19. Posen criminal police headquarters personnel review, July 4, 1940, BA-ZA, ZR 213; recommendation for decoration, Mar. 22, 1944, BAB, R 70 Italien/20; interrogation of Theo Saevecke, Oct. 6, 1965, BAL, B 162/3174, p. 3056f.

Best was from Armsheim in Rhenish Hesse, and did not join the "movement" quite as early as Saevecke did. He joined the NSDAP on June 1, 1931, and became a member of the SS at the same time. After training to become a mechanical engineer, he made a career change in November 1933 and was appointed administrative officer of the Mainz Gestapo. Best worked in Rauff's *Amt* VI F at the RSHA after 1939; his transfer to the Einsatzkommando may have been at the initiative of his superior.[20] Heinrich Harder, the third new SS officer ordered to Tunisia, was born in Frankfurt. He joined the Hitler Youth at 16, and then as a 17-year-old, at the end of 1931, transferred to the SS. After training and several years of practical experience as a clerk in Frankfurt, Harder moved to Berlin.[21]

In addition to the expansion of the officer corps, the rest of the personnel structure of the SS Einsatzkommando was enlarged as well in January 1943. After the first weeks of the mission, in which it became clear that the unit was understaffed, considering its many and varied tasks, the Berlin headquarters responded by approving an increase in the total strength of Rauff's unit to 100 men. This composition seems to have been maintained until the commando was withdrawn from North Africa.[22] As reinforcements, for example, 16 German nationals who were former members of the French Foreign Legion were assigned to the Einsatzkommando; they were to be used "in large-scale activist operations during bright moonlit nights."[23]

Jews had been living in Tunisia for 2,000 years. In the mid-1930s their community numbered approximately 85,000, of whom 5,000 held Italian citizenship. The Tunisian Jews lived primarily in the larger cities, among a majority population of 2,330,000 Muslims; Tunis alone was home to more than half of all the Jews in the country.[24] Anti-Semitic activities and assaults occurred there long before the Germans arrived. Within a few months after the outbreak of World War II, the Muslim population had carried out repeated attacks in many cities, causing damage to businesses and homes and injuries to individuals. In addition, Vichy introduced a series of special anti-Semitic laws in the Maghreb. The Christian-oriented Admiral Estéva prevented their implementation, how-

---

20. SS membership card, BAB, SSO Georg Best; curriculum vitae, Dec. 1, 1934, BAB, RuSHA Georg Best; interrogation of Georg Best, Oct. 29, 1964, BAL, B 162/16674; Abitbol, p. 132, is incorrect in the assumption that Georg Best was the brother of Dr. Werner Best, the temporary Reich plenipotentiary in Denmark; on his origins: Herbert, p. 42; Petrick, p. 60f.

21. SS membership card, BAB, SSO Heinrich Harder; curriculum vitae, June 23, 1935, BAB, RuSHA Heinrich Harder.

22. CdS/II C 1 to head of RK, April 22, 1943, BAB, R 58/860; Pz.AOK 5/Ic war diary, Jan. 11, 1943, BA-MA, RH 21-5/27.

23. RSHA VI to RFSS adjutancy, Jan. 7, 1943, BAB, NS 19/3787.

24. Carpi, *Mussolini*, p. 198; Mejcher, p. 634f.; EdH, vol. 3, p. 1438.

ever, allowing the Tunisian Jews to remain largely unaffected.[25] This benign attitude was by no means shared by all French nationals, though. In April 1943, the Axis troops' Abwehr officer reported that French youth groups based in Tunisia were so radically politicized that "even today, at great risk, they openly champion the idea of European solidarity against Anglo-Saxons, Jews, and Bolsheviks."[26]

The SS Einsatzkommando began its activities against the local Jews shortly after it arrived in Tunisia on November 24.[27] Just days earlier, leading community members had been arrested by the Germans but then released quickly when the French resident-general interceded. In his memoirs, Rahn claimed to have taken the decision personally, in opposition to Rauff. But since the Einsatzkommando was not even in Tunis at the time of the arrests, the responsibility for the arrests would much more likely have come from the civilian administration and thus directly with Rahn himself.[28] The diplomat's credibility as "rescuer of the Jews" is further damaged by his own reports to the Foreign Office. On November 22, he had requested Arabic radio broadcasts with an "anti-Jewish bias."[29] Then, on January 13, 1943, he spoke of his "extremely close collaboration" with Rauff. He did not lack for initiatives of his own, either. One week later, Rahn reported that he had seized all radios in Jewish possession because the owners were using the equipment to transmit Allied propaganda.[30]

At a December 6 meeting with Nehring, in which Rahn and Rauff also participated, the representatives of the Wehrmacht, the security police, and the Foreign Office agreed upon a large-scale deployment of Jewish forced laborers to work on the front lines.[31] Moishe Borgel, the Jewish community council chairman, and Haim Bellaïche, the chief rabbi—the two leading Jewish representatives in Tunis—were subsequently summoned to meet with Rauff. He informed them of Nehring's order that the community council be disbanded and that all Jews were to perform forced labor for the Axis. Rauff ordered the immediate formation of a nine-member Jewish council that would implement the German directives. The Obersturmbannführer also demanded the immediate preparation of a list of 2,000 persons fit for work. He threatened the

25. EdH, vol. 3, p. 1438f.; Metzger, p. 641; Mejcher, p. 635; on the reaction of the North African Jews: Abitbol, p. 38f.
26. Report by HGr Afrika/Ic, April 19, 1943, BA-MA, RH 2/600.
27. Pz.AOK 5/Ic war diary, Nov. 24, 1942, BA-MA, RH 21-5/25.
28 Abitbol, p. 127; Rahn, p. 203f.; OKW/WFSt/HStb.Übs. to Dt.Gen.b.HQu.It.Wehrm., Nov. 26, 1942, BA-MA, RW 5/690; Greiselis, p. 178, also presumes the arrests took place "in the initial zeal" of the Einsatzkommando.
29. Rahn/AA to AA, Nov. 22, 1942, PAAA, R 27766.
30. Ibid., Jan. 13, 1943, PAAA, R 27766; Ibid., Jan. 20, 1943, PAAA, R 27766.
31. Pz.AOK 5/Ic war diary, Dec. 6, 1942, BA-MA, RH 21-5/25.

instant arrest of 10,000 Jews if the community failed to cooperate. Finally, Rauff also ordered the Jewish forced laborers to wear yellow stars on their backs, so that they could always be recognized and could be shot if they tried to escape.[32]

After Admiral Estéva, who had been notified in the meantime, succeeded in extending the German ultimatum deadline by 24 hours, Rauff called for the 2,000 Jewish laborers to be supplied the following morning. Given the short amount of time, the Jewish council was unable to comply with the order; a hastily publicized appeal brought in only 128 Jews on December 9. After Rauff had confirmed the result, he threatened furiously to shoot everyone present and then rushed with his men to the main synagogue, where he arrested all the worshippers. Numerous arrests were also made at other community facilities. All those arrested were transported by the SS to the Cheylus camp 65 kilometers from Tunis. On the way there, one of the Germans from the escort commando murdered a handicapped boy.[33]

In the meantime, Rauff summoned Borgel again, berated him, and disclosed to him that he had already had numerous Jews killed in Poland and in the occupied Soviet Union; he would soon do the same in Tunisia. Members of the SS Einsatzkommando then appeared in the Jewish town hall, arrested all those present, and demanded a list of 100 persons who would serve as hostages to ensure that the German demands were carried out. Given Rauff's repressive approach, the newly constituted Jewish council saw no alternative but to issue an appeal urging all men from 18 to 27 years of age to report for work.[34] As a result, Rahn telegraphed Berlin on December 9 with the message, "Jewish labor service initiated."[35]

In addition to Estéva, who had repeatedly interceded, the Italians also interfered with the implementation of the anti-Jewish measures from the outset. Rahn's report on the initiation of forced labor thus contained the important qualification that the Italian consulate general had resolutely opposed the involvement of Jews having Italian citizenship.[36] In early September, the Axis partner had already protested against the application of the anti-Semitic laws to the Italian Jews living in Tunisia, based on their important economic contribution—which would come to an end in the event of the planned "Aryaniza-

32. Carpi, *Mussolini*, p. 234; Abitbol, p. 129f.
33. Abitbol, p. 130f.; EdH, vol. 3, p. 1440.
34. Abitbol, p. 131f.; Carpi, *Mussolini*, p. 234.
35. Rahn/AA to AA, Dec. 9, 1942, PAAA, BA 61134; in the areas occupied by Italian troops, the Axis partner refused the intervention of the Einsatzkommando and insisted on interning all Jews itself, telex from OKW/WFSt/Qu.IV to AA, Dec. 4, 1942, PAAA, BA 61134.
36. Rahn/AA to AA, Dec. 9, 1942, PAAA, BA 61134.

tion," to Italy's detriment.[37] In view of their ally's attitude, the Germans were forced to dispense with the use of Italian Jews for forced labor and to generally exempt them from the special measures.[38]

The hostile stance of many Italians toward the German Jewish policy and the opposition of the French resident-general were no doubt influential factors in the SS Einsatzkommando's failure to organize mass murder in Tunisia. There were also disproportionately worse conditions for implementation than, for example, in German-occupied Eastern Europe. The restricted area of the North African bridgehead and the proximity of the Allied troops presented the danger that the extermination of the Jews could become quickly revealed. As an alternative to on-site killings, Rauff could have deported the Tunisian Jews directly to the extermination camps in occupied Poland. This option was not a viable solution either, however, due to limited transport capacity and Allied control of most air and sea routes.

If the conditions in the bridgehead had been more favorable and less consideration necessary for the Italian allies, Rauff would doubtless have been ready to engage in mass murder in Tunisia as well—or so his earlier actions strongly suggest. An assessment by Rahn, who explicitly praised the "extraordinarily energetic and successful activity of Obersturmbannführer Rauff," also indicates that Rauff's pursuit of his true convictions in Tunisia was constrained against his will.[39] Rather than killing the Jews, the SS Einsatzkommando in North Africa was primarily engaged in registering, robbing, and terrorizing the Jews, as well as using them extensively as forced laborers for the Axis powers. Even though the mass murder of the Tunisian Jews remained unimplemented, Rauff and the rest of the occupation command structure nevertheless established a true reign of terror during their five-month presence.[40]

After the initiation of the forced labor program, the Obersturmbannführer entrusted the direct oversight of the arrangements' execution to his staff. Saevecke and Pohl maintained contact with the Jewish community in Tunis after December 10; both issued specific instructions twice a day. Outside the capital, Best was the contact for the community in Sfax. He was also responsible for the Jews living in Sousse, although Saevecke often appeared there as well.[41] The forced labor system was steadily expanded. Those born in

37. IB Berlin to AA, Sept. 2, 1942, PAAA, R 29837.
38. Note by Woermann/AA, Nov. 24, 1942, PAAA, R 29948; note by Woermann/AA, Nov. 25, 1942, PAAA, R 29948; Woermann/AA to Schnurre/AA, Dec. 4, 1942, PAAA, R 29948; Carpi, *Mussolini*, p. 234; Abitbol, p. 128; Greiselis, p. 178.
39. DG Italy to HöSSPF Italy, April 15, 1944, BAB, R 70 Italien/19.
40. OKW/WFSt/Qu.IV to RFSS, Dec. 8, 1942, BAB, NS 19/1775; OK HGr Afrika/Ic to OKH/GenStdH/Op.Abt., April 19, 1943, BA-MA, RH 2/600; recommendation for decoration by HöSSPF Italy, Feb. 25, 1945, BAB, R 70 Italien/19; cf. Longerich, p. 255f.; Hilberg, p. 685ff.
41. Abitbol, p. 132f.

the years 1912 to 1915 were taken in December, followed continuously by new conscriptions until April 21, 1943, when the Germans pressed into service those born between 1900 and 1908.[42] There were ultimately more than 30 labor camps for men conscripted in the capital alone, with appalling conditions prevailing in many of them. Only the camps operated by the Italians seem to have had better conditions.[43] The forced labor arrangements organized by the Einsatzkommando in other Tunisian cities differed, sometimes significantly, from the situation in Tunis. In Sousse all Jewish men between the ages of 18 and 50 were required to report for repair work at the harbor every morning, while in Sfax 100 Jews were assigned to build bomb shelters and unload military transports. Plans even called for the construction of a concentration camp in Sfax, but they were not realized, due to the impending military defeat.[44]

In addition to the forced labor program, the occupying power in Tunisia began to rob the Jewish communities. In December, with the justification that "international Jewry" was responsible for the Allied bomb attacks on Tunisian cities, a compulsory levy of 20 million francs was imposed to repair the resulting damage.[45] In April 1943, the amount extorted totaled was at least 50 million francs.[46] On February 13, a sum of 10 million francs was demanded of the long-established Jewish community on the island of Jerba. When the people were unable to raise the funds, they were given the alternative of handing over 50 kilograms of gold. They succeeded in collecting 43 kilograms, which were delivered to the Germans.[47] Official coercive measures such as these were hardly distinguishable from the countless additional private acts of plundering.

In view of the steady Allied advance, the Tunisian Jews began to hope, by March at the latest, for an early victory over the Axis powers. Escaping and going into hiding now appeared to be promising options for those who wanted to avoid risking their lives in the forced labor program or being deported to an uncertain fate by the Germans at the last minute. For this reason, the number of Jewish forced laborers in the Italian zone dropped from 930 to 160 at the end of March. Likewise, in the German-controlled area the figure declined to just 1,556 by the end of April.[48] On April 12, due to the flight of numerous Jews and the increased labor requirements brought about by the precarious

42. Ibid., p. 137; Carpi, *Mussolini*, p. 235.
43. Abitbol, p. 138ff.; Carpi, *Mussolini*, p. 237; for a map with the locations of the forced labor camps: Carpi, *Mussolini*, p. 196.
44. EdH, vol. 3, p. 1440; Abitbol, p. 138.
45. Rahn/AA to AA, Dec. 22, 1942, PAAA, R 27766; Metzger, p. 642.
46. Ibid., April 6, 1943, PAAA, R 27767; Greiselis, p. 178.
47. Abitbol, p. 142.
48. Ibid., p. 141; Carpi, *Mussolini*, pp. 235, 238; in mid-April the Wehrmacht still estimated the number of Jewish forced laborers at 7,000, report by HGr Afrika/Ic, April 19, 1943, BA-MA, RH 2/600.

military situation, the Axis powers extended the work obligation (which had previously applied only to the Jewish communities) to the entire Tunisian civilian population.[49]

Until the end, the reaction of Tunisia's Muslim majority population to the treatment of the Jews seems to have been characterized by widespread indifference. Gestures of support and active assistance for the minority being disenfranchised, plundered, and conscripted into forced labor were very rare.[50] Others also unmistakably showed their hatred for the Jews. Arab passersby would publicly insult and physically attack individuals; however, these types of anti-Semitic outbursts do not seem to have been a mass phenomenon.[51] Nevertheless, Einsatzkommando Tunis reported in early December regarding the areas occupied by the Allies that "the native population in North Africa is extremely agitated because of the release of the communists and Jews, and for this reason experts believe that intensifying the Arabic radio propaganda now would have a great impact, especially if it were to stress more heavily the opposition between Arabs and Jews."[52]

Among the Muslims, Amin el-Husseini was probably the first to attempt to promote collaboration with the Axis in Tunisia and the neighboring North African countries. The day after the Allied landing, he offered to deliver a radio address to help mobilize the Arabs; it was broadcast two days later from the transmitters in Bari and Zeesen.[53] On November 18, he also authored a memorandum in which he warned about the power of Allied propaganda and cautioned against a decline in support for the Axis in the Maghreb countries. As the cornerstone of a promising policy for the Germans and Italians, he suggested the formation of a "Maghreb liberation army" consisting of prisoners of war and North African laborers. The Mufti also argued, in accordance with his well-known strategy, that all possible means must be employed to incite uprisings in the areas held by the British and Americans. To create a favorable turning point for the Axis and a new power base for himself, el-Husseini revived one of his old demands. He suggested that the Maghreb be publicly promised freedom and independence, guaranteed by an appropriate agreement. The Arabs drawn to the Axis side in this way, announced the Mufti optimistically, would "deliver at least half a million brave soldiers experienced in warfare in those areas" for Germany and Italy. With regard to the basic motives of the Arabs, he concluded, "If the Maghreb sympathizes with the

---

49. Rahn/AA, April 12, 1943, PAAA, R 27767; Abitbol, p. 147; Greiselis, p. 175f.
50. Satloff, p. 33.
51. Abitbol, p. 147.
52. Head of RSHA VI to AA, Dec. 3, 1942, PAAA, R 101101.
53. Greiselis, p. 134.

Axis, it is only because these powers are former enemies of France and are fighting the Jews, the manipulators of the Anglo-Americans."[54] From Tunis, Rahn supported such plans; the diplomat was under no illusions about the outcome. "Consequences of arming the Arabs, such as the plundering of French settlements or pogroms against the Jews, would be accepted," he declared to the Foreign Office in early December.[55]

In parallel to his memorandum, el-Husseini offered another suggestion. To help oppose the British-American landing, he proposed directing an appeal to the North African Arabs, warning them against collaboration with the Allies. The text, which he included as a draft, again had an exclusively anti-Semitic orientation and focused on the Jews' supposed position of power in the United States. "Ever since the Jewish influence in America began to increase after the Great War," it said, "that country has become a serious obstacle to freedom for the Arabs. America has always supported the Zionist movement, both politically and financially, in order to turn Palestine into a Jewish state." The Mufti then attempted to make a case for the North Africans' hostile behavior toward the Allies. On this subject, the paper included the following statement: "The North Africans know very well what misfortune the Jews have brought them. They know that the Jews were the champions of the imperialism that has mistreated North Africa for so long. They know to what extent the Jews served the imperialists as spies and accomplices, and how they appropriated the sources of power in the North African areas, sucked out their wealth, and corrupted them in every way."[56]

Not least because of the precarious military situation, the Wehrmacht commander-in-chief received el-Husseini's proposals with great interest and declared that Arab collaboration and the incitement of uprisings against the Allies in North Africa would be "extraordinarily valuable." The Foreign Office was promptly requested to establish the corresponding political framework for Arab collaboration and, in particular, to review questions relating to a declaration of independence by the Axis.[57] The high esteem in which the Mufti was still held by the Wehrmacht was also revealed at a December 8 meeting in Berlin between el-Husseini and Canaris. The latter subsequently averred that in Tunisia, thanks to the involvement of the Mufti, "active support by the native population" had already been achieved "in all Abwehr affairs."[58]

---

54. Memorandum by Mufti, Nov. 18, 1942, PAAA, BA 61124.
55. Rahn/AA to AA, Dec. 5, 1942, PAAA, R 27766.
56. DG Rome to AA, Nov. 19, 1942, PAAA, R 29866.
57. OKW/Ausl/Abw to AA, Dec. 3, 1942, PAAA, R 29867; note by Woermann/AA, Dec. 8, 1942, PAAA, BA 61124.
58. Head of OKW/Ausl/Abw to chief of OKW, Dec. 9, 1942, PAAA, R 29867.

As with his numerous prior attempts to influence the Axis powers' policies in the Middle East, el-Husseini doubtless saw in the German-Italian intervention in Tunisia a new opportunity to promote Arab nationalism and the creation of an empire under his leadership—which would be brought about by the Third Reich in opposition to the Allies. Many times he repeated his request for the publication of a declaration of independence for the Maghreb.[59] Mussolini, who had also heard about the Mufti's plans, of course, flatly refused to issue a declaration of independence because it would damage French interests—and, not least, thwart his own intentions in North Africa as well. In December, out of consideration for both their Italian ally and France, the Germans finally rejected all these wishes as well and endeavored to assure Italy of its primacy in the region.[60] In early March 1943, however, el-Husseini again attempted to induce the Axis powers to guarantee the independence of the Arab countries. His proposal regarding this matter naturally contained the requisite reference to Palestine. He framed it as follows: "The Axis powers are ready to abolish the Jewish national home in Palestine, which is in opposition to the interests of the Arab and Islamic world."[61]

As he had done during Rommel's advance in Egypt, the Mufti offered in November 1942 to travel to North Africa himself in order to capitalize upon his influence among Arab circles on behalf of the Axis.[62] Hitler ultimately decided to prohibit the trip to Tunisia in order to avoid further irritating the already mistrustful Italians with a dubious policy in their claimed sphere of interest.[63] In collaboration with el-Husseini and other Arab exiles in Germany, however, extensive propaganda activities were developed, the products of which found wide distribution in the countries of the Maghreb. Regarding the character of the Germans in the Maghreb, a leaflet on the behavior of Wehrmacht personnel toward the North African population stated: "The Arab esteems and respects the Germans! He sees in German soldiers the best soldiers in the world."[64]

But because Germany's positive image was hardly sufficient for a promising campaign, the propagandists availed themselves of the familiar anti-Western resentments and again resorted primarily to anti-Semitism: "Hear ye,

---

59. Mufti to RAM, Jan. 28, 1943, PAAA, BA 61125; Prüfer/AA to RAM, Feb. 10, 1943, PAAA, BA 61125; draft by Mufti (undated/Mar. 1943), PAAA, BA 61125; on his motives for creating an Arab empire: head of RSHA VI to AA, Oct. 20, 1942, PAAA, R 27332.

60. DG Rome to AA, Dec. 11, 1942, PAAA, BA 61134; Greiselis, p. 138ff.

61. Draft by Mufti (undated/Mar. 1943), PAAA, BA 61125.

62. Head of Amt Ausl/Abw to chief of OKW, Dec. 9, 1942, PAAA, R 29867; when el-Husseini realized that his wishes for Axis-guaranteed independence for the Arab countries would again not be granted by Germany and Italy, he even offered to travel to North Africa without preconditions, note by StS./AA, Dec. 10, 1942, PAAA, BA 61124; StS./AA to RAM, Dec. 12, 1942, PAAA, BA 61124.

63. Carpi, *Mufti*, p. 127.

64. Draft of leaflet (undated/Jan. 1943), BA-MA, RH 21-5/27.

noble Arabs!" began an appeal targeted at the Arab population. "Free yourselves from the English, the Americans, and the Jews! Defend your families,
your property, and your faith! Because the English, Americans, Jews, and their
allies are the Arabs' and Islam's greatest enemies!"[65] A text prepared by the
Foreign Office in early December for distribution via leaflets and radio in
Morocco included the following: "What do the Americans want? They want to
help the Jews. The Americans are enemies of Germany because Germany
wants to eliminate the Jewish threat, for you and for all peoples. [...]
Moroccans! If you work for America, you are working for the Jews and en-
slaving yourselves further. [...] You know that you have powerful friends in
Adolf Hitler and his soldiers [...]. Take up weapons, wherever you find them.
Inflict damage on the enemy wherever you can. Practice sabotage!"[66] Such
appeals were not without results. An American pilot shot down over Tunisia
stated during his interrogation in early January 1943 that the Allied supply convoys often suffered slashed tires and punctured fuel tanks. With regard to the
attitude of the Muslim population, the prisoner declared that the Allies in
North Africa saw themselves facing an "unanticipated Arab problem" as the
war continued.[67]

The German consulate general in Tangier, which was to distribute the
above-mentioned sabotage appeal, was so active that Spain, the protectorate
power, had to fend off British protests. The SS, which belonged to the staff of
the German representation, had repeatedly attracted attention in the city
because of its extremely provocative behavior and had organized extensive
propaganda activities. For this reason, in August 1943 Great Britain demanded
that Spain immediately close the consulate general—a demand that the Franco
dictatorship complied with in May of the following year.[68] At the end of
December 1942, Rieth, a member of that German diplomatic representation,
suggested to his superiors in the Foreign Office that a propaganda campaign be
launched to promote pro-Axis attitudes in Morocco. He drafted the key content himself. The diplomat believed the propagation of the following line of
thought would be particularly effective: "Thanks to the heroic resistance of
your Arab brothers in Palestine, England's attempt—carried out with savage
means—to deliver this entire country to the Jews has failed. Now Roosevelt
has promised the Jewish leaders that he will make a Jewish national home out
of Morocco. The American soldiers are your enemies! Behind every one of
them stands a Jew who will remain when the soldier leaves. Moroccans! Prove

---

65. Translation of leaflet (undated/Jan. 1943), BA-MA, RH 21-5/27.
66. Propaganda appeal (undated/Dec. 1942), PAAA, R 29867.
67. Rahn/AA to AA, Jan. 20, 1943, PAAA, R 27766.
68. Storch de Gracia, p. 7f.

yourselves worthy of your brothers in Palestine!"[69] Almost identically worded propaganda was distributed that same month in French Morocco as well. The leaflets in mass circulation there read, "Consider that behind every U.S. soldier stands a Jew who is waiting in America to come to Morocco in order to take away your land and rob you, even worse than the French did."[70]

In their propaganda campaigns, the Germans again availed themselves of the Koran as well as Muslim symbolism. A leaflet whose text was framed by a Hand of Fatima quoted a sura from the Islamic holy book and then continued in a similar style: "'You will find that the worst enemies of the believers are the Jews and the idol worshipers.' (Sura 5:85) The Jews and usurers, they take from the believers what they own, and for that they should be punished. The Americans and English who have invaded the Maghreb are friends of the Jews; Roosevelt and Churchill eat out of the Jews' hands. Whoever is against the Jews must also be against the Americans and English."[71] By disseminating propaganda content such as this, the Germans in the region hoped to incite revolts against the Americans and the British; they also set out quite purposefully to foment anti-Semitism and spur the Arabs to attack the Jewish minority. In the German instructions for "whisper propaganda" in Morocco, one of these strategies is stated quite explicitly: "(2) The Jewish element provides another starting point for the outbreak of hostilities between the population and the American occupiers. The native population is to be encouraged to engage in anti-Jewish violence; because the Americans will then be forced to take on the protection of the Jews, this will bring about the desired conflict between the Americans and the natives: [...] Approved terminology for 2: Instigation of demonstrations, clashes, and pogroms against Jews. Calls to loot Jewish businesses and refusal to pay interest and repay loans. Reestablishment of the mellahs (ghettos) and the obligation to wear Jewish dress, etc. Noguès as protector of the Jews."[72]

It is not difficult to imagine that the German efforts bore fruit and had an immediate impact in the Maghreb. In late November 1942, the above-mentioned Rieth reported as follows to the Foreign Office regarding the situation in Morocco: "Because of the recent repeated incidents, the American occupation authorities in Casablanca ordered the military to block off the Jewish quarter, the so-called mellah. For the time being, the measure is valid for two weeks. By doing this, they hope to prevent new violence by the Moroccan

69. DGK Tangier to AA, Dec. 30, 1942, PAAA, R 60650.
70. DGK Tangier to AA, Dec. 19, 1942, PAAA, R 60660.
71. Translation of propaganda postcard (undated), BA-MA, RH 21-5/26.
72. Schmieden/AA, Nov. 29, 1942, approved terminology for whisper propaganda in Morocco, PAAA, R 29867.

population against the Jews." Not least because of these anti-Jewish excesses, the Americans also imposed a strict weapons ban.[73]

One of the Arab factions that the Germans hoped to win over to the Axis side was the Tunisian Neo-Destour Party, a nationalist party founded in 1934. The majority of its leaders, who had named their organization after the Arabic word for "constitution," had been imprisoned by the French. After the first Neo-Destourians were released from French captivity as a result of German intervention and greeted with great enthusiasm on the streets, the crowd demanded the release of the party leaders who were still in prison in France.[74] The demand had its supporters among the Germans as well. Eitel Friedrich Moellhausen, Rahn's deputy, argued that the Arabs could be incited to action "against Jews and Anglo-Saxons" through the release of the prisoners in Marseille, without the Germans having to provide specific assurances concerning independence.[75] Woermann also speculated about sparking a revolt "of modest scope" upon the prisoners' arrival in Tunisia; as a result, "minor acts of sabotage," the "affiliation of small units" with German formations in a "guerrilla war," and an increasing refusal to support the Allies could be expected.[76]

Among the Neo-Destourians imprisoned in Marseille was the party leader Habib Bourguiba, the future president of Tunisia. His release, as well as that of six of his fellow party members, was arranged by the German Foreign Office in early December.[77] On December 18, Klaus Barbie, the Gestapo chief from Lyon, appeared personally in Bourguiba's cell, had him taken to Chalon-sur-Saône, and finally delivered him to the Italians in January 1943.[78] Bourguiba, together with his fellow party members, was not able to return to his homeland until April 7. He immediately went into hiding to avoid being captured by the Axis again. Unlike many other Neo-Destourians, he was one of the few Arab leaders who did not unquestioningly make common cause with the Axis powers and actually judged their chances of success very skeptically.[79]

In addition to pro-Arab propaganda, the release of nationalists, and the attempts to spark uprisings against the Allies in the Maghreb states, the German leadership believed it held another trump card in the form of the

---

73. DGK Tangier to AA, Nov. 24, 1942, PAAA, R 29866.
74. Rahn/AA to AA, Dec. 1, 1942, PAAA, R 27766; Rahn/AA to AA, Dec. 2, 1942, PAAA, BA 61134.
75. Note by Moellhausen/AA, Dec. 8, 1942, PAAA, BA 61134.
76. Note by Woermann/AA, Dec. 14, 1942, PAAA, BA 61134.
77. Schröder, *Deutschland*, p. 213; Greiselis, p. 143; Carpi, *Mufti*, p. 129.
78. Greiselis, p. 143f.; Faligot/Kauffer, p. 99; on Bourguiba's contacts with Italian fascism: Faligot/Kauffer, p. 100.
79. DG Rome to AA, Jan. 20, 1943, PAAA, R 27766; DG Rome to AA, April 6, 1943, PAAA, R 27768; Rahn/AA to AA, Feb. 1, 1943, PAAA, R 27768; Greiselis, p. 147f.; Metzger, p. 650f.

frontline deployment of the Arab volunteer units in Tunisia, which would be used to establish a sustainable alliance on the ground with forces willing to collaborate. On November 23, el-Husseini had called for the deployment of the German-Arab Battalion, and the OKH had considered, at least since early December, transferring it from the Eastern Front via Italy to Tunis, where it could be used as the core of a new, larger volunteer unit of North African Muslims.[80] When the Italian government found out about the German plans, it suspiciously asked to what extent the Arab unit would be exploited for propaganda purposes in Tunisia.[81] Then, in Tunis, an Iraqi in German uniform, apparently a member of the Brandenburg regiment, gave a fiery nationalist speech on his own initiative before an enthusiastic Arab public and waved the Tunisian flag. This incident immediately led to complaints by the Italians, who were concerned about their sphere of influence. They claimed that the Germans did not involve either the Italian military or the foreign ministry enough in the decision-making processes in Tunisia. The Germans then felt compelled to again explicitly recognize Italian primacy in North Africa.[82]

Preparations for deploying the Arab volunteers moved ahead regardless. At the end of December, the unit was en route to the North African front, and on January 17, 1943, the commander-in-chief of the 5th Panzer Army reported from Tunisia that the German-Arab Battalion was on location.[83] After the end of March, based on an order from the OKH, the unit's only assignment was to serve as replacement troops for the newly created Arab volunteer units that the Germans in the Tunisian bridgehead had been ambitiously forming for weeks.[84] After a poor start, more than 2,000 Arabs had volunteered for service by February. Three battalions—Tunisia, Algeria, and Morocco—were formed; however, only Algeria qualified for the required readiness for action.[85] Their frontline deployment after the beginning of April remained, to general disappointment, far below expectations. Right from the start, a sizable number of Arabs defected to the enemy side. The remaining men in the Arab companies fought downright poorly on the front, in the estimation of a German staff

80. Note by Grobba/AA, Dec. 4, 1942, PAAA, BA 61125; Tillmann, p. 429.
81. IB Berlin to AA, Dec. 24, 1942, PAAA, BA 61125.
82. Rahn/AA to AA, Dec. 10, 1942, PAAA, BA 61134; Rahn/AA to AA, Dec. 13, 1942, PAAA, R 27766; memorandum by RAM, Dec. 14, 1942, PAAA, R 27766.
83. Grote/AA to Rahn/AA, Dec. 12, 1942, PAAA, R 27767; note by Woermann/AA, Dec. 24, 1942, PAAA, BA 61125; note by Prüfer/AA, Jan. 12, 1943, PAAA, BA 61125; OKW/WFSt to GenStdH/Op.Abt., Jan. 17, 1943, BA-MA, RH 2/602.
84. Order by chief of OKW, Mar. 29, 1943, BA-MA, RH 2/597; cf. note by Ritter/AA, Dec. 14, 1942, PAAA, R 27827.
85. Greiselis, p. 152f.

officer. As a result of these sobering realizations, the volunteer companies in North Africa were subsequently used only as labor units.[86]

The negative experience with the Arab units was in any case one of the Axis troops' minor problems. With the arrival of spring, the military situation in the Tunisian theater of war became increasingly precarious. On February 23, Rommel was named commander-in-chief of Army Group Africa, which had just been created by merging the two panzer armies.[87] After the successful but then discontinued offensive in western Tunisia at the end of February, Rommel ordered an attack to the south, to counter the threat posed there by Montgomery's 8th Army. The operation, under the code name "Capri," ended in defeat. At Medenine, on the morning of March 6, the weak Axis troops reached the fortified positions of the far superior British, who repelled the enemy; Rommel lost one-third of his remaining 150 panzers.[88] The field marshal's days on the African continent were now numbered. On March 9, he flew to meet with Hitler at his headquarters. Two days later, Hitler relieved Rommel of his command of the army group. On March 4, Hitler had already said that he considered the Tunisian theater to be lost. Despite the disaster at Stalingrad a few weeks earlier, he was again unable to decide for an organized withdrawal, which could have saved the men and the war matériel. The fate of Army Group Africa was thus sealed.[89]

The 8th Army under Montgomery launched a new offensive in the south on March 20; during this operation, on April 7, the army successfully joined up with Eisenhower's troops. A large-scale attack by the Allies followed on May 6. They broke through the German-Italian front, and Tunis and Bizerte fell in the next few days. The remains of Army Group Africa retreated to the headland of Cape Bon, where, in a hopeless situation, the last troops surrendered on May 13. Because a large-scale evacuation could not be organized at the end, due to Hitler's order not to retreat and the Allies' complete air and naval supremacy, 250,000 soldiers were taken as prisoners of war. Among them were the two commanders-in-chief of the Axis troops, Arnim and Messe.[90] The German and Italian military presence in Africa had come to an end.

During the Allied advance in Tunisia in the spring of 1943, Rauff's SS Einsatzkommando had also progressively lost its field of operation, and initial preparations were made for evacuation. Due to the chaotic situation in the rapidly constricting pocket, the SS were unable to implement the original plan

---

86. Note by Schnurre/AA, June 26, 1943, PAAA, R 27332; Greiselis, p. 153; Tillmann, p. 445.
87. Keegan, p. 497.
88. Gundelach, vol. 2, pp. 540–544; Fraser, *Rommel*, p. 385ff.
89. Fraser, *Rommel*, p. 387ff.; Keegan, p. 498f.; Gundelach, vol. 2, p. 544f.
90. Gundelach, vol. 2, pp. 548–554, 577-584; Hirszowicz, *Reich*, p. 305; Keegan, p. 498f.

of deporting the leading representatives of the Jewish community in Tunis to Germany. Borgel had been warned of the planned action in advance by a leading Muslim dignitary in Tunis, who also offered him refuge in his house.[91] However, the attempt to save approximately 20 Jewish and non-Jewish resistance fighters was unsuccessful. They were carried off to concentration camps in Germany, where some of them were killed.[92]

On May 9, four days before the final surrender of the Axis troops, Rauff and all his men were flown out of Tunis. The unit was taken to Naples, and then to Corsica for a few weeks on a security police assignment.[93] In early September 1943 Rauff was assigned to the commander of the security police and SD for Italy, where, as commander of the Northern Italy-West group, his responsibilities included "partisan control."[94] One of his subordinates in Italy, Saevecke, also became chief of the security police in Milan. In early August 1944, the underground carried out a bomb attack on a German military truck. Although no German soldiers were injured, six Italian civilians were killed. As "retribution," Saevecke had 15 Italian hostages shot in Milan's Piazzale Loreto on August 10.[95]

---

91. Abitbol, p. 148; Satloff, p. 33.
92. Abitbol, p. 146.
93. Rauff to HGr Afrika/Ic, May 11, 1943, NAK, HW 19/271.
94. Recommendation for decoration by HöSSPF Italy, Feb. 25, 1945, BAB, R 70 Italien/19; interrogation of Kurt Loba, Oct. 27, 1964, BAL, B 162/16690; on the methods of "partisan control" there: Gentile, pp. 188–195.
95. Schenk, p. 269.

Chapter XIII

Muslim Units in the Wehrmacht, SD, and Waffen-SS

Even before the Mufti went to Berlin, the Wehrmacht had begun developing an Islamic unit within its ranks, in response to the urgent need for personnel because of Operation Barbarossa. By the end of November 1941 the Germans had already suffered losses of 743,112 dead, injured, or missing soldiers; this corresponded to 23.12 percent of the entire Eastern Army.[1] Given this bloodletting, individual army formations had long started to add local auxiliary volunteers into the rear logistical services and to some degree into frontline units as well, and on November 15 the quartermaster general authorized the formation of groups of 100 "prisoners of war of Turkistani and Caucasian ethnicities" in the rear echelons of Army Group South's operating area.[2] The shortage of security forces compelling the Germans to "use all indigenous elements hostile to the Soviet system in the occupied eastern territories" was also the basis for the order issued on January 9, 1942, that an additional group of 100 "trustworthy released prisoners of war and local residents" should be raised in every army.[3] This was the beginning of the Eastern legions.

---

1. KTB Halder, vol. 3, p. 318.
2. OKH/Gen.Qu. to Berück Süd, Nov. 15, 1941, BA-MA, RH 22/198.
3. OKH/Org.Abt. (II) to HGr, Jan. 9, 1942, BA-MA, RH 19 III/492.

On January 13, 1942, the chief of ordnance and commander of the replacement army ordered the military commander of the Generalgouvernement to raise a Turkistani legion and a Caucasian Muslim legion.[4] By August 1942 two additional Islamic units, a North Caucasian legion and a Volga Tatar legion, had been raised as well. The Eastern legions' formation staff at the Rembertów training area (in Radom after the summer of 1942) constituted their leadership. The regulations for raising the Eastern legions, issued on April 24, defined these formations, which in any event would be headed by German commanders, as "units of volunteers fighting for the liberation of their homeland from Bolshevism and for freedom to follow their beliefs."[5] The ethnic insignia that the legionnaires wore on the right arm of their German field uniforms also indicated their Islamic roots, as it featured a crescent moon, a mosque, and crossed scimitars.[6] "The armed deployment of the legions should not only save German blood," concluded the commander-in-chief of Army Group South, "but also serve as a political weapon to subvert and weaken the enemy's resistance."[7]

In the Crimea, the 11th Army even went a step further. The Tatars, who represented 20 percent of the total population, were the only Muslim group on the peninsula. They had immediately joined up with the Germans and were therefore, "due to their voluntary enlistment, integrated into the units of the 11th Army"—that is, as an integral component of the Wehrmacht—at the beginning of 1942.[8] By the end of January, 3,000 Tatars had already signed up.[9] In March 1942, as many as 20,000 volunteers fought in the ranks of the 11th Army. Thus, one in ten Crimean Tatars was in the German army.[10] Such an undertaking cannot be confused with nonideological military service, as is evidenced by the directives developed for the Tatars' training: "Following topics will be addressed: (a) Bolshevism, the oppressor of national and individual freedom. The role of the Jews in Bolshevism."[11]

By 1943, in the Generalgouvernement and in Mirgorod in the Ukraine— where a second formation and training staff, the 162nd Infantry Division, emerged in the spring of 1942—78 reinforced Eastern legion infantry battal-

4. OKH/Chef HRüst u. BdE, Jan. 13, 1942, raising the Turkistani and Caucasian Muslim legion, BA-MA, RH 12-21/7.

5. Ibid., April 24, 1942, regulations for raising the Eastern legions, BA-MA, RH 19 V/108.

6. Hoffmann, *Ostlegionen*, pp. 25–39.

7. OK HGr Süd order, May 19, 1942, BA-MA, RH 19 V/108.

8. AOK 11/O.Qu./Qu. 2 order, Jan. 6, 1942, BA-MA, RH 20-11/407; cf. Oldenburg, p. 119ff.; Kunz, pp. 207ff., 237f.

9. AOK 11/IV Wi, report for Dec. 1, 1941–Jan. 31, 1942, BA-MA, RH 20-11/415.

10. Sonderführer Siefers to OKH/Gen.Qu., Mar. 20, 1942, raising Tatar and Caucasian formations in the area of AOK 11, BA-MA, RH 19 V/108.

11. AOK 11/1c, Feb. 18, 1942, propagandistic training of the Tatar volunteers, BA-MA, RH 20-11/457.

ions had been formed and sent to the front in three waves; 54 of them were Islamic.[12] In addition, a large number of construction and supply units, pack trains, and similar units were formed, to which legionnaires were assigned who were not fully physically fit for combat. Similar numbers would have applied to these units. The total number of Eastern legionnaires recruited in this way amounted to at least 150,000 to 170,000;[13] approximately two-thirds of them would have been Muslims. The Wehrmacht rewarded their commitment by providing mullahs down to the battalion level and with the observation of Islamic dietary and burial rules.[14] Because the Eastern legions were gradually dispersed throughout the army's entire European operational area, the need increased for consistent top leadership. For this reason, in 1943 the Army High Command named Ernst Köstring as commanding general of the Eastern troops—general of the volunteer units as of January 1, 1944.[15] In September 1944 he commanded at least 160,000 soldiers, whom he would ultimately deploy in the hot spots of the French and Italian invasion fronts. As the final unit, he formed an Eastern Muslim regiment.[16] Three Turkic battalions fought to the last man in Stalingrad, several in the Caucasus, and six battalions outside Berlin in 1945.[17]

The security police and SD took their slice of the Islamic pie as well. The Ic officer of the 11th Army ordered Otto Ohlendorf's Einsatzgruppe D to recruit the Crimean Tatars on January 2, 1942, and the very next day the "first official meeting of the Simferopol Tatar committee on the topic of beginning to enlist the Crimean Tatars for the common struggle against Bolshevism" took place. The mullah of the community declared that the Tatars' religion and their faith demanded that they take part in this holy struggle together with the Germans, and the committee chair professed, "It is an honor for us to be able to fight under the Führer Adolf Hitler, the greatest man of the German nation." Then the assembled Tatars stood up and repeated after their mullah: "1st command: For attainment of a rapid victory and the common goal, as well as for long life for the Führer Adolf Hitler." Of the 9,255 men enlisted by mid-February, the Einsatzgruppe diverted 1,632 volunteers to its own ranks and organized them into 14 Tatar security companies distributed across the peninsula. They were "decidedly oriented against Bolshevism, Jews, and gypsies" and

---

12. Hoffmann, *Kaukasien*, pp. 51, 55.
13. Ibid., p. 56.
14. Hoffmann, *Ostlegionen*, p. 136ff.
15. Ibid., p. 52; cf. Teske.
16. Memorandum by Mende/RMbO, Sept. 18, 1944, meeting with Dr. Oltzsche/SSHA on Sept. 13, BAB, R 6/143.
17. Hoffmann, *Kaukasien*, p. 156ff.; Krecker, p. 220f.

"often went as far as deliberate denunciation," praised Ohlendorf.[18] Two months later, he judged that they had "proven themselves admirably" in fighting the partisans.[19]

The SD foreign intelligence service also made use of the Islamic sounding board inside the Soviet Union. During Operation Zeppelin, which was launched in early 1942, *Amt* VI C recruited prisoners of war and defectors from the Red Army, trained them in camps and then either dropped the newly minted "activists" behind the front lines by parachute or smuggled them toward the interior through gaps in the main battle line. Their tasks alternated between sabotage and subversion, reconnaissance, and propaganda.[20] To prepare the Muslim "Turkistanis" for deployment east of the Volga or in western Kazakhstan, a pre-camp was established in Legionowo, near Warsaw,[21] and a main camp in Oswitz, near Breslau.[22] From there, they also visited the mosque in Berlin-Wilmersdorf in 1942.[23]

In Western and Central Europe, the security police and SD were also in a position to recruit Muslims to their ranks. In the summer of 1944, a unit consisting of Arabs and Moroccans under Hauptsturmführer Helmut Retzek, the former deputy commander of the security police and SD in Bordeaux and Toulouse, was deployed in southern France to fight the resistance.[24] In the fall the unit withdrew to Baccarat in the Vosges, where it perpetrated its last murders.[25] In February 1945, *Amt* Mil—the former Abwehr, which in 1944 was incorporated into *Amt* VI of the RSHA—still maintained numerous "training camps for Arab informers from Morocco, Algiers, Tunis, Palestine, Iraq, Iran," in which identification, reporting, and radio operations were taught, along with sabotage and insurrection. Screening was performed by confidants of the Mufti, and training by Palestinian Germans.[26] "An improvement in the performance of Arabs deployed as informers is easy to achieve through training, because we guide the Arabs in a particular direction politically and intellec-

18. Einsatzgruppe D, recruitment of the Crimean Tatars, status on Feb. 15, 1942, BA-MA, RH 20-11/433; cf. Einsatzgruppe D to AOK 11, Feb. 26, 1942, descriptions and locations of the Tatar self-security companies, BA-MA, RH 20-11/344; AOK 11/Qu. 2, Jan. 31, 1942, entries in war diary, BA-MA, RH 20-11/407; AOK 11/IV Wi, report for Mar. 1–31, 1942, BA-MA, RH 20-11/415; Angrick, p. 467ff.; Hoffmann, *Ostlegionen*, p. 39ff.
19. Einsatzgruppe D to AOK 11, April 16, 1942, BA-MA, RH 20-11/488.
20. Mallmann, "Krieg," p. 325ff.; Angrick, p. 477ff.
21. MiG/Ia, April 18, 1942, Operation Zeppelin, BA-MA, RH 53-23/36; RSHA VI C/Z to VI A 4 (undated/Aug. 1942), BA-ZA, RH 920/1.
22. Breslau-Oswitz camp to RSHA VI C/Z, April 15, 1943, BA-ZA, ZR 920/1.
23. Querg, p. 272f.
24. BAL, B 162/Vorl. AR 3606/65; BAL, B 162/Vorl. AR 3617/65.
25. BdS France to RSHA I, Oct. 27, 1944, BAB, R 70 Frankreich/1; Erich W. to Cologne public prosecutor's office, July 12, 1971, BAL, B 162/8433, p. 235ff.
26. Report by Kommando-Melde-Gebiet Stuttgart, Feb. 26, 1945, training camp for noncommissioned officers, Pfedelbach, Krs. Öhringen, BAB, R 58/116.

tually, such that their and our interests are parallel," summed up a German in the Stuttgart training camp for noncommissioned officers. "This is not difficult with regard to the constellation of enemy powers, as the Arabs are ab ovo sworn enemies of the Jews, the French, and to some degree also the English."[27]

For the Waffen-SS, the essential conditions for the formation of Islamic units were created in February 1943. On the 10th of the month, Hitler ordered that an SS division of Bosnian Muslims be raised in Croatia under the supervision of the Prinz Eugen, an existing ethnic German SS division.[28] In Croatia, which was led by the puppet regime of Ante Pavelić, and also in Serbia, a fierce guerrilla war had raged since the German occupation began in April 1941, tying up large numbers of troops. For this reason, it was in the German interest to look for collaborators who were willing to work against Tito's communist partisans and against the nationalist, royalist Serbian Chetniks. Three days after the Führer issued his order, Himmler charged the commander of the Prinz Eugen SS division, Gruppenführer Artur Phleps, with the formation of such a division. Although the Croatian puppet regime, after much negotiation, formally indicated its agreement, in reality the fascist Ustaši in particular torpedoed the SS plans to form the division. They feared that the self-confidence of the despised Muslims would be strengthened if the Germans formed a Muslim division, and wanted to prevent this.[29]

The Mufti again appeared on the scene in connection with the issue of arming the Muslims. He claimed to be concerned with the situation of his fellow believers in the Balkans "for a long time" and promptly appointed himself as their advocate with the Germans.[30] In late March 1943, el-Husseini went to Croatia and Bosnia for an official visit; he flew in the aircraft of Kurt Daluege, the chief of the regular police.[31] On the two-week trip he was accompanied by several SS officers from the RSHA and SS headquarters, among others. In Zagreb, Banja Luka, and Sarajevo, the Mufti met with representatives of the Croatian government, high-level religious leaders, and local dignitaries, as well as representatives of the German and Italian occupation authorities. However, one of the primary reasons for the trip, communication with the Croatian government, appeared to be a failure right from the start, as Pavelić's attitude toward el-Husseini was entirely uncooperative. Not until Berger intervened by

27. Report by Kommando-Melde-Gebiet Stuttgart, Feb. 26, 1945, Operation Conrad, BAB, R 58/116.
28. RFSS to Kdr. 7. SS-Div., Feb. 13, 1943, BAB, NS 19/2601; SSFHA order, April 30, 1943, BAB, NS 19/3523; on the 7th SS Division Prinz Eugen: Casagrande.
29 . Schnurre/AA to SS-Ostubaf. Riedweg/SSHA, Feb. 20, 1943, PAAA, R 100998; chief of SSHA to RFSS, Mar. 9, 1943, BAB, NS 19/3523; DG Zagreb to AA, Mar. 23, 1943, PAAA, R 100998; DG Zagreb to AA, July 8, 1943, PAAA, R 100997; Klietmann, p. 187.
30. Note by Mufti (undated/April 1943), PAAA, R 100998; on the Mufti's initiative in the formation of the SS Division Handschar: cf. Faligot/Kauffer, p. 144f.
31. Chief of SSHA to RFSS, Mar. 27, 1943, BAB, NS 19/2255.

telephone with the Croatian ambassador in Berlin was Pavelić's attitude "reversed."[32] Though el-Husseini avoided making any requests for independence for the Bosnian Muslims when meeting with the Croatian officials, the supporters of autonomy appeared noticeably stronger after his departure.[33] As the chief of the SS headquarters emphasized in a report to Himmler, the visit ultimately had "an extremely positive effect in every way, including politically, and should contribute significantly to pacifying this area." He also pointed out that the visit showed that the Mufti enjoyed "immense esteem in the Mohammedan world."[34]

As a precondition for the creation of a Muslim SS division, the self-proclaimed National Socialist military elite first had to further soften their racial selection criteria. In the future, the ideal of the Nordic Aryan would no longer constitute an imperative within the strictly anticlerical Waffen-SS; instead, men of "foreign race"—practicing Muslims at that—would become part of the armed SS. Without further ado, Himmler classified the Balkan Muslims among the "racially valuable peoples of Europe." However, they still had to win their place at the side of the Aryans. Now it was up to them, said Himmler, "to prove their future right to live in the framework of a National Socialist Europe by fighting and assisting in the reorganization of Europe."[35]

To smooth the way for the future SS soldiers as faithful party followers of National Socialism, some religious and cultural peculiarities would be maintained. Thus, several positions were created for imams for the division, as these were seen as essential for the men's morale.[36] In addition, Himmler personally attended to the procurement of a headdress for the Muslim recruits, which was specially made by forced laborers. After the first designs had been proposed, he required changes because the "fezes" were too similar in shape and color to those of the Moroccans and therefore needed to be "recolored and trimmed a bit."[37] He also inquired of the Mufti regarding what "Islam prescribes for its soldiers with regard to diet." When the Mufti requested a diet without alcohol or pork, a cooking course was set up near Graz.[38] Himmler afforded the Muslims the "iron-clad special right" to forgo pork and alcoholic beverages and obligated his SS officers to strictly adhere to this arrangement. As justification, he explained that the Muslims had joined the German side "out of hatred

---

32. Chief of SSHA to RFSS, April 19, 1943, BAB, NS 19/2255.
33. DG Zagreb to AA, April 28, 1943, PAAA, R 100998.
34. Chief of SSHA to RFSS, April 19, 1943, BAB, NS 19/2255.
35. RFSS order, Nov. 10, 1943, IfZ, Nbg. Dok., No-3577.
36. Chief of RFSS personal staff to Wagner/AA, May 13, 1943, PAAA, R 100998.
37. RFSS to head of WVHA, Nov. 26, 1943, BAB, NS 19/2601.
38. RFSS to chief of SSHA, July 22, 1943, BAB, NS 19/2601; chief of SSHA to RFSS, July 26, 1943, BAB, NS 19/2601.

for the common Jewish-English-Bolshevik enemy and out of veneration and loyalty to the Führer Adolf Hitler, who was revered by all of them," and for this reason they must be treated with great respect. He peremptorily forbade "any of the jokes popular in other circles or teasing the Mohammedan volunteers."[39]

Although there was "great readiness" among the Bosnian Muslims for service in the Waffen-SS, the number of volunteers enlisting in Croatia remained below expectations, even after the Mufti's visit.[40] The coarse promotional methods used by the Germans bore some of the responsibility; in addition, it turned out that the project was also being torpedoed by Croatian officials.[41] Phleps reported to Berlin that the Croatian government would "use all available means to prevent or at least delay the formation of the unit."[42] The original plan, to raise an entirely Muslim division, could not be realized in practice. Thus, a large contingent of approximately 15 percent Catholic recruits was incorporated into the volunteer unit.[43] The local difficulties ultimately led to the transfer of all the recruits and the division staff, under SS-Oberführer Karl-Gustav Sauberzweig (characterized by Himmler as a "total National Socialist"), to the south of France in the area of Le Puy.

The division was raised and trained there in the following months.[44] The change of location soon led to new problems, however. In the summer of 1943, Tito's partisans launched a large-scale offensive in Bosnia, and approximately 210,000 people soon took flight. The men in training in France were concerned about the fate of their relatives—particularly because they had originally been assured that they could serve in their homeland. During the night of September 16, open mutiny broke out. Roughly a thousand Bosnians participated in killing some of their superiors. The revolt was quickly put down, with 15 Muslim SS members losing their lives. Aside from a few death sentences, the mutineers generally received a relatively light punishment.[45]

The division was subsequently transferred for further training to the Neuhammer grounds in Silesia.[46] By early 1944, its formation had progressed to the

39. RFSS order, Aug. 6, 1943, BAB, NS 19/3285.
40. Chief of SSHA to AA, April 2, 1943, PAAA, R 100998; Bev.AA.b.Mil.befh.Serb. to AA, May 18, 1943, PAAA, R 100998.
41. RFSS to RFSS representative in Croatia, July 1, 1943, BAB, NS 19/3523; DG Zagreb to AA, July 8, 1943, PAAA, R 100997.
42. Kdr. 7. SS-Div. to chief of SSFHA, April 19, 1943, BAB, NS 19/2601.
43. Ritter/AA to AA, Feb. 21, 1943, PAAA, R 100998; DG Zagreb to AA, May 5, 1943, PAAA, R 100998; Ritter/AA to AA, May 29, 1943, PAAA, R 100998.
44. Order by chief of SSFHA, July 2, 1943, BAB, NS 19/3523; RFSS to PK, Nov. 2, 1943, BAB, NS 19/2252; Stein, p. 163f.; Klietmann, p. 187f.
45. Chief of SSHA to RFSS, Sept. 25, 1943, BAB, NS 19/2601, Gensicke, p. 190f.
46. Kdr. 13. SS-Div. to chief of SSHA, Sept. 30, 1943, BAB, NS 19/2601; note by Reichel/AA, Oct. 7, 1943, PAAA, R 100998; chief of SSHA to Reichel/AA, Oct. 11, 1943, PAAA, R 100998.

point that deployment in Yugoslavia could be considered. Both the Germans and the Muslims had high expectations; when the division arrived in February, the Germans organized a regular propaganda tour through Bosnian cities.[47] Leaflets were also distributed to inform the population about the arrival of the soldiers. "A new dawn is breaking. We are coming!" read one draft.[48] Another version proclaimed: "We bring peace to our homeland. We come as brave, free, proud SS men, united with our German comrades."[49] After recruiting additional members, the Muslim SS unit was deployed in northern Bosnia in March, against Tito's partisans.[50] In May the unit received its own name. Hitler conferred the name "Handschar" on the 13th SS Division, after the local word for the Arab scimitar.[51]

Despite raising the first Muslim SS division, the Germans did not succeed in containing the partisans in Yugoslavia, and interest in additional collaboration units soon grew. In this context, the Albanian Muslims also came into increased consideration, as several thousand men had already volunteered for service in the 13th SS Division. To accelerate recruitment for the Waffen-SS, Berger spread the rumor in October 1943 that British agents were under way in the country "with a great deal of gold," intending to win the men over to the enemy cause.[52] After Hitler had provided the necessary authorization in February, Himmler gave the official order on April 17, 1944, to raise the 21st Waffen Mountain Division of the SS, the Skanderbeg.[53] The unit was assembled in Kosovo during the months that followed. It included Albanians from the Handshar division, Albanian POWs and ablebodied men were also recruited. The volunteers mobilized by the Albanian National Committee and subsequent enlistments in the region totaled 6,500.[54] Regarding the Albanians' combat-readiness, Himmler said they had previously "proved themselves very well in their deployment," so in the future "great military benefit can be expected from them."[55] In reality, serious difficulties were involved in the formation of the Skanderbeg division from the start. In addition to inadequate equipment and weapons, there was also a shortage of German personnel to

---

47. DG Belgrade to AA, Jan. 31, 1944, PAAA, R 100984; circular by Kdr. 13. SS-Div., Feb. 25, 1944, BAB, NS 19/2601.

48. 13. SS-Div. leaflet draft (undated/spring 1944), BAB, NS 19/2601.

49. 13. SS-Div. leaflet draft (undated/spring 1944), BAB, NS 19/2601.

50. DG Zagreb to AA, Feb. 22, 1944, PAAA, R 100984; circular by Kdr. 13. SS-Div., Mar. 27, 1944, BAB, NS 19/2601; Stein, p. 164.

51. Führer order, May 15, 1944, BAB, NS 19/2601.

52. Chief of SSHA to Reichel/AA, Oct. 11, 1943, PAAA, R 100984.

53. Order by chief of OKW, Feb. 12, 1944, PAAA, R 100984; DG Tirana to AA, Mar. 5, 1944, PAAA, R 100984; Klietmann, p. 229.

54. Chief of SSHA to Reichel/AA, Feb. 5, 1944, PAAA, R 100984; order by chief of OKW, Feb. 12, 1944, PAAA, R 100984; DG Belgrade to AA, Mar. 5, 1944, PAAA, R 100984; chief of SSHA to RFSS, April 13, 1944, BAB, NS 19/2071; Klietmann, p. 229.

55. Wagner/AA to RAM, April 14, 1944, PAAA, R 100679.

train the recruits.[56] The only combat-ready battalion had in the meantime already been deployed against the partisans during the summer and fall.[57]

After October 1943, there were also initiatives to raise a third Muslim SS division. After consulting with *Amt* VI of the RSHA, Berger asked Himmler for permission to form an SS division of "Turkic peoples"; with this initiative, the Waffen-SS placed itself in open competition with the Wehrmacht with regard to recruiting.[58] The core of the unit was to be comprised of the Wehrmacht's Turkic Battalion 450, commanded by Sturmbannführer Andreas Mayer-Mader, one of the Wehrmacht officers transferred to the Waffen-SS.[59] In terms of the location in which to raise the division, one of the centers of partisan activity in Eastern Europe seemed most appropriate, as the recruits could obtain the necessary combat practice there already during training. Berger argued for Minsk and spoke of his project as a "political matter of the greatest significance and consequence," through which an additional part of the Muslim world could be won for National Socialism. In this way, it could also be demonstrated to the Mufti "that we are serious about friendship with the Mohammedan world." Even though, as Berger noted, the unit would be comprised of "savage peoples," the steadily expanding Waffen-SS would thus be strengthened by another division.[60] On May 2, 1944, Himmler then issued the formal order to raise an "Eastern Muslim" division of the Waffen-SS.[61]

El-Husseini quickly became involved in these preparations as well. On December 14, 1943, in the presence of Mayer-Mader's officers, he was introduced to the planned unit and took the opportunity to make himself its advocate. Following the discussion, the Mufti sought an appointment with Berger and submitted the wishes of the Turkmen to him. The Muslims were to be treated like the men in the Bosnian division with regard to issues such as receiving spiritual support from imams and the specific Muslim diet. The Mufti had also already thought about further strengthening the unit and suggested that all the members of "Turkic peoples" still serving in the Wehrmacht be assigned to the SS.[62] The influence that el-Husseini exerted, in this case as well, on the future Muslim officers is demonstrated in a memorandum by one of the officers from the SS headquarters concerning the meeting. Regarding the reac-

56. Klietmann, p. 229.
57. Report by Kdr. 21. SS-Div., July 7, 1944, BAB, NS 19/2071.
58. Chief of SSHA to RFSS, Oct. 15, 1943, BAB, NS 31/43; chief of SSHA to RFSS, Jan. 25, 1944, BAB, NS 19/297.
59. RFSS to Gen. Zeitzler, Nov. 8, 1943, BAB, NS 19/297; Mayer-Mader to chief of SSHA, Jan. 20, 1944, BAB, NS 19/297; Hoffmann, *Kaukasien*, pp. 138f., 145ff.
60. Chief of SSHA to RFSS, Oct. 15, 1943, BAB, NS 31/43.
61. RFSS to chief of SSHA and SSFHA, May 2, 1944, BAB, NS 19/2839.
62. Memorandum by SSHA A I, Dec. 15, 1943, BAB, NS 31/44; Mufti to chief of SSHA, Dec. 15, 1943, BAB, NS 31/44.

tion to the Mufti's statements, he noted: "Not until after the remarks by His Eminence did the Turkmen officers recognize the significance of the deployment for all of Islam; previously, from the narrower horizon of their prior missions, they had not thought of the orderly formation of a division, but only of a legion-like combat unit."[63]

To train the clerics for the Muslim SS divisions, an "imam institute" was opened under the direction of the Mufti in April 1944. SS headquarters provided el-Husseini with the house, a small hotel in Guben, Saxony.[64] In the opening address, given on April 21 in the presence of Berger, the Mufti expressed his pleasure at the creation of the institute, which was a testament to "the success of the collaboration between the Muslims and the Greater German Reich" and was based on "common interests and goals." He called upon the future imams to lead "your comrades, just like yourselves, in the Islamic merits and virtues that have contributed to the betterment of mankind, as history shows."[65] In practice, the imams worked closely with the ideological education officers from Germany. The Muslim Waffen-SS concept appeared to bear fruit quickly. Division commander Sauberzweig reported in April 1944, with regard to his 13th SS Division, that the recruits embraced "National Socialist teachings [...] only too readily." Euphorically, the Brigadeführer saw his work advance to the point "that the Muslims—SS men of the division and civilians—are beginning to see in our Führer the coming of a second prophet."[66]

The content of the division's ideological education confirmed the commander's positive assessment. During a four-day political short course at the end of March, the men gave presentations with telling titles such as "National Socialism and Islam," "The Life of Our Führer," and "The Meaning of This War."[67] At the end, a written exercise was included in the program, containing a total of twenty questions to be answered. The sixth question, regarding the awareness Hitler had gained in Vienna, was answered as follows by SS-Sturmmann Stefan Windisch: "In Vienna the Führer learned on the one hand to know the workers and their work, and on the other, the Marxist idea. That is when he began to hate the Jews."[68] The question concerning the reasons for the common struggle of National Socialism and Islam was answered in the

---

63. Memorandum by SSHA A I, Dec. 15, 1943, BAB, NS 31/44.
64. RFSS to chief of SSHA, Nov. 24, 1943, BAB, NS 19/2601; response, April 22, 1944, BAB, NS 19/2637.
65. Transcript of Mufti's speech, April 21, 1944, BAB, NS 19/2637.
66. Kdr. 13. SS-Div. to chief of SSHA, April 16, 1944, BAB, NS 19/2601.
67. Service schedule for 13. SS-Div./Abt. VI, Mar. 29, 1944, BAB, NS 19/2601.
68. Exam questions for 13. SS-Div./Abt. VI, April 1, 1944, BAB, NS 19/2601; written exam of Stefan Windisch, April 1, 1944, BAB, NS 19/2601.

following manner by Rottenführer Josip Vukelić: "They have the same enemies: Bolshevism, the Jews, the Anglo-Americans, the Freemasons, and political Catholicism."[69] On the basis of such promising results, the Mufti arranged
with the SS headquarters to avoid attempting to synthesize National Socialism
and Islam. Instead, the foundation for the ideological education of the Muslim
Waffen-SS was recorded as follows: "National Socialism will be communicated
to the Muslims as the ethnically determined ideology of the Germans, and
Islam as the ethnically determined Arab ideology." The common enemies—
with "the Jews" listed in first place, then "the Anglo-Americans," and only in
third place "communism"—were to be featured separately.[70]

Despite the expense and the numerous special rules, the practical value of
the Muslim SS formations proved to be modest. In the operational area assigned to his division, Sauberzweig had a "general peace order" proclaimed,
which, with its many regulations, in effect abrogated the authority of the
Croatian central administration—resulting in furious protests not only from
the Croatians but also from the Germans.[71] Even Berger finally had to admit
that the situation had "created a great deal of bad blood."[72] During their
missions, all the Muslim SS formations committed numerous war crimes. The
Skanderbeg division, for example, reported in July 1944 that it had taken
drastic and wide-ranging measures "against the Jews" in its area of activity.
Between May 28 and July 5 alone, "a total of 510 Jews, communists, and gang
supporters and political suspects were incarcerated as a preventive measure in
the division's own detention camp." Through "retribution measures for cases
of sabotage as well as the arrests carried out, [...] acting energetically will
strengthen the prestige of the German Wehrmacht."[73]

Regarding the conduct of the Handschar division, Hermann Fegelein,
Himmler's liaison officer in Hitler's headquarters and himself a mass murderer
of 10,000 civilians, provided his Führer a telling insight in April 1944 during a
briefing. He described how, given the Muslims' approach, "the others will run
away with everything whenever they intervene. They only kill with knives.
There was a man there who was wounded. He had his arm bound and still took
out 17 opponents with his left hand. There are also cases in which they cut out
the enemy's heart." After the description of such details, however, Hitler was

69. Translation of written exam of Josip Vukelić, April 5, 1944, BAB, NS 19/2601.
70. SSHA A I report, May 19, 1943, BAB, NS 19/2601.
71. Kdr. 13. SS-Div., Mar. 9, 1944, "Richtlinien für die Sicherung des Landfriedens in Bosnien" ["Guidelines
for Safeguarding the General Peace in Bosnia"], BAB, NS 19/2145.
72. Chief of SSHA to RFSS, Aug. 4, 1944, BAB, NS 19/1492.
73. Report by Kdr. 21. SS-Div., July 7, 1944, BAB, NS 19/2071.

entirely unimpressed. With an "I don't care!" he turned to the order of the day.[74]

The experiences with the Handschar division were not nearly as satisfactory as Fegelein attempted to assure his listeners. The unit was deployed in the region until the end of September 1944; however, Himmler could not fulfill the Wehrmacht's wishes that the division be transferred to the Yugoslav-Hungarian border to prevent a threatening merger between the Red Army and Tito's partisans.[75] It became apparent that the Muslims, fixated on defending their homeland, could not be sent to any other theater of war. But there were unmistakable signs of disintegration appearing even in the increasingly critical war situation in Yugoslavia. The men appeared to be progressively less convinced of a Nazi victory. By the beginning of October, 2,000 SS troops had defected to Tito; then another 740 followed by the end of the month.[76] Himmler therefore decided to disband the Handschar 13th Waffen Mountain Division of the SS. Some of the equipment was used elsewhere, while the primarily German command personnel were deployed as Battle Group Hanke in the defensive battles in Hungary.[77] The mission of the Skanderbeg division did not proceed as hoped either. Instead of fighting loyally and selflessly alongside the Germans as the Mufti had envisioned, the Albanians disappeared in droves. By October 1, 1944, 3,500 Muslims had deserted from the unit. Based on alarming reports such as these, the Muslim Albanian SS division was disbanded that same month. The German staff would also fight in the defensive battles in Hungary during the following months.[78]

Preparations for raising a Turkic division of the Waffen-SS also came to a standstill during the final stages of the war. Mayer-Mader, who had previously served as commander of the planned formation, was replaced because, as Berger argued, the position required "an officer who knows the Eastern Turkic-Islamic world." The choice fell on Harun el-Rashid, a German convert to Islam who was a former colonel in the Turkish general staff. He had already had the opportunity to demonstrate his knowledge in a significant position. In 1944, as Weise's successor, el-Rashid worked as RSHA liaison officer to the

---

74. Heiber, p. 560 (midday situation conference, April 6, 1944); on Fegelein as an individual and the mass crimes he committed in Central and Eastern Europe: Cüppers, *Wegbereiter*.

75. Stein, p. 163f.; Klietmann, p. 187f.

76. Chief of SSHA to RFSS, Aug. 17, 1944, BAB, NS 19/2148; Thadden/AA conversation note, Oct. 5, 1944, PAAA, R 100998; DG Zagreb to AA, Oct. 28, 1944, PAAA, R 100998.

77. DG Zagreb to AA, Oct. 27, 1944, PAAA, R 100998; DG Zagreb to AA, Oct. 28, 1944; Wagner/AA to AA, Dec. 7, 1944, PAAA, R 100998; Stein, p. 165.

78. Klietmann, p. 229.

Mufti.[79] After October 20, Himmler charged el-Rashid with raising the Eastern Turkic unit of the Waffen-SS.[80] In fact, this division was never formed. In the summer of 1944, however, in Poniatowa, near Lublin, the 1st Eastern Muslim Regiment was formed from the two Turkic battalions, 450 and I/90, with additional Wehrmacht personnel. Shortly thereafter, the regiment assisted in putting down the Warsaw uprising, together with the infamous Sonderregiment Dirlewanger. The plan was to create a division out of the Muslim unit in the fall; however, in the chaos of the final months of the war, the plan never came to pass.[81] The plans to form a fourth Waffen-SS division, consisting primarily of Muslims, ultimately met a similar fate. The 23rd Waffen Mountain Division of the SS, Kama, was raised in June 1944 with Muslim volunteers and in-dividual Handschar units. After mass desertions, however, the formation was disbanded in October.[82]

Other lofty plans for German-Muslim engagement against the Allies were likewise overtaken by events. After Churchill disclosed in the House of Commons on September 28, 1944, that several Jewish brigades were being formed within the British army, the Mufti immediately suggested the creation of an Arab Islamic army in Germany. El-Husseini's idea was that the army "would be formed of Arab and Muslim volunteers and merged with the existing Arab Islamic units."[83] In reality, the results of these grandiose projects were virtually nil. In response to an inquiry from the Foreign Office, the SS was forced to concede that just 300 Arabs were available for the Arab Islamic army. According to statements by the chief of the SS headquarters, "a greater number were anticipated," but these men never appeared.[84] Consequently, the Mufti's dreams of an Arab army disintegrated in the final phase of the war.

79. Chief of SSHA to RFSS, July 14, 1944, BAB, NS 19/2838; BAB, SSO Harun el-Rashid; Hoffmann, *Kaukasien*, p. 153.

80. RFSS order, Oct. 20, 1944, BAB, NS 19/3537.

81. Chief of SSHA to SSFHA, Aug. 10, 1944, BAB, NS 31/43; Klietmann, p. 381f.

82. Klietmann, p. 243f.

83. Personal aide of RFSS to AA, Oct. 18, 1944, BAB, NS 19/2637; Schechtman, p. 136; Cooper, "Policy," p. 70.

84. Personal aide of RFSS to AA Oct. 23, 1944, BAB, NS 19/2637.

Chapter XIV

Endgame:

Agents and Infiltrators

Even after the German defeats at El Alamein, Stalingrad, and Tunis had enabled the Middle East to escape from the clutches of the Third Reich, the region remained a target for infiltration attempts. Literally until the end of the war, the Mufti and the German military agencies focused on sabotage and subversion, attempting to tie up enemy forces and weaken the opponent's ability to support the war effort. Their goal and their hope was still jihad, an Arab uprising against the British and the Jews. In the spring of 1944, the Mufti concluded a radio address with the appeal, "We will create an independent state that will have no room for even a single Jew or Jew's accomplice."[1] With these words, he anticipated the Arabs' rallying cry in 1948: "Drive them into the sea!"[2] Holy war thus remained the precept through 1945—and beyond.

While al-Gailani's influence continued to weaken, el-Husseini basked in the favor of the powers that be. "The Führer has approved Dr. Goebbels's support of the Grand Mufti, giving him general power to do everything possible to

---

1. Draft AA/Inland II, Palästina – Machtprobe zwischen England und Juda. Die Auseinandersetzung um das brit. Palästina-Weißbuch [Palestine: Showdown between England and Judah. The Conflict Over the British Palestine White Paper.] (undated/1944), PAAA, R 99389.
2. Cf. Lewis, "Meer," p. 232ff.

strengthen the Grand Mufti's influence," Berger reported to the Reichsführer-SS in the spring of 1944.[3] But despite the great esteem in which the Mufti was held, German power was not sufficient to fulfill his every wish. For example, when the Mufti requested that a secret transmitter be set up "for the entire Mohammedan world,"[4] the Germans had to tell him that the project was not within the realm of "current technical possibility."[5] He also frequently asked too much of the Luftwaffe, which was facing an increasing shortage of aircraft and a disastrous fuel situation. "An air attack on Tel Aviv, the citadel of the Palestinian Jews and their emigration, has been repeatedly suggested by the Arabs, particularly the Grand Mufti, in the last six months," noted the Luftwaffe command staff in the fall of 1943. Although Göring had personally rejected the plan on July 17, el-Husseini was not satisfied with this decision and suggested bombing Jewish targets on November 2, the anniversary of the Balfour Declaration.[6] When he again requested an air strike for April 1, 1944, the Germans pointed out that the Mufti had "already repeatedly proposed bomb attacks against Tel Aviv and Jerusalem, in order to harm the Palestinian Jews and achieve a propagandistic effect in the Arab world with these attacks. Thus far, we have never agreed to these suggestions."[7] Even anti-Semitic fantasies of omnipotence reached their limits in the final stage of the war.

The Mufti was more successful in the maintenance of his intelligence service. When the Turkish government gradually moved away from the Axis after the turning point in the war, and in the summer of 1943 deported all Arabs suspected of having worked for the Third Reich, Ettel noted that "the Grand Mufti's previously effective intelligence service to and from the Arab countries has become ineffective." In the fall of that same year, however, el-Husseini sent his colleague Dr. Mustafa al-Wakil, the former vice president of the Young Egypt party,[8] to Istanbul with a German diplomatic passport to initiate the development of a new intelligence network that would assist the Arab Affairs department of *Amt* VI.[9] India specialist Obersturmführer Otto Heyer had served as its interim leader since the summer of 1943. He was also a young SD employee. Heyer came from the Bielefeld SD district and, as a candidate for superintendent, had been assigned to Einsatzkommando 6 in the

---

3. Chief of SSHA to RFSS personal staff, May 27, 1944, BAB, NS 19/2181.
4. Chief of SSHA to RFSS, Dec. 4, 1943, BAB, NS 19/1896.
5. Note by AA, Mar. 20, 1944, PAAA, R 101101.
6. Conversation note by LFSt/Ic, Oct. 29, 1943, telephone conversation with 1st Lt. Zetsche regarding air attacks in the Palestinian area, BA-MA, RL 2 II/496.
7. Ibid., Mar. 30, 1944, proposal by the Grand Mufti for a bomb attack on Tel Aviv on April 1, BA-MA, RL 2 II/496.
8. Cf. Jankowski, *Rebels*, pp. 27f., 82, 84ff.
9. Note by Ettel/AA, Dec. 10, 1943, IfZ, Nbg. Dok., NG-2997; cf. report by informer "Aladin," Oct. 20, 1943, PAAA, BA 61125.

Ukraine, so he had experience in matters relating to the killing of Jews. In 1942, as part of Operation Zeppelin, he had led the deployment of agents in Transcaucasia. In December 1944, he was to become head of *Amt* VI in the headquarters of the commander of the security police and the SD in Bratislava.[10] Heyer, by his own admission, also sent agents to Syria, Egypt, Iraq, and Lebanon. The Athens branch of *Amt* VI, under Obersturmführer Eylitz, generally served as the starting point for these missions. The agents either took the land route via Anatolia or traveled along the Turkish coast in small boats. Most of those agents were not Germans.[11]

Another fact, clearly, is that in 1943–44 numerous mixed German-Arab commandos were air-dropped into the Middle East in order to perform acts of sabotage for the Abwehr and *Amt* VI and to smuggle in weapons for the jihad. Schellenberg confirmed this in his testimony at Nuremberg,[12] and Berger also reported to Himmler in the spring of 1944 "a new plan regarding the deployment of his men for sabotage cases in North Africa and Palestine," which the Mufti had suggested to Schellenberg.[13] Schulze-Holthus, in his report on the mission in Iran, included the following sentence from Kurmis: "Commandos like us have been air-dropped everywhere now...in Iraq, Palestine, and Syria...a brilliant, brand-new program for the Orient...the Reichsführer-SS and Kaltenbrunner direct the matter themselves."[14] And in a special British internment camp for German paratroopers, he also spoke with members of commandos "that Abwehr II air-dropped in Palestine and a Kurdish area, from bases on the Greek islands."[15] It is also certain that the 1st Squadron in the test formation of the commander-in-chief of the Luftwaffe under Major Edmund Gartenfeld— renamed Bomber Wing 200 in February 1944—was responsible for agent insertions of this type.[16]

The number, timing, and results of these missions are difficult to confirm, however. The most specific information available concerns an *Amt* VI commando unit that was captured by the British in the Jordan Valley on October

---

10. SS membership card, BAB, SSO Otto Heyer; curriculum vitae, BAB, RuSHA Otto Heyer; interrogation of Otto Heyer, April 30, 1947, and May 10, 1948, BAL, B 162/16685; interrogation of Otto Heyer, Oct. 15, 1973, BAL, B 162/Vorl. AR-Z 131/70, p. 321ff.

11. Extract from Middle East Security Summary No. 203, Oct. 11, 1944, NAK, KV 2/400; S.I.M.E. Report No. 1, Oct. 14, and No. 2, Oct. 24, 1944, NAK, KV 2/162; interrogation of Otto Heyer, May 10, 1948, BAL, B 162/16685.

12. Kempner, p. 299.

13. Chief of SSHA to RFSS, April 22, 1944, BAB, NS 19/2637.

14. Schulze-Holthus, *Iran*, p. 278.

15. Schulze-Holthus, *Fälschung*, p. 23.

16. RML u. ObdL, Feb. 12, 1944, Umgliederung des Versuchsverbandes des OBdL u. Aufstellung des Kampfgeschwaders 200 [Reclassification of the Test Formation of the Commander-in-Chief of the Luftwaffe and the Raising of Bomber Wing 200], BA-MA, RL 2 III/58; Gellermann pp. 11f., 33ff., 212ff.

16, 1944.[17] The five paratroopers were briefed by el-Husseini himself, who compared Islam to National Socialism and assured them that the struggle in Palestine would help Germany. He hoped that all the Arab nations would now unite in fighting the Jews.[18] After taking off from Athens, the paratroopers jumped near Jericho during the early morning hours of October 6. Their failure to find several of their cargo parachutes would be their undoing. Three days later, the British police discovered the air-dropped cargo and set out to find the unit. Although the men attempted to hide the purpose of their mission, their equipment gave them away: submachine guns, dynamite, radio equipment, a duplicating machine, and a German-Arabic dictionary.

The composition of the unit was just as significant. Its leader was Lieutenant Kurt Wieland, a Palestinian-German from Sarona. He succeeded Eugen Faber as head of the Palestinian Hitler Youth in 1938,[19] joined the Brandenburg regiment in 1940, accompanied Grobba to Iraq one year later,[20] and since then had been part of Sonderstab F. Lieutenant Werner Frank was designated as radio operator. Frank, a Palestinian-German born in Haifa, joined the Hitler Youth there in 1934 and became a Brandenburger in 1940.[21] Staff sergeant Friedrich Deininger, who escaped capture, was also from Palestine. He was to serve as weapons instructor. He spoke Arabic well and also joined Sonderstab F via the Brandenburg regiment.[22] Abdul Latif, in contrast, the fourth member of the unit, came from Jerusalem. He belonged to the Mufti's milieu and had edited the Mufti's radio addresses in Berlin. He was to establish contact with the Arab underground in Palestine. He claimed that when he had asked why three Germans were to come along on the mission, el-Husseini responded that it was to make sure the weapons would be used correctly—that is, against the Jews. The fifth participant, Hassan Salama, also managed to go into hiding. He had been a guerrilla leader near Nablus during the Arab revolt.[23] Altogether, it was a veritable mixture of German and Arab radicalism that fell into British hands.

Operation Mammoth, planned by Abwehr II, is also well documented. The operation was to parallel the German invasion of Iran and, supported by the Kurdish tribes in northern Iraq, result in the seizure of the oil fields and re-

17. Report by press department of AA, Oct. 21, 1944, PAAA, R 101101.
18. Chief of SSHA to RFSS, Sept. 28, 1944, BAB, NS 19/1503; S.I.M.E. Report No. 1, Oct. 30, 1944, interrogation of Kurt Wieland, NAK, KV 2/400; S.I.M.E. Report No. 1, Oct. 31, 1944, interrogation of Werner Frank, NAK, KV 2/400.
19. Balke, p. 238.
20. Schröder, *Irak*, p. 70.
21. S.I.M.E. Report No. 1, Oct. 31, 1944, interrogation of Werner Frank, NAK, KV 2/400.
22. Ibid.; S.I.M.E. Report No. 1, Oct. 30, 1944, interrogation of Kurt Wieland, NAK, KV 2/400.
23. S.I.M.E. Report No. 1, Oct. 23, and Nov. 3, 1944, interrogation of Abdul Latif, NAK, KV 2/400.

fineries at Kirkuk.[24] Preparations for the mission continued even after Hitler had ordered (during the night of December 27–28, 1942) Army Group A to withdraw from the Caucasus.[25] However, the commando—three Germans and a Kurd—did not depart from the Crimea until June 16, 1943. One month later, news reached Berlin that all the men had been captured at Arbil, near their landing point.[26] On November 27, 1944, a Ju290 from the 1st Squadron of Bomber Wing 200 took off from Vienna and, after a stopover in Rhodes, dropped five Iraqis near Mosul by order of the Mufti; their fate remains unknown.[27] Other verifiable missions include the air-dropping of Arab subversives and spies in Algeria and Tunisia in June, July, and October 1944,[28] as well as the insertion of agents to blow up railway lines in Morocco.[29] Other commandos also appear to have been sent to Palestine.[30]

Although El Alamein without a doubt produced a shock in the Arab world, the Axis retreat did not imply abandonment of long-held dreams. In Palestine, a reorganization of the underground began in 1943.[31] Agent reports "characterize the situation there as serious and alarming," noted the German embassy in Turkey in March 1944. "Arabic treatises distributed throughout the country attack the Jews and the Americans, and call upon the Arabs to take up arms against the Jews and destroy Tel Aviv with fire and sword."[32] Shortly thereafter, *Amt* VI reported on "constant disruptions to the oil pipelines in Syria, Transjordan, and Palestine" and concluded, "The continuous unrest in Palestine has caused the English authorities to reinforce British troops, especially since an intensification of the Arab-Jewish conflict is expected."[33] In North Africa, as well, peace did not return even with the American-British landing. "Despite the welcome dollars, a certain reserve toward the Americans can be observed among upper-class Muslims, which has its roots in the increasing Jewification of the country," reported Amt VI in the fall of 1943, regarding Morocco.[34] The German consulate in Tangier stated six months later that "representatives of nationalist groups as well as members of prominent tribes have repeatedly applied to the offices located here, requesting the

24. Lt. Müller/[OKW] Ausl/Abw II, Operation Mammoth, Dec. 5, 1942, BA-MA, RW 5/271.
25. [OKW]Ausl/Abw II order, Jan. 14, 1943, BA-MA, RW 5/271.
26. [OKW]Ausl/Abw II war diary, July 22, 1943, BA-MA, RW 5/498.
27. Gellermann, p. 92ff.
28. Gen. Koller diary, June 27, 1944, BA-MA, RL 2 I/24; Gellermann, pp. 30f., 75f., 84ff.
29. Quarterly report by III/44 Amt Mil D and Front Reconnaissance Troops II, Dec. 19, 1944, BA-MA, RW 49/145; Gellermann, p. 96.
30. S.I.M.E. Report No. 1, Nov. 3, 1944, interrogation of Abdul Latif, NAK, KV 2/400; Dekel, p. 239f.; Cooper, *Palestinian*, p. 20.
31. Kiernan, p. 106ff.
32. DG Istanbul, Mar. 25, 1944, PAAA, R 99432.
33. Middle East weekly report, July 1–7, 1944, BAB, R 58/1129.
34. CdS VI B 2 to AA, Oct. 15, 1943, PAAA, R 101023.

delivery of weapons."[35] The reference was to the Abwehr and *Amt* VI branches in Tangier. Rauff also boasted in January 1945 that the "opposition groups that we cultivated are still actively working against the enemy in North Africa."[36]

It was symptomatic that the Egyptian prime minister, Ahmed Maher, was shot by a nationalist fanatic when he declared war on Germany and Japan in the Cairo parliament on February 26, 1945.[37] And other events pointed straight to the future: on November 2 of that year, protest demonstrations against the Balfour Declaration in Cairo and Alexandria turned into anti-Jewish pogroms, with businesses plundered and synagogues set on fire, and five people killed.[38] These were harbingers of the forced exodus of 500,000 Sephardic Jews out of the Arab world after the founding of the state of Israel.

35. DK Tangier to AA, Mar. 7, 1944, PAAA, R 101023.
36. Rauff to Wenner, Jan. 20, 1945, BAL, B 162/Vorl. Dok.Slg. Versch. XVI.
37. Middle East situation report, Mar. 3–10, 1945, BAB, R 58/1129.
38. Krämer, *Jews*, p. 162f.

Epilogue

The Allied victory over the Third Reich effectively cancelled all the plans for the "liberation" of Arab lands by the Germans as well as the murder of the Jews who were living there. By May 1945, the protagonists of these efforts were attempting to find a safe haven to avoid capture and prosecution by the Allies.

Walter Rauff was being held as a prisoner of war in Rimini, Italy, until December 1948, when he succeeded in escaping to Syria with the help of the Catholic Church. Shortly after, he traveled to South America. In Argentina, his SD intelligence-service reputation landed him a job as contact person for the Gehlen Organization and later the Federal Intelligence Service BND. The German connection was severed only in 1962, when the West German judiciary began investigating former Nazis responsible for the gas vans.[1] Rauff then relocated to Chile. He settled in Punta Arenas, in the south of the country, and became wealthy as a successful industrialist. At 66 years of age, the former SS officer was questioned, with his express consent, in connection with the investigation of Bruno Streckenbach that was being conducted in West Germany. Rauff knew full well that the German judiciary could do him no harm in Chile, since the Federal Republic's first extradition request had been denied by the Chilean Supreme Court in February 1963.[2]

On June 28, 1972, in the chambers of the German embassy in Santiago, he met with the examining magistrate and a prosecutor from the Hamburg state court to chat once again about old times and take the opportunity to emphasize the significance of his own previous role. While he minimized his

---

1. Banach, p. 258; Schenk, p. 348, note 750.
2. Farías, p. 300f.

responsibility for the use of the gas vans and hinted only very vaguely at his SS-Einsatzkommando Africa, he did provide details about the RSHA from an insider's viewpoint, reporting on intrigues and describing Reinhard Heydrich at length. He did not fail to mention that Heydrich "could be a very charming and gracious host."[3] After his defense before the German judiciary, Rauff continued to live undisturbed. Simon Wiesenthal attempted in August of that year to persuade the socialist president Salvador Allende to extradite Rauff, but the request was denied.[4] In September 1973, the mass murderer witnessed the military coup against Allende by the military under the orders of General Augusto Pinochet. Chile's shift to a dictatorship would not have displeased him; his move to the capital shortly thereafter suggests this at least. As the owner of a cannery, he lived in great comfort there as well. He eventually died of cancer in May 1984.[5]

Most of the former officers in Rauff's Einsatzkommando survived the war as well. The Middle East specialist Wilhelm Beisner, according to American sources, was living in Cairo in 1952 with other former SS men under the false name of Jäger. In Egypt, years later, he supposedly trained Algerian volunteers for the fight for independence against France. Beisner was apparently also involved in extensive arms trade with the Algerian Front de Libération Nationale (FLN). In October 1960, in Munich, an explosive device was detonated under a car, and the driver was seriously injured. It was clear that Beisner was the intended target but he was only injured. The authors of the attack were operatives of the Main Rouge, the French terror organization created by the SDECE and directed against the Algerian independence movement.[6] Several days later, the former Sturmbannführer was questioned in the hospital by the Bavarian state police but was released after his recovery.[7]

After the German defeat, Hans-Joachim Weise settled in Bergisch Gladbach, where he worked as an administrator. In an examination of witnesses in 1965, he recounted in detail his assignment with Rauff's Einsatzkommando—knowing that his participation in a mass murder that was ultimately never carried out (though it was specifically prepared for) would have no negative consequences for himself.[8] The administrative specialist Kurt Loba was transferred to the Waffen-SS in the final phase of the war, in February 1945, and

---

3. Interrogation of Walther Rauff, June 28, 1972, BAL, B 162/3637, pp. 76–91.
4. Farías, pp. 291–299.
5. Ibid., p. 314.
6. Bavarian state police headquarters memorandum, Sept. 5, 1961, BAL, B 162/Vorl. AR 1650/67, p. 17f.; FAZ, Oct. 21, 1960; Faligot/Kauffer, pp. 195f., 205–208.
7. Interrogation of Wilhelm Beisner, Nov. 4, 1960, BAL, B 162/Vorl. AR 1650/67, pp. 6–9.
8. Interrogation of Hans-Joachim Weise, Jan. 12, 1965, BAL, B 162/16704.

was assigned to the command staff of the Reichsführer-SS in Salzburg. After another transfer, he was taken prisoner by the British. He was released in October 1948 to a new life in postwar Germany. He settled in Düsseldorf and, in keeping with his former administrative skills, became an office manager. Loba was questioned once in October 1964 by the North Rhine-Westphalian state police regarding his previous activity as an SS officer; then he was allowed to continue his postwar life undisturbed.[9] Waldemar Menge also returned safely from the war and built himself a new life as a clerk in Frankfurt.[10] Franz Hoth was not as lucky after the end of National Socialism. After his return from Tunis, he temporarily served as commander of the security police and the SD in Paris. In early November 1943, Kaltenbrunner assigned him to serve as provisional head of operations for the commander of the security police and the SD in Nancy.[11] His initiatives there led to his death sentence by a French military court in Metz on February 19, 1949. He was executed five months later, on July 28.[12]

George Best did not escape Allied justice either. After his missions under Rauff in Tunisia and then Corsica, he was transferred to Paris. In late 1944 he became a commander of the Wehrwolf force under the Higher SS and Police Leader in Wiesbaden.[13] In this role, he was responsible for organizing Nazi acts of terror to be carried out in the period after the likely defeat and to pursue the fierce fight against the opponents of the collapsing system. Like several of his SS comrades, Best had problems after May 8, 1945, due to the murder of captured Allied pilots during the final phase of the war.[14] Because he passed on an order relating to this matter, he was sentenced in March 1947 to 15 years in prison by an American military court in Dachau. He served 7 years of this sentence in Landsberg am Lech and was released at the end of March 1954. The former SS-Sturmbannführer then settled in Mainz, his wife's home town, and worked as a mechanical engineer, the occupation for which he had originally trained.[15] Heinrich Harder, in contrast, who like Best and Saevecke did not join Rauff's Einsatzkommando until Tunis, did not survive to see the end of the war. He was killed in combat in Italy.[16]

Theo Saevecke had a colorful life after 1945. He was captured by the Allies in April and spent three years interned in the former concentration camp at

---

9. Interrogation of Kurt Loba, Oct. 27, 1964, BAL, B 162/16690.
10. Interrogation of Waldemar Menge, Dec. 14, 1961, BAL, B 162/1325, p. 429.
11. CdS to SSPHA, Nov. 8, 1943, BAB, SSO Franz Hoth.
12. BAL, central file, Franz Hoth file card.
13. Ibid., Georg Best file card.
14. Cf. Mallmann, "Volksjustiz."
15. Interrogation of Georg Best, Oct. 29, 1964, BAL, B 162/16674.
16. Interrogation of Waldemar Menge, Dec. 14, 1961, BAL, B 162/1325, p. 431.

Dachau. After his release he went to Berlin, where his previous profession helped him obtain a position working with the American intelligence service. In December 1951 Saevecke was hired by the newly established Federal Criminal Police Office, where he was soon active in investigations again.[17] At the beginning of April, the former SS-Hauptsturmführer conducted a remarkable interrogation at Frankfurt police headquarters. In connection with the attempted bomb attack against Federal Chancellor Konrad Adenauer,[18] German investigators had received a tip that a Jew, Samuel B., who was living in Frankfurt, had provided a room for the alleged bomb courier. They quickly decided to make an arrest. They searched the house in the early morning of April 6, without results, and the husband and wife were then questioned separately.[19] Saevecke interrogated B., who came from what was formerly eastern Poland. B. had managed to escape the extermination measures when the Germans invaded in 1941, joined the partisans and ultimately survived the Holocaust. He went to Darmstadt as a displaced person in 1946; four years later he moved to Frankfurt, where he operated a wholesale textile business. Without realizing that he was speaking to a former SS officer, he affirmed his innocence. Saevecke—who, according to the consul general in Milan, was characterized by the citizens there as "a cold, cruel, and brutal tormentor"—could find no incriminating evidence against the suspect, and released B.[20]

Later on Saevecke pursued a respectable career in the Federal Criminal Police Office. In August 1952 he was promoted to detective superintendent and four years later to detective. A disciplinary proceeding initiated in 1954 based on his role in the Nazi regime came to nothing.[21] In any case, he later became deputy head of the Bonn Sicherungsgruppe (secret investigation unit). In this role, he was in charge (because of the absence of his superior, who was abroad on business) of the action taken on October 27, 1962, against the news magazine *Der Spiegel*, which became one of the greatest scandals in postwar Germany.[22] After revelations about Saevecke's SS past surfaced, even the Bundestag, in its March 6, 1963, session, became involved.[23] A second disciplinary proceeding—this time regarding the shooting of hostages in Milan in 1944 and the deportation of Jews in Tunisia and Italy—was, as in the first case, abandoned due to a purported lack of evidence. Additional investigations into

---

17. Schenk, p. 269.
18. For greater detail on this: Sietz.
19. Ibid., p. 64.
20. Quoted in Wagner, p. 178; Sietz, pp. 58f., 64ff.
21. Wagner, p. 179.
22. Schenk, p. 261ff.; Wagner, p. 178.
23. Schenk, p. 264.

crimes he had committed took place in Italy, however, leading to a 1999 trial when a Turin military court sentenced the accused to life in prison in absentia. This would not have greatly troubled the former SS officer, who was protected from extradition by German law, because he had retired in 1971. Saevecke's twilight years were quiet, and he died of old age in 2000.[24]

Erwin Ettel, the staunch anti-Semite and radical supporter of the Mufti in the Foreign Office, finally, after much urging, received permission from Ribbentrop at the end of 1943 to "prove" himself at the front. He promptly reported to the Waffen-SS. To his regret, however, he was never sent into combat; instead, he served as an instructor in various schools for armored troops. The SS-Brigadeführer survived the war, somehow managed to avoid internment and denazification, and, in 1950, was hired as an editor in the foreign policy department of the weekly newspaper *Die Zeit* under the assumed name of Ernst Krüger. There he became the archenemy of political editor Marion Gräfin Dönhoff, who left the paper temporarily in August 1954—not least because of the attitude of Ettel/Krüger, of whose previous true identity she was unaware.[25]

In his journalistic activity, Ettel tirelessly focused on his old ideological enemies. He entitled an article about the Knesset's protest against the agreement with Germany "Disagreeable Israel," and references to Menachem Begin were routinely accompanied by the commentary "head of the Jewish terrorist group Irgun Zwai Leumi." Ettel referred to Nazis by contrast simply as the "so-called war criminals."[26] In the mid-1950s, the climate within *Die Zeit* began to change; the publisher, Gerd Bucerius, and Gräfin Donhöff took the paper in a distinctly more liberal direction, and Ettel/Krüger was forced to leave the editorial staff. He retired and soon arranged to have himself, as a former diplomat, paid the pension benefits of a legation counselor, first class. Even in retirement, he admitted his National Socialist ideas to his circle of friends and voted for a radical right-wing splinter party in the Bundestag elections of 1965.[27]

Ettel's former rival Dr. Fritz Grobba temporarily went into retirement in June 1944 but continued to attempt to influence the Arab policy of the Foreign Office. Released for an assignment during the last months of "total war," he then worked in Dresden for the government of the state of Saxony. Immediately after the end of the war, Grobba took a position as a lawyer in Meiningen, in southern Thuringia. In the Soviet occupation zone, however, he

24. Ibid., p. 269f.
25. Bajohr, pp. 241, 246f.
26. Ibid., p. 248f.
27. Ibid., p. 251f.

was arrested on a probably unfounded suspicion of espionage. He was initially held in Dresden, then taken to Moscow, interrogated, and sentenced to many years' detention in a prison camp. Soviet authorities released him after 10 years and allowed him to return to Germany. He subsequently wrote commentaries on the Nazi-Arab policy for the Americans. His political memoirs were published in 1967.[28]

After many years of exile in Germany and Italy, the Mufti returned to the Arab world. In March 1945 he told his German caretakers that he wished to visit Berlin again, but he was talked out of it because of the massive bombings the city was undergoing. Instead, he and his entourage moved out of the overcrowded Bad Elster health resort to Bad Gastein.[29] On May 7 he flew across the border to Bern; from there, however, he was quickly handed over to France. Initially he was held in custody in Paris, but for various reasons none of the Allied powers showed any great interest in charging el-Husseini with war crimes and thus risking a conflict with the Arab world. So time passed, and the Mufti lived under "house arrest" with servants and personal chauffeurs in a villa on the edge of Paris.[30]

While el-Husseini's future was still being debated in Europe, his followers returned to Palestine in November 1945 to reestablish the Arab Higher Committee, which the British had dissolved. The position of president was held open for the Mufti, and he soon was given the opportunity to take office. When no one on the Allied side demanded judicial retribution for his many crimes, the Mufti again took his fate into his own hands and using false documents flew to Cairo on May 29, 1946, where he was quickly granted asylum. His return to the Middle East demonstrated that his leadership role in promoting the Palestinian cause was still entirely undisputed. Supported by the Arab League, which had been established in March 1945, he directed the operations of the Arab Higher Committee from Cairo.[31] The fact that el-Husseini could be considered a legitimate representative of the Palestinians, despite his close collaboration with the National Socialists and his continued uncompromising anti-Semitic mind-set, no doubt played a role in preventing a possible reconciliation between Jews and Palestinians at that time.[32]

El-Husseini never distanced himself from Nazism. Although he wrote while still in exile near the end of the war in 1944 that he never would have

---

28. Schwanitz, "Geist," pp. 139–145; cf. Grobba.
29. Memorandum by Dörnberg/AA, Mar. 3, 1945, PAAA, BA 61199.
30. Gensicke, p. 151f; Faligot/Kauffer, p. 146; Schechtman, p. 167.
31. Schiller, p. 173; Gensicke, p. 253ff.; Küntzel, "Zeesen," p. 286.
32. See Morrison, p. 157ff.

gone to Germany if another Arab country had been ready to take him in in 1941,[33] his words reflect more a disappointment at the failure of the common project than a sudden distancing from his allies. Back in Cairo, he in any case imme-diately devoted himself to his primary concern, the struggle against the Jews. In the postwar Middle East as well, he soon advocated the view that the Arabs "should attack the Jews together and destroy them."[34] In Palestine he called together thousands of volunteers to put that idea into practice after the expected departure of the British. He tirelessly established new international alliances to help him achieve his goals. At a Muslim world conference in 1951, el-Husseini acted as chair, and four years later, he also participated in the first Afro-Asian Conference in Bandung, Indonesia.[35]

He remained extremely popular among the Palestinians as well; thousands lined the streets in Jerusalem during his visit in March 1967.[36] Finally, he also addressed the issue of identifying a worthy successor. As early as 1952, he encouraged his distant relative, Yasser Arafat, to run for president of the Palestinian student union, thus beginning a promising political career. The two met and spoke regularly through the end of the 1960s, when the Mufti seems to have concluded that Arafat would be a capable leader for a future Palestinian nation.[37] El-Husseini died on July 4, 1974, in Beirut. Tens of thousands of supporters attended his funeral in Lebanon and—true to the general direction of his life's work—turned the event into a mass demonstration against the Jews.[38]

Like the Mufti, Rashid Ali al-Gailani left Germany in early May 1945 and crossed the border into Switzerland. By way of Belgium, he then went to France, where he remained until mid-July. Using false documents, he suc-ceeded in boarding a French ship for Beirut, then traveled on to Damascus and, after a brief stay there, reached the Saudi capital of Riyadh by the end of September. King Ibn Saud granted al-Gailani asylum; a return to Iraq was out of the question because the regent, Abdul Illah, would never forgive him during his lifetime for either the 1941 coup or the revolt against the British. Even when the Iraqi monarchy was overthrown in July 1958, making a home-coming possible, the former prime minister did not return to the country of his birth. Instead, he spent his final years on the Arabian Peninsula without making another political appearance in Baghdad.[39]

33. Carpi, "Mufti," p. 101.
34. Quoted in Gensicke, p. 254.
35. Lewis, "Meer," p. 191.
36. Jbara, p. 192.
37. Küntzel, *Djihad*, p. 114f.
38. Jbara, p. 192.
39. Khadduri, *Irak*, p. 242.

In contrast to most of his like-minded friends, the Syrian Fawzi al-Qawuqji did not flee before the victorious Allies in the spring of 1945. Instead, he simply remained with his family in his home in the eastern part of the capital. He was not arrested by the Soviets until May 1946. Initially interned in the Biesdorf camp, the former terrorist leader was interrogated many times by Russian officers. After a temporary transfer to another detention facility, al-Qawuqji was released in early 1947; however, Soviet authorities stipulated that he not leave the eastern sector of the city. With French help, he obtained false documents that allowed him, his wife, and his adjutant to escape to Paris in early February. That same month he traveled on to Beirut.[40] In the year that followed, he again had the opportunity to actively work toward his vision of a Palestine free of Jews. In the period preceding the Arab attack on the soon-to-be-established state of Israel, the head of the Arab League awarded him command over the Arab Liberation Army, a volunteer formation created especially to fight the Jews. Al-Qawuqji took over the command, and he and his unit, together with the other armies, invaded Israel only hours after the state was proclaimed in May 1948. Following his initial offensive in the direction of central Galilee, he operated largely unsuccessfully against the newly formed Israel Defense Forces, which defeated his troops during the war and ultimately expelled him from the territory of the Jewish state. His career of fighting the British, the Yishuv, and finally Israel was then over.[41]

After 1945, the Arab world's affinity for National Socialism continued largely unabated. There were few calls for a change in thinking; indeed, episodes such as the failure to prosecute the Mufti seemed to indicate the complete absence of any Arab guilt and underline the legitimacy of the shared ideas. The founding of the state of Israel in 1948 and the defeat—considered impossible—of the Arab armies, further fueled hatred of the Jews and radicalized the entire Arab world. Historical reminiscences of National Socialism showed a continuity of those ideological affinities. A Muslim Brotherhood newspaper in Damascus summed up the continuing close relationship to the German Führer when it stated in 1956: "One cannot forget that Hitler enjoys high esteem in the Arab world, unlike in Europe. His name awakens sympathy and enthusiasm in the hearts of our supporters."[42] In 1953, rumors emerged that Hitler might still be alive after all, and hiding in Brazil. Anwar el-Sadat, in an imaginary letter to the object of his admiration, wrote quite bluntly, "I con-

---

40. Höpp, "Zwischenspiel," p. 37f.
41. Ibid., p. 38; O'Brien, p. 184f.; Jbara, p. 192.
42. Quoted in Wistrich, p. 315.

gratulate you with all my heart, because although you appeared to have been defeated, you were the real victor."[43]

On April 24, 1961, shortly before the start of Adolf Eichmann's trial in Jerusalem, the Jordanian *Jerusalem Times* published an open letter to the accused, claiming that the co-organizer of the annihilation of the European Jews had proven to be "a real blessing to humanity." The letter continued, "This trial will one day find its conclusion with the liquidation of the remaining six million..."[44] Noteworthy statements regarding the Nazi persecution of the Jews were also made in a conversation, reproduced in the Beirut press in June 1974, between Lebanese politician Kamal Jumblatt and Syrian president Hafez al-Assad. After the Syrian emphasized that the Arabs remembered Hitler "in a positive way," Jumblatt eagerly concurred: "At least he saved us from the Zionists. We cannot take a strong position against National Socialism [...]. National Socialism should be revived a bit [...]. Some studies suggest that the number of Jews killed by the Nazis was grossly overstated. There were huge groups that managed to escape from Germany."[45]

Countless pieces of evidence such as these point to rampant anti-Semitism in the Arab world, as well as the lingering nostalgia for National Socialism and its plans to exterminate the Jews. The persistence of these attitudes after 1945 had far-reaching consequences, in particular for the long-established Jewish communities in Arab countries. Years after the German defeat in the war, anti-Jewish riots occurred in numerous locations; prospects were dim for the Jews in these areas. As a result, mass emigration took place between the late 1940s and early 1950s, primarily to Israel. Of the once 300,000 Jews in Morocco, only 18,000 remained in the country; of the 55,000 Yemeni Jews, only 1,000 remained. Of 135,000 Algerian, 125,000 Iraqi, and 75,000 Egyptian Jews, only a few hundred of each remained in their homelands.[46]

After Israel had successfully defended itself against the destructive will of its Middle Eastern neighbors, Arab propagandists displayed an increasing tendency to draw a direct analogy between the Jewish state and National Socialism. In the 1982 Lebanon War, for example, the Egyptian newspaper *Al-Ahram* expressed the view that the actions of the Israeli army were comparable to the murder of European Jews in the gas chambers of the German extermination camps.[47] Even a relatively new radical anti-Zionist regime such as the Islamic Republic of Iran soon made use of such rhetoric. For the founder of

---

43. Quoted in Lewis, "Meer," p. 193.
44. Quoted in Wistrich, p. 334; cf. Küntzel, "Zeesen," p. 285.
45. Quoted in Küntzel, "Zeesen," p. 194.
46. Lewis, *Juden*, p. 170.
47. Rabinovich, p. 253.

the state, Ayatollah Khomeini, Zionism had always been "an enemy of mankind."[48] In propagating hatred of the Jews, however, the Arabs dug even deeper into the reservoir of anti-Semitism when necessary. A series of articles printed in 1984 in *Imam*, the newspaper published by the press department of the Iranian embassy in London, ended with the statement, "The effects of the policy of Israel and the Western states, in particular the USA, [...] prove that Jewish-influenced Western governments are following *The Protocols of the Elders of Zion* word for word."[49]

In the meantime, at least nine translations of the *Protocols* were in print—mass circulation, as measured by typical book sales—in the Muslim world. In the past, various Arab leaders liked to quote or recommend this shoddy piece of work, and even in 2002, Egyptian state television broadcast a 41-part prime-time series for which the anti-Semitic classic served as the script.[50] In the West, and particularly in Germany, such connections are not exactly considered the appropriate components of the collective consciousness. In past decades, the preference was to classify the freely interchangeable travel stories from Casablanca, Cairo, Damascus, or Baghdad, in which tourists recognized as Germans were enthusiastically greeted with "Heil Hitler," into the category of obscure idiosyncrasy instead of taking such expressions seriously as political statements. But the post-World War II Arab world represents a region in which radical anti-Semitism is more pervasive than anywhere else; looking to the future, only this kind of awareness will offer useful approaches to effectively fight the phenomenon—suppressing it or playing it down will not help.

Even in historical and Islamic research, the close connection between National Socialism and the Arab world received little serious attention until very recently. The comment that in Palestine "there were actually approving and, according to isolated reports, sometimes even enthusiastic reactions to Hitler and National Socialism by the Arabs"[51] may suggest a somewhat superficial knowledge of the sources, but other interpretations point in a much more ominous direction. While confirmations of the Mufti's radical anti-Semitism, his obvious admiration for the Third Reich, and his continuing readiness to collaborate are extremely numerous and easily accessible, analyses that emphasize the defining characteristics of his relationship with Nazi Germany are very rare even today.[52]

---

48. Wistrich, p. 321.
49. Quoted in ibid.
50. Lewis, "Antisemitism," p. 57f.; Wistrich, pp. 316–321; *Die Welt*, Oct. 11, 2005.
51. Wildangel, p. 124.
52. Positive examples include again Gensicke; Küntzel, *Djihad*; Lewis, "Meer"; Wanner; Wiesenthal; Wistrich; the criticism of Höpp, "Gefangene," p. 15, that Gensicke wished "only to confirm prejudgments [...] by piling up mountains of facts" is typical.

A deliberately different and considerably more common view argues instead that the Mufti attached himself to National Socialism only out of "opportunism,"[53] and even in more detailed monographs concerning el-Husseini hardly a word is written about his extremely active collaboration with the Germans.[54] In fact, colleagues who do not suppress the close connection between the Mufti and the National Socialists are attacked. One author, for example, asserted that "Zionists" had "exaggerated" the Mufti's dealings with National Socialism.[55] Or it is simply claimed that his propaganda appeals in the Arab world remained largely unsuccessful and inconsequential.[56] Scholarly publications contain praise for his "pronounced leadership capability," his "honesty," and the "absence of corruption of any kind," and discussions of his exile in Germany stress that el-Husseini was "not blinded by Germany's racial doctrine," which "was incompatible with his convictions as a Muslim and a believer."[57] With regard to preserving the Mufti's memory in the Palestinian autonomous territories, the same author noted with regret that there were no days of mourning for him and no refugee camps or streets named after him.[58]

One historiographer of the Palestinian nationalist movement found it completely unacceptable that the British mandatory power had compelled the "charismatic and influential leader" to flee because of his efforts in the Arab revolt. Other culprits were then quickly identified: "The Mufti was styled as the archenemy of British policy in the Middle East, and Great Britain—together with the Zionist movement, then after 1948 with Israel, and eventually with Emir Abdullah as well—began a targeted defamation and delegitimation campaign against him, coupled with a delegitimation of Palestinian nationalist aims and the Palestinians in general as a nation." Appalled—and far from the truth—the author writes about the perpetrator who for her had become the victim: "Hajj Amin became a sort of 'pariah politician.'"[59]

The interpretation of al-Gailani's policy as "primarily of a pragmatic nature" and representing a "policy of neutrality" between the power blocs is, if nothing else, unconvincing and above all fails to address the heart of the problem. The claim that the Iraqi politician did not recognize the dilemma of his entanglement with National Socialism would seem to give him undue credit, as it largely disregards his actual actions, which he performed with complete

---

53. Mattar, Hajj, *The Mufti of Jerusalem,* p. 107.
54. Ibid.; in this 160-page study of the Mufti, just 6 pages are devoted to his time in exile in Germany in 1941–45.
55. Ibid., p. 99.
56. Mattar, "The Mufti of Jerusalem and the Politics of Palestine," p. 237.
57. Dayyeh, pp. 35, 41.
58. Ibid., p. 46.
59. Baumgarten, p. 36.

awareness.[60] The characterization of the first jihadist, al-Qassam, as "a notable representative of the Salafi Islamic reform movement" appears just as unhelpful[61] as this conclusion from the same text: "In his activism, which culminated with an act of martyrdom, lay the new, the fascinating, and also the surprising, which awakened admiration and imitation well beyond religious circles."[62]

With regard to the Arabs' willingness to collaborate, which sometimes cannot be denied, it is said that the relationship was strictly opportunistic and—directed against the English colonial power and the Zionists—followed the simple logic of "the enemy of my enemy is my friend." It is then claimed that the Arabs didn't care about the true character of National Socialism,[63] or the idea is worded somewhat differently, as a general exculpation: "Very few Arabs appear to have thought about it very carefully at the time."[64] Even just the title of one publication, *Arabs in the Second World War: Collaboration or Patriotism?*, allows for conclusions to be drawn about the author's way of thinking.[65] In the text, "Eurocentrism" is promptly identified as the cause of widespread unjustified criticism of Arab attitudes and is countered with the seemingly wise but in reality meaningless argument that, yes, "life is rich and complicated."[66] Another criticism is that the field of study has unfortunately become a "conflict topic" that is primarily used "for reciprocal accusations of collaboration."[67] As an alternative, the author suggests an "unemotional view,"[68] which, however, considering the above-cited paradigm would likely miss the heart of the matter by a long shot.

Whenever the Middle East's open admiration for National Socialism is historiographically proven, the immediate response is the excuse that support for National Socialism merely corresponded with the wish for national liberation.[69] Such reasoning undoubtedly falls short as well. Apart from that, researchers happily devote themselves to other aspects of German-Arab relations. However, it is precisely the works on the history of Arab colonial soldiers, on Arabs in German prisoner-of-war camps, and even on Arabs as prisoners in

---

60. Dieterich, "Kailānī," p. 73ff.
61. Krämer, *Geschichte*, p. 303.
62. Ibid., p. 307.
63. Steppat, p. 271; also Aries, p. 49: "How did a 40-year-old religious scholar cope with such a life in 1937? He did what Wallenstein did in the Thirty Years' War. He sought allies and found them where others were fighting against his enemies. Thus, al-Husseini helped the National Socialists with the fervor of desperation that became hatred."
64. Höpp, "Alī," p. 571.
65. Höpp, *Araber*, p. 86.
66. Ibid., p. 86f.; the following claim in Höpp, Gefangene, p. 14, comes across as similarly meaningless: "The Mufti and his environment must be placed in their many historical, political, social, and cultural contexts."
67. Höpp, "Araber," p. 88.
68. Ibid., p. 92.
69. Harras, p. 207.

concentration camps that collectively demonstrate that these realities were marginal phenomena in comparison to actual cooperation and the readiness of parts of the Arab world to collaborate.[70]

By contrast, the ominous potential for anti-Semitism in the region is hardly recognized or is often misinterpreted. An artificial argument to trivialize the Muslim affinity for the Third Reich is illustrated in the claim that the racial component of National Socialist ideology would have created a barrier between the Germans and the Arabs.[71] However, there is a dearth of evidence that could reveal to what degree the Nazi racial ideology was perceived as objectionable in the Arab world and perhaps actually hindered the joint German-Arab scheme to "eliminate the Jewish national home in Palestine." Analysis attempts claiming, based on meager supporting sources, that Muslim anti-Semitism was "in all significant aspects an import from Europe"[72] are also quite dubious. Finally, a classical inversion of cause and effect takes place when historians argue that in the Palestinian nationalist movement, nascent anti-Semitism was "unquestionably a reflex against the systematic policy of crowding out" by the Zionists.[73]

The reader must be prepared for anything when a book on the social history of the Palestinian conflict, widely read and highly regarded in Germany, begins with the malicious sentence, "The Jews, who in their thousands of years of history have suffered more than almost any other people, today cause others to suffer in the Middle East." Adapting the often-stated vague assumption that Israel's policy is geared exclusively toward profiting from the Holocaust, the author adds that the crimes of the Germans at that time "have given carte blanche to the Jews in the Middle East."[74] He also skillfully manages to write about the Arab "protests," "unrest," and "strikes" in 1921, 1929, and 1937 without wasting even a single word on Arab terror and its victims of that time.[75] Presented in such a manner, the founding of the Jewish state could logically only be classified as "injustice": "After National Socialism had already collapsed politically, it found another indirect victim; the Arabs suffered for German fascism's crimes against the Jews."[76]

Distancing itself from such spitefulness, the present study has shown that during the Nazi regime, the Germans tried much more concretely than pre-

---

70. Cf. Höpp, "Diskurs."
71. Kiefer, p. 83.
72. Holz, p. 15.
73. Kiefer, p. 70; with this same orientation: Holz, p. 81.
74. Hollstein, p. 9.
75. Ibid., pp. 110f., 128f.
76. Ibid., p. 126.

viously supposed to physically destroy the Jews of Palestine and forever prevent the founding of an independent state for the Yishuv. Extensive documentation has also been presented to show that these endeavors would have received widespread and active support from the Arabs. What is worth highlighting, based on this finding alone, is the categorical insistence on defending the existence of the state of Israel. The authors have repeatedly emphasized a broader connection that has been demonstrated time and again in the decades since the end of World War II, including in the Middle East: all chances of understanding are destroyed when the principles of civilized cooperation are abandoned in favor of action founded on irrational mind-sets aimed at stigmatizing human individuals or social groups based on supposed inherent characteristics. Nazi Germany and parts of the Arab world saw themselves in a common struggle against "imperialist" England, and the Jews were denounced as instigators and accomplices. Because no rational negotiation was possible in the face of such delusional thinking, the descent into disaster was already looming.

In such a context, it is totally beside the point to introduce the view of different cultural practices as a form of absolution for the Arabs. Such an argument means nothing less than reducing individuals and their actions to different rigid cultural circles and thus excusing them, and also denying the subjects any serious reflection on human action. But to counter the criticism of such frivolous considerations with the charge of "Eurocentrism" amounts to a form of censorship against any kind of thinking. This issue has nothing to do with Eurocentrism; in this case, universalism is of essential importance in reaching a verdict on the Arabs' collaboration with Nazi Germany.[77]

Western thinking would be impossible without the achievements of the Enlightenment, which enabled the acceptance of the universal value of all human beings beyond the limits of religion, economic wealth, or gender. Today, this attribution of universal value is in fact the defining foundation of modern civilized societies. For every individual, the ability to trust a guarantee of this universality must be grounded in existence. A distinguishing characteristic of this initial condition, however, must also make sure that the public is aware that such a civilizing ideal does not yet exist in some communities, and that some nations, such as Germany, even voluntarily renounced it at some stage in their history. In no way can this lead to declarations of understanding for Arab societies that, although well on their way to obtaining national independence, were prepared to realize that goal through an alliance with Nazi Germany and through the commission of mass crimes. It is precisely because

---

77. Cf. Groß/Konitzer; *Welzer*, pp. 16f., 48ff.

of the universality of the human condition that no one can be released from such responsibility.

When scholarship no longer strives to distinguish between thoroughly legitimate aspirations of national independence and the recourse to prejudice-based ideologies such as anti-imperialism, anti-Zionism, and anti-Semitism, the danger arises that the difference between enlightened thinking and the alternative road to barbarism may be lost. The full awareness of the 20th century's crimes against humanity resides precisely in this ability to differentiate, which should be defended at all costs.

Abbreviations

Ia—Erster Generalstabsoffizier (Taktische Führung)
first general staff officer (tactical leadership)

Ic—Dritter Generalstabsoffizier (Feindnachrichten/Abwehr)
third general staff officer (enemy intelligence)

AA—Auswärtiges Amt
Foreign Office

AAS
Asian and African Studies

Abt.—Abteilung
department, section, detachment

ADAP—Akten zur Deutschen Auswärtigen Politik
Archives of German Foreign Policy

Amt—Mil Militärisches Amt
Military Department (of the RSHA)

AOK—Armeeoberkommando
field army command

AR—Amt Rosenberg
Alfred Rosenberg's Center for National Socialist Ideological and Educational Research

ASQ
Arab Studies Quarterly

Ausl/Abw—Amt Ausland/Abwehr
the Abwehr (Germany's intelligence organization)

BAB—Bundesarchiv Berlin
Federal Archives, Berlin

BAK—Bundesarchiv Koblenz
Federal Archives, Koblenz

BAL—Bundesarchiv-Außenstelle Ludwigsburg
Federal Archives, Ludwigsburg Branch

BA-MA—Bundesarchiv-Militärarchiv Freiburg im Breisgau
Federal Archives/Military Archives, Freiburg im Breisgau

BA-ZA—Bundesarchiv-Zwischenarchiv Dahlwitz-Hoppegarten
Federal Archives/Interim Archives, Dahlwitz-Hoppegarten

BdE—Befehlshaber des Ersatzheeres
commander of the replacement army

BdS—Befehlshaber der Sicherheitspolizei und des SD
commander of the security police and the SD

Bev.AA.b.Mil.befh.Serb.—Bevollmächtigter des Auswärtigen Amts beim Militärbefehlshaber Serbien
Foreign Office representative with the military commander for Serbia

BPK—Bildarchiv Preußischer Kulturbesitz Berlin
Image Archive of the Prussian Cultural Heritage, Berlin

Capt.
Captain

CdS—Chef der Sicherheitspolizei und des SD
chief of the security police and the SD

DAK—Deutsches Afrikakorps	German Afrika Korps
DG—Deutsche Gesandtschaft	German embassy
DGK—Deutsches Generalkonsulat	German consulate general
Div.	Division
DK—Deutsches Konsulat	German consulate
DNB—Deutsches Nachrichtenbüro	German News Agency (official central news agency of the Third Reich)
Dok.—Dokument(e)	document(s)
DRZW—Das Deutsche Reich und der Zweite Weltkrieg	German Reich and the Second World War
Dt.Gen.b.HQu.It.Wehrm.—Deutscher General beim Hauptquartier der Italienischen Wehrmacht	German general at the headquarters of the Italian armed forces
DVK—Deutscher Vizekonsul	German vice consul
EdH—Enzyklopädie des Holocaust	Encyclopedia of the Holocaust
Feldgend.—Feldgendarmerie	field (military) police
FHW—Abteilung Fremde Heere West	Foreign Armies West department
Gen.	General
Gen.kdo.—Generalkommando	general headquarters
Gen.Qu.—Generalquartiermeister	quartermaster general
GenStdH—Generalstab des Heeres	army general staff
Gestapa—Geheimes Staatspolizeiamt	Secret State Police Office
Gestapo—Geheime Staatspolizei	Secret State Police
HGr—Heeresgruppe	army group
HRüst—Heeresrüstung	ordnance
HöSSPF—Höchster SS- und Polizeiführer	Supreme SS and Police Leader
HSSPF—Höherer SS- und Polizeiführer	Higher SS and Police Leader
HStb.Übs.—Heimatstab Übersee	home staff overseas
Hstuf.—Hauptsturmführer	Waffen SS captain
IB—Italienische Botschaft	Italian embassy
IfZ—Institut für Zeitgeschichte, München	Institute for Contemporary History, Munich
JCH	*Journal of Contemporary History*
JMES	*Journal of Middle Eastern Studies*
JMH	*Journal of Modern History*
Kdo.—Kommando	command, commando

Kdr.—Kommandeur	commander
Kp.—Kompanie	company
KTB—Kriegstagebuch	war diary
LBIYB	Leo Baeck Institute Year Book
Lt.	Lieutenant
LFSt—Luftwaffenführungsstab	air force command staff
Maj.	Major
MEJ	*The Middle East Journal*
MES	*Middle Eastern Studies*
M.I.3	British Military Intelligence Section 3
MiG—Militärbefehlshaber im Generalgouvernement	military commander in the General government
NAK	National Archives, Kew, Great Britain
NARA	United States National Archives and Records Administration, College Park, Maryland
Nbg. Dok.—Nürnberger Dokument	Nuremberg document
NSDAP—Nationalsozialistische Deutsche Arbeiterpartei	National Socialist German Workers' Party (Nazi Party)
OB—Oberbefehlshaber	commander-in-chief
OBdL—Oberbefehlshaber der Luftwaffe	air force commander-in-chief
OK—Oberkommando	high command
OKH—Oberkommando des Heeres	Army High Command
OKW—Oberkommando der Wehrmacht	Armed Forces High Command
Op.Abt.—Operationsabteilung	operational department
O.Qu.—Oberquartiermeister	deputy chief of general staff
Org.Abt.—Organisationsabteilung	organizational department
Ostubaf.—Obersturmbannführer	Lieutenant Colonel (Waffen SS)
PAAA—Politisches Archiv des Auswärtigen Amtes Berlin	Political Archives of the Foreign Office, Berlin
PK—Parteikanzlei	party chancellery
PzAA—Panzerarmee Afrika	Afrika Korps
PzGr—Panzergruppe	panzer group
Qu.—Quartiermeister	quartermaster
RAM—Reichsaußenminister	Reich foreign minister
RFSS—Reichsführer-SS	Commanding General of the SS (H. Himmler)
RK—Reichskanzlei	Reich chancellery
RMbO—Reichsministerium für die besetzten Ostgebiete	Reich Ministry for the Occupied Eastern Territories
RMI—Reichsministerium des Innern	Reich Ministry of the Interior

RML—Reichsminister(ium) für Luftfahrt	Reich Minister/Ministry for Aviation
RMVP—Reichsminister(ium) für Volksaufklärung und Propaganda	Reich Minister/Ministry for Education and Propaganda
RSHA—Reichssicherheitshauptamt	Reich Security Office
RuSHA—Rasse- und Siedlungshauptamts-Akte	Race and Settlement Department files
SA—Sturmabteilung	Storm Troopers
SD—Sicherheitsdienst Reichsführer-SS	Secret Section of the Reichsführer-SS
SDHA—SD-Hauptamt	SD headquarters
SG—Sozial. Geschichte	Social History
S.I.M.E.	Special Intelligence Middle East
Slg.—Sammlungcollection	
SPN—Sonderdienst Politischer Nachrichten	Special Political Intelligence Service
SS—Schutzstaffel	Protection Unit
SSFHA—SS-Führungshauptamt	SS Operational Headquarters
SSHA—SS-Hauptamt	SS Main Office
SSO—SS-Offiziers-Akte	SS officers' files
SSPHA—SS-Personalhauptamt	SS Main Personnel Office
StS.—Staatssekretär	secretary of state
SZ	*Studies in Zionism*
U.—Und	and
USHMM	United States Holocaust Memorial Museum, Washington, D.C.
VAA—Verbindungsoffizier Auswärtiges Amt beim Armeeoberkommando	Foreign Office liaison officer to the field army command
Versch.—Verschiedene(s)	various
VfZ—Vierteljahrshefte für Zeitgeschichte	*Journal for Contemporary History*
WFSt—Wehrmachtführungsstab	Armed Forces Command
WI—Die Welt des Islam	The World of Islam
WVHA—Wirtschaftsverwaltungshauptamt	Economic Administration Office
YVA	Yad Vashem Archives, Jerusalem
YVS	*Yad Vashem Studies*
zbV.—zur besonderen Verwendung	for special use
ZfP—Zeitschrift für Politik	Political history publications

Archival Sources

Bundesarchiv Berlin (Federal Archives, Berlin, Germany)

NS 19—Persönlicher Stab Reichsführer-SS	personal staff of the Reichsführer-SS
NS 31—SS-Hauptamt	SS headquarters
R 6—Ministerium für die besetzten Ostgebiete	Ministry for the Occupied Eastern Territories
R 43 II—Reichskanzlei	Reich chancellery
R 58—Reichssicherheitshauptamt	RSHA
R 70 Frankreich—SS- und Polizeidienststellen in Frankreich	SS and police departments in France
R 70 Italien—SS- und Polizeidienststellen in Italien	SS and police departments in Italy
RuSHA—Rasse- und Siedlungshauptamts-Akten	Race and Settlement Department files
SSO—SS-Offiziers-Akten	SS officers' files
3200—NSDAP-Zentralkartei	NSDAP central files

Bundesarchiv-Militärarchiv Freiburg/B (Federal Archives/Military Archives, Freiburg im Breisgau, Germany)

RH 2—Chef des Generalstabes des Heeres	chief of the Army General Staff
RH 12-21—Feldzeuginspektion	ordnance inspectorate
RH 19 III—Heeresgruppe C, Nord, Kurland	Army Group C, North, Courland
RH 19 V—Heeresgruppe A, Südukraine, Süd, Ostmark	Army Group A, Southern Ukraine, South, Austria
RH 19 VIII—Panzerarmee Afrika	Afrika Korps
RH 20-11—11. Armee	11th Army
RH 21-5—5. Panzerarmee	5th Panzer Army
RH 22—Befehlshaber rückwärtige Heeresgebiete	commander of rear army areas
RH 23—Kommandanten rückwärtige Armeegebiete	commandant of rear army areas
RH 24-68—Sonderstab Felmy	
RH 24-200—Deutsches Afrikakorps	German Afrika Korps
RH 53-23-Militärbefehlshaber im Generalgouvernement	military commander in the Generalgouvernement
RL 2 I—Chef des Generalstabes der Luftwaffe	chief of the Air Force General Staff

RL 2 II—Luftwaffenführungsstab	Luftwaffe command staff
RL 2 III—Generalquartiermeister der Luftwaffe	Luftwaffe quartermaster general
RL 7-Truppenführungsstäbe Gesamtluft- waffe	troop command staffs of the combined air forces
RM 7—Seekriegsleitung	naval warfare
RW 4—Wehrmachtführungsstab	Wehrmacht command staff
RW 5—OKW, Amt Ausland/Abwehr	OKH, Abwehr
RW 34-OKW, Deutsche Waffen- stillstandskommission	OKH, Armistice Commission
RW 49—OKW, Dienststellen und Ein- heiten der Abwehr	OKH, Abwehr offices and units
N 316—Nachlaß Eberhard Weichold	Eberhard Weichold estate
N 475—Nachlaß Werner Junck	Werner Junck estate

Bundesarchiv Koblenz (Federal Archives, Koblenz, Germany)

N 1146—Nachlaß Paul Leverkuehn	Paul Leverkuehn estate

Bundesarchiv, Außenstelle Ludwigsburg (Federal Archives, Ludwigsburg Branch, Germany)

B 162—Zentrale Stelle der Landesjustiz- verwaltungen zur Aufklärung von NS- Verbrechen	Central Office of the State Justice Administration for the Investigation of National Socialist Crimes (Because the original file reference numbers are currently undergoing conversion, con- sistent designations cannot be pro- vided.)

Bundesarchiv-Zwischenarchiv Dahlwitz-Hoppegarten (Federal Archives/Interim Archives, Dahlwitz-Hoppegarten, Germany)

ZR— Dokumente zu RSHA und SD	documents concerning the RSHA and SD

Politisches Archiv des Auswärtigen Amtes Berlin (Political Archives of the Foreign Office, Berlin)

BA 61123-68998—Akten des Auswärtigen Amtes, Dauerleihgabe aus dem Bundesarchiv Berlin	Foreign Office files, on permanent loan from the Federal Archives, Berlin
R 27185—Dienststelle Ribbentrop	Ribbentrop Office
R 27266—Chef Auslandsorganisation	head of the foreign organization
R 27322-27333—Handakten Ettel	Ettel reference files
R 27772-27828—Handakten Ritter	Ritter reference files
R 28877—Büro Reichsaußenminister	office of the Reich foreign minister
R 29533-29857—Büro Staatssekretär	office of the secretary of state

R 29866-29948—Büro Unterstaatssekretär	office of the undersecretary of state
R 60601-67674—Kulturabteilung	Cultural Department
R 78325-78338—Abteilung III	Department III
R 98813—Abteilung Inland I-D	Interior Department I-D
R 99342-100134—Abteilung Inland II-A/B	Interior Department II-A/B
R 100702-101101—Abteilung Inland II geheim	Interior Department II classified
R 102806-102974—Abteilung Pol. II	Political Department II
R 104776-104791—Abteilung Pol. VII	Political Department VII
R 105187-105192—Abteilung Pol. XIII	Political Department XIII

Institut für Zeitgeschichte München (Institute for Contemporary History, Munich, Germany)

Nbg. Dok.—Nürnberger Dokumente	Nuremberg documents

National Archives, Kew, Great Britain
FO 371
HW 19
KV 2
WO 208

United States National Archives and Records Administration, College Park, Maryland, U.S.
Foreign Military Studies
RG 226—Records of the Office of Strategic Services

United States Holocaust Memorial Museum, Washington, D.C., U.S.
RG 71.005.D7—Robert Kempner estate

Yad Vashem Archives, Jerusalem, Israel
TR 3—Eichmann trial document collection

Bibliography

Abbasi, Nezam al-. *Die Palästinensische Freiheitsbewegung im Spiegel ihrer Presse von 1929 bis 1945,* Diss. Freiburg 1981.

Abitbol, Michel. *Les Juifs d'Afrique du Nord sous Vichy,* Paris 1983.

Aglion, Raoul. *The Fighting French,* New York 1943.

Akten zur deutschen auswärtigen Politik 1918–1945 (ADAP), ser. D (1937–1941), 13 vols., ser. E (1941–1945), 8 vols., Baden-Baden et al. 1950–1979.

Altoma, Salih J. "The Image of the Jew in Modern Arabic Literature 1900–1947," in: *Al-Arabiyya* 11 (1978), pp. 60–73.

Angrick, Andrej. *Besatzungspolitik und Massenmord. Die Einsatzgruppe D in der südlichen Sowjetunion 1941–1943,* Hamburg 2003.

Antonius, George. *The Arab Awakening,* London 1938.

Arendt, Hannah. *Eichmann in Jerusalem. Ein Bericht von der Banalität des Bösen,* Munich and Zurich 1986.

Aries, Wolf D. Ahmet. "Hadj Amin al-Husseini—eine Herausforderung an die Gegenwart," in: *Zimmer-Winkel, Araber,* pp. 47–49.

Arnoni, Menachem S. *Arab Nationalism and the Nazis,* Tel Aviv 1970.

Arnon-Ohanna, Yural. "The Bands in the Palestinian Arab Revolt, 1936–1939: Structure and Organization," in: *AAS* 15 (1981), pp. 229–247.

Aronson, Shlomo. *Hitler, the Allies, and the Jews,* Cambridge 2004.

Arsenian, Seth. "Wartime Propaganda in the Middle East," in: *MEJ* 2 (1948), pp. 417–429.

Avriel, Ehud. *Open the Gates,* New York 1975.

Awaisi, Abd Al-Fattah Muhammad el-. *The Muslim Brothers and the Palestine Question 1928–1947,* London and New York 1998.

Baida, Jamaa. "Die Wahrnehmung der Nazi-Periode in Marokko. Indizien für den Einfluß der deutschen Propaganda auf die Geisteshaltung der Marokkaner," in: *Popp,* pp. 193–196.

Bajohr, Frank. "Im übrigen handle ich so, wie mein Gewissen es mir als Nationalsozialist vorschreibt." Erwin Ettel—vom SS-Brigadeführer zum außenpolitischen Redakteur der ZEIT, in: *Matthäus/Mallmann,* pp. 241–255.

Baker, Robert L. *Oil, Blood, and Sand,* New York 1942.

Balke, Ralf. *Die Landesgruppe der NSDAP in Palästina,* Diss. Essen 1997.

Ball-Kaduri, Kurt Jakob. "Illegale Judenauswanderung aus Deutschland nach Palästina 1939/40—Planung, Durchführung und internationale Zusammenhänge," in: *Jahrbuch des Instituts für Deutsche Geschichte* 4 (1975), pp. 387–421.

Banach, Jens. Heydrichs Elite. *Das Führerkorps der Sicherheitspolizei und des SD 1936–1945,* Paderborn et al. 1998.

Barbour, Neville. "Broadcasting to the Arab World. Arabic Transmissions from the B.B.C. and Other Non-Arab Stations," in: *MEJ* 5 (1951), pp. 57–69.

Barkai, Avraham. "German Interests in the Haavara-Transfer Agreement 1933–1939," in: *LBIYB* 35 (1990), pp. 245–266.

Bauer, Yehuda. "From Cooperation to Resistance: The Haganah 1938–1946," in: *MES* 2 (1966), pp. 182–210.

―――. *Present-Day Antisemitism*, Jerusalem 1988.

―――. *From Diplomacy to Resistance. A History of Jewish Palestine 1939–1945*, Philadelphia 1970.

Baumgarten, Helga. *Palästina: Befreiung in den Staat. Die palästinensische Nationalbewegung seit 1948*, Frankfurt 1991.

Beckman, Morris. *The Jewish Brigade. An Army with Two Masters 1944–1945*, Staplehurst 1998.

Beer, Matthias. "Die Entwicklung der Gaswagen beim Mord an den Juden," in: *VfZ* 35 (1987), pp. 403–417.

Bentwich, Norman/Bentwich, Helen. *Mandate Memories, 1918–1948*, New York 1965.

Berg, Nicolas. *Der Holocaust und die westdeutschen Historiker. Erforschung und Erinnerung*, Göttingen 2003.

Bessis, Juliette. *La Méditerranée Fasciste, L'Italie Mussolinienne et la Tunisie*, Paris 1981.

Bethell, Nicholas. *Das Palästina-Dreieck. Juden und Araber im Kampf um das britische Mandat 1935–1948*, Frankfurt et al. 1979.

Björkman, Walther. "Die neuesten Erfolge der Arabischen Nationalbewegung" in: *ZfP* 27 (1937), pp. 350–356.

―――. "Der Mufti von Jerusalem," in: *ZfP* 28 (1938), pp. 306–311.

Black, Edwin. *The Transfer Agreement. The Untold Story of the Secret Agreement Between the Third Reich and Jewish Palestine*, New York and London 1984.

Black, Ian/Morris, Benny. *Mossad, Shin Beit, Aman. Die Geschichte der Israelischen Geheimdienste*, Heidelberg and Palmyra 1994.

Blum, Howard. *Ihr Leben in unserer Hand. Die Geschichte der Jüdischen Brigade im Zweiten Weltkrieg*, Munich 2002.

Bouman, Johan. *Der Koran und die Juden. Die Geschichte einer Tragödie*, Darmstadt 1990.

Bowden, Tom. "The Politics of the Arab Rebellion in Palestine 1936–1939" in: *MES* 11(1975), pp. 147–174.

Breitman, Richard/Goda, Norman J. W./Brown, Paul. "The Gestapo," in: Richard Breitman/Norman J. W. Goda/Timothy Naftali/Robert Wolfe: "U.S. Intelligence and the Nazis," *Cambridge et al.* 2005, pp. 137–172.

Brenner, Y. S. "The 'Stern Gang' 1940–1948," in: *Kedourie/Haim*, pp. 114–142.

Brockdorff, Werner. *Geheimkommandos des Zweiten Weltkrieges. Geschichte und Einsätze der Brandenburger, der englischen Commands und SAS-Einheiten, der amerikanischen Rangers und sowjetischer Geheimdienste*, Wels, no date.

Browder, George C. "Walter Schellenberg. Eine Geheimdienstphantasie," in: *Smelser/Syring*, pp. 418–430.

Buchheit, Gert. *Der deutsche Geheimdienst. Geschichte der militärischen Abwehr*, Munich 1966.

Cao-Van-Hoa, Edmond. *"Der Feind meines Feindes …." Darstellungen des national-sozialistischen Deutschlands in ägyptischen Schriften*, Frankfurt et al. 1990.

Caplan, Neil. "The Yishuv, Sir Herbert Samuel, and the Arab Question in Palestine, 1921–25," in: *Kedourie/Haim*, pp. 1–51.

Carell, Paul. *Die Wüstenfüchse. Mit Rommel in Afrika*, Hamburg 1958.

Carmel, Alex. *Die Siedlungen der württembergischen Templer in Palästina 1868–1918*, Stuttgart 1973.

Carpi, Daniel. "The Mufti of Jerusalem, Amin al-Husseini, and His Diplomatic Activity During World War II (October 1941–July 1943)," in: *SZ* 7(1983), pp. 101–131.

———. *Between Mussolini and Hitler. The Jews and the Italian Authorities in France and Tunisia*, Hannover and London 1994.

———. "The Diplomatic Negotiations Over the Transfer of Jewish Children from Croatia to Turkey and Palestine in 1943" in: *YVS* 12 (1977), pp. 109–124.

Casagrande, Thomas. *Die volksdeutsche SS-Division "Prinz Eugen." Die Banater Schwaben und die nationalsozialistischen Kriegsverbrechen*, Frankfurt et al. 2003.

Churchill, Winston S. *Der Zweite Weltkrieg*, Frankfurt 2003.

Cohen, Hayyim J. "The Anti-Jewish Farhūd in Baghdad, 1941," in: *MES* 3 (1966), pp. 2–17.

Cohen, Michael J. "Direction of Policy in Palestine, 1936–1945," in: *MES* 11 (1975), pp. 237–261.

———. *The Origins and Evolution of the Arab-Zionist Conflict*, Berkeley et al. 1987.

———. "Origins of the Arab States' Involvement in Palestine," in: *MES* 19 (1983), pp. 244–252

———. *Palestine: Retreat from the Mandate. The Making of British Policy, 1936–1945*, London 1978.

———. "The British White Paper on Palestine, May 1939. Part II: The Testing of a Policy, 1942–1945," in: *The Historical Journal* 19 (1976), pp. 727–758.

———. "British Strategy in the Middle East in the Wake of the Abyssinian Crisis, 1936–39," in: *Cohen/Kolinsky*, pp. 21–40.

———. "British Strategy and the Palestine Question 1936–39," in: *JCH* 7 (1972), pp. 157–183.

———. Kolinsky, Martin. *Britain and the Middle East in the 1930s. Security Problems, 1935–1939*, Basingstoke et al. 1992.

Cohen, Naomi W. *The Year After the Riots. American Responses to the Palestine Crisis of 1929–30*, Detroit 1988.

Cohn, Norman. *"Die Protokolle der Weisen von Zion." Der Mythos der jüdischen Weltverschwörung*, Baden-Baden and Zurich 1998.

Collet, Anne. *Collet des Tcherkesses*, Paris 1949.

Colvin, Ian. *Vansittart in Office. An Historical Survey of the Origins of the Second World War Based on the Papers of Sir Robert Vansittart*, London 1965.

Connell, John. *Wavell. Scholar and Soldier*, New York 1965.

Cooper, Elias. "Forgotten Palestinian: The Nazi Mufti. Roots of the Bitterness in the Arab-Israeli Conflict," in: *The American Zionist* 68 (1978), pp. 5–35.

———. "Nazi Policy in the Middle East," 1939–1945, in: *Midstream* 10 (1964), pp. 61–75.

Cüppers, Martin. *Wegbereiter der Shoah. Die Waffen-SS, Der Kommandostab Reichsführer-SS und die Judenvernichtung 1939–1945*, Darmstadt 2005.

Dann, Uriel (ed.). *The Great Powers in the Middle East 1919–1939*, New York and London 1988.

Dayan, Moshe. *Die Geschichte meines Lebens*, Vienna et al. 1976.

Dayyeh, Suleiman Abu. "Hadj Amin al-Husseini—Ein palästinensicher Führer und Kämpfer," in: *Zimmer-Winkel, Araber*, pp. 35–46.

Deakin, Frederick William. *Die brutale Freundschaft. Mussolini, Hitler und der Sturz des italienischen Faschismus*, Cologne and Berlin 1964.

Dekel, Efraim. Shai. *The Exploits of Hagana Intelligence*, New York and London 1959.

Dessouki, Mohamed-Kamal el-. *Hitler und der Nahe Osten*, Diss. Berlin 1963.

Der Dienstkalender Heinrich Himmlers 1941/42. Edited by Peter Witte/Michael Wildt/ Martina Voigt/Dieter Pohl/Peter Klein/Christian Gerlach/Christoph Dieckmann/ Andrej Angrick, Hamburg 1999.

Dieterich, Renate. "Rāšīd ᶜAlī al-Kailānī in Berlin—ein irakischer Nationalist in NS-Deutschland," in: *Al-Rafidayn* 3 (1995), pp. 47–79.

———. "in der warmen Jahreszeit ist ein Lagern im Freien überall möglich": "Die deutsch-transjordanischen Beziehungen bis zum Ende des Zweiten Weltkriegs," in: *Schwanitz, Deutschland*, pp. 66–85.

Döscher, Hans-Jürgen. *Das Auswärtige Amt im Dritten Reich. Diplomatie im Schatten der 'Endlösung'*, Berlin 1987.

Eade, Charles. *Winston Churchill's Secret Session Speeches*, New York 1946.

Eckman, Lester S./Hirschler, Gertrude. *Menachem Begin. Vom Freiheitskämpfer zum Staatsmann*, Bergisch Gladbach 1979.

Elpeleg, Zvi. *The Grand Mufti. Haj Amin al-Hussaini, Founder of the Palestinian National Movement*, London 1993.

Enzyklopädie des Holocaust (EdH). *Die Verfolgung und Ermordung der europäischen Juden, 3 vols. and an index vol.*, edited by Israel Gutman/Eberhard Jäckel/Peter Longerich/ Julius H. Schoeps, Berlin 1993.

Eppler, John W. *Geheimagent im Zweiten Weltkrieg. Zwischen Berlin, Kabul und Kairo*, Preußisch Oldendorf 1974.

———. *Rommel ruft Kairo. Aus dem Tagebuch eines Spions*, Gütersloh 1959.

Epstein, Albert K. *Palestine at War*, Washington 1943.

Erlich, Haggai. "British Internal Security and Egyptian Youth," in: *Cohen/Kolinsky*, pp. 98–112.

Faligot, Roger/Kauffer, Rémi. *Le croissant et la croix gammée. Les secrets de l'alliance entre l'Islam et le nazisme d'Hitler à nos jours*, Paris 1990.

Farías, Víctor. *Die Nazis in Chile*, Berlin and Vienna 2002.

Feilchenfeld, Werner/Michaelis, Dolf/Pinner, Ludwig. *Haavara-Transfer nach Palästina und Einwanderung deutscher Juden 1933–1939*, Tübingen 1972.

Fischer-Weth Kurt. *Amin al-Husseini Großmufti von Palästina*, Berlin 1943.

Flacker, Edgar. *Fritz Grobba and Nazi Germany's Middle Eastern Policy 1933–1942*, Diss. London 1998.

Flores, Alexander. *Nationalismus und Sozialismus im arabischen Raum. Kommunistische Partei und arabische Nationalbewegung in Palästina, 1919–1948*, Münster 1980.

Fraser, David. "Generalfeldmarschall Erwin Rommel," in: Gerd R. Ueberschär (ed.): *Hitlers militärische Elite* vol. 2, *Vom Kriegsbeginn bis zum Weltkriegsende*, Darmstadt 1998, pp. 184–193.

————. *Rommel, Die Biographie*, Berlin 1995.

Friedman, Jonathan C. "The Politics of Collaboration: A Historiography of Arab-German Relations, 1933–1945," in: Saul S. Friedman (ed.): *Holocaust Literature*, Westport and London 1993, pp. 459–469.

Fröhlich, Elke (ed.). *Die Tagebücher von Joseph Goebbels*, Teil II, Diktate 1941–1945, vol. 8, April–Juni 1943, Munich et al. 1996.

Fromkin, David. *A Peace to End All Peace. The Fall of the Ottoman Empire and the Creation of the Modern Middle East*, London 1989.

Gelber, Yoav. "Central European Jews from Palestine in the British Forces," in: *LBIYB* 35 (1990), pp. 321–332.

Generalstab des Heeres, *Abteilung für Kriegskarten und Vermessungswesen, Militärgeographische Angaben über Palästina und Transjordanien*, booklet, Oct. 15, 1941.

Gensicke, Klaus. *Der Mufti von Jerusalem, Amin el-Husseini, und die Nationalsozialisten*, Frankfurt et al. 1988.

Gentile, Carlo. "Walter Reder—ein politischer Soldat im 'Bandenkampf in: *Mallmann/Paul*, pp. 188–195.

Gerber, Haim. *Ottoman Rule in Jerusalem 1890–1914*, Berlin 1985.

Gessler, Philipp. *Der neue Antisemitismus. Hinter den Kulissen der Normalität*, Freiburg et al. 2004.

Glasneck, Johannes/Kircheisen, Inge. *Türkei und Afghanistan—Brennpunkte der Orientpolitik im Zweiten Weltkrieg*, East Berlin 1968.

Green, Elliott A. "Arabs and Nazis—Can It Be True?" in: *Midstream* 40(1994), pp. 9–13.

Greiselis, Waldis. *Das Ringen um den Brückenkopf Tunesien, 1942/43. Strategie der "Achse" und Innenpolitik im Protektorat*, Frankfurt and Bern 1976.

Grobba, Fritz. *Männer und Mächte im Orient. 25 Jahre diplomatischer Tätigkeit im Orient*, Göttingen et al. 1967.

Groscurth, Helmuth. *Tagebücher eines Abwehroffiziers 1938–1940. Mit weiteren Dokumenten zur Militäropposition gegen Hitler*, edited by Helmut Krausnick and Harold C. Deutsch, Stuttgart 1970.

Gross, Raphael/Konitzer, Werner. "Geschichte und Ethik. Zum Fortwirken der nationalsozialistischen Moral," in: *Mittelweg* 36, 8 (1999), no. 4, pp. 44–67.

Gruchmann, Lothar. "Die "verpassten strategischen Chancen" der Achsenmächte im Mittelmeerraum 1940/41," in: *VfZ* 18 (1970), pp. 456–475.

————. *Der Zweite Weltkrieg*, Munich 1990.

Gundelach, Karl. *Die deutsche Luftwaffe im Mittelmeer 1940–1945*, 2 vols., Frankfurt et al. 1981.

Haim, Sylvia G. "Aspects of Jewish Life in Baghdad under the Monarchy," in: *MES* 11 (1975), pp. 188–208.

Halder. (Generaloberst) *Kriegstagebuch* (KTB Halder). *Tägliche Aufzeichnungen des Chefs des Generalstabes des Heeres 1939–1942*, edited by Hans-Adolf Jacobsen, 3 vols., Stuttgart 1962–1964.

Hamdi, Walid M. S. *Rashid Ali Al-Gailani and the Nationalist Movement in Iraq 1939–1941. A Political and Military Study of the British Campaign in Iraq and the National Revolution of May 1941*, London 1987.

Harras, Mokhtar el-. "Die Printmedien und das Deutschlandbild in der spanischen Protektoratszone von Nordmarokko (1934–1945)," in: *Popp*, pp. 197–207.

Hartmann, Richard. "Der Mufti Amin al-Husaini," in: *ZfP* 31 (1941), pp. 430–439.

Heiber, Helmut (ed.). *Hitlers Lagebesprechungen. Die Protokollfragmente seiner militärischen Konferenzen 1942–1945*, Stuttgart 1962.

Henke, Josef. *England in Hitlers politischem Kalkül 1935–1939*, Boppard 1973.

Hentig, Werner Otto von. *Mein Leben eine Dienstreise*, Göttingen 1962.

Herbert, Ulrich. Best. *Biographische Studien über Radikalismus, Weltanschauung und Vernunft, 1903–1989*, Bonn 1996.

Hest, Heinrich. *Palästina: Judenstaat? England als Handlanger des Weltjudentums*, Berlin 1939.

Hilberg, Raul. *Die Vernichtung der europäischen Juden*, 3 vols., Frankfurt 1990.

Hildebrand, Klaus. *Vom Reich zum Weltreich. Hitler, NSDAP und koloniale Frage 1919–1945*, Munich 1969.

Hillgruber, Andreas. *Hitlers Strategie. Politik und Kriegsführung 1940–1941*, Frankfurt 1965.

———. "The Third Reich and the Middle East, 1933–1939," in: *Dann*, pp. 274–282.

Hirschfeld, Yair P. *Deutschland und Iran im Spielfeld der Mächte. Internationale Beziehungen unter Reza Schah 1921–1941*, Düsseldorf 1980.

Hirszowicz, Łukasz. "Germany and Italy in the Arab East," in: *Acta Poloniae Historica* 6 (1962), pp. 55–88.

———. *The Third Reich and the Arab East*, London and Toronto 1966.

Hitler, Adolf. *Mein Kampf*, Munich 1930.

Hoffmann, Joachim. *Kaukasien 1942-43. Das deutsche Heer und die Orientvölker der Sowjetunion*, Freiburg 1991.

———. *Die Ostlegionen 1941–1943. Turkotataren, Kaukasier und Wolgafinnen im deutschen Heer*, Freiburg 1981.

Hollstein, Walter. *Kein Frieden um Israel. Zur Sozialgeschichte des Palästina-Konflikts*, Berlin 1984.

Holz, Klaus. *Die Gegenwart des Antisemitismus. Islamistische, demokratische und antizionistische Judenfeindschaft*, Hamburg 2005.

Höpp, Gerhard. "Nicht, Alī zuliebe, sondern aus Hass gegen Mu' Āwiya." "Zum Ringen um die "Arabien-Erklärung" der Achsenmächte 1940–1942," in: *Asien Afrika Lateinamerika* 27 (1999), pp. 569–587.

———. "Araber im Zweiten Weltkrieg—Kollaboration oder Patriotismus?," in: *Schwanitz, Legenden*, pp. 86–92.

———. "Der verdrängte Diskurs. Arabische Opfer des Nationalsozialismus," in: *Höpp/Wien/Wildangel*, pp. 215–268.

————. "Der Gefangene im Dreieck. Zum Bild Amin al-Husseinis in Wissenschaft und Publizistik seit 1941. Ein bio-bibliographischer Abriß," in: *Zimmer-Winkel, Araber*, pp. 5–16.

————. "Der Koran als 'Geheime Reichssache.' Bruchstücke deutscher Islampolitik zwischen 1938 und 1945," in: Holger Preißler/Hubert Seiwert (ed.): Gnosis-forschung und Religionsgeschichte. Festschrift für Kurt Rudolph zum 65." *Geburtstag, Marburg* 1994, pp. 435–446.

———— (ed.). *Mufti-Papiere. Briefe, Memoranden, Reden und Aufrufe Amin al-Husainīs aus dem Exil, 1940–1945*, Berlin 2001.

————. "Muslime unterm Hakenkreuz. Zur Entstehungsgeschichte des Islamischen Zentralinstituts zu Berlin e.V.," in: *Moslemische Revue* 14 (1994), pp. 16–27.

————. "Ruhmloses Zwischenspiel. Fawzi al-Qawuqji in Deutschland, 1941–1947," in: *Al-Rafidayn* 3 (1995), pp. 19–46.

————/Wien, Peter/Wildangel, René. *Blind für die Geschichte? Arabische Begegnungen mit dem Nationalsozialismus*, Berlin 2004.

Hubatsch, Walther. *Hitlers Weisungen für die Kriegsführung 1939–1945*. Dokumente des Oberkommandos der Wehrmacht, Koblenz 1983.

Hüber, Reinhard. Rashid Ali El-Gailani, in: "Arabische Führergestalten," *Heidelberg* 1944, pp. 153–159.

Hurewitz, Jacob Coleman. *The Struggle for Palestine*, New York 1950.

Hyamson, Albert M. *Palestine Under the Mandate 1920–1948*, Westport 1976.

Jäckel, Eberhard. *Frankreich in Hitlers Europa. Die deutsche Frankreichpolitik im Zweiten Weltkrieg*, Stuttgart 1966.

Jankowski, James P. *Egypt's Young Rebels. "Young Egypt" 1933–1952*, Stanford 1975.

————. "The Government of Egypt and the Palestine Question, 1936–1939," in: *MES* 17 (1981), pp. 427–453.

————. "Egyptian Responses to the Palestine Problem in the Interwar Period," in: *JMES* 12 (1980), pp. 1–38.

Jaschinski, Klaus. "Das deutsch-iranische Verhältnis im Lichte der alliierten Invasion in Iran 1941," in: *Schwanitz, Deutschland*, pp. 151–172.

Jbara, Taysir. *Palestinian Leader Hajj Amin Al-Husayni. Mufti of Jerusalem*, Princeton 1985.

Jochmann, Werner (ed.). *Adolf Hitler. Monologe im Führerhauptquartier 1941–1944. Die Aufzeichnungen Heinrich Heims*, Hamburg 1980.

Jorda, Iwo. *Araber-Aufstand. Erlebnisse und Dokumente aus Palästina*, Vienna 1943.

————. "Fauzi el-Kawukschi—der Held der Wüste," in: *ZfP* 32 (1942), pp. 261–265.

Kahn, David. *Hitler's Spies. German Military Intelligence in World War II*, New York 1978.

Kaiser, Wolf. *Palästina—Erez Israel. Deutschsprachige Reisebeschreibungen jüdischer Autoren von der Jahrhundertwende bis zum Zweiten Weltkrieg*, Hildesheim et al. 1992.

Kalkas, Barbara. The Revolt of 1936: A Chronicle of Events, in: Ibrahim Abu-Lughod (ed.): "The Transformation of Palestine. Essays on the Origin and Development of the Arab-Israeli Conflict," *Evanston* 1971, pp. 237–274.

Kannapin, Norbert. *Die deutsche Feldpostübersicht 1939–1945. Vollständiges Verzeichnis der Feldpostnummern in numerischer Folge und deren Aufschlüsselung*, vol. 1, Osnabrück 1980.

Katz, Samuel. *Tage des Feuers. Das Geheimnis der Irgun*, Königstein 1981.

Kedourie, Elie. "The Bludan Congress on Palestine, September 1937," in: *MES* 17 (1981), pp. 107–125.

——. *England and the Middle East. The Destruction of the Ottoman Empire 1914–1921*, London and Boulder 1987.

——. "Great Britain and Palestine: The Turning Point," in: *Kedourie, Islam and the Modern World*, London 1980, pp. 93–170.

——. *Arabic Political Memoirs and Other Studies*, London 1974.

——, Haim, Sylvia G. (eds.). *Zionism and Arabism in Palestine and Israel*, London and Totowa 1982.

Keegan, John. *Der Zweite Weltkrieg*, Berlin 2004.

Kempner, Robert M. W. *SS im Kreuzverhör. Die Elite, die Europa in Scherben schlug*, Nördlingen, 1987.

Khadduri, Majid. *Independent Iraq 1932–1958. A Study in Iraqi Politics*, London et al. 1960.

——. "General Nūrī's Flirtations with the Axis Powers," in: *MEJ* 16 (1962), pp. 328–336.

Khalaf, Issa. *Politics in Palestine. Arab Factionalism and Social Desintegration, 1939–1948*, Albany 1991.

Khoury, Philip Shukry. *Syria and the French Mandate. The Politics of Arab Nationalism 1920–1945*, Princeton 1987.

Kiefer, Michael. *Antisemitismus in den islamischen Gesellschaften: Der Palästina-Konflikt und der Transfer eines Feindbildes*, Düsseldorf 2002.

Kiernan, Thomas. *Arafat. The Man and the Myth*, New York 1976.

Kimche, Jon. *Seven Fallen Pillars. The Middle East, 1915–1950*, London 1950.

——/Kimche, David. *The Secret Roads. The "Illegal" Migration of a People 1938–1948*, Westport 1976.

Kiram, Zeki. "Ein Moslem über das neue Deutschland. Hitler ist der berufene Mann," in: *Moslemische Revue* 1938, p. 59f.

Kirk, George. *The Middle East in the War*, London et al. 1952.

Kisch, Frederick. *Palestine Diary*, London 1938.

Klee, Karl. *Das Unternehmen "Seelöwe." Die geplante deutsche Landung in England 1940*, Göttingen et al. 1958.

Klein, Peter (ed.). *Die Einsatzgruppen in der besetzten Sowjetunion 1941/42. Die Tätigkeits- und Lageberichte des Chefs der Sicherheitspolizei und des SD*, Berlin 1997.

Klietmann, Kurt-Gerhard. *Die Waffen-SS. Eine Dokumentation*, Osnabrück 1965.

Koestler, Arthur. *Promise and Fulfilment, Palestine 1917–1949*, New York 1949.

Kogon, Eugen/Langbein, Hermann/Rückerl, Adalbert et al. (eds.). *Nationalsozialistische Massentötungen durch Giftgas. Eine Dokumentation*, Frankfurt 1986.

Kohlhaas, Wilhelm. *Hitler-Abenteuer im Irak. Ein Erlebnisbericht*, Freiburg et al. 1989.

Kolinsky, Martin. "The Collapse and Restoration of Public Security," in: *Cohen/Kolinsky*, pp. 147–168.

——. *Law, Order and Riots in Mandatory Palestine, 1928–35*, Basingstoke and London 1993.

————. "Reorganization of the Palestine Police after the Riots of 1929," in: *SZ* 10 (1989), pp. 155–179.

Kossak-Raytenau, Karl L. *Mord und Brand im "heiligen" Land. Ein Tatsachenbericht mit 55 meist eigenen Aufnahmen des Verfassers, einem Faksimile und einer Karte*, Munich 1939.

Kostiner, Joseph. Britain and the Challenge of the Axis Powers in Arabia: "The Decline of British-Saudi Cooperation in the 1930s," in: *Cohen/Kolinsky*, pp. 128–143.

Krämer, Gudrun. *Geschichte Palästinas. Von der osmanischen Eroberung bis zur Gründung des Staates Israel*, Munich 2002.

————. *The Jews in Modern Egypt, 1914–1952*, Seattle 1989.

————. "Die Juden als Minderheit in Ägypten, 1914–1956. Islamische Toleranz im Zeichen des Antikolonialismus und des Antizionismus," in: *Saeculum* 34 (1983), pp. 36–69.

Krausnick, Helmut. *Hitlers Einsatzgruppen. Die Truppe des Weltanschauungskrieges 1938–1942*, Frankfurt 1985.

————. *Holsteins Geheimpolitik in der Ära Bismarck 1886 bis 1890*, Hamburg 1942.

Krecker, Lothar. *Deutschland und die Türkei im Zweiten Weltkrieg*, Frankfurt 1964.

Kuhlmann, Jan. *Subhas Chandra Bose und die Indienpolitik der Achsenmächte*, Berlin 2003.

Kühn, Volkmar. *Rommel in the Desert*, West Chester 1991.

Küntzel, Matthias. *Djihad und Judenhaß. Über den neuen antijüdischen* Krieg, Freiburg 2002.

————. "Die zweite Spaltung der Welt. Die Holocaust-Leugnung des iranischen Präsidenten hat Methode," in: *Internationale Politik* 4 (2006), pp. 75–83.

————. "Von Zeesen bis Beirut. Nationalsozialismus und Antisemitismus in der arabischen Welt," in: Doron Rabinovici/Ulrich Speck/Natan Sznaider (eds.): "Neuer Antisemitismus? Eine globale Debatte," *Frankfurt 2004*, pp. 271–293.

Kunz, Norbert. *Die Krim unter deutscher Herrschaft (1941–1944). Germanisierungsutopie und Besatzungsrealität*, Darmstadt 2005.

Kupferschmidt, Uri M. *The Supreme Muslim Council. Islam under the British Mandate for Palestine*, Leiden et al. 1987.

Lachman, Shai. "Arab Rebellion in Palestine 1929–39. The Case of Sheikh Izz al-Din al-Qassam and His Movement," in: *Kedourie/Haim*, pp. 52–99.

Laqueur, Walter. *Der Weg zum Staat Israel. Geschichte des Zionismus*, Vienna 1975.

Lesch, Ann Mosely. *Arab Politics in Palestine, 1917–1939. The Frustration of a Nationalist Movement*, Ithaca and London 1979.

Leverkuehn, Paul. *Der geheime Nachrichtendienst der deutschen Wehrmacht im Kriege*, Frankfurt 1957.

Lewis, Bernard. "Antisemitism in the Arab and Islamic World," in: *Bauer, Antisemitism*, pp. 57–66.

————. *Die Juden in der islamischen Welt. Vom frühen Mittelalter bis ins 20.* Jahrhundert, Munich 2004.

————. *"Treibt sie ins Meer!", Die Geschichte des Antisemitismus*, Frankfurt and Berlin 1987.

————. *Die Wut der arabischen Welt. Warum der jahrhundertelange Konflikt zwischen dem Islam und dem Westen weiter eskaliert*, Frankfurt and New York 2003.

Lia, Brynjar. *The Society of the Muslim Brothers in Egypt. The Rise of an Islamic Mass Movement 1928–1942*, Reading 1998.

Longerich, Peter (ed.). *Die Ermordung der europäischen Juden. Eine umfassende Dokumentation des Holocaust 1941–1945*, Munich and Zurich 1989.

Lozowick, Yaakov. *Hitlers Bürokraten. Eichmann, seine willigen Vollstrecker und die Banalität des Bösen*, Zurich and Munich 2000.

Luca, Anthony R. De. "Der GroßMufti' in Berlin: The Politics of Collaboration," in: *International Journal of Middle East Studies* 10 (1979), pp. 125–138.

Lucas, James. *Afrika Korps*, London 1977.

MacDonald, Callum A. "Radio Bari: Italian Wireless Propaganda in the Middle East and British Countermeasures 1934–38," in: *MES* 13 (1977), pp. 195–207.

Madani, S. Djalal. *Iranische Politik und Drittes Reich*, Frankfurt et al. 1986.

Mallmann, Klaus-Michael. "Der Krieg im Dunkeln. Das Unternehmen "Zeppelin" 1942–1945," in: *Michael Wildt (ed.): Nachrichtendienst, politische Elite und Mordeinheit. Der Sicherheitsdienst des Reichsführers SS, Hamburg 2003*, pp. 324–346.

———. Menschenjagd und Massenmord. "Das neue Instrument der Einsatzgruppen und -kommandos 1938–1945," in: *Paul/Mallmann*, pp. 291–316.

———. "Die Türöffner der "Endlösung." Zur Genesis des Genozids," in: *Paul/Mallmann*, pp. 437–463.

———. "Volksjustiz gegen anglo-amerikanische Mörder"—"Die Massaker an west-alliierten Fliegern und Fallschirmspringern 1944/45," in: *Alfred Gottwaldt/ Norbert Kampe/Peter Klein (eds.): NS-Gewaltherrschaft. Beiträge zur historischen Forschung und juristischen Aufarbeitung, Berlin* 2005, pp. 202–213.

———, Cüppers, Martin. "Beseitigung der jüdisch-nationalen Heimstätte in Palästina." "Das Einsatzkommando bei der Panzerarmee Afrika 1942," *in: Matthäus/Mallmann*, pp. 153–176.

———, Musial, Bogdan (eds.). *Genesis des Genozids: Polen 1939–1941*, Darmstadt 2004.

———, Paul, Gerhard (eds.). "Karrieren der Gewalt. Nationalsozialistische Täterbiographien," *Darmstadt* 2004, pp. 188–195.

———, Rieß, Volker/Pyta, Wolfram (eds.). *Deutscher Osten 1939–1945. Der Weltanschauungskrieg in Photos und Texten*, Darmstadt 2003.

Marcus, Ernst. "The German Foreign Office and the Palestine Question in the Period 1933–1939," in: *YVS* 2 (1958), pp. 179–204.

Marlowe, John. *The Seat of Pilate. An Account of the Palestine Mandate*, London 1959.

Marston, Elsa. "Fascist Tendencies in the Pre-War Arab Politics. A Study of Three Arab Political Movements," in: *Middle East Forum* 35 (1959), pp. 19–22, 33, 35.

Mattar, Philip. "Amin Al-Husayni and Iraq's Quest for Independence," in: *ASQ* 4 (1984), pp. 267–281.

———. *The Mufti of Jerusalem. Al-Hajj Amin al-Husayni and the Palestinian National Movement*, New York 1988.

———. "The Mufti of Jerusalem and the Politics of Palestine," in: *MEJ* 42(1988), pp. 227–240.

———. "The Role of the Mufti of Jerusalem in the Political Struggle Over the Western Wall, 1928–1929," in: *MES* 19 (1983), pp. 104–118.

Matthäus, Jürgen/Mallmann, Klaus-Michael (eds.). *Deutsche, Juden, Völkermord. Der Holocaust als Geschichte und Gegenwart,* Darmstadt 2006.

McKale, Donald M. Curt Prüfer. *German Diplomat from the Kaiser to Hitler,* Kent and London 1987.

———. *The Swastika Outside Germany,* Kent 1977.

———. *War by Revolution. Germany and Great Britain in the Middle East in the Era of World War I,* Kent 1998.

Meinertzhagen, Richard. *Palestine Diary 1917–1956,* London 1960.

Mejcher, Helmut. "North Africa in the Strategy and Politics of the Axis Powers 1936–1943" in: *Cahiers de Tunisie* 39 (1981), pp. 629–648.

Melka, Robert L. *The Axis and the Arab Middle East: 1930–1945,* Diss. University of Minnesota 1966.

———. "Nazi Germany and the Palestine Question," in: *JMES* 5 (1969), pp. 221–233.

Mendel, Miloš/Müller, Zdeněk. "Fascist Tendencies in the Levant in the 1930s and 1940s," in: *Archív Orientální* 55 (1987), pp. 1–17.

Metzger, Chantal. *L'Empire Colonial Français dans la Stratégie du Troisième Reich (1936–1945),* Brüssel et al. 2002.

Michaelis, Meir. "Italy's Mediterranean Strategy, 1935–39," in: *Cohen/Kolinsky,* pp. 41–60.

Michman, Dan. "Araber, Zionisten, Bishara und der Holocaust," in: *Zimmer-Winkel, Araber,* pp. 42–47.

———. "Täteraussagen und Geschichtswissenschaft. Der Fall Dieter Wisliceny und der Entscheidungsprozeß zur 'Endlösung,'" in: *Matthäus/Mallmann,* pp. 205–219.

Mildenstein, Leopold von. *Rings um das brennende Land am Jordan. Eine Fahrt bis zu den Quellen des flüssigen Goldes,* Berlin 1938.

———. *Naher Osten—vom Straßenrand erlebt. Ein Reisebericht mit sechzehn Farbbildern,* Stuttgart 1941.

Mitchell, Richard P. *The Society of the Muslim Brothers,* London 1969.

Morris, Benny. *Righteous Victims. A History of the Zionist-Arab Conflict, 1881–2001,* New York 2001.

Morrison, S. A. "Arab Nationalism and Islam," in: *MEJ* 2 (1948), pp. 147–159.

Moyzisch, Ludwig C. *Der Fall Cicero. Die sensationellste Spionageaffäre des Zweiten Weltkrieges,* Frankfurt and Heidelberg 1950.

Mühlen, Patrick von zur. *Zwischen Hakenkreuz und Sowjetstern. Der Nationalismus der sowjetischen Orientvölker im Zweiten Weltkrieg,* Düsseldorf 1971.

Nafi, Basheer M. *Arabism, Islamism and the Palestine Question 1908–1941. A Political History,* Reading 1998.

———. "The Arabs and the Axis: 1933–1940," in: *ASQ* 19 (1997), pp. 1–24.

———. "Shaykh, Izz al-Dīn al-Qassām "A Reformist and a Rebel Leader," in: *Journal of Islamic Studies* 8 (1997), pp. 185–215.

Neitzel, Sönke. *Abgehört. Deutsche Generäle in britischer Kriegsgefangenschaft 1942–1945,* Berlin 2005.

Neubert, Friedrich. *Die deutsche Politik im Palästina-Konflikt 1937/38,* Diss. Bonn 1977.

Nevo, Joseph. "Al-Hajj Amin and the British in World War II," in: *MES* 20(1984), pp. 3–16.

―――. "Palestinian-Arab Violent Activity During the 1930s," in: *Cohen/Kolinsky*, pp. 169–189.

Nicosia, Francis R. J. "Arab Nationalism and National Socialist Germany, 1933–1939: Ideological and Strategic Incompatibility," in: *MES* 12 (1980), pp. 351–372.

―――. *Central Zionist Archives, Jerusalem 1939–1945*, New York and London 1990.

―――. *Hitler und der Zionismus. Das Dritte Reich und die Palästinafrage 1933–1939*, Leoni 1989.

―――. "Fritz Grobba and the Middle East Policy of the Third Reich, in: Edward Ingram (ed.): National and International Politics in the Middle East," *Essays in Honour of Elie Kedourie, London and Totowa 1986*, 206–228.

Nordbruch, Götz. "Antisemitismus als Gegenstand islamwissenschaftlicher und Nahost-bezogener Sozialforschung," in: *Werner Bergmann/Mona Körte (eds.): Antisemitismusforschung in den Wissenschaften*, Berlin 2004, pp. 241–269.

O'Brien, Conor Cruise. *Belagerungs Zustand. Die Geschichte des Zionismus und des Staates Israel*, Vienna 1988.

Odermann, Heinz. "Taktik gewinnt Schlachten—Strategie des Krieges. Zu einigen Aspekten der deutschen Nahost- und Nordafrikapolitik und -propaganda (1940–1942)," in: *Schwanitz, Legenden*, pp. 93–110.

Ofer, Dalia. *Escaping the Holocaust. Illegal Immigration to the Land of Israel, 1942–1944*, New York and Oxford 1990.

Oldenburg, Manfred. *Ideologie und militärisches Kalkül. Die Besatzungspolitik der Wehrmacht in der Sowjetunion 1942*, Cologne et al. 2004.

Omissi, David. "The Mediterranean and the Middle East in British Global Strategy, 1935–1939," in: *Cohen/Kolinsky*, pp. 3–20.

Osta, Abdel al-. *Die Juden in der palästinensischen Literatur zwischen 1913 und 1987*, Berlin 1993.

Overy, Richard. *Die Wurzeln des Sieges. Warum die Alliierten den Zweiten Weltkrieg gewannen*, Stuttgart and Munich 2000.

Owen, D. L. Lloyd. *Providence their Guide. A Personal Account of the Long Range Desert Group 1940–45*, London 1980.

Pail, Meir. "A Breakthrough in Zionist Military Conceptions: 1936–39," in: *Cohen/Kolinsky*, pp. 190–205.

Papen, Franz von. *Der Wahrheit eine Gasse*, Innsbruck 1952.

Paul, Gerhard/Mallmann, Klaus-Michael (eds.). *Die Gestapo im Zweiten Weltkrieg. "Heimatfront" und besetztes Europa*, Darmstadt 2000.

Peres, Schimon. *Shalom*. Erinnerungen, Stuttgart 1995.

Peters, Joan. *From Time Immemorial. The Origins of the Arab-Jewish Conflict over Palestine*, New York 1984.

Petersen, Jens. *Hitler-Mussolini. Die Entstehung der Achse Berlin-Rom 1933–1936*, Tübingen 1973.

Petrick, Fritz. "Werner Best. Ein verhinderter Generalgouverneur," in: *Smelser/Syring*, pp. 60–76.

Pfullmann, Uwe. "Die deutsch-saudischen Beziehungen und die Akteure aufder Arabischen Halbinsel 1924–1939," in: *Schwanitz, Deutschland*, pp. 86–106.

Piekalkiewicz, Janusz. *Rommel und die Geheimdienste in Nordafrika 1941–1943*, Munich and Berlin 1984.

Pohl, Dieter. "Die Einsatzgruppe C 1941/42," in: *Klein*, pp. 71–87.

―――. "Ukrainische Hilfskräfte beim Mord an den Juden, in: Gerhard Paul (ed.): Die Täter der Shoah. Fanatische Nationalsozialisten oder ganz normale Deutsche?," *Göttingen* 2002, pp. 205–234.

Poliakov, Léon/Wulf, Joseph (eds.). *Das Dritte Reich und die Juden. Dokumente und Berichte*, Wiesbaden 1989.

Polkehn, Klaus. "The Secrets Contacts: Zionism and Nazi Germany, 1933–1941," in: *Journal of Palestine Studies 5(1976)*, pp. 54–82.

Popp, Herbert (ed.). *Die Sicht des Anderen. Das Marokkobild der Deutschen, das Deutschlandbild der Marokkaner*, Passau 1994.

Porath, Yehoshua. "Al-Hājj Amīn Al-Husaynī, Mufti of Jerusalem—His Rise to Power and the Consolidation of His Position," in: *AAS* 7 (1971), pp. 121–156.

―――. *The Emergence of the Palestinian-Arab National Movement 1918–1929*, London 1974.

―――. *The Palestinian Arab National Movement. From Riots to Rebellion, 1929–1939*, London and Totowa 1977.

―――. *In Search of Arab Unity 1930–1945*, London 1986.

Pratt, Lawrence. "The Strategic Context: British Policy in the Mediterranean and the Middle East, 1936–1939," in: *Dann*, pp. 12–26.

Querg, Thorsten. *Spionage und Terror—Das Amt VI des Reichssicherheitshauptamtes 1939–1945*, Diss. Berlin 1997.

Rabinovich, Itamar. "Antisemitism in the Muslim and Arab World," in: *Bauer, Antisemitism*, pp. 253–268.

―――. "Germany and the Syrian Political Scene in the Late 1930's," in: *Wallach*, pp. 191–198.

Rabl, Hans. "Der Nahe Osten auf dem Weg zur Einigung," in: *Zeitschrift für Geopolitik 13 (1936)*, pp. 293–302.

―――. "Nah-Ost-Nachtrag," in: ibid., pp. 402–404.

Rahn, Rudolf. *Ruheloses Leben. Aufzeichnungen und Erinnerungen*, Düsseldorf 1949.

Das Deutsche Reich und der Zweite Weltkrieg (DRZW), published by Militärgeschichtlichen Forschungsamt, 9 vols., Stuttgart 1979–2005.

Reile, Oscar. *Geheime Ostfront. Die deutsche Abwehr im Osten 1921–1945*, Munich and Wels 1963.

Reinhardt, Klaus. *Die Wende vor Moskau. Das Scheitern der Strategie Hitlers im Winter 1941/42*, Stuttgart 1972.

Rejwan, Nissim. *The Last Jews in Baghdad. Remembering a Lost Homeland*, Austin 2004.

Reuth, Ralf Georg. *Entscheidung im Mittelmeer. Die südliche Peripherie Europas in der deutschen Strategie des Zweiten Weltkrieges 1940–1942*, Koblenz 1985.

―――. *Erwin Rommel. Des Führers General*, Munich and Zurich 1987.

————. "Erwin Rommel—Die Propagandaschöpfung," in: Ronald Smelser/Enrico Syring (eds.): "Die Militärelite des Dritten Reiches." *27 biographische Skizzen, Berlin and Frankfurt* 1995, pp. 460–475.

Roosevelt, Kermit. "The Partition of Palestine. A Lesson in Pressure Politics," in: *MEJ* 2(1948), pp. 1–16.

Rose, Norman Anthony. "The Arab Rulers and Palestine, 1936: The British Reaction," in: *JMH* 44(1972), pp. 213–231.

Roshwald, Aviel. *Estranged Bedfellows. Britain and France in the Middle East during the Second World War,* New York and Oxford 1990.

Roth, Karl Heinz. "Vorposten Nahost: Franz von Papen als deutscher Türkei-botschafter 1939–1944," in: *Schwanitz, Deutschland,* pp. 107–125.

Rutherford, Ward. *The Biography of Field Marshal Erwin Rommel,* London et al. 1981.

Sadat, Anwar el-. *Unterwegs zur Gerechtigkeit,* Vienna et al. 1977.

————. *Revolt on the Nile,* New York 1957.

Sammons, Jeffrey L. (ed.). *Die Protokolle der Weisen von Zion. Die Grundlage des modernen Antisemitismus— eine Fälschung.* Text und Kommentar, Göttingen 1998.

Satloff, Robert. "In Search of 'Righteous Arabs,'" in: *Commentary* 118 (2004), pp. 30–35.

Schattenfroh, Franz. *Britenfaust und Judengeist. Eine Reise durch Aegypten und Palästina im Schatten des Krieges,* Berlin et al. 1940.

Schechtman, Joseph B. *The Mufti and the Fuehrer. Rise and Fall of Haj Amin el-Husseini,* New York and London 1965.

Scheffler, Wolfgang. "Die Einsatzgruppe A 1941/42," in: *Klein,* pp. 29–51.

Schellenberg, Walther. *Memoiren,* Cologne 1959.

Schenk, Dieter. *Auf dem rechten Auge blind. Die braunen Wurzeln des BKA,* Cologne 2001.

Schiller, David Th. *Palästinenser zwischen Terrorismus und Diplomatie. Die paramilitärische palästinensische Nationalbewegung von 1918 bis 1981,* Munich 1982.

Schmidt, H. D. "The Nazi Party in Palestine and the Levant 1932–9," in: *International Affairs 28* (1952), pp. 460–469.

Schmitz-Kairo, Paul. *Die Arabische Revolution,* Leipzig 1942.

Schnabel, Reimund. *Mißbrauchte Mikrofone. Deutsche Rundfunkpropaganda im Zweiten Weltkrieg. Eine Dokumentation,* Vienna 1967.

Schölch, Alexander. "Das Dritte Reich, die zionistische Bewegung und der Palästina-Konflikt," in: *VfZ* 30 (1982), pp. 646–674.

Schröder, Bernd Philipp. *Deutschland und der Mittlere Osten im zweiten Weltkrieg,* Göttingen et al. 1975.

————. *Irak 1941,* Freiburg 1980.

Schröder, Josef. "Die Beziehungen der Achsenmächte zur Arabischen Welt," in: Funke, Manfred (ed.): Hitler, Deutschland und die Mächte. Materialien zur Außen-politik des Dritten Reiches," *Düsseldorf 1976,* pp. 365–382

Schulze-Holthus, Julius Berthold. "Eine groteske Fälschung," in: *Die Nachhut no. 7, 1969,* pp. 18–26.

————. *Frührot in Iran. Abenteuer im deutschen Geheimdienst,* Esslingen 1952.

Schwanitz, Wolfgang G. (ed.): *Deutschland und der Mittlere Osten,* Leipzig 2004.

————. "Djihad 'Made in Germany': Der Streit um den Heiligen Krieg 1914–1915," in: *SG* 18(2003), pp. 7–34.

————. "'Der Geist aus der Lampe': Fritz Grobba und Berlins Politik im Nahen und Mittleren Osten," in: *Schwanitz, Deutschland*, pp. 126–150.

———— (ed.). *Germany and the Middle East 1871–1945*, Frankfurt and Madrid 2004.

———— (ed.). *Jenseits der Legenden*. Araber, Juden, Deutsche, Berlin 1994.

————. "Max von Oppenheim und der Heilige Krieg. Zwei Denkschriften zur Revolutionierung islamischer Gebiete 1914 und 1940," in: *SG* 19 (2004), pp. 28–59.

————. "Paschas, Politiker und Paradigmen. Deutsche Politik im Nahen und Mittleren Orient, 1871–1945," in: *Schwanitz, Deutschland*, pp. 22–45.

Schwipps, Werner. *Wortschlacht im Äther. Der deutsche Auslandsrundfunk im* Zweiten Weltkrieg, Berlin 1971.

Segev, Tom. *Es war einmal ein Palästina. Juden und Araber vor der Staatsgründung Israels*, Munich 2005.

Seidt, Hans Ulrich. *Berlin Kabul Moskau. Oskar Ritter von Niedermayer und Deutschlands Geopolitik*, Munich 2002.

Seifert, Hermann Erich. *Der Aufbruch in der arabischen Welt*, Berlin 1941.

Seubert, Franz. "Der GrossMufti von Jerusalem und die Abwehr," in: *Die Nachhut* no. 4, 1968, pp. 2–7.

Shamir, Shimon. "The Influence of German National-Socialism on Radical Movements in Egypt," in: *Wallach*, pp. 200–209.

————. "The Middle East in the Nazi Conception," in: *Wallach*, pp. 167–174.

Sheffer, Gabriel. "The Involvement of Arab States in the Palestine Conflict and British-Arab Relationship Before World War II," in: *AAS* 10 (1974), pp. 59–78.

————. "Principles of Pragmatism: A Reevaluation of British Policies Toward Palestine in the 1930s," in: *Dann*, pp. 109–127.

Shlaim, Avi. *The Politics of Partition. King Abdullah, the Zionists and Palestine 1921–1951*, Oxford 1990.

Sietz, Henning. *Attentat auf Adenauer. Die geheime Geschichte eines politischen Anschlags*, Berlin 2003.

Simon, Reeva Spector. *Iraq Between the Two World Wars. The Militarist Origins of Tyranny*, New York 2004.

Sivan, Emmanuel. "Islamischer Fundamentalismus und Antisemitismus," in: Herbert A. Strauss/Werner Bergmann/Christhard Hoffmann (eds.): *Der Antisemitismus der Gegenwart*, Frankfurt and New York 1990, pp. 84–98.

Sluglett, Peter. *Britain in Iraq 1914–1932*, Oxford 1976.

Smelser, Ronald/Syring, Enrico (eds.). *Die SS: Elite unter dem Totenkopf.* 30 Lebensläufe, Paderborn et al. 2000.

Spaeter, Helmuth. *Die Brandenburger. Eine deutsche Kommandotruppe*, Düsseldorf 1991.

Stang, Knut. "Kollaboration und Völkermord. Das Rollkommando Hamann und die Vernichtung der litauischen Juden," in: *Paul/Mallmann*, pp. 464–480.

Stark, Freya. *The Arab Island. The Middle East 1939–1943*, New York 1945.

Stein, George H. *Geschichte der Waffen-SS*, Düsseldorf 1967.

Steppat, Fritz. "Das Jahr 1933 und seine Folgen für die arabischen Länder des Vorderen Orients, in: Gerhard Schulz (ed.): Die große Krise der dreißiger Jahre. Vom Niedergang der Weltwirtschaft zum Zweiten Weltkrieg," *Göttingen* 1985, pp. 261–278.

Stewart, Norman. *German Relations with the Arab East 1937–1941*, Diss. Saint Louis 1975.

Stewart, Richard A. *Sunrise at Abadan. The British and Soviet Invasion of Iran, 1941*, New York et al. 1988.

Storch de Gracia, J. M. "Die Abwehr und das deutsche Generalkonsulat in Tanger," in *Die Nachhut* no. 2, 1967, p. 7f.

Swedenburg, Ted. *Memories of Revolt. The 1936–1939 Rebellion and the Palestinian National Past*, Minneapolis and London 1995.

———. "The Role of the Palestinian Peasantry in the Great Revolt (1936–1939)," in: Edmund Burke/Ira Lapidus (eds.): *Islam, Politics and Social Movements, Berkeley et al.* 1988, pp. 169–203.

Sykes, Christopher. *Kreuzwege nach Israel. Die Vorgeschichte des jüdischen Staates*, Munich 1967.

———. *Orde Wingate*, London 1959.

Teske, Hermann (ed.). *General Ernst Köstring. Der militärische Mittler zwischen dem Deutschen Reich und der Sowjetunion 1921–1941*, Frankfurt, no date (1965).

Theil, Edmund. *Rommels verheizte Armee. Kampf und Ende der Heeresgruppe Afrika von El Alamein bis Tunis*, Vienna et al. 1979.

Tibi, Bassam. *Nationalismus in der Dritten Welt am arabischen Beispiel*, Frankfurt 1971.

Tillmann, Heinz. *Deutschlands Araberpolitik im Zweiten Weltkrieg*, East Berlin 1965.

Trentow, Bernd/Kranhold, Werner. "Im Dienst imperialistischer Weltherrschaftspläne. Zum Orient-Einsatz des faschistischen Rundfunks im zweiten Weltkrieg," in: *Beiträge zur Geschichte des Rundfunks* 7 (1973), no. 4, pp. 22–51.

Vernier, Bernard. *La Politique Islamique de l'Allemagne*, Paris 1939.

Wagner, Patrick. *Ehemalige SS-Männer am "Schilderhäuschen der Demokratie"? Die Affäre um das Bundesamt für Verfassungsschutz 1963/64, in*: Gerhard Fürmetz/Herbert Reinke/Klaus Weinhauer (eds.): Nachkriegspolizei. Sicherheit und Ordnung in Ost- und Westdeutschland 1945–1969, Hamburg 2001.

Waldschmidt, Julius. "Al-Alamein—Die Wende im Wüstenkrieg 1942," in: *Schwanitz, Legenden*, pp. 111–120.

Wallach, Jehuda L. (ed.). *Germany and the Middle East 1835–1939*, Tel Aviv 1975.

Wanner, Jan. "Amin al-Husayni and Germany's Arab Policy in the Period 1939–1945," in: *Archív Orientální* 54 (1986), pp. 226–245.

Warlimont, Walter. *Im Hauptquartier der Deutschen Wehrmacht 1939–1945*, Frankfurt 1964.

Warner, Geoffrey. *Iraq and Syria 1941*, London 1974.

Wasserstein, Bernard. *The British in Palestine. The Mandatory Government and the Arab-Jewish Conflict 1917–1929*, London 1978.

Watt, D.C. "German Ideas on Iraq, 1937–1938," in: *MEJ* 12 (1958), pp. 195–204.

Weber, Frank G.: *The Evasive Neutral. Germany, Britain and the Quest for a Turkish Alliance in the Second World War*, Columbia and London 1979.

Weizmann, Chaim. *Memoiren. Das Werden des Staates Israel,* Zurich 1953.

Welzer, Harald. Täter. *Wie aus ganz normalen Menschen Massenmörder werden,* Frankfurt 2005.

Wendt, Bernd-Jürgen. *Großdeutschland. Außenpolitik und Kriegsvorbereitung des Hitler-Regimes,* Munich 1987.

Wien, Peter. ""Neue Generation" und Führersehnsucht, Generationenkonflikt und totalitäre Tendenzen im Irak der dreißiger Jahre," in: *Höpp/Wien/Wildangel,* pp. 73–114.

Wiesenthal, Simon. *Großmufti*—Großagent der Achse, Salzburg and Vienna 1947.

Wild, Stefan. "Judentum, Christentum und Islam in der palästinensischen Poesie," in: *WI* 23–24 (1984), pp. 259–297.

———. ""Mein Kampf" in arabischer Übersetzung," in: *WI* 9 (1964), pp. 207–211.

———. "National Socialism in the Arab Middle East between 1933 and 1939," in: *WI* 25 (1985), pp. 126–173.

———. "Die arabische Rezeption der "Protokolle der Weisen von Zion," in: Rainer Brunner/Monika Gronke/Jens Peter Laut/Ulrich Rebstock (eds.): Islamstudien ohne Ende. Festschrift für Werner Ende zum 65." *Geburtstag, Würzburg 2002,* pp. 517–528.

Wildangel, René. "Der größte Feind der Menschheit." "Der Nationalsozialismus in der arabischen öffentlichen Meinung in Palästina während des Zweiten Weltkrieges," in: *Höpp/Wien/Wildangel,* pp. 115–154.

Wildt, Michael. *Generation des Unbedingten. Das Führungskorps des Reichssicherheitshauptamtes,* Hamburg 2002.

——— (ed.). *Die Judenpolitik des SD 1935 bis 1938.* Eine Dokumentation, Munich 1995.

Wirsing, Giselher. *Engländer Juden Araber in Palästina,* Jena 1938.

Wistrich, Robert. *Der antisemitische Wahn. Von Hitler bis zum Heiligen Krieg gegen Israel,* Munich 1987.

Yamak, Labib Zuwiyya. *The Syrian Social Nationalist Party. An Ideological Analysis,* Cambridge 1966.

Yisraeli, David. "The Third Reich and Palestine," in: *MES* 7 (1971), pp. 343–353.

———. "The Third Reich and the Transfer Agreement," in: *JCH* 6 (1971), pp. 129–148.

Zimmer-Winkel, Rainer (ed.). *Die Araber und die Shoah. Über die Schwierigkeiten dieser Konjunktion,* Trier 2000.

——— (ed.). Eine umstrittene Figur: *Hadj Amin al-Husseini. Mufti von Jerusalem,* Trier 1999.

Zweig, Ronald. *Britain and Palestine During the Second World War,* Woodbridge and Dover 1986.

———. "The Palestine Problem in the Context of Colonial Policy on the Eve of the Second World War," in: *Cohen/Kolinsky,* pp. 206–216.

———. "The Political Use of Military Intelligence: Evaluating the Threat of a Jewish Revolt Against Britain During the Second World War," in: Richard Langhorne (ed.): *Diplomacy and Intelligence During the Second World War,* Cambridge et al. 1985, pp. 109–125.

Index